A STRUCTURAL HISTORY OF ENGLISH

A Structural
History of English

John Nist

AUBURN UNIVERSITY

ST. MARTIN'S PRESS · NEW YORK

For Jo, Brian, Brice, and Brent.

Preface

A Structural History of English combines a traditional history-of-the-language approach with modern linguistic analysis. In its account of the historical evolution of English, this book also describes the major features of the language at each stage of development: in phonology, morphology, syntax, and formal stylistics.

The first two chapters deal with the present status and structure of the language; the next eight chapters delineate the historical and structural factors that have shaped the English of today. Since present-day English is dominated by its speakers in the United States, Chapter 11 returns to the present through the evolution of American English. The final chapter undertakes to assess the future course of the language in usage, influence, and academic study.

By its discussion of the social forces that have helped determine the patterns of growth and change in the language and its various national, dialectal, and regional versions, this book differs from other history-of-English texts. It also insists on interpreting and evaluating, from an analysis of the poetic cadences of Old English to a discussion of the oral influences on the evolution of a classic informality in Mark Twain. The thesis that English belongs to the people who speak it, and is thus primarily psychological rather than logical, leads to an appraisal of the mathematically prescriptive methods of present-day generative grammar.

A Structural History of English has several useful pedagogic features.

1) A linguistic key, which gives an overview of the historical evolution of English phonology.

2) Summary historical sections, which list at the outset of each major phase of English the important dates, outstanding persons, and major attributes of the language.

3) A selective bibliography at the end of each chapter.

4) A selective glossary at the end of the book, which defines fundamental terms and illustrates basic principles of modern linguistic science.

5) Questions for research and discussion at the close of each chapter, to stimulate both classroom liveliness and personal mastery of significant linguistic issues.

Depending upon the amount of supplementary reading and the number of individual reports and research papers assigned, this book can form the basis for either a one-semester or a two-semester course in the English language.

I am indebted to Professor Harold Whitehall of Indiana University and to Professor Albert H. Marckwardt of Princeton University for their assistance in reading the manuscript and in making recommendations for its improvement. My most personal expression of thanks goes to Mrs. Patricia Wyatt, who solved every secretarial problem connected with drawing up a final draft, and to my wife, who offered constant encouragement and support.

Contents

A Linguistic Key

PHONEMES	KEY WORDS
/p/	*p*an, na*p*
/b/	*b*an, na*b*
/m/	*m*ob, bu*m*
/f/	*f*ive, li*f*e
/v/	*v*an, gi*v*e
/θ/	*th*ane, wi*th*
/ð/	*th*is, wi*th*in
/t/	*t*an, gna*t*
/s/	*s*and, ga*s*
/d/	*d*en, be*d*
/z/	*z*oo, oo*z*e
/n/	*n*ip, pi*n*
/l/	*l*ook, coo*l*
/ķ/	*c*ēap (Old English)
/c/	*ch*in, lun*ch*
/š/	*sh*awl, wa*sh*
/r/	*r*ow, oa*r*
/ĝ/	e*cg* (Old English)
/j/	*j*am, nu*dg*e
/ž/	lo*g*e, rou*g*e
/x/	ni*h*t (Old English)
/h/	*h*igh, *h*oo (offset glide)
/k/	*k*ing, boo*k*
/ɤ/	ā*g*an (Old English)
/g/	*g*ain, na*g*
/ŷ/	*g*ēar (Old English)
/y/	*y*ou, *y*oung (offset glide)
/ɒ/	ri*ng*, so*ng*
/w/	*w*ane, *w*ing (offset glide)

PHONEMES	KEY WORDS
/ł/	b*ur*r, s*ir*
/u/	b*oo*k, b*oo*r
/e/	b*e*t, b*ea*r
/ə/	b*u*t, c*u*d
/ő/	*oe*xen (Old English)
/o/	b*oa*t (New England)
/æ/	b*a*t, c*a*d
/a/	b*a*h, b*a*r
/ɔ/	b*a*ll, b*o*re
/i:/	h*ī*d (Old English)
/iy/	b*ee*, b*ea*t
/iw/	r*u*de (Middle English)
/ih/	r*ee*d (Early Modern English)
/y:/	dr*ȳg*e (Old English)
/ł:/	l*io*ht (Old English)
/ły/	b*ee* (Cockney)
/łw/	s*u*e (Early Modern English)
/łh/	f*ur* (Eastern New England)
/uy/	b*uoy*, p*u*sh (Southern U.S.)
/u:/	h*ū*s (Old English)
/uw/	b*oo*, b*oo*t
/uh/	t*oo*th (Early Modern English)
/e:/	sp*ē*d (Old English)
/ey/	b*ay*, b*ai*t
/ew/	h*ou*se (Tidewater Virginia)

/i/	b*i*t, b*ee*r	/e˘/	b*ea*ten (Middle English)
/y/	c*y*nn (Old English)		
/eh/	n*a*me (Early Modern English)	/æw/	*ou*t (Eastern U.S.)
		/æh/	b*aa*
/əy/	b*i*rd (Brooklynese)	/ay/	b*u*y, b*i*te
/ə:/	s*ēo*ðan (Old English)	/aw/	b*ou*gh, b*ou*t
/əw/	b*eau* (Southern British)	/a:/	d*ēa*f (Old English)
/əh/	b*u*rr (r-less dialect)	/a˘/	l*a*me (Middle English)
/oy/	b*o*y (Middle English)	/ah/	b*a*lm, p*a*lm
/o:/	r*ō*d (Old English)	/ɔy/	c*oi*n, t*o*y
/ow/	g*o*, g*oa*t	/ɔw/	l*a*w (Southeastern U.S.)
/o˘/	b*oa*t (Middle English)		
/oh/	p*ou*r, p*aw* (r-less dialect)	/ɔ:/	b*ā*n (Old English)
/æ:/	h*ǣ*lan (Old English)	/ɔh/	w*a*r (Northern Middle Western)
/æy/	p*a*ss (Southeastern U.S.)		

LINGUISTIC SYMBOLS

ā   A *macron* over a vowel (ā) in Old English indicates tension, as applied by the glide /:/.

ẹ   A *iota subscript* under a vowel (ẹ) in Middle English indicates "open" articulation (with a wide opening above the tongue).

/ /   Two slash lines indicate a phonemic transcription.

/:/   The Old English glide of tension, the rough equivalent of any of the present-day offset glides /y w h/, depending upon vocalic environment.

/˘/   The Middle English centering glide of tension, the rough equivalent of the present-day offset glide /h/.

/´/   The suprasegmental phoneme of *maximum* stress.

/ˆ/   The suprasegmental phoneme of *major* stress.

/ˋ/   The suprasegmental phoneme of *minor* stress.

/˘/   The suprasegmental phoneme of *minimum* stress.

/+/   Open juncture, which discriminates morphemic boundaries of stressed elements.

/|/   Optional internal close juncture, which discriminates word-group boundaries. Is not punctuated in writing.

/‖/	Obligatory internal close juncture, which discriminates phrasal and clausal boundaries. Must be punctuated in writing.
/#/	Obligatory terminal close juncture, which discriminates sentence boundaries. Must be punctuated in writing.
/4/	Highest intonation (pitch) level; highest attention demanded.
/3/	High intonation (pitch) level; high attention demanded.
/2/	Normal intonation (pitch) level; normal attention demanded.
/1/	Low intonation (pitch) level; low attention demanded.
↗	Indicates *rising* intonation pattern.
↘	Indicates *falling* intonation pattern.
*	Signifies a non-permitted structure.
{ }	A pair of braces indicates a morpheme under analysis.
-	Indicates a bound morpheme when preceded or followed by an affix or base.
→	Indicates a rewrite rule in the direct representation of phrase structure in generative grammar.
=>	Indicates a transform made from kernel sentences in the indirect representation of transformation in generative grammar.

A STRUCTURAL HISTORY OF ENGLISH

CHAPTER 1

The Present Status of English

⟶◈⟵

IMPORTANT DATES

1914–1918 Increased Anglo-American influence enhances the prestige of the English language.

1920 on Growth of mass-media communication of the spoken word accelerates the development of informal usage in English.

1933 With the publication of Leonard Bloomfield's *Language*, linguistic science becomes the *avant-garde* basis for the study of English.

1939–1945 World War II brings about the international dissemination of the English language.

1945 on The Atomic Age deepens the scientific impact on specialist vocabularies and the use of English.

1948 on The rise of commercial television exerts an enormous influence on English through the "folk poetry" of its advertising.

1951 In America the battle between structural analysis and traditional prescription and proscription in the academic study of English is intensified by the publication of Trager and Smith's *An Outline of English Structure*.

1957 on The Space Age, as evidenced by sputnik, further strengthens the scientific impact on specialist vocabularies and the use of English.

1962   With the publication of the second edition of Noam Chomsky's *Syntactic Structures*, generative grammar becomes a major basis for the modern study of English.

OUTSTANDING PERSONS

Leonard Bloomfield (1887–1949)   Father of modern linguistics in America.

Noam Chomsky (b. 1928)   Chief proponent of generative grammar.

e. e. cummings (1894–1962)   Leading practicer of concretism in modern American poetry.

T. S. Eliot (1888–1965)   Epitome of modern critical temperament and creative obliqueness in English.

Ernest Hemingway (1898–1961)   Modern English prose stylist par excellence.

Gerard Manley Hopkins (1844–1889)   Great metrical innovator and master of the oldest poetic resources of the English language, discovered via posthumous publication in 1918.

Roman Jakobson (b. 1896)   Leading modern theoretical linguist.

Otto Jespersen (1860–1943)   Pioneer of modern approaches to the scientific study of the English language.

James Joyce (1882–1941)   Perfecter of the expressive continuum in the modern English novel: stream of consciousness.

Rudyard Kipling (1865–1936)   First Nobel laureate in literature of the English language.

H. L. Mencken (1880–1956)   Popular pioneer in the study of American English.

Dylan Thomas (1914–1953)   Reviver of oral bardic poetry in English.

George L. Trager (b. 1906) and Henry Lee Smith, Jr. (b. 1913)   Central figures in the modern structural study of English.

William Butler Yeats (1865–1939)   Master of lyric refrain and mythic projection in modern English poetry.

MAJOR ATTRIBUTES OF THE LANGUAGE

Worldwide importance.
Immense cosmopolitan vocabulary.
Inflectional simplicity.
Natural gender.
Difficult idiomatic structures.

Poor correspondence of orthography with phonology.
Analytic and hypotactic syntax.
Functional fixed word order of essentials.
Syntactical movability of non-essentials.
Overwhelming importance of stress in determining pitch, juncture, word groups, and cadences.

TODAY, IN THE LATTER HALF of the twentieth century, the English language is at a pinnacle of linguistic prestige and power. It commands an importance out of proportion to the number of its native speakers, for they constitute only about 10 percent of the population on earth. Yet at least 70 percent of the world's mail is addressed in English and at least that much of its business is conducted in the present version of the tongue that Shakespeare spoke.

Although more people speak Chinese (the Mandarin dialect only) than speak English as their first language, most of the civilized world looks to the Western tongue for leadership in the expression of every form of human culture. When we consider that Chinese is splintered into various dialects and hampered by a ponderous ideographic system of writing, we can understand why English overwhelms Chinese in its use as a second language. There are from half to three-quarters of a billion speakers of some form of Chinese; against that range, English has about three hundred million native speakers, plus an immediate potential of at least a billion people more who either use English as their second tongue or will soon be able to do so. Outside of Mandarin Chinese, English outranks every other language in the number of native speakers. The following chart of the twelve leading languages of the world makes clear this numerical supremacy of English:

LANGUAGE	NUMBER OF NATIVE SPEAKERS
Mandarin Chinese	450–500 million
English	275–300 million
Spanish	140–150 million
Russian	130–140 million
German	100–105 million
Japanese	95–100 million
Arabic	85–90 million
Portuguese	80–85 million
Bengali	75–80 million
Urdu	75–80 million
French	65–70 million
Hindi	65–70 million

English has not only a numerical edge but also a *distributional* advantage over the other major tongues. Mandarin, Russian, Japanese, German, Arabic, Bengali, Urdu, and Hindi are all concentrated in a single area. Spanish, Portuguese, and French have a wider distribution, but they are limited mainly to the Western world. English, on the other hand, is spoken as a first language on all the continents, including Oceania and Antarctica. This immense distribution of English is both racial and religious.

CHARACTERISTICS OF PRESENT-DAY ENGLISH

The importance of English, as indicated by its vast number of speakers and its global distribution, has been established through a complex set of factors: commercial, military, linguistic, and cultural. The prestige of any language is determined by the answer to this basic question: Who speaks the language? From 1415, when the longbowmen of Henry V put an end to medieval chivalry at the English victory over the French at Agincourt, to 1945, when American airmen dropped the first atomic bomb, the course of Anglo-Saxon civilization has been one of repeated and continued success. The outgoingness of that civilization and its language, necessary at first by the lack of self-sufficiency of Britain's island kingdom, and later enhanced by the intercontinental salesmanship of restless Yankee ingenuity, has established English in its present-day prestige, speaking for the greatest economic and military power on earth.

Language, like man, is primarily *psychological* rather than *logical*. English is therefore an accurate mirror of the psychological factors that have helped to establish the leadership of that Anglo-Saxon civilization. As the most vigorous and economical language on earth, present-day English is the product of centuries of energy, which, in turn, has fostered a *flexibility* that has kept English rich in creative idioms and new constructions, and free from the authoritarian dictates of an Academy or a narrow-minded pedantry in usage.

Much of the strength of English depends upon its *economy*—a pragmatic and utilitarian trait. This economy begins with the backbone of the language: its consonantal system. The English consonants, which require a good deal of stress energy to pronounce, are—in contrast with the slurring of Danish and the palatalizing of Russian—well defined in themselves and undergo little modification through vowel environment. The English vowel system itself is noted for its phonetic symmetry, clear-cut distinctness, even balance between *lax* simple phonemes and *tense* complex diphthongs, and historical evolution toward ever more stability— all signs of economy. This economy in English is also responsible for morphological clipping (*natch*) and syntactical shortening (*I will if you will*). Such economy keeps monosyllables at the core of the language, curtails the use of the definite article (*love is best*), regularizes all new verbs, and reduces inflectional forms (grammatical affixes). It joins with a normal British predilection for litotes (understatement) and an intonational pattern far less violent in range than that of any Romance language.

STRESS. The most important single factor in the historical development of English and its present-day structure is stress. Centuries before the Teutonic Invasion of Britain began in 449 A.D., the Germanic prototypes of English experienced a stress shift, whereby emphasis was placed on the root syllable. Since the root syllable was almost always the first syllable, this emphasis on the essential amounted to a *forwarding of stress*. To this day, the English language forwards its stress pattern whenever it can.

With the Norman Conquest of 1066, the official language of Britain— in King's Council, Parliament, law court, church, and school—became French, a language noted for its refined and metrically pale system of accent. Threatened with a displacement of their native stress patterns by the aristocratic domination of French, the English peasants maintained the forward position of accent. The result was the Anglicizing of Norman and Parisian imports. Such Anglicizing produced not only a change in the accentual patterns of Romance words but also a radical shift in their sound structures, for *stress is phonemic*, that is, fundamental to the shaping of sound and sense. Chaucer and Shakespeare prove this point in their different pronunciations of the same woman's name: *CriSEYde* and *CRESSida*.

The importance of stress in English, however, runs far deeper than its impact on either spelling or pronunciation. For stress—by means of its phonemic, morphological, syntactical, rhetorical, rhythmical, and semantic modifications—is the key determinant of most of the major attributes of Modern English: simple inflectional system, natural gender, analytic syntax and fixed word order, poor correspondence between spelling and pronunciation, word-group cadences, and the enormous flexibility of functional shifts due to the placing of accents.

In the phonology (sound structures) of Modern English, two laws are central: *stress yields full vowel coloring;* and *lack of stress yields vowel transmutation to either schwa* (ə) *or colorless i* (ɨ). (The *schwa* is heard in unaccented *the;* the *colorless i,* in the second syllable of *women.*) These laws are the result of centuries of English insistence on the forwarding of stress, a practice which in turn led to the *zeroing*—the loss of *-a-* in the British pronunciation of *secondary*—of many relatively stressless syllables. Since most of these relatively stressless syllables were the inflectional endings of Anglo-Saxon, these inflections were among the first items to be sacrificed by the English resistance to the Norman Conquest. With the loss of inflections, something other than case endings in a predominantly substantive language had to serve as function determiner. So *position in the syntax* came to be the most important factor in the evolution toward analytic Modern English.

If *-em*, let us say, represents the accusative case and therefore determines the function of the direct object, then we may report a blow struck in any of the following ways: *John hit Billem; hit Billem John; John Billem hit; Billem John hit; hit John Billem; Billem hit John.* Such syntactical groupings were possible in Old English, but if Bill is to get whacked in Modern English, the speaker has very little choice other than the standard active version: *John hit Bill.* Thus stress modifications helped to produce the syntactical order and consistency—further marks of economy—that prevail in Modern English.

In English, stress determines both noun and verb functions of the same homographs, words written alike: for example, *ADdress* is noun, *AdDRESS* is verb. Nouns have a *falling* stress pattern: *EXport, IMpact, REBel;* verbs have a *rising* stress pattern: *exPORT, imPACT, reBEL.* Stress differentiates *noun word groups* from *noun compounds;* noun word groups (*the little red HEN*) have a rising stress pattern, whereas noun compounds (*BLACKbird*) have a falling stress pattern.

Stress further determines the suprasegmental (intonation) features of English: *pitch* (levels of intonation), *juncture* (pause values), *prolongation* (quantitative emphasis), and *pacing* (speed of speech delivery). As a rule, in English speech the peaks of stress energy are also the peaks of pitch height and prolongation. Major junctures, which determine rhythmical patterns and pacing of delivery, are intimately connected with the placing of maximum stresses. Thus the collocations of maximum stress divide the following simple sentence into three rhythmical groupings, according to the dictated major junctures: *The very bad BOY | gave the very good GIRL | a box of delicious CANdy.*

Even more important is the role of stress as a movable semantic interpreter. In the statement *Give me the book*, the speaker may stress each of the four words in turn and get four different meanings, for meaning is primarily a matter of emphasis: 1) GIVE, don't *lend* or *sell;* 2) ME, not *Billy;* 3) THE book we talked about: *War and Peace*, not *The Catcher in the Rye;* 4) BOOK, rather than *lecture* on it or *review* about it.

Apart from the immense cosmopolitan vocabulary of present-day English, other major attributes of the language have been determined in large measure by the principle of stress: inflectional simplicity (a minimum of grammatical affixes); natural gender; analytic (word order determines function) and hypotactic (subordinating constructions predominate) syntax; fixed word order of essentials (in which subject, verb, inner complement, and outer complement appear usually in this exact order); syntactical movability of non-essentials (as in the placing of the adverbial modifier *only* either before the verb, after the verb, or after the direct object); word-group cadences (the basic units of English rhythm); difficult—for foreigners—idiomatic structures; and a poor correspondence between orthography (spelling) and phonology (pronunciation). The insistence on forwarding stress led to the eventual dropping of inflectional endings, which in turn emphasized syntactical placing to determine function in both English speech and writing. With the loss of inflectional endings, English nouns and adjectives could no longer maintain a grammatical gender dictated by those endings. Hence the great advantage of natural or logical gender came into being. With the added emphasis on syntactical positioning, English prose style could concentrate more on the interdependence and proper subordination of ideas.

The movement away from parataxis (the syntax of coordination), seen most clearly in Old English, to hypotaxis (the syntax of subordination) was greatly furthered by the periodic rhythms made possible by the word-group patterns dictated by maximum stresses and their attendant junctures. The introduction of *schwa* and *colorless i* in stressless positions into the phonology of English helped to precipitate enormous changes in the basic pronunciation of the language. These changes took place during the worst possible time, when the spelling of the language jelled from 1550 to

1650. Thus, for the most part, present-day English spells like a post-Chaucerian and pronounces like a post-Shakespearean. A similar lack of correspondence exists *on a logical level* between the literal and the figurative meanings of English idioms. Thus an immigrant to America may very well have a hard time understanding how a *SHOWdown* may be *shaping UP*.

COSMOPOLITAN VOCABULARY.   The history of the English language, in a lexical sense, is a study in the growth of its cosmopolitan vocabulary, for the breed of English spoken today is mongrel. With the exception of a few Celtic place-names, a larger list of Latin terms introduced by Christian missionaries, and about eighteen hundred Scandinavian loans and cognates, English until 1066 was basically West Teutonic in its word stock. With the Norman Conquest, however, that word stock became a hybrid, a cross between Anglo-Saxon base and Latinic transplant. French, which made its greatest gains in England in the reign of Henry III, was a beachhead for the invasion of Latin and its Greek uncle and Romance nephews—a vast army of words that swelled the vocabulary ranks of English from the thinly populated Anglo-Saxon (50,000 to 60,000 words), through the growing Middle English (100,000 to 125,000 words) and the commercial Renaissance English (200,000 to 250,000 words), to the immense international British, American, and Commonwealth English of today (650,000 to 750,000 words, at least). Not only has the size of the English vocabulary grown persistently; but so also has the hybrid quality of its content. So cosmopolitan has the English language become that a random sampling of its vocabulary is sufficient to indicate the universal character of its borrowing. The following list of twenty-six Modern English words constitutes an ABC of imports:

WORD	SOURCE
amen	Hebrew
bandana	Hindustani
canyon	Spanish
dengue	Swahili
emotion	French
focus	Latin
gimmick	German
henna	Arabic
igloo	Eskimo
jute	Sanskrit

WORD	SOURCE
kamikaze	Japanese
lilac	Persian
mahogany	West Indian
nougat	Provençal
opossum	North American Indian
pickaninny	Portuguese
quirt	Mexican Spanish
rocket	Italian
salt	Indo-European
they	Old Norse
ukulele	Hawaiian
vassal	Celtic
welcome	Anglo-Saxon
xylophone	Greek
yen	Chinese
zebra	Bantu

This list, of course, is somewhat misleading: although it shows something of the tremendous range of borrowing, it fails to show the ratios of concentration. Eskimo, as represented by *igloo,* for example, exerts on Modern English only a fraction of the influence of Anglo-Saxon, as represented by *welcome.* Nor can Japanese begin to match the importance of French in English imports, or Arabic that of Latin, or Swahili that of German. Much more significant than the extent of borrowing are the ratios of concentration of that borrowing at the various levels of Modern English usage: basic spoken and written, informal spoken and written standard, formal spoken and written standard, regional and dialect variants, literary learned, scientific specialist, and the several forms of substandard: slang, jargon, argot, and illiteracy. These ratios demonstrate that English remains preëminently Anglo-Saxon at its core: in the suprasegmentals of its stress, pitch, and juncture patterns and in its vocabulary. No matter whether a man is American, British, Canadian, Australian, New Zealander, or South African, he still *loves his mother, father, brother, sister, wife, son, and daughter; lifts his hand to his head, his cup to his mouth, his eye to heaven, and his heart to God; hates his foes, likes his friends, kisses his kin, and buries his dead; draws his breath, eats his bread, drinks his water, stands his watch, wipes his sweat, feels his sorrow, weeps his tears, and sheds his blood; and all these things he thinks about and calls both good and bad.*

So Anglo-Saxon is the emotional heart of the language, the basis of its everyday communication and Sunday communion, of its pragmatic work and ideal dream, of its businesslike prose and Biblical poetry. Even though 51 percent of Chaucer's 8,000-word vocabulary committed to print is Romance in origin, less than 20 percent of that total vocabulary is not basic English in actual density of occurrence. The cosmopolitan vocabulary of English has, by means of a vast system of synonyms and parallel developments, structured itself into the following major strata of usage, each with its characteristic derivation:

STRATUM	DERIVATION
Basic English	Anglo-Saxon
Literary	French
Learned	Latin
Scientific	Latin and Greek
Technological	Greek
Specialist:	Depends on Specialty:
Art	Italian, Dutch
Cooking	French
Drama	Greek
Law	French
Medicine	Greek
Military	French
Music	Italian
Poetry	Greek
Seafaring	Anglo-Saxon, Norse, Dutch
Theology	Latin, Greek, Hebrew

STRUCTURAL INFLUENCES.   The genius of English in its use of other languages runs deeper than a simple borrowing of words to enrich its expressive potential. Scandinavian, for example, helped bring order out of chaos in the English pronoun system with the gifts of *they*, *their*, and *them*. It also supplied *are* as the present plural verb form of *to be*. In addition, Scandinavian is responsible for the -*s* inflection of active verbs in the third person singular, present indicative, and for the principle of strong stress on the preposition, which makes possible the very modern habit of first forming *idiomatic verbs* with the preposition, strongly stressed, functioning as a directive adverb and of then forming an *idiomatic noun* from the verb by forwarding the stress pattern. To illustrate: if someone says, "Let's cook OUT tonight," he invents an idiomatic verb. When his wife changes his original statement to read, "Let's have a COOKout tonight," she is inventing an idiomatic noun.

Both forms are partially attributable to the influence of Scandinavian in a *structural* manner.

Latin also has had considerable structural influence on the evolution of English. Beyond the vast number of its loans it has exercised a tremendous impact on a major *morphological process* (method of word formation) of English—*affixing*. So great, in fact, was the penetra*tion* of Latin *af*fixing during the Renaiss*ance* that it quite *un*did the Anglo-Saxon habit of *com*pounding as the leading means of word form*ation* in English. So brief a list as the following shows how impoverished English would be without its complex system of Latin prefixes and suffixes: *ab-, ad-, bi-, com-, con-, contra-, de-, dis-, pre-, pro-; -able, -al, -ance, -ation, -ble, -ent, -ion, -ive, -ous, -ty*. Ten examples of each, of course, barely scratch the surface of the contribution of Latin affixing, but they do prove the point.

Greek, on the other hand, revived compounding as a central morphological process in English. Because the system of compounding in Ancient Greek is so much like that of the Germanic languages its terms become so readily resorted to and easily absorbed by the various specialist vocabularies of Modern English, especially those of science and technology. Thus the native *wis-dom* of Anglo-Saxon is analogous to the borrowed *philo-sophy* of the formal followers of Socrates. And so one language enhances its own strength, economy, and flexibility with such adoptions from another as *astrophysics, psychotherapy, thermonuclear; seismograph, telephone, parthenogenesis; helicopter, stichomythia, teleology; electrophysiology, hieroglyphics*, and *philanthropy*.

Yet despite the important structural influences of Scandinavian, Latin, and Greek, French has exerted the greatest impact on the English language. With the Norman Conquest, the social prestige of French guaranteed the extension of its vocabulary into administrative, ecclesiastical, and scholarly circles. Such extension, however, is but a portion of the story, for the combinations formed from French stems and English affixes or from English stems and French affixes are a deeper indication of linguistic influence. Hybrid terms like *bountiful, falseness, governorship, gentleman, laughable, wondrous*, and *shepherdess* tell more about the French impact than do purist borrowings like *exploit, enchantment, glory, horror, question, sacred*, and *virtue*. The hybrids show the eventual fusion of the two languages. With the suppression and loss of the West-Saxon written prose standard and the mixed poetic dialect, French dominance permitted the free play of English dialects, upset—as Harold Whitehall has said—"the linguistic equilibrium" of the language, forced a revision of its traditional orthography, and completely changed the source and basis of its literary tradition. Thus it is that the *Canterbury Tales* and not *Beowulf* forms the fountainhead of English literature.

Ironically and paradoxically, the most profound impact of French on the English language was exerted by failure rather than by success: the failure of the French suprasegmental system to permanently penetrate and control the natively Germanic basis of English pronunciation. Just as the early influx of missionary Church Latin stimulated the native resources of Anglo-Saxon to respond with a further enrichment of word formation, so the challenge of French patterns of stress, intonation, and juncture strengthened the resolve of the English peasants to enforce their own patterns upon every new word introduced into their language. Beset with a large-scale invasion of aristocratic Norman and Parisian French words, idioms, and expressions, scarcely understanding the simplest statements in the courts of law, despising the "affected" language of their feudal masters and social betters, the middle and lower classes of Britain stuck to their linguistic guns, defending their right to "mispronounce" by Anglicizing everything.

By overstating their case, the English peasants transformed the language in the course of three or four centuries. Because of the native insistence on a forwarding of stress, we speak an English noted for its inflectional simplicity, natural gender, and analytic syntax: all products of a foreign challenge that, in its ultimate success of failure, may be called "The French Linguistic Revolution." Without this revolution, present-day English would in all likelihood sound like some special dialect of Low German.

INFLECTIONAL SIMPLICITY.   The inflectional simplicity of present-day English is an evolutionary result of the French challenge and the forwarding of stress. With the phonemic weakening induced by unstressed positions in Middle English, the case endings of Anglo-Saxon nouns and adjectives dropped off rapidly. By the same principle, though more slowly, English verb forms also silenced their person and mood indicators. In this process of simplification, as Albert C. Baugh said, "English has gone further than any other language in Europe." The inflectional vestiges from the Anglo-Saxon and Middle English past may be listed as follows:

INFLECTION	MEANING
-ed	past tense
	past participle
-er	comparative, originally
	a dual marker
-est	superlative
-ing	present participle
-s	plural
	third person singular
	present indicative
-'s	possession

NATURAL GENDER.   With the loss of inflectional endings from English nouns, case forms ceased to determine gender. Once gender could no longer be sustained on *grammatical* principles, it sought its rationale on *logical* grounds. Thus came an advantage English has over many other languages: natural gender based upon simple logic. In Modern English, *woman* is feminine; in Anglo-Saxon, however, she (*wīf*) was neuter. Even when married, in German she (*Weib*) remains neuter, just as she was when a *maiden* (*Mädchen*) and a *child* (*Kind*). The three grammatical genders of German, in fact, are anything but logical.

The uninflected adjective and the unchanging definite article *the* are two more indications of the economy of English. Nor is that economy threatened by the fact that the Romance languages have only two genders: masculine and feminine. Such reduction from three to two, on a grammatical basis, confuses the issue even more, for it permits an indiscriminate absorption of the neuter. And the division of all nouns between the two genders is often arbitrary and even silly. Except for the occurrence of *covert* gender (sailboat as *she*, eagle as *he*), which is a matter of conversational attribution, in English *meaning* determines gender. Hence nouns of all living things are masculine or feminine according to their sex; lifeless things are neuter *its*.

ANALYTIC SYNTAX.   As an inevitable outgrowth of the loss of inflectional endings, English syntax evolved from a rather loosely knit *synthetic* to a very tightly woven *analytic*. Word order replaced case endings in the expression of grammatical relationships. With that replacement, English syntax—unlike that of many languages—became truly functional, another mark of strength and economy. Position in the syntax now determines emphasis and meaning more than any other device. So strict has English syntax become in its order and consistency that positional poetic license for the sake of rhyme is often either strained or amateurish. Order and consistency are great assets in advancing English as the lingua franca of the world, for it is relatively easy for the foreigner to master the one-two-three-four syntactical positioning of Modern English. One, the *subject*, together with all its modifiers, fore and aft; two, the *verb*, together with all its auxiliaries and modifiers, fore and aft; three, the *inner complement*, together with all its modifiers, fore and aft; four, the *outer complement*, together with all its modifiers, fore and aft. Thus so simple a sentence as

1	2	3	4
The man	gave	the woman	a book.

may be expanded to

1

The tall, dark, and handsome young man, who was
a member of Phi Beta Kappa from Duke University
and now a graduate student at Harvard,   2

                                           had just decided
to give, with all the flourishes of his own inimitable
style,   3

            the sweet and petite young woman from Radcliffe,
an institution she had dearly loved, both for its own
sake and for that of her recently deceased grandmother
(God rest her soul!),   4

                             a leather-bound and gold-embossed
deluxe (what else can you call it at fifty dollars a copy?)
edition of that most famous little book of poems out of
late Victorian England: A. E. Housman's *A Shropshire Lad.*

without any basic change in structure. The functional positioning remains the same.

This one-two-three-four word order in the analytic syntax of Modern English is, as Jespersen pointed out, a major trait of the language. In *Beowulf*, the percentage of this analytic word order is only sixteen; in the prose of King Alfred, merely forty. Old English was obviously synthetic in its word order. Against the low percentages of its analytic syntax, we can project, as a means of contrast, the high percentages of analytic syntax of some outstanding writers in Modern English:

AUTHOR	PROSE	POETRY
Byron	93	81
Carlyle	87	
Dickens	91	
Macaulay	82	
Pinero	97	
Shelley	89	85
Swinburne		83
Tennyson		88

GREAT VOWEL SHIFT.   In addition to the changes wrought in the inflectional system, gender, and syntax of the language, the forwarding of stress and its resultant phonemic weakening in unstressed positions eventually brought about a revolution in pronunciation that marked the end of Middle English and the beginning of Modern English. The Great Vowel Shift in Renaissance English was a clockwise movement, according to tongue height and oral-cavity positioning during articulation, from high-front and high-back to low-central and from low-central to mid-front *on the first formant elements of diphthongs.* That is to say, the shift took place on *long* (tense) vowels rather than on *short* (lax) vowels *in stressed positions.* In unstressed positions, all vowels—tense and lax—tended to end up as mid-central. Some displacements in pronunciation were more dramatic than others, but the direction of shift remained constant. Thus Chaucer's *boot* was pronounced like Tennyson's *boat*, his *bleed* like Byron's *blade*, his *ride* like Wordsworth's *read*, his *day* like Pope's *die*. By listing several words common to both Middle and Modern English and their corresponding present-day rhymes, the following list illustrates the major changes in pronunciation that resulted from the Great Vowel Shift:

WORD	PRESENT-DAY RHYMES	
	Middle English	*Modern English*
house	goose	louse
bite	sweet	light
blood	road	mud
meat	fate	sweet
fly	sea	sigh
debate	pot	eight
love	groove	of
rout	cute	pout
wait	height	late
blow	sue	so

ORTHOGRAPHY.   Because the revolution in English pronunciation took place when its spelling was solidifying, the present-day orthography of the language is a poor indication of its phonology. Although Middle English looks much like it sounds, Modern English does not. Indeed, the spelling practices of Modern English are the worst of any major language of the world. For example, *ghoti* equals *fish*—that is to say, the *gh* as in *rough*, the *o* as in *women*, and the *ti* as in *nation* all add up to the phonetic structure of the word that signifies the scaled inhabitants of water. Because it conflicts with normal phonemic distribution, *ghoti* could never actually occur; but this hypothetical illustration is only the beginning of the phonetic chaos in English. Thus it is bad enough to have the vowel sound of *bee* represented by the following variant spellings: gr*ie*ve, dec*ei*ve, m*ea*n, mach*i*ne, h*e*, and h*ee*l; yet it is even worse to have the same vowel spellings produce different pronunciations: s*ie*ge, s*ie*ve; b*ea*k, br*ea*k; al*i*ve, rel*i*ve; g*o*ne, sh*o*ne; sl*au*ghter, l*au*ghter; f*ou*l, gh*ou*l, s*ou*l; dr*ea*m, dr*ea*d; l*ai*d, s*ai*d; w*a*ter, w*a*der; gl*o*w, gl*o*wer; f*oo*l, f*oo*t.

To complicate this phonetic disorder, the consonants of Modern English are a welter of confusion. As Baugh points out, there are fourteen spellings for the sound of *sh*: *shoe, sugar, issue, mansion, mission, nation, suspicion, ocean, nauseous, conscious, chaperon, schist, fuchsia, pshaw.* As a further demonstration of this confusion among the English consonants, one may cite the differences in sound between the *c* in *call* and the *c* in *cell*, the *g* in *give* and the *g* in *gyve*, the *ng* in *sing* and the *ng* in *singe*, the *s* in *concise* and the *s* in *advise*, the *wh* in *what* and the *wh* in *who*. The silencing of certain English consonants further widens the gap between orthography and phonology. Chaucer's *knight*, therefore, rhyming as it does with German *richt* and pronouncing its initial *k*, makes spelling sense; Eliot's *knight*, rhyming with *trite* and no longer pronouncing its initial *k*, does not make spelling sense.

Even though linguistic experts claim that changing the present graphemic English alphabet to a phonemic one would save the average grammar school pupil two years of study in mastering the fundamentals of his language, such a change is unlikely, because conservative forces—linguistic, cultural, and aesthetic—generate immense pressure to preserve, protect, and defend the status quo in English spelling. First of all, there is the *inertia of tradition*—in the orthographic practices of the language and the psychological habits of its speakers. Second, there is the *visual demand of silent reading*, which minimizes dialect and regional differences within the English language.

When William Caxton made printing a cultural force in England in 1476, he elevated the Spoken British Standard of London to that of the Written British Standard. Thus the visual morpheme became a power in reducing differences of pronunciation to a single written version. The three major forms of Modern English—British, American, and Commonwealth—are very nearly identical on the printed page, a great source of the linguistic unity and cultural solidarity of Anglo-Saxon civilization. If English spelling suddenly became phonemic, however, it would tend to fragment and divide that civilization. If all speakers of the language wrote exactly as they talked, a far more dangerous confusion would soon emerge: an inability to communicate with ease. What difficulty the Texan would have in reading the letters from his New York cousin; how hard it would be for the Lancashire farmer to decipher the reports of an Australian soil physicist; with what sweat a South African novelist would study the lines of an Irish poet! The traditional orthography of English, with its standard appeal to the eye, in its role as cultural unifier lends a great support to other conservative forces that operate for the maintenance of the present non-phonemic system of spelling.

Third among the conservative forces that favor the present method of English spelling is the *etymological factor*. The current spelling of an English word is an indication of its etymology, the source of its original linguistic derivation and of its historic semantic evolution. The sacramental term *Eucharist*, for example, shows through its traditional spelling that the ultimate basis of its morphological compounding is Greek: *eu-* (*well*) plus *charizesthai* (*show favor to*); together these two formant elements produce the Greek term *eucharistia*, which means *gratitude* or *thankfulness*. Now since thanksgiving is included with adoration, contrition, and supplication among the four acts of worship in the Mass, the early Christian Church specialized the term *Eucharist* to signify the best means of conveying thanksgiving—that of Holy Communion. The very word is an indication that the Mass itself was of Greek invention. Phonemic spelling of this sacramental term /yuwkərist/ would blur the clear lines of its etymology, reduce the value inherent in its long history, and lessen the emotional impact generated by its original derivation. Men could still use the word to *communicate*, but in its phonemic form the chances are that they would not feel that they could *commune* properly with it.

And this feeling is of the utmost importance, for it shows once again that language is primarily psychological rather than logical.

This psychological factor underlies the fourth conservative force favoring the present system of spelling: a great reluctance to witness the translation of literary masterpieces into an alphabetical system not native either to the writers or to the readers or to the language itself. With the adoption of a phonemic alphabet, the resultant need for such translation would run head-on into powerful vested interests, which long have supported the present system of spelling.

The first vested interest standing against such translation into a phonemic alphabet is financial: how much will it cost? The answer goes far beyond a simple dollars-and-cents reckoning. The cost in money of course would be staggering. Even more significant would be the cost in time and human effort expended to reduce the whole of English literature worth keeping to the print of the new system—that is, if men could ever agree on what that system should be. That they could not agree on a particular system is probable because of the recalcitrance of human nature, and the fact that there is no unique phonemic solution for the problem of pronunciation.

But even if men could agree on some international phonemic or phonetic alphabet, a bigger source of difficulty would remain—deciding on an international standard of spelling based on pronunciation. Whose standard would it be: that of the reader from London? Edinburgh? Dublin? Montreal? Chicago? Kingston? Auckland? Sydney? Johannesburg? Hong Kong? or New Delhi? The difficulty of deciding on a standard is conveyed in the sense of this anecdote: An Englishman and an American were arguing over the pronunciation of the word *neither*; "It's *nigh*ther," said the Englishman; "Oh, no, it's *nee*ther," said the American; then an Irishman, who had overheard the argument, spoke up and said, "It's really *nay*ther!" A democratic spirit in pronunciation militates against the reduction of present-day English orthography to one of greater correlation with phonology. It is a powerful vested interest; it defends the principle that the language belongs to everybody speaking it, not just to the few. This democratic spirit also permits one linguistically to have his cake and eat it too, for *though the spoken word may vary, the written word remains constant*. This variable constancy is a great advantage attributable directly to the so-called poor spelling practices of Modern English.

Ironically enough, by maintaining these practices, the language serves another vested interest at the far end of the scale from the democratic spirit, *snobbism*. If A can spell better than B, by virtue of either a better education or a keener memory, he can enjoy the delusion that the language really belongs to him and to men of his class.

IDIOMATIC LANGUAGE.   Modern English idioms, like poor orthography, hinder the spread of English as the lingua franca of the world. They also indicate the enormous flexibility and inventive vitality of the language. English, like every other form of living speech, must constantly renew itself; idiomatic expressions, because they are so close to the heart of slang and the simple poetry of metaphor, constitute an excellent means for such renewal. They are also the despair of foreign students of English. A German-born professor, for example, now an American citizen and teaching in a major university, was commenting on the beauty of his remembered Old World flame. Wishing to be breezy and up-to-date for the benefit of his graduate assistants, the professor exclaimed: "Boy, was she stuffed!" The students who laughed at the slip on *stacked* were reminded of the difficulty of English idioms in a linguistics class, where the American-born professor demonstrated the loving creativity inherent in Juliet's desire to cut Romeo *out* in little stars; had the heroine said *up*, her idiom would have carried a different connotation.

The idiomatic preposition is a good illustration of the rich inventiveness and the great difficulty encountered in using Modern English idioms. The idiomatic preposition itself functions in both word groups and compounds. When converted to a directive adverb in word groups, which always have rising stress patterns, the preposition is part of the verb idiom and is therefore *predicative: Will you blow UP the bridge?* While purists carry *on* over each fresh predicative use of the idiomatic preposition, the wagging tongues of invention carry *off* their innovations well —simply by carrying *on*. Thus doting grandparents may indulge in loving pride and make *over* a favorite grandchild, but a pouting lover had better make *up* with his sweetheart first; his chances of making *out* are otherwise slim. An imbiber, on the other hand, can conceivably be sleeping *in* while sleeping *out* for the sole sake of sleeping it *off*. Perhaps that is why one of the favorite maxims chilly age offers to flaming youth runs like this: Be careful how you live it *up;* you may never live it *down!* And he who goes all *out* in tracking down the tricky idiomatic preposition will soon find himself all *in*.

But of this fact he can be sure: if the preposition does not attach itself to the verb or its morphological equivalent, then the preposition remains part of another word group—the prepositional phrase—and is *attributive* and therefore not idiomatic. In compounds, which usually have falling stress patterns, the idiomatic preposition converts the verb into a noun formant and is therefore *substantive: Will there be another BLOWup?* Poets and punsters especially enjoy the substantive use of the idiomatic preposition. They delight in the fact that a cheap hood appears in a police show*up* because he couldn't resist being a show*off* in a mob show*down*. One too many in the Saturday night hang*out* inevitably leads to the Sunday morning hang*over*. How often does the Internal Revenue ask for a run*down* on past earnings only to get the run*around?* When a center fielder says he's a hold*out*, often the front office swears he means a hold*up*. Pity the husband who makes the usual male slip*up* by buying a slip*over* when the little woman wanted a slip*on*. Present-day speakers of American English make good use of lay*down* in bridge, lay*away* in marketing, lay*over* in traveling, lay*off* in economic recession, lay*up* in basketball, and lay*out* in advertising and in gangster architecture. Hence, for idiomatic prepositions acting as substantives in compounds, it may be said that

> Some are actively up-and-about,
> While others are passively down-and-out.

Ever since the end of World War I, the vitality of the idiomatic preposition in English has been matched by the acceptance of its usage in new constructions. From about 1920 to the present, the growth of mass-media communication of the *spoken* word has accelerated both the development and the sanction of the informal in the language. This acceleration, in turn, is an extension of the process of elevation of the colloquial to the accepted standard, a process that had its start in 1816 with the establishment of the first cheap newspaper in England. Today a new word (*egghead*) or phrase (*wise up*) gets locked into print for mass distribution with amazing speed, simply because the new word or phrase tends to receive instantaneous acceptance by countless millions of native English speakers upon its broadcast via radio, television, or the cinema.

Oral English today invades and conquers *visual* English with a speed unparalleled in history. Consequently, as Bergen Evans has said in a 1962 review of *Webster's Third New International Dictionary*, "Ideas of what is proper to use in serious, dignified speech and writing are changing—and with breathtaking rapidity. This is one of the major facts of contemporary American English." This is a major fact concerning all national forms of English, for the language is worldwide and so are the mass-media communications that disseminate it with such swiftness. Despite some academic preferences for maintaining the eighteenth-century divorce between the spoken and the written word, a quick acceptance of the informal in usage is demanding a remarriage of the two.

Since mass-media communications are global in their importance and influence, they are immediate indicators of the fact that present-day English is spoken from London to Sydney, from Dublin to Hong Kong, from New York to Johannesburg, from Gibraltar to Manila, in three leading versions: *British, American,* and *Commonwealth.* They bear witness to the enormous vitality of the language, with many national, regional, and local dialect forms. If the *sch* of *schedule* sounds like the *sh* in *shoe,* chances are that a Canadian is speaking. Should somebody be dying of a fever that sounds like *favor,* probably an Irishman is reporting the tragic event. A *bison* is a concave vessel that an Austr*e*y*e*lian warshes his *fice* in. The Scottish burr is unmistakable; so also is the higher pitch of South African intonation. Oriental influences are heard in Hawaiian Pidgin, and the syncopation of calypso music is a distinct factor in the stress dislocations of the English of the Caribbean. So thick is the tongue of a true Cockney, an East End Londoner born—according to legend— within the sound of the bells of St. Mary-le-Bow Church, that his speech habits have become the despair of his fellow Englishmen.

To compound the difficulty of interpreting what he says, today the Cockney has established an elaborate system of oblique references by means of rhymes—for example, *storm and strife* may signify *wife, life,* or *knife,* depending upon the context. But when the Cockney says, "Watch your *loaf!*" he means *bread,* which rhymes with *head,* his real intent. Thus he is developing a new system, one step removed from rhyme. If his American counterpart in Brooklyn is not so inventive, he is almost as strange and colorful in the peculiarities of pronunciation. An accident at the ballpark might be reported in the following Brooklynese: "Hurt got hoit at t'oid in de t'oid!" What the fan is saying is this: that a player named Hoyt was injured at third base in the third inning. Thus English, though so widely distributed and universally standardized in written form, is subject to local flavor.

BRITISH ENGLISH.   Local flavor has long been a determining factor in the evolution of British English. Anglo-Saxon had four major dialects: *Northumbrian, Mercian, Kentish*, and *West Saxon*. Middle English supported at least six dialect variants: *Northern, Northeast Midland, West Midland, Southeast Midland, Kentish*, and *Southern*. From the Southeast Midland dialect—the language of London—evolved the present-day Received Standard British: the speech of the universities and boarding schools, of Crown and Parliament, of BBC radio and television commentators, of the actors at Old Vic. It is the speech of most refined and well-educated Britons. The development and adoption of Received Standard British was making a virtue of necessity, for the various dialects of the British Isles have impeded general communication for centuries.

It is in maintaining true dialects under its Received Standard that British English differs so much from American English. American English knows *regionalisms* (or *speech varieties*), not dialects. Dialects obstruct communication; regionalisms do not. Hence there has never been the felt need for adopting a Received Standard American English in the United States. In Britain where roughly 90 percent of the population is exposed to some sort of dialect, general education in the proper phonology of the Standard is fundamental. A key lesson in Shaw's *Pygmalion* is that failure to master the Standard places a terrible limitation—social, educational, and financial—upon the individual. Since failure is to be avoided whenever possible, one naturally is led to ask, "What are the central traits of Received Standard British?"

The British speak with more tension than the Americans, and through a smaller oral aperture. As a result of these habits, British English may be characterized by the following central traits: 1) the development of a grave ("muffled") back-vowel pronunciation in such words as *blast, fast, half*, and *path* so that *rather* rhymes with *father, aunt* and *can't* nearly rhyme with *want;* 2) the flattening of the tongue on final *r* in such words as *rather, father, brother, learn, core, fork*, and *bark* to produce what is called an *r*-less kind of articulation; 3) the tendency to reduce major stress to minor and minor to minimum so that *secondary* sounds like *second'ry, tertiary* like *terti'ry, dictionary* like *diction'ry, stationary* like *station'ry*, and *territory* like *territ'ry;* 4) because of the greater tension in pronunciation, the wider latitude of tongue height and depth on diphthongs, and the constant intonation pressures of the various dialects, a resultantly more dramatic range of pitch patterns than in American English, which tends, by contrast, to be flat, nasal, and less musical.

In British English an indefinite singular pronoun controls a plural reference ("Let *everyone* do *their* duty!") and a collective singular noun governs a plural verb ("Her Majesty's *Government are* considering the proposal"). British English, at least in its Received Standard version, is less dynamic in idiomatic creation, less informal in usage, more traditional in morphology, and more given to understatement than American English, which revels in exaggeration. If American English reflects its pioneering spirit and impatience with tradition in inventive functional shifts, blends, and clippings, then British English mirrors its much longer history in an elegant conservatism, which for sheer euphony cannot be matched by the liberal breeziness of its exuberant cousin. The style, the grace, the dignity of British English all mark it as indeed the King's English.

Although British and American English agree on a vast majority of words native to them both, they also support certain vocabulary differences. These differences reflect the gradual divergence of two independent cultures: the one rather pure in racial stock and national origin, the other a heterogeneous mixture of peoples from several races and many countries; the one topographically limited to an island world, small and scenically tame, the other sprawling over half a continent and spilling into three oceans and two other major bodies of water, with climates ranging from subtropic to subpolar; the one officially maintaining a class society under a reigning monarch who does not rule, the other officially opposing all class distinctions in a constitutional republic where public opinion often plays the tyrant; the one somewhat impoverished in natural resources but extremely rich in historical achievements, the other rich in land and minerals yet disproportionately poor in social legislation; the one diplomatically more sophisticated than its waning armed strength would seem to indicate, the other militarily mightier than its political naïveté would apparently warrant; the one a preserver of tradition, the other a worshiper of novelty.

Thanks to the exhaustive research of H. L. Mencken, we may demonstrate a brief portion of the vocabulary differences between British and American:

AMERICAN	BRITISH
billion	milliard
broiled	grilled
carnival	fun fair
commuter	season ticket holder
corporation	limited liability company
cracker	biscuit
eraser	Indian rubber
filling station	petrol pump
garbage can	dust bin
hash	shepherd's pie, mince
installment plan	hire-purchase system
monkey wrench	adjustable spanner
oatmeal	porridge
pantry	larder
radio	wireless
squash	vegetable marrow
subway	underground, tube
surplus	reserve
ticket agent	booking clerk
touchdown	try
truck farmer	market gardener
T.V.	telly
water heater	geyser
weather bureau	meteorological office
white-collar	blackcoat

AMERICAN ENGLISH. Differences in vocabulary do not constitute the only distinction between American and British English. American English is less musical in its intonation patterns, preserves full pronunciation value on stressless syllables, and supports less tension in articulation. It also maintains a more conservative phonology in the following speech characteristics: 1) general preference for the "flat" *a* (as in *man*) rather than for the "broad" *a* (as in *father*) before *f, sk, sp, st, ss, th,* and *n* as the first element in certain consonantal clusters; 2) the retention of final *r* in the pronunciation of most Americans (except in New England and in the South); 3) a lower and unrounded pronunciation of the *o* (except in Eastern New England, Western Pennsylvania, and along the Ohio River) in such words as *cot, hot, lot, not,* and *process;* 4) a somewhat archaic use of either a lax vowel or vocalic *l* in the second syllable of words like *fertile* and *sterile,* which are diphthongized in British English to rhyme with *smile;* 5) a rather pedantic articulation in words like *figure* and *ate*, spoken as *figger* and *et* in Britain.

American English also prefers a lax pronunciation of *been* so that it rhymes with *sin*, rather than with *seen*, as in British English, and a tense pronunciation of *leisure* so that it rhymes with *freeze your* rather than with *pleasure*. Much more important, however, is the conservatism of American English in grammar and usage, as fostered by its Puritan beginnings, a genteel literary tradition, the cultural insecurity of immigrant learners of the language, the snobbism of suburbia, and the dominance of the rules of the eighteenth-century grammarians in the teachings of the schools. Yet in direct opposition to this conservatism, American English enjoys a greater liberality in word and idiom formation. Thanks to Benjamin Franklin and Noah Webster, American English also spells with economy and innovation, preferring *-or* to *-our* in such words as *color, honor, savior; -er* to *-re* in terms like *center, meter, theater;* single consonants in words like *reveler, traveler,* and *wagon;* the use of *s* for *c* in such terms as *defense,* and *offense;* and graphemic modernity in spellings like the following: *ax, jail, medieval,* and *plow.*

Arrested as some regional aspects of American English may be, they cannot begin to match the extreme conservatism, indeed the archaic flavor, of the British dialects. No version of the language in the United States can imitate the whine of Suffolk, the clipping of Yorkshire, the guttural throatiness of Northumberland, the glottal stopping of Lancashire, the bardic pitch patterns of Wales, or the Gaelic thickness of the Scottish Highlands. A simple question in South Staffordshire, for example, betrays ancient Germanic influence on syntax and Middle English control of pronunciation: *"Bist tha bi guwin' uwt?"* ("Are you to be going out?"). A fundamental command by a Cockney, on the other hand, might run to such incomprehensible limits: *"Pu' th' 'ud i' th' o'!"* ("Put the wood in the hole!"—i.e., "Shut the door!"). Because American regionalisms, unlike British dialects, are no hindrance to communication, they constitute a major feature of American English. These ten regionalisms, discussed at length in Chapter 11, are Eastern New England, New York City, Middle Atlantic, Western Pennsylvania, Southern, Appalachian, Central Midland, North Central, Northwest, and Southwest.

COMMONWEALTH ENGLISH.   Commonwealth English is very young in the prestige of its independent status. With time, it will grow both in numbers of speakers and in influence, for it has a vast potential backed by an enormous population (as in India and Pakistan), immense resources in land and minerals (as in Canada and Australia), a rapidly expanding industrial base, a rising standard of living, a zeal for independence (as in the emerging African states), a proud tradition to uphold, and an emerging culture of world stature to disseminate. In the wide range of its geographical distribution, its variant pronunciations and intonation patterns, its colorful idioms and local slang, its national psychologies and creative temperaments, Commonwealth English has an exciting future. Now, it is a loose confederation of national versions of English that have evolved through the origin of immigrant speakers, local modifications and immediate foreign influences, and the object of imitation and emulation: American or British.

Canadian English is the product of a colonial culture similar to that of the United States, but resulting in a different kind of nationalist autonomy and therefore in different sentimental ties with Britain. Though Canadian English wants to be free of both American and British control, its original common source of immigrant speakers (generally Southern England, of middle and lower classes) and its subsequently similar local modifications have combined to make it much more like American than British. Excluding the prevalence of French in Quebec, there are reasons for Canadian differences from American English—a continuous flow of immigration from the British Isles and a resultantly more homogeneous society; strong British habits of speech; the preservation of conservative Northern forms by immigrant Scots; loyalty to the Crown and therefore greater receptivity to English manners, customs, and institutions. Some of these Canadian differences from American English are 1) a general tendency to lower and broaden the pronunciation of *o* as in *pod* to equal the *aw* of *pawed;* 2) the development of two variants for the diphthongs *ai* and *ow* (*rite/ride, out/loud*); 3) the preservation of conservative British spelling in words like *cheque* and *centre;* 4) a native system of stressing on foreign terms like French *CORnet;* 5) Anglicized pronunciations of such words as *economics* (*eekuhnomiks*), *lieutenant* (*leftenant*), and *clerk* (*clark*).

Australian English is much more like nonstandard British than is either American, Canadian, or New Zealand English, for the Australians are heirs to the Cockney vowel system, introduced into the island continent by the criminal exiles shipped out to its penal colony. With this Cockney vowel system, Australian English also enjoys an American-like informality of usage and its own imaginative slang—for example, *billy* (tin pot for heating water), *donk* (fool), *fork* (jockey), *hunk* (large man), *larrikan* (rowdy street loafer), *to mizzle* (to complain), *rest* (year in jail), *smoodger* (flatterer), *swagman* (tramp with a bundle), and *wowser* (sanctimonious and prohibiting Puritan).

The speech of the South Africans is much like that of the Australians but shows the foreign influence of Afrikaans, the name for Dutch in that region. New Zealand English (heavily influenced by the conservative habits of Scots immigrants) did not inherit such peculiar patterns of pronunciation; the great local influence on the New Zealanders' language is Maori, the tongue of the indigenous Polynesians of the same name. Hence the various national versions of Commonwealth English evolve according to their own historical and cultural conditions.

CULTURAL PRESTIGE.   Important as the high cultural achievements of Anglo-Saxon civilization have been in strengthening the prestige of English, they cannot match the popular culture of that civilization in establishing the language as the lingua franca of the world. British and American troops have taken the language to common folk everywhere. With the language, they have taken ways of living, with emphasis on mass production of goods and mass media. As a result of popular culture penetration, today English is *the* international language of airways communication and *the* linguistic exegete of jazz. Indeed the Communist nations confirm the universality of English by resorting to it for propaganda broadcasts to East Africa and the Far East and by sending hundreds of highly trained teachers of English to Africa south of the Sahara. Russian exports to the Near East bear the English legend "Made in U.S.S.R."

The written word itself is a great force behind the present prestige of English. In 1907, Rudyard Kipling became the first writer in the language to win the Nobel Prize for Literature. Today the list of Nobel laureates in English runs as follows:

YEAR	AUTHOR	NATION
1907	Rudyard Kipling	Great Britain
1913	Rabindranath Tagore	India
1923	William Butler Yeats	Ireland
1926	George Bernard Shaw	Great Britain
1930	Sinclair Lewis	United States
1932	John Galsworthy	Great Britain

YEAR	AUTHOR	NATION
1936	Eugene Gladstone O'Neill	United States
1938	Pearl Buck	United States
1948	Thomas Stearns Eliot	Great Britain
1949	William Faulkner	United States
1950	Bertrand Russell	Great Britain
1953	Winston Churchill	Great Britain
1954	Ernest Hemingway	United States
1962	John Steinbeck	United States

When Sinclair Lewis became the first American to win the Nobel Prize in Literature in 1930, he was a symbol that the written word of his countrymen had come of age and been recognized as worthy of international status.

THE MODERN STUDY OF ENGLISH.   Since the end of World War I, English has undergone the vital study of modern linguistic science: in its phonology, morphology, systematic structures, semantics, geographic distribution, and social usage. In 1919, H. L. Mencken published his first edition of *The American Language*, a seminal document in what Ravin I. McDavid, Jr., has called the basic tradition of American linguistics: "objectivity in observing and classifying the evidence and free and generous co-operation in research and in exchange of information." Though intuitive and impressionistic by temperament, Mencken commanded a wealth of information, and he knew what to do with it in a style noted for masculine vigor and satiric wit. Often under attack, he nevertheless was the first great student of American English as a form distinctly different from British and therefore a major world dialect of the language, possessing its own uniformity, freedom in usage, and inventive genius.

In 1925 Mencken's study was joined by George P. Krapp's two-volume *The English Language In America*, the first comprehensive and professional treatment of the subject. By 1931 work had begun on *Linguistic Atlas of the United States and Canada*, an important document in modern dialectology. In 1933, Leonard Bloomfield published his monumental *Language*, the one book that can be called the foundation of modern linguistic science in the United States. Bloomfield, an anthropologist with expert knowledge of Cree Indian dialects and a professor of Germanic philology, demonstrated that every language is *phonemic, referential, systematic, symbolic, semantic*, and *complete*. English is, therefore, a set of human conventions, unique in pronunciation, grammar, and vocabulary, undergoing constant change, so that what is "correct" depends mainly upon usage.

By 1940 C. C. Fries was demonstrating Bloomfield's principles of description in *American English Grammar*. With the publication of Hans Kurath's *A Word Geography of the Eastern United States* in 1949, a linguistic landmark in the scientific study of American regionalisms had been established. Two years later George L. Trager and Henry Lee Smith, Jr., published their now famous *An Outline of English Structure* and intensified the war of objective observation against preconceived norms. The latest major weapon available in the struggle against the prescriptive and proscriptive legacy of the eighteenth-century grammarians is the 1962 publication of *Syntactic Structures* by Noam Chomsky, the father of generative grammar.

QUESTIONS FOR RESEARCH AND DISCUSSION

1. Listen to ten major news commentators on radio and television and study their speech patterns. What differences can you detect in diction, intonation levels, stress volume, speed of delivery, pause values, and local dialect flavor? In what ways do the ten commentators sound alike? What does this investigation tell you about the impact of mass-media communications upon both the delivery and the reception of present-day American English? Do you have any evidence to show that the same general process is occurring in both British and Commonwealth English?

2. Analyze the commercials on television for two weeks and write a critical paper on the central stylistic features that constitute their "folk poetry." How important are such items as alliteration, rhyme, rhythm, metaphor, symbol, and myth?

3. Draw up your own ABC of English Imports from twenty-six languages. What do the specialization of each term and the date of its entry indicate about the importance of the language-culture that did the lending? Are the borrowings of the English language a socio-linguistic history of the world in miniature? Explain your answer.

4. What new words were introduced into the English language during World War I? World War II? the Korean War? How do these words reflect the enormous growth in technology and the practical applications of science? Is language an accurate mirror of man, moment, and milieu? Develop your answer in detail.

5. Illustrate the tremendous fecundity of Greek and Latin in the formation of scientific terminology in Modern English. Concentrate your attention upon such subjects as medicine, physics, chemistry, psychology, and linguistics.

6. Gather two lists of specialist vocabularies that indicate the fresh linguistic coinages of the atomic age and the space age. Do experts in these areas of scientific research and technological experiment have their own slang? Illustrate your answer.

7. If asked to state and define twenty-five current idiomatic constructions in American English most likely to baffle foreign students of the language, which would you select? Does your list coincide with those of your classmates? Are there differences in definition of the idioms themselves? Discuss the linguistic moral of this lesson assignment.

8. What are the key contributions of Leonard Bloomfield to the development of linguistic science in the United States? Organize a class project of individual reports on the various chapters of his famous book *Language.*

9. Discover twelve leading authorities on Modern English not mentioned in this chapter and briefly discuss their major contributions to the study of the language. What does this project tell you about the vitality of the subject in question? Develop your answer in detail.

10. Challenge one of your classmates to a debate on the subject of "English Spelling: To Phonemicize or Not To Phonemicize." Let the class itself divide into pro and con and join in on the intellectual battle. Now write a paper of critical analysis on the central issues of this continually vexing problem.

11. Coleridge once defined poetry as putting the right words in the right order. Compare and contrast the syntactical artistry of Dylan Thomas and e. e. cummings. Do these two modern poets support Coleridge's thesis, modify it, or negate it? Defend your answer in detail.

12. Investigate the contributions of James Joyce to modern artistic prose style. Discuss Joyce as an individual embodiment of the enormously creative potential of the English language in the twentieth century.

SELECTED BIBLIOGRAPHY

Baugh, Albert C. *A History of the English Language.* Second Edition. New York: Appleton-Century-Crofts, 1957. See especially Chapter 1, pp. 1–16. An indispensable text—strong in historical backgrounds and cultural features.

Bloomfield, Leonard. *Language.* New York: Henry Holt and Company, 1933. See especially Chapter 4, pp. 57–73. The pioneer classic in the field of language study in America.

Bloomfield, Morton W., and Leonard Newmark. *A Linguistic Introduction to the History of English*. New York: Alfred A. Knopf, 1963. See especially Chapter 1, pp. 3–26. Up-to-date and sound in scholarship.

Chomsky, Noam. *Syntactic Structures*. The Hague: Mouton, 1957, 1962. The bible of generative grammar.

Francis, W. Nelson. *The Structure of American English*, with a chapter on "American English Dialects" by Ravin I. McDavid, Jr. New York: The Ronald Press Company, 1958. An excellent popular text.

Jespersen, Otto. *Growth and Structure of the English Language*. Ninth Edition. New York: Doubleday, Anchor Books, 1955. See especially Chapter 1, pp. 1–17. An imaginative and challenging classic.

Mencken, H. L. *The American Language*. The Fourth Edition and the Two Supplements, abridged, with annotations and new material, by Raven I. McDavid, Jr., with the assistance of David W. Maurer. New York: Alfred A. Knopf, 1963. The best one-volume study on the subject—a genuine masterpiece.

Robertson, Stuart, and Frederic G. Cassidy. *The Development of Modern English*. Second Edition. Englewood Cliffs, New Jersey: Prentice-Hall, 1954. See especially Chapters 11 and 12, pp. 327–417. A sound and well-written text, with a fine "Glossary of Linguistic Terms."

Whitehall, Harold. "The English Language." In *Webster's New World Dictionary of the American Language*. College Edition. Cleveland and New York: The World Publishing Company, 1964. Pp. xv–xxxiv. This brilliant essay analyzes the English language, both synchronically and diachronically, with economy and clarity.

CHAPTER 2

The Present Structure
of English

—⸎—

PHONOLOGY

LANGUAGE IS PRIMARILY AN ACT of oral communication—meaningful sounds from the human throat and mouth. Man has been talking about a hundred times longer than he has been scribbling. English, therefore, is first of all a set of sounds developed, refined, and changed—to be further developed, refined, and changed over centuries of social interaction among men. Children in each new generation learn these sounds by imitating their elders. Later on, should they become serious students of the language, they realize that the sounds of English are in several ways just like the sounds of any other tongue: 1) in the arbitrary and unpredictable correlation between themselves in their *difference* from one another and with the objects of the outside world that are their *referential* meaning; 2) in the fact that all language sounds occur *systematically* and hence form *substitution frames* rather than mere *units*; 3) in the *symbolic* stimulus and response of "displaced speech" (i.e., talk about *absent* things) which these sounds make to develop a "universe of discourse"; 4) in their expansible combinations that make them completely adequate for their cultural tasks, for every language is, as Archibald A. Hill has said, "a model of a culture and its adjustment to the world." Any study of the present structure of English must begin with an analysis of the sound patterns (i.e., phonology) of the language.

In languages like Spanish, Bohemian, Polish, and Finnish, the alphabet spells what the speakers pronounce. Not so in English, for its orthography is far from phonemic. Indeed in present-day English, 5 alphabetic vowels and 2 alphabetic semivowels are the poor representatives of at least 36 different vocalic nuclei, 9 simple and 27 complex. The entire range of these 36 vocalic nuclei—as heard in the various regionalisms and dialects of Modern English—may be demonstrated in the following 30 words: *pit, pet, pat, just, cut, cot, put, home, wash, bee, bay, pass, bird, buy, buoy, boy, few, house, moon, go, do, law, dear, yeah, baa, fur, palm, boor, paw, war*. Thus the student of conventional English must orient himself away from the concept of the *grapheme*, the basic unit of writing, and toward the *phoneme*, the minimum unit of *distinctive* sound-feature. As minimum units of distinctive sound, the phonemes are the non-graphemic bases of English language as it is spoken throughout the world today.

As metaphysics has demonstrated, everything below the level of God is characterized by a matter-form, potential-actual relationship. Modern linguistics and literary criticism prefer to call this type of union as one of *texture* and *structure*. A phoneme, then, as a minimum unit of distinctive sound in any given language, is the product of just such a texture-structure relationship. As *sound*, a phoneme is texture; as *specific* sound, it is structure. Every phoneme becomes the textural constituent of the larger structure of a *morpheme*, the minimum unit of meaning in any given language. In English, for example, the free morpheme *cat*, when spoken, is the structural union of three textural constituents: the phonemes /k/, /æ/, and /t/—/kæt/. Such a morpheme, in this case coterminal with a word, becomes a textural constituent of a larger structure: the word group, or *syntagmeme* (e.g., *the little black cat*). The word group, in turn, is a textural constituent of the larger structure of the *sentence*, which becomes texture for the *paragraph*, which becomes texture for the *discourse*. From such an evergrowing texture-structure relationship, we can analyze and describe the present structures of the English language. This analysis and description, of course, must begin with the minimum units of distinctive sound.

CONSONANTS.   Consonants are formed with more effort and a greater obstruction of the breath current than are vowels. According to their positions of formation and the articulators involved, the 24 phonemic Modern English consonants are either *labial* (formed by the lips), *labiodental* (formed by lower lip and upper teeth), *interdental* (formed by tongue between upper and lower teeth), *alveolar* (formed by tongue against dental ridge), *alveolopalatal* (formed by tongue and breath moving from hard palate to dental ridge), *palatal* (formed by breath striking hard palate), or *velar* (formed by breath striking soft palate). If the consonants are *tense* in articulation, they are *voiceless;* if *lax* in articulation, they are *voiced.* Moving from the front of the mouth to the back, we may isolate and illustrate the 24 phonemic Modern English consonants as follows:

Labial

Voiceless:	/p/	pain, pie
Voiced:	/b/	bane, buy
	/m/	main, my

Labiodental

Voiceless:	/f/	fain, fie
Voiced:	/v/	vain, vie

Interdental

Voiceless:	/θ/	thane, thigh
Voiced:	/ð/	thy, thine

Alveolar

Voiceless:	/t/	ta'en, tie
	/s/	sane, sigh
Voiced:	/d/	Dane, die
	/z/	Zane, zoo
	/n/	nigh, new
	/l/	lane, lie

Alveolopalatal

Voiceless:	/c/	chain, chew
	/š/	Shane, shy
Voiced:	/r/	rain, rye
	/j/	Jane, Jew
	/ž/	loge, rouge

Palatal

Voiceless:	/h/	high, hoo
	/k/	cane, coo
Voiced:	/g/	gain, guy
	/y/	yi, you

Velar

Voiced:	/ŋ/	ring, sing
	/w/	wane, Wye

As can be seen from the isolating pairs, sound is its own meaning. Since *pie* and *buy* differ in their initial consonants, they also differ in what they signify. Thus an important law in linguistics: *phonemic is morphemic*.

To indicate the localized positions of the 24 Modern English consonants as they occur in articulation, we may diagram their distribution among the speech articulators of man. These articulators include the lips, the teeth, and the four major areas of the tongue: point, blade, front, and back. Through the employment of these articulators the present-day English consonants are positionally distributed as follows:

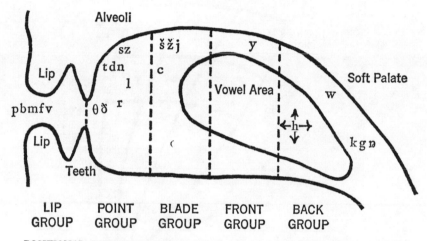

POSITIONAL DISTRIBUTION OF LATE MODERN ENGLISH CONSONANTS

From the diagram it can be seen that the phoneme /h/, surrounded by arrows, is a nonlocalized consonant usually occurring within the vowel area; it is therefore often employed as a semivowel glide, with the tendency to both center and widen the preceding vowel. The other two semivowel glides among the consonants are /y/ and /w/; these two glides tend to raise and narrow the preceding vowel, but with this fundamental difference: /y/ fronts the vowel and /w/ backs it. As for the other consonants, they also indicate the importance of *phonemic environment*—especially through the possibilities of their initial and final clusters. Among the possible initial consonantal clusters of Modern English are /pl pr py pw tr tw kl kr ky kw bl br by dr dw gl gr gy gw fl fr fy θr θy θw hy hw vy my sl sw sp st sk sf sv sm sn šl šr šw šn spl spr spy str skl skr sky skw ty dy sy zy sty ts/; the possible final clusters, on the other hand, include such consonantal groupings as /ps ts ks fs θs bz dz gz vz ðz mz nz ŋz lz rz ns ls rs mp nt nd ŋk mps nts ndz ŋks nθ mf nc nj lp lt lk lps rst mpst ntst ŋkst hrldz/.

VOWELS.   The phonemic vowels of English are, in contrast with the consonants, all voiced. The vowels do, however, support the same tense-lax distinction: a tense vowel is "long" and for the most part *complex;* a lax vowel, "short" and *simple.* Since all the complex vocalic nuclei of

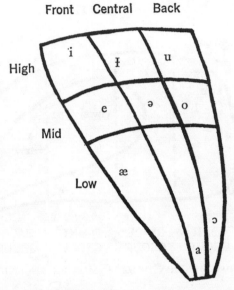

POSITIONAL DISTRIBUTION OF THE SIMPLE VOWELS

Modern English are formed by use of the simple vowels in conjunction with any of the three offset glides /y w h/, these simple "basic" vowels must be examined first. The simple English vowels are characterized by two attributes of articulation: tongue height and oral positioning. These vowels are therefore either *high, mid,* or *low* in the first category and either *front, central,* or *back* in the second. By analysis according to tongue height and oral positioning, then, we may catalogue the simple vowels of present-day English as follows:

High-Front: /i/   bit, beer
High-Central: /ɨ/   burr, sir
High-Back: /u/   book, boor

Mid-Front:	/e/	bet, bear
Mid-Central:	/ə/	but, cud
Mid-Back:	/o/	boat, road (New England)
Low-Front:	/æ/	bat, cad
Low-Central:	/a/	bah, bar
Low-Back:	/ɔ/	ball, bore

These simple English vowels, according to the research of Trager and Smith, have allophonic variations in length: "longest before voiced spirant, rather long before voiced stop and nasal, somewhat long before voiceless spirant, short before voiceless stop . . . ." Apart from their phonemic environment, of course, these simple vowels tend to occur upon the tongues of all English speakers in the positional distribution as diagrammed on page 36. But like consonants, simple vowels have a phonemic environment. When this environment includes one of the 3 offset glides /y w h/, then a complex vocalic nucleus is created.

Since all 9 of the simple vowels of present-day English may occur with each of the 3 semivowel offset glides /y w h/, the complex vowels (diphthongs) are 27 in number. Although no speaker of current Late Modern English actually uses all 27 of these nuclei in his normal speech habits, these complex vowels do exist as a portrait of the vocalic range of the language on a worldwide scale. The nuclei may be listed and illustrated as follows:

/iy/	bee, beat	/əw/	beau, boat (Southern British)
/ɨy/	bee, beat (as in Cockney English)	/ow/	go, goat
		/æw/	house, out (Eastern and Southern U.S.)
/uy/	buoy		
/ey/	bay, bait	/aw/	bough, bout
/əy/	bird (Brooklynese)	/ɔw/	awe, law (Southeastern U.S.)
/oy/	boy, Hoyt (in regional variation with /ɔy/)	/ih/	beer, dear (in all r-less dialects and regionalisms)
/æy/	bait, pass (Southeastern U.S.)	/ɨh/	burr, fur (in Eastern New England)
/ay/	buy, bite	/uh/	boor, poor
/ɔy/	wash (at headwaters of the Ohio River)	/eh/	bear, dare
		/əh/	burr, fur (in variation with simple /ɨr/)
/iw/	few (old-fashioned variation on /yuw/)	/oh/	pour, paw (r-less dialect)
/ɨw/	moon (in Philadelphia)	/æh/	baa
/uw/	boo, boot	/ah/	balm, palm
/ew/	house, out (in Tidewater Virginia)	/ɔh/	war, paw (Northern Middle Western)

From this catalogue, we see that the complex vowels of present-day English are formed from a union of a simple vowel with one of the 3 semivowel offset glides /y w h/. Nine of these nuclei—formed in union with the centering and lowering /h/—are *wide*, whereas 18—those formed in union with fronting and raising /y/ and with backing and raising /w/—are *narrow*. The most interesting phonological history in English has to do with these narrow nuclei, for English is basically a "high tongue" language, and the tendency for its tense vowels has been one of rising and breaking. The lax vowels, in contrast, have tended to remain stable or to lower slightly. Thus what Otto Jespersen called the Great Vowel Shift is primarily the result of change in the first formant element of the tense vocalic nuclei, for the semivowel glides have continued fairly constant.

DISTINCTIVE ACOUSTIC FEATURES.   At the level of the phoneme, every language has a series of basic oppositions of sound structure that may be termed *distinctive acoustic features*. In Late Modern English these basic oppositions are seven; they may be listed and described as follows:

1) *Vocality vs. Consonantality*. A simple distinction between *syllabic* and *non-syllabic* phonemic nuclei: vowels and semivowels in opposition to consonants.

2) *Tension vs. Laxness*. In the vowels, an automatic long/short distinction; in the consonants, an automatic voiced/voiceless.

3) *Interruption vs. Continuance*. A basic contrast between phonemes which impede the flow of breath in pronunciation and those which do not: *stops* /p t c k/ and *obstruents* /b d j g/ in opposition to *fricatives* /f v θ ð h s š z ž/, *nasals* /m n ŋ/, *liquids* /l r/, and all vowels and semivowels.

4) *Gravity vs. Acuteness*. A simple distinction between grave *back* vowels /u o ɔ/ and acute *front* vowels /i e æ/; between grave *labial* consonants /p b m f v/ and acute *apical* and *post-apical* consonants /s š z ž t c d j θ ð n l r/. Gravity or "muffling" is a secondary and redundant feature in the back consonants /h k g ŋ/ and the semivowel /w/.

5) *Compactness vs. Diffuseness*. A basic contrast between the presence of and the absence of a central formant region: *low*

vowels /æ a ɔ/ against *high* vowels /i ɨ u/; *back* consonants /h k g ŋ w/ against *apical* and *post-apical* consonants /s š z ž t c d j θ ð n l r/.

6) *Nasality vs. Orality.* A simple distinction characterized by whether the nasal passage is used as a formant region: the *nasals* /m n ŋ/ in contrast with the oral obstruents /b d g/.

7) *Stridency vs. Mellowness.* A basic contrast between *muffling* and *non-muffling* in the fricatives: /s š z ž/ are strident; /θ ð/ are mellow.

These seven distinctive acoustic features are central not only to the phonemic structure of Modern English, but also to the sound-pattern exploitations inherent in the great aesthetic statements of its poets. When we read the following two lines fom Tennyson's "Come Down, O Maid":

> The moan of doves in immemorial elms
> And murmuring of innumerable bees.

we immediately feel a vague satisfaction with our own awareness of the poet's control of sound. Linguistic analysis, however, can turn vague satisfaction into clear delight at understanding what Tennyson has achieved with three simple phonemic devices: complete *voicing, intermediate compactness* in the vowels, and *nasalization* in the consonants. The distinctive acoustic features of English are, when properly used by a genius, the source of artistic transfiguration in the language. These features are also a means whereby modern literary criticism can isolate the *biographical indices* in an author's lines and analyze the *textural intensity* of his work.

From an analytical mastery of these seven basic distinctive-feature oppositions in English, the literary critic and the student of poetry equip themselves for accurate appraisals of the sound-pattern values which obtain in the work of any poet. When one probes the oral-tradition achievements in the language of Edgar Allan Poe, he will see beyond Poe's obvious control of alliteration, assonance, consonance, onomatopoeia, and repetition and refrain. Through careful study, the critic will appreciate Poe's creative predilection for liquids and nasals, his fondness for laxness and continuance, his avoidance of interruption and tension. Such an understanding of the language of Poe casts sharp light upon his personal poetic style and upon those eccentricities in his psyche which brought such a style into being. D. H. Lawrence says in his *Studies in Classic American Literature* that the critic must not believe the author (for the author often lies to himself), but that the critic must believe the author's literary artifacts. And the poems and stories of Poe show that he wanted love and life, as Lawrence indicates, without resistance. The distinctive features of his language establish Poe's sentimentality and psychic softness, his mythic projection toward fantasy and escape. Because of their psychological implications at the phonemic level of language, the distinctive acoustic features are biographical indices.

More important than psychological implications and biographical indices are the critical approaches that distinctive-features control makes available to the student and the critic for an appreciation of *textural intensity*. Textural intensity is the aesthetic control of language that turns sound into form, meaning, and value. To illustrate: Lady Macbeth tells her husband to appear the harmless flower to King Duncan but to be the serpent hiding under that flower. A soliloquy by Macbeth shortly thereafter begins thus:

> if the assassination
> Could trammel up the consequence and catch
> With his surcease success . . .

The distinctive feature of these lines is the stridency of the phoneme /s/; the hissing of the serpent has already begun, and the intelligent auditor knows that no matter what arguments Macbeth gives himself for not committing murder, he will nevertheless redden his hands with the blood of Duncan. Shakespeare is a master of textural intensity. So is Gerard Manley Hopkins, who in the subdued meditative lyric "Spring and Fall: To a Young Child" achieves acute moral significance with the fusion of strident /s/ with diphthongal /ay/:

> MÁRGARÉT, are you gríeving
>
> Over Goldengrove unleaving?
>
> Leáves, líke the things of man, you
>
> With your fresh thoughts care for, can you?
>
> Áh! ás the heart grows older
>
> It will come to such sights colder
>
> By and by, nor spare a sigh

Though worlds of wanwood leafmeal lie;

And yet you wíll weep and know why.

Now no matter, child, the name:

Sórrow's spríngs áre the same.

Nor mouth had, no nor mind, expressed

What heart heard of, ghost guessed:

It ís the blight man was born for,

It is Margaret you mourn for.

The sense of spiritual rending in diphthongal /ay/, as conveyed by Hopkins in this poem, is substantiated in the prose of Ernest Hemingway, for in *The Old Man and the Sea*, when the sharks come to attack the magnificent marlin, it is the exact cry of anguish from the lacerated heart of Santiago. And Hemingway says, "There is no translation for this word and perhaps it is just a noise such as a man might make, involuntarily, feeling the nail go through his hands and into the wood." This diphthong runs the complete gamut of the phonemic spectrum of vowels in English. As a piece of textural intensity in both the poetry of Hopkins and the prose of Hemingway, diphthongal /ay/ is aesthetic evidence of that constant texture-structure relationship between simple phonemics and complex metaphysics. One of the greatest challenges for linguistics and literary criticism in the latter half of the twentieth century is to analyze that relationship.

THE SUPRASEGMENTAL PHONEMES. The 33 phonemic units that constitute the distinctive acoustic features of present-day English are all part of the linear sequence of speech; they are therefore *segmental*. But the language also communicates by means of an intonational system that forms a vertical "simultaneous" axis to cut that of horizontal successiveness. The phonemes that occur along this axis of simultaneity are therefore *suprasegmental*. These suprasegmental phonemes are 12 in number: 4 deal with *stress*, or the loudness of an utterance; 4 have to do with *pitch*, or the frequency at which voiced sounds vibrate from the glottis; the remaining 4 are the methods of *juncture*, the marking of division points in speech by means of prolongation and pause. Since phonemic is morphemic, these 12 suprasegmentals are constantly involved in the problem of meaning. They form a basis for semantic implication and inference.

In Late Modern English, stress is both phonemic and morphemic. Maximum stress tends to give vowels their full phonemic value; minimum stress tends to reduce that value to either /ə/ or /ɨ/. Thus when the definite article *the* bears rhetorical stress as in *Give me THE book*, its full phonemic content is /ðiy/; without that stress its reduced phonemic content is /ðə/. An unhappy couple may decide to /sepəreyt/; if they do, chances are that he will pay her /seprɨt/ maintenance. The stress patterns make all the difference in pronunciation. Such patterns also make all the difference in meaning.

The three words *light* and *house* and *keeper* may combine into at least three distinct semantic spectra, depending upon the various collocations of the following four English stress phonemes:

Maximum Stress	(loudest)	/ˊ/
Major Stress	(next to loudest)	/ˆ/
Minor Stress	(next to softest)	/ˋ/
Minimum Stress	(softest)	/˘/

If the three words listed above combine to indicate the man who keeps a lighthouse near the entrance to a harbor, the stress pattern will run like this:

líghthoùse kêepĕr

If the same three words unite to signify the occupant of a small apartment, then the stress pattern will read as follows:

lìght hóusekèepĕr

If the speaker wishes to complicate the morphology somewhat by describing the occupant of such an apartment as either the slender one or the blonde by means of the modifier *light*, then the stress pattern takes on this slight variation:

lîght hóusekèepĕr

These three different meanings, of course, show that stress modifications produce morphological modifications. The two words *long* and *house* further demonstrate this linguistic principle. If the house isn't short, it is a *word group* with a rising stress pattern that looks like this:

thĕ lòng hóuse

If the house is an Indian council hall, it is a *compound* with a falling stress pattern that looks like this:

     the lŏnghòuse

Stress determinations differentiate two-syllable verbs from their homographic nouns and word groups from their equivalent compounds. The verbs are like the word groups in that they have rising stress patterns; the nouns are like the compounds in that they have falling stress patterns. These differences may be illustrated as follows:

Verb	Noun	Word Group	Compound
subjéct	súbject	a smôkĭng jáckĕt	a smôkĭng jàckĕt
contrást	cóntrast	a wôrkĭng gírl	a wórkĭng gìrl
prodúce	próduce	a dâncĭng téachĕr	a dâncĭng tèachĕr

In addition to their morphological modifications, the stress phonemes of Late Modern English have direct bearing upon the phonemes of the other two categories of the intonational system: pitch and juncture.

With Desdemona strangled and Emilia banging at the door for admission to the bedroom where a murder is miscalled a sacrifice, Othello says:

     'Tis like she comes to speak of Cassio's death.
     The noise was high.

Shakespeare dramatically illustrates what every native speaker of English intuitively realizes—namely, that the various *pitch levels* of the human voice are true indicators of the importance of what is being said and therefore of the amount of attention demanded. Parallel with its four degrees of phonemic stress, present-day English has four levels of phonemic pitch, which may be symbolized and briefly described as follows:

Highest Pitch:	/4/	(highest attention demanded)
High Pitch:	/3/	(high attention demanded)
Normal Pitch:	/2/	(normal attention demanded)
Low Pitch:	/1/	(low attention demanded)

Like the four degrees of stress, the four levels of pitch are relative rather than absolute. A child's /1/ may be much higher than a male adult's /4/, but despite the number of vibrations per second the /1/ will be heard as /1/ and the /4/ as /4/. Since pitch is closely related to semantics, the listener will detect urgency only in the male adult's voice, because pitch level /4/ is that of emotional agitation, whether shock, anger, panic, or pain. The child's /1/, in all probability, will indicate the close of a speech continuum that may properly be called a *sentence*. The listener, in turn, will interpret both situations with effortless ease, simply because he has been conditioned for years to the different meanings of the various pitch patterns. It is precisely because these pitch patterns are the *built-in voice gestures of the language* that they are so vital in conveying that extra-linguistic significance which may be called *psychological tone*. Hence the high-pitched patterns of a shrill-voiced shrew will label her as hysterical, and television uses the deadly monotone of a professional gunman to mark him as emotionally phlegmatic.

Since the most common pitch pattern for an English sentence is /2/-/3/-/1/ (start at normal level, then rise to high on the stressed syllable, and fall to low at the end), any departure from this pattern indicates a special psychological tone. Native speakers of the language grow accustomed to the *terminal contour* of a fall from high pitch to low pitch, with an accompanying *voice fade* and *breath intake*, as the intonation behavior of an ordinary semantics. This falling terminal contour of /3/-/1/ occurs most often in the following linguistic situations:

On *single words* functioning as declarative sentences:

/3/-----/1/
Naturally.
/3/-/1/
Sleeping.
/3/-/1/
Goodbye.

On the *last stressed word* of any word-group functioning as a declarative sentence:

/3/-/1/
The high and the mighty.
/3/-/1/
Better late than never.
/3/-/1/
Down in Dallas.

Normally on a *single interrogative:*

/3/-/1/
Where?

/3/-/1/
When?

/3/-/1/
Why?

Normally on the *last stressed word* of a question introduced by either an *interrogative* or *interrogative word order:*

/3/-/1/
What was his position?

/3/-/1/
Where did he work?

/3/-/1/
Did they go to the movie?

The second terminal contour is that of the high pitch level /3/ rising toward the highest /4/. This intonation pattern indicates one of the three following general meanings: *you better pay attention, notice my surprise,* or *I expect or even demand an answer.* Such a demonstrative pitch movement from /3/ to/4/ occurs in the following linguistic situations:

On the last stressed word of questions occurring in a normal declarative word order:

/3/-/4/
You gave him an option?

/3/-/4/
He took you out dancing?

/3/-/4/
Your fish got away?

On a *single interrogative* that either *expresses surprise* or *calls for a repeated answer:*

/3/-/4/
How?

/3/-/4/
Why?

/3/-/4/
Who?

On the last stressed word of a question introduced by an interrogative or by interrogative word order when the question either *expresses surprise* or *calls for an answer:*

/3/-/4/
Where was the explosion?
/3/-/4/
Was that his answer?
/3/-/4/
Did you dig that hairdo?

Usually, on the *stressed words of series:*

/3/-/4/ /3/-/4/ /3/-/4/ /3/-/4/
I want the following men: Jackson, Jones, Rogers, Smith,
/3/-/1/
and Williams.

As distinct from the high falling pitch pattern, the high rising is accompanied by *abrupt voice cutoff* rather than by gradual voice fade. A reversal of this cutoff may be seen in the shouted /2/-/4/ pattern employed by every mother on her tardy son:

/2/-/4/
Junior!

If Junior hears this unusual intonation, he knows it means "Get in here on the double!"

A few other unusual pitch patterns, with their special semantics in parentheses, may be listed as follows:

/2/----------/4/-/1/
What are you doing?   (Panic)

/2/-/3/-/2/-/3/-/1/
What are you doing?   (Exasperation)

/3/-/1/------/1/
What are you doing?   (Insistence)

/3/-/2/----/3/-/1/
What are you doing?   (Persistence)

As one oralizes these statements, he realizes how intimately pitch is associated with stress. Stress is also a companion of juncture.

The third major feature of the Late Modern English intonational system is *juncture,* the means whereby the flow of speech is interrupted momentarily for the sake of morphological and syntactical clarity. Parallel to the four degrees of stress and the four levels of pitch are four kinds of phonemic juncture, which may be named, symbolized, and described as follows:

Open Juncture:	/+/	Defines morphemic and word boundaries on stressed elements: *that + stuff* *that's + tough* *gray + day* *Grade + A* *see + Mable* *seem + able*
Optional Internal Close Juncture:	/|/	Defines word-group boundaries without the need for written punctuation: *The handsome man | gave the pretty girl | a box of chocolate candy.*
Obligatory Internal Close Juncture:	/||/	Defines phrasal and clausal boundaries with the need for written punctuation: *Joe Jackson || the handsome man who worked at Ford's || gave Mary Smith || the pretty GM stenographer || a box of chocolate candy.*
Obligatory Terminal Close Juncture:	/#/	Defines sentence boundaries with the need for written punctuation: *The bullet struck him # Then he fell # Dead upon the instant # Even before his aides could turn around #*

Since the three types of close juncture all occur after maximum-stressed elements in their respective grammatical constructions, they are marked by distinctive pitch patterns. The optional internal /\|/ produces a /2/-/2/ intonation movement at a *constantly steady level*. The obligatory internal /\|\|/ is responsible for an *upturn* to the first /2/ pitch level before continuing with the second /2/. The pitch difference between these two close junctures is readily heard in the following different statements:

$$/2/-/2/ \qquad\qquad /2/-/2/$$
The man who was strong pulled the sled.

$$/2/ \nearrow /2/ \qquad\qquad /2/ \nearrow /2/$$
Tom Wilson who was strong pulled the sled.

The obligatory terminal /#/ is unmistakable in its usual pitch pattern of /3/-/1/ that finally *falls even lower into silence:*

/3/-/1/↘
He won't be going.

Just as the native speaker of English correctly interprets the four degrees of stress and the four levels of pitch, so he also responds intelligently to the four kinds of juncture.

Summary. Late Modern English has 33 segmental phonemes that constitute its axis of successiveness: 21 consonants, 9 vowels, and 3 semivowel glides. These 33 segmentals, which form a distinctive-acoustic-features spectrum of 7 basic sound oppositions, are supported by 12 suprasegmental phonemes—4 of stress, 4 of pitch and 4 of juncture—that constitute the intonational system. Within this system operate 4 major pitch contours: 2 terminal (high falling and high rising) and 2 internal (normal steady and normal rising). The 2 terminal contours are accompanied by either gradual voice fade or abrupt voice cutoff. Since phonemic is morphemic, the structures of English phonology are the textural constituents of the morphology of the language.

MORPHOLOGY

THE SMALLEST, AND THEREFORE, BASIC, unit of meaning in any language is a *morpheme*. In present-day English a morpheme may be either a *word*, a *base*, or an *affix*. The basic unit *man* is a word in the following simple sentence: *The man runs.* In the word *manliness*, the morpheme *man* is a base to which are affixed two other morphemes: *-li-* and *-ness*. The morpheme *man* may occur alone or combined with other morphemes of its type to form compounds (*mankind, showman*). Hence *man* is a *free* morpheme. The morphemes *-li-* and *-ness* may not occur alone (except in special semantic situations like this present one, wherein they always bear maximum stress) or combine with other morphemes of their type to form compounds; consequently, *-li-* and *-ness* are classified as *bound* morphemes. Since the verb inflection *-s* (/z/) in the sentence *The man runs* is also a minimum unit of meaning, it too is a morpheme. Late Modern English morphemes thus classify into the following categories: *phonemic, syllabic*, and *word simple*. The phonemic and syllabic morphemes are bound, whereas the word simple morphemes are free.

The number of *bound phonemic morphemes* in present-day English is very small, for the phonemic morphemes are closely allied with the vestigial inflections. So compact and economical has the phonemic morphology of the language become under the pressures of its historical evolution that the morphemes themselves tend to be homophonic. The outstanding examples of this tendency are the phonemic morpheme /z/ and its voiceless equivalent /s/, which operate with a different meaning in each of the following statements:

John/z/ other wife.   Jack/s/ other wife.
There are three John/z/ here.   There are three Jack/s/ here.
How fast John run/z/!   How fast John skip/s/!
Who said John/z/ going?   Who said Jack/s/ going?

The four meanings of the phonemic morpheme /z/ and its voiceless equivalent /s/, as illustrated above, are possession, plurality, third person singular present indicative of a finite verb, and contraction of the empty verb auxiliary *is* in the progressive form of *go*. If one says,

John/z/ gone!   Jack/s/ gone!

then the /z/ and /s/ may mean either *is* or *has*.

The phonemic morpheme /t/ also has more than one meaning, as can be seen from the following examples:

I stop/t/ the car.
I have stop/t/ smoking.
I can/t/ stop loving you.

Thus /t/ may signify past tense, past participle, or contraction of the negative adverb *not*. In the following three illustrations, the phonemic morpheme /d/ means past tense, past participle, and contraction of the verb auxiliary *would*:

I sue/d/ the company.
Mr. Jones has been sue/d/.
He/d/ make a good candidate.

Regardless of meaning, the phonemic morpheme—whether /z/, /s/, /t/, or /d/—attaches itself as an *enclitic* modification of a stressed base. As an enclitic, the phonemic morpheme has no independent syllabic status. Neither does its internal equivalent of *vowel transmutation* to indicate such morphological changes as past tense from present in irregular verbs (*break/broke*) and past participle from past tense in those same verbs (*sang/sung*), or the plural from the singular in the stems of irregular nouns (*goose/geese, louse/lice*), or the noun from the verb in cognates (*heal/health, lift/loft, sing/song*).

The *bound syllabic morphemes* in Late Modern English are immense in number and constantly growing in form and function. A few syllabic morphemes are part of the vestigial inflectional system of the language. In their inflectional usage, these morphemes indicate seven basic meanings—past tense, past participle, comparative form, superlative form, present participle, plural number, and possession—seen in the following examples:

> George want/ɪd/ a drink.
> The c͟ ͟minal has been want/ɪd/ for years.
> Did they find the sunk/ɪn/ ship?
> Joe's much fast/ɪr/ afoot.
> That's the bigg/ɪst/ farce ever.
> He'll be go/ɪŋ/ home now.
> Were all his s/ɪz/ clearly written?
> Mr. Jones/ɪz/ dog woke the neighbors.

Far beyond their limited inflectional usage, however, the bound syllabic morphemes of English dominate the language under a system strengthened by the Norman Conquest and refined by the resultant influences of Latin and Greek: *affixing*. The possible number of varying combinations of Latin prefixes joining to Latin bases in Modern English is staggering. A few such prefixes combined with the base -*duce* (from *ducere*, "to lead") convey a sense of this linguistic phenomenon: *adduce, conduce, deduce, induce, produce, reduce, seduce,* and *traduce*.

In the sentence

> John is going away.

the *a-* is a bound syllabic morpheme acting as prefix in the *derivative* word *away*. In the sentence

> John has a way home.

the *a* is a morpheme word known as an indefinite article. In this latter function, *a* is free morphologically, but it is bound syntactically to its word group. In both cases *a-* and *a* do not usually carry stress and are normally pronounced /ə/. The number of word groups that *a* as an indefinite article may appear in is immense. Far more restricted is the use of *a-* as a prefix in words of derivation, like *aboard, abroad, adown, afloat, agog, aground, akin, aloft, amuck, around, asunder, atwitter, awhile*. As an indefinite article, the insertion of *a* into the following ambiguous statement brings immediate clarity:

> Ship sails today.
> A ship sails today.

Here *a* serves as a free word simple restricted solely to *grammatical function*. It is a symbol of the fact that present-day English words may be classified according to *form* and *function*.

FORM.   Modern English words are, according to their form, *morpheme words, compounds*, or *derivatives*. Morpheme words are free morphemes, their boundaries coinciding with those of a word. Such morpheme words as *bird, black, bread, chicken, coop, dog, horse, man, ship*, and *sweet* are thus minimum units of free meaning. When they combine with one another, they become compounds:

blackbird	bird dog
sweetbread	chicken coop
horseman	shipman

Such compounds are accompanied by a *falling stress modification*, from maximum /ˊ/ to minor /ˋ/. If one combines *horse* and *man* and *ship*, he makes a derivative, for *-ship* in this instance is a bound morpheme, that is, a noun suffix meaning "state, condition, or quality of." This *-ship* can sail nowhere alone; it is not a morpheme word. Neither is the *-duce* in *reduce* nor the *-ceive* of *deceive*. But both *reduce* and *deceive* are derivatives.

As the third kind of English word according to its form, a derivative is a word derived from the combination of a bound morpheme with some other morpheme(s). The *base* of a derivative, therefore, may be any of the following:

> A morpheme word: *love* in *lovely*.
> A compound: *salesman* in *salesmanship*.
> Another derivative: *manly* in *manliness*.
> A bound morpheme: *-ject* in *project*.

Regardless of their bases, derivatives share an attribute with compounds: they may be classified as either *transparent* in their formation or *obscure*. Thus *salesmanship* is morphologically clearer to the average speaker of Late Modern English than is *project*. Both compounds and derivatives, regardless of their clarity, share an attribute with morpheme words in their role as form: they participate in the morphological (word-formation) processes of the language.

MORPHOLOGICAL PROCESSES.   The morphological processes of present-day English are several and varied. Some, like compounding and affixing, are as old as the language, time-honored and traditional; others, like telescoping and acronyming, are of recent development, young, jazzy, and brash. An illustrated listing of the major morphological processes of the language runs as follows:

1) *Compounding*. The combining of free morphemes with a falling (maximum to minor) stress modification: *baseball, clubhouse, horsehide, jack-in-the-box, kingpin, lover boy, muttonhead, racing form, streetcar, ticket agent, X-ray*. Compounds may be written together, hyphenated, or separate.

2) *Affixing*. The combining of bound morphemes with either free morphemes, compounds, derivative words, or other bound morphemes to form derivatives: *abject, banishment, contort, deceive, extract, intervention, kingly, laughable, manhood, obstruction, productivity, recession, statesmanship, unwise, vaccination, wholesomeness, yesterday, zoneless*.

3) *Internal Modification*. The replacing of phonemes within a word by other phonemes in order to indicate changes of meaning and/or function: for example, to *gild* with *gold;* two *geese* for one *goose; spoke* for past of *speak, sung* for past participle of *sing*.

4) *Stress Modification*. The mutual morphemic interchange of rising and falling stress patterns to distinguish a) *noun* (falling stress) from *verb* (rising stress) in two-morpheme words: *ADdress/adDRESS, IMport/imPORT;* b) *compounds* (falling stress) from *word groups* (rising stress) of the same form: *that FRENCHman/that French MAN, it's SWEETbread/it's sweet BREAD;* c) *full* and *substitute* (falling stress) word compounds

from *empty* (rising stress) word compounds; *bláckbìrd* and *sómeòne* vs. *ǔntìl* and *wǐthòut;* d) *genuine* (falling stress) compounds from *quasi-* (rising stress) compounds: *HUMP*back and *RED*head vs *hand-TOOLED* and *clip-FED.*

5) *Reduplication.* The doubling of a word, usually with internal modification on either vowel or consonant (though not always, especially in baby talk), for the sake of emotional emphasis— generally of an echoic nature, whether humorous, derogatory, or diminutional: *antsy-pantsy, boo-boo, criss-cross, dilly-dally, fiddle-faddle, harum-scarum, helter-skelter, killer-diller, mish-mash, namby-pamby, piffle-paffle, pitter-patter, razzle-dazzle, riff-raff, sing-song, wishy-washy.*

6) *Replacement.* A meaning identification of one morpheme with another, but with no conceivable phonemic connection: for example, the use of *went* as past tense of *go;* the use of *am, is, are, was, were* as parts of the verb *be;* the use of such personal substitute forms as *me* for *I, us* for *we,* and *her* for *she.*

7) *Zeroing.* The absence of an addition to or a modification of morphological form, with some important meaning implied by such absence: for example, the lack of suffix *-s* in *will, shall, can, may, need, dare* indicates a grammatical state of *non-actuality;* the lack of suffix *-s* in *bear, deer, fish, quail,* and other game indicates *non-distinctive number.*

8) *Onomatopoeia.* The process of forming words in imitation of natural sounds: *bang, crack, drip, fizz, gurgle, hiss, jingle, mumble, pop, sizzle, splash, swish, tinkle, whiz, zoom.*

9) *Acronyming.* The formation of a word by means of combining the initial letters (*UNESCO*) or syllables and letters of a series of words or a compound term (*radar*): *Anzac, Ascap, CARE, Gestapo, NATO, SEATO, Socony, TAC, UNRRA, WAC, Wave.*

10) *Clipping.* The morphological shortening of polysyllabic words: *ad, bus, curio, cute, doc, goodbye, hoax, mend, mob, phone, piano, spaniel, still, tawdry, zoo.*

11) *Back Formation.* A morphological process closely allied to clipping, in which the use of formative elements is reversed upon source words *that look as if they carry bound morphemes: edit* from *editor, beg* from *beggar, rove* from *rover, hawk* from *hawker,* and *enthuse* from *enthusiasm.*

12) *Telescoping.* The morphemic and/or phonemic interpenetration of two words to become one word, in the formation of either portmanteau witticisms (*slanguage*) or serious blends (*astronaut*): *Audiophile, brunch, chortle, dumbfound, flurry, grumble, heliport, insinuendo, jamwich, nucleonics, radiotrician, sneet, sportscast, teleprompter, travelogue.*

13) *Idea Naming.* The transferring of the name of a person or place to indicate the meaning of an idea-thing: *ampere, babel, china, dunce, hector, maudlin, meander, pander, quisling, roentgen, sandwich, simony, watt.*

14) *Imagery.* The creation of words by means of metaphor, figures of speech, and poetic slang: for example, *beatnik, blues, flattop, heater, Jack-in-the-pulpit, mouthpiece, numskull, pipsqueak, pill, quack, rat on, stool pigeon, tinhorn, woolgatherer, yak.*

15) *Functional Shift.* The assumption of a new syntactic function by a word, usually without any change in morphology except in the verb form: a) from *adjective* to *noun* in "the village *green*," "he's either a *pink* or a *red*," "the *main* burst," and "it's a *natural*"; b) from *verb* to *noun* in "take the British *lift*," "to hold *sway*," "count the *yield*"; c) from *noun* to *verb* in Shakespeare's "he *childed* as I *fathered*," or "Joe *candies* the apple," "Bill *mans* the watch," and "Tom *DDT's* the fields"; d) from *preposition* and *directive adverb* to *noun* in "we're on the *outs*," "they're on the *ups*," "it's fourth *down*"; e) from *adjective* to *adverb* in "drive *slow*," "hold *tight*," "think *straight*"; f) from *adverb* to *adjective* in "*lowly* job," "*sickly* child," and g) from *noun* to *adverb* in "drive *home*."

An extension of this list would include *creation from nothing* (as in *kodak*), *borrowing from other languages* (*sputnik*), *lengthening* (as in the addition of *d* to make *thunder* and *sound*), *metathesis* (as in the modern formation of *bird* and *walrus*), and *folk etymology* (as in *sourcastic*, *Welsh rarebit, penthouse,* and *teetotal*). But the fifteen methods of word formation outlined above are the major ones of Late Modern English.

FUNCTION. Words do not exist only according to their form; they also exist according to their function. Indeed their function helps to determine both their meaning and their form. According to their semantic and/or syntactic function, then, present-day English words separate into three major classes: *full* words, *empty* words, and *substitute* words.

Full words are determined by the following attributes: they *always* carry stress, they hold *practical* meaning, they *may not be omitted* from a statement, they *do not violate* literal sense except in figures of speech. The five leading categories of full words in Modern English are *nouns* and their *adjectives, verbs* and their *verbals* and *adverbs:* the nuclei of the various word-group constructions of the language.

Empty words are determined by these attributes: they *seldom* carry stress, they hold *grammatical* meaning only, they *may be omitted* from a statement, they *often violate* literal sense by simple contradiction (e.g., "*pretty* ugly," "*awfully* good," "*terribly* pretty"), and they are frequently *encliticized* to full words. The leading categories of empty words include *verb auxiliaries, prepositions, conjunctions, transitionals, intensives,* and *articles.*

Substitute words resemble both full words and empty words in their *systematic* usage: they are like empty words in that their meaning is merely grammatical and therefore defined by the person, number, and gender of their antecedents or postcedents; they are like full words in that they bear stress and ultimately represent the practical meaning of the expressions for which they are the substitutes. The leading categories of systematic substitute words are the *pronouns* (personal, possessive, and reflexive), the *expletives* and the *deictic* (pointer) *adverbs* of time and place.

Full words and even their word groups, however, may serve as *parallel* substitutes in any of the following constructions:

> 1) After *than* or *as*, nouns may substitute for antecedent predicates with noun complements: *George can swing a bat better than Tom. Mary dances the jig as well as Cynthia.*

2) The verb *do* may substitute for antecedent predicates: *I will go swimming if you do.*

3) Verb modals and timers may substitute for antecedent predicates in which they have already functioned: *Byron had loved more women than Wordsworth had. I can cross the river if you can.*

4) Word groups may substitute for antecedent predicates the complements of which are of the same structure: *Her kisses were honey'd lies; her lies, poisoned honey.*

5) Modifiers may substitute for antecedent noun groups: *I like fried eggs better than scrambled.*

6) A noun and its preposition may substitute for a following noun and its preposition plus objective noun group: *I see no dominance over or pressure upon the general by the colonel.*

7) Verbs and verbals may substitute for postcedent verbs and verbals with their complements: *He had actually witnessed but not really seen the terrible accident. To love is to forgive your enemy. Running is losing that race.*

These seven general categories of parallel substitutes do not begin to exhaust the subject, for in these constructions morphology becomes grammar. The successive axis of grammar is *syntax*.

SYNTAX

IN THE CONTINUAL UNION OF texture and structure at every linguistic level of present-day English, the following equations prevail: phonemic is morphemic; morphemic is semantic; semantic is syntactic. The native speakers of the language do more than merely make significant sounds with their mouths; they also arrange these sounds in an arbitrary and conventional order for the purpose of achieving an organic value that transcends the mechanical value of added parts. That is, the spoken sounds make related statements rather than unrelated noise. Underlying and supporting the structures of all such statements are the principles of Late Modern English syntax. As the phoneme is the minimum unit of distinctive sound and the morpheme the minimum unit of bound meaning and the word the minimum unit of free meaning, so the *word group* is the minimum unit of statement.

The word groups of English are not only the building blocks of its syntax, but also the determiners of its prose rhythms and poetic meters. The chief reasons for such syntactical and rhythmical importance are two: every word group is capable of carrying at least one maximum stress (/´/); and every word group may have its close marked by any one of the three *major* junctures (/| || #/). Operating between major junctures and carrying their own stress collocations, the word groups of the language may be further characterized by whether they contain a *word nucleus* that may substitute for the entire group without any loss of basic meaning. Those word groups that do contain such a nucleus are *endocentric;* those that do not are *exocentric.*

ENDOCENTRIC WORD GROUPS.   The principal kinds of endocentric word groups in Late Modern English subdivide into three basic types: *nucleus back, nucleus front,* and *compound nucleus.* Regardless of the type of endocentric word group, every nucleus is a full word, and can therefore carry maximum stress. By capitalizing the nucleus and italicizing the entire word group in which it appears, we may outline the endocentric types in this manner:

1) *Nucleus Back.*
   a) Noun Word Group:
      The pretty little HOUSE is mortgaged.
      All these crisp red APPLES taste good.
   b) Verb Word Group:
      John's cow *will soon be GIVING* good milk.
      George *could undoubtedly have HIT* a home run.

2) *Nucleus Front.*
   a) Modifier Word Group:
      She wrote in a style *most DIFFICULT to imitate.*
      They want a franchise *OPEN to everyone over twenty.*
   b) Verbal Word Group:
      SINGING sentimental old songs is a pleasant pastime.
      I want *TO DANCE a slow statuesque tango.*

3) *Compound Nucleus.*
   a) Noun Conjunctional:
      The black CAT and the red DOG fought each other.
      Francis was *both BEGGAR and SAINT.*

    b) Verb Conjunctional:

        She *has been PACING* the deck and *SIPPING* brandy
        for hours.

        George *will either DRIVE the car or STAY home.*

    c) Modifier Conjunctional:

        Lee wanted an army *QUICK to attack and SLOW to
        retreat.*

        She drew a salary *neither HARD to spend nor EASY to
        save.*

    d) Verbal Conjunctional.

        SINGING songs and PLAYING games are both fun.

        TO LOVE pain and TO HATE pleasure are the twins
        of masochism.

Disregarding the few minor modifications possible (as with the pronoun substitutes, for example), these then are the major endocentric word groups of Modern English. Whether short or long, they are all *phrasal* in nature.

EXOCENTRIC WORD GROUPS.   There are only two major exocentric word groups, but they are extremely important. Indeed one of them is not only a basic unit of statement, but also the very principle of statement. The *subject-predicate* word group is the *clausal* determinant of whether a statement is an independent sentence or merely a dependent subsentence. As the only clausal structure among all the present-day English word groups, the subject-predicate group can incorporate every other group into its total sentence-level patterns. Hence the subject-predicate construction may exist as either a word group, a clause, or a sentence. All three levels of this existence are demonstrated in the following examples:

    1) Subject-Predicate Word Group:

        "*Jesus wept*" is a famous Biblical statement.

        She saw the words "*Joe died*" in the telegram.

    2) Subject-Predicate Clause:

        If it doesn't rain tomorrow, I'll drive to Chicago.

        His answer was "*When and if I inherit the house.*"

    3) Subject-Predicate Sentence:

        I love you.

        The boy bought the girl a silver bracelet.

As we expand the subject-predicate constructions to sentence level, we discover that we cannot escape using the second major class of exocentric word groups: the *prepositional*. The well-developed system of prepositional word groups in Late Modern English is a result of the syntactical evolution of the language from highly inflected synthetic to almost uninflected analytic. The loss of case endings as markers of function necessitated refining and extending the prepositions of the language to substitute for case endings and therefore to function as allies of syntactical positioning and stress. Since prepositions take objects, which may in turn carry modifiers, the prepositions themselves initiate *syntactical linking;* they link their word groups to other antecedent word groups and thereby continue the expanding relationship of statement in the sentence:

> The man *at the window* saw the girl *of his dreams* step
> *from the stalled city bus.*
> "*In the event of war,*" he said, "fire *on the enemy.*"

PHRASES AND CLAUSES.   Word groups do not exist in isolation from one another; they unite to form larger linguistic units known as *phrases* and *clauses.* Thus *in the event* and *of war* are both prepositional word groups, but together they form one *complex* prepositional phrase that is dominated by one maximum stress:

> in thĕ evênt ŏf wár

In like manner, *the girl*, a noun word group, combines with the prepositional group *of his dreams* to form one *substantive* phrase with one maximum stress:

> thĕ gîrl ŏf hĭs dréams

Similarly, *fire* is a truncated subject-predicate word group (the *you* is understood) and *on the enemy* a prepositional word group; together they constitute a simple clause controlled by one maximum stress:

> fîre ŏn thĕ énemy

In the subject-predicate word group that is also a sentence, the same feature of one maximum stress to indicate clause holds true:

> Jêsŭs wépt.

The principle of maximum stress underlies and determines the phrasal and clausal constructions of which the word groups are the immediate constituents. This principle can be heard at work in the major junctures that it dictates. So the following sentence divides into one phrase and two clauses:

"In the event of war" || he said || "fire on the enemy" #

The phrase and the two clauses are alike in that each is a minimum unit of rhythm. This unit of rhythm, whether in prose or poetry, is properly known as a *cadence*.

MODERN ENGLISH CADENCE.   In present-day English, a cadence is that rhythmical pattern or accentual collocation which occurs between two actualized major junctures. Since these major junctures may be actualized only after a maximum-stressed element, the nucleus of every cadence is a maximum stress. Read aloud in a normally paced voice attentive to the dictates of the word groups, which are the basic factors in the rhythm of the English language, Alexander Pope's famous line scans itself like this:

The proper study of mankind | is man #

The traditional distortion of this line into a so-called "regular iambic pentameter" of the heroic couplet has emphasized a stressless word (*of*), turned a noun compound (*mankind*) into a noun word group, and not indicated the quickened pacing of contiguous minimum stresses (as in study *of*). Even worse than these failures of traditional scansion is its absolute ineptitude to indicate the basic rhythmical structure of the line: two cadences, with one maximum stress each.

Traditional scansion will not allow for the variation that can occur under slower-than-normal conditions of reading (e.g., in dictation), in which the line would structure itself according to the dictates of its word groups into three cadences with one maximum stress each:

The proper study | of mankind | is man #

Thus the cadence—and not the classical foot—is the basic unit of metrical structure in the English language. Shakespeare's blank verse, therefore, indicates a line of from nine to eleven syllables (this is its *unity*) within which operates a number of excitingly different accentual patterns (this is its *variety*). Indeed the resources of the language as well as Shakespeare's genius conspired to keep him from the iambic monotony of dee-dum dee-dum dee-dum dee-dum dee-dum.

NON-DECLARATIVE SENTENCES.   Because a maximum stress is the nucleus of a Modern English cadence and because the end of a cadence is marked by a major form of juncture and because one of these junctures may be obligatory terminal /#/, a cadence of one maximum-stressed syllable may be a *non-declarative sentence*. The word *yes* is a sentence cadence when it carries maximum stress and dictates an obligatory terminal juncture accompanied by either a high rising or a high falling terminal pitch contour. So when Mary asks John if he needs the car for Saturday, he may answer in a *completional sentence: Yes*. His cadence is different, but his sentence is of the same general pattern, when he answers her question about what he wants for breakfast with this classic completional: *Ham and eggs*. Both answers demonstrate the fact that in spoken discourse a sentence is determined by terminal contour rather than by some handbook statement about the need for a subject and a verb to state a complete and independent thought.

The several different kinds of nondeclarative sentences, as indicated by their terminal contours, may be named and illustrated as follows:

Completional sentences:
(When will you leave?) Tomorrow.
(Are you sure you love me?) Uh-huh.
(Will you sign this petition?) If you will.
(What'll you have?) A cheeseburger deluxe.

Questional sentences:
Positive?
No fooling?
On the level?
You sure?

Equational sentences:
The sooner, the better.
The more, the merrier.
Like father, like son.
First up, then down.

Exclamational sentences:
    Boy-oh-boy!
    Way out, man!
    Shibby-dibby-doo!
    Ouch!

Interjectional sentences:
    Oh-oh.
    Aw, nuts.
    For crying out loud.
    Says who?

Imperatival sentences:
    Now, Joe, now!
    Scram.
    Beat it!
    Steady.

Reportal sentences:
    The police notes read as follows:
    From thirty-five to forty.
    Five-eight.
    About 165.
    Brown bald.

DECLARATIVE SENTENCE TYPES.   Despite the several kinds of non-declarative sentences in Late Modern English, the declarative sentence of subject-predicate construction is the outstanding form of both spoken and written statement. Employing its analytical word order so that the subject appears in position one, the verb in position two, the indirect object or its complement equivalent in position three, and the direct object or its complement equivalent in position four, the declarative sentence of one independent clause subdivides into three basic types: with no complement, with one complement, and with two complements.

With no complement:

subject	verb
His car	stalled.
Her struggle for life	failed.
The boys	were still fighting.
The worst possible thing	finally happened.

With one complement:

subject	verb	complement
To love	is	to die.
The professors	graded	their papers.
George	reported	exactly what had happened.
He	fell	on his face.

With two complements:

subject	verb	inner complement	outer complement
The President	sent	Congress	a message.
Tom Jones	bought	his wife	some flowers.
Stonewall	led	a flank march	on the enemy.
The Allies	considered	their invasion	a success.

Since this subject-verb-inner-complement-outer-complement word order is the dominant one for all clauses, whether independent or dependent, it is the major method of syntactical positioning in all Late Modern English sentences: active or passive in voice, simple or compound or complex in structure. Any departure from this fixed word order is an act of rhetorical emphasis or aesthetic variety, an act of formal stylistics.

FORMAL STYLISTICS

WRITING DERIVES FROM SPEECH. AS a derivation it is language in a secondary and non-immediate sense. Just as symphonic notes on scored sheets remain rhythmical mathematics until an orchestra turns them into completed music, so black letters and punctuation marks on a printed page remain speech symbols until some oralizing reader turns them into completed language. And the danger in both music and language is the same—the incompetent interpreter. Arturo Toscanini once remarked to an admiring matron that it was no wonder she so enjoyed his version of a Brahms symphony: this was the first time that she had really ever heard Brahms. What the maestro meant was that other conductors took such liberties with the composer's marked intentions that they played themselves rather than Brahms.

And so it can be with a piece of great writing. A Whittier reading of some poetry of Whitman would have been aesthetic murder, for so antipathetic was Whittier to Whitman's verbal artistry that he threw his gift copy of *Leaves of Grass* into the fire. But there need not be such temperamental odds against a writer to make trouble in communication. The writer has trouble by the very fact that he is committing his language creations to written form, for as a derivation and therefore a representation of speech, writing lacks the communicative completeness of voice and gesture and their intellectual and emotional nuance of tone and mood. As incomplete language, then, writing must carry within itself its own best means of clarification. These means are all part of the formal stylistics of the written word.

The written word is a bully. If a person does not say what he means, then he most assuredly ends up by meaning what he says. In the following sentence, for example, a dangling modifier makes a serious statement ridiculous: *If thoroughly stewed, the patients will enjoy the prunes.* The author forgot the first law of written communication: *Write so that you cannot possibly be misunderstood.*

In order to avoid misunderstanding, the formal stylistics of present-day English depends upon three major attributes to achieve written clarity: *unity, coherence,* and *emphasis.* When a piece of writing is unified in the substance of its structure, maintains an integrity in the development of its texture, and achieves a perfect proportion of parts to whole and means to ends, then it strikes the reader with that transcendental radiance that may properly be called *beauty.*

UNITY.   The unity in a piece of writing is its quality of "oneness," that which clearly delimits it as uniquely itself. A historian, for instance, does not begin an account of the French Revolution with an essay on the political corruption in Japan in the nineteenth century. Similarly, a novelist writing a story on World War I in the historical present and with a German private as hero does not suddenly shift to past tense and adopt the sensibility of a French general as the dominant point of view. Nor does a cookbook give directions on how to bake a cake in the imperative mood and then change at the separation of yolks and whites into the indicative. All such blemishes vitiate the sense of oneness in writing. To maintain that sense of oneness, the formal stylistics of Late Modern English relies heavily upon three major systems of unity: of subject; of point of view; of verb structures.

The *unity of a subject* in writing is controlled by the *thesis:* the central idea to be developed, fact to be proved, process to be demonstrated, statement to be analyzed, or argument to be executed. Whether the thesis takes ten volumes or ten pages in the proving, it is supported constantly by *topic ideas*, all related to the thesis, though varying in length of demonstration from a paragraph, through a chapter, to a volume.

The *unity in the point of view* of a piece of writing is maintained by a faithful adherence to one person, one vantage point, one genre mood, and one audience tone. In *War and Peace*, for example, Tolstoy writes in the third person, from an omniscient vantage point (though heavily biased toward the Russians), in an epic novel of serious and philosophic mood, but with a violation of tone: his fiction often gives way to his sermonizing—an early indication of the growing religious fanaticism that was to end his career as a creative artist.

The *unity of verb structures* in a written discourse achieves a constant sense of oneness in the dominant choices of *tense, mood,* and *voice.* A good writer does not indiscriminately shift from past to future or from imperfect to perfect tense; he does not move from indicative to imperative, to hortatory, to subjunctive, to optative, and back to indicative in the course of a paragraph or two; and he does not jump back and forth between active and passive voice without considering the dictates of coherence and emphasis.

COHERENCE.   The coherence in good writing is the quality of integrity in the development of texture, which ultimately becomes structure. Indeed the very unity of good writing is dependent upon this quality of integrity, for nothing can be itself, one and entire, if it constantly keeps falling apart at the seams. To maintain integrity, the formal stylistics device of coherence depends primarily upon four grammatical systems: *selection, substitution, connection,* and *punctuation.*

Selection is the grammatical means by which one word (or word group) dictates the choice of form in another word. The only words that exercise this selection in present-day English are nouns, pronouns, verbs, and prepositions. Since the four grammatical relations indicated by such selection are *number, gender, person,* and *case,* the personal pronouns alone show the full range of this system for maintaining coherence. Within the system itself the following few basic principles operate: *a)* a subject and its verb must agree in number and person; *b)* a pronoun reference must agree with its antecedent in number, person, and gender;

c) any pronoun capable of showing "case endings" must be in the "objective" form when it follows a preposition or a transitive verb (*who* is becoming an exception); *d*) any pronoun following a form of the linking verb *to be* must usually appear in the "nominative" case (exceptions are growing rapidly, however—e.g., "*It's me.*" "*That's him!*"); *e*) the demonstratives *this/these* and *that/those* must agree in number with their postcedent nouns.

Substitution is the grammatical means that uses either words or word groups as fill-ins for antecedent or postcedent constructions in the context of a statement. As previously outlined, substitution is a major method of maintaining written coherence with the factor of economy.

Connection is the grammatical means whereby empty words are used to join words, word groups, phrases, clauses, sentences, and paragraphs to other similar constructions. The major connectives of Late Modern English are *prepositions, coordinating conjunctions, subordinating conjunctions, relative pronouns*, and *transitional words and phrases*. Just as heat is necessary for the welding of metals, so proper use of the connectives of the language is necessary for achieving a well-joined coherence of written structure.

Punctuation in writing is the typographical means whereby an author indicates the exact placing of the various forms of major obligatory juncture in speech. As an arbitrary means of correlating the visual with the spoken, punctuation is at best only an approximation. In the use of quotation marks, hyphen, apostrophe, and abbreviation period, punctuation is not associated with major juncture. There are basically four primary functions of punctuation in its role of helping maintain coherence: a) *linking* sentences, clauses, series phrases, and word parts: the semicolon (;), the colon (:), the linking dash (—), the linking hyphen (-); b) *separating* sentences and sentence parts: the period (.), the question mark (?), the exclamation point (!), and the separating comma (,); c) *enclosing* sentence parts: paired commas (,. . .,), paired dashes (—. . .—), paired parentheses [(. . .)], paired brackets ([. . .]), and paired quotation marks (". . ."); d) *indicating omissions:* the apostrophe ('), the omission period (.), the omission dash (—), the non-terminal ellipsis (. . .), and the terminal ellipsis (. . . .).

EMPHASIS.   Emphasis in good writing is simply the act of putting first things first and last things last. Emphasis, therefore, is a constant exercise in the critical judgment of proportioning stress energy to the importance of the subject. If everything is emphasized, nothing is emphasized; thus the good writer plays up his most significant ideas and plays down his least. He will not place his leading statements in either dependent constructions or subordinate positions. The following simple sentence, for example, violates the attribute of emphasis: *John won the race with a final burst of speed.* But John could have walked across the finish line; what really matters is that he won the race. So the sentence should read: *With a final burst of speed, John won the race.* The first version of this statement is *loose;* the second, *periodic.*

Spoken discourse, relying heavily on complete communication aided by voice and gesture, employs loose constructions as a natural habit; written discourse, handicapped by incomplete communication and forced to rely upon formal stylistics, must cultivate the periodic construction and make it second nature. An author must construct his sentences along the same general principles that govern the layout of the front page of a good newspaper: the far right column or end position is that of the most emphatic; the far left column or beginning position is that of the next most emphatic; the central columns or middle positions are those of the least emphatic.

With these general principles in mind, we may outline the major stylistic devices for achieving written emphasis as follows:

Repetition and Refrain. Under the stress of emotion, all men tend to repeat themselves as a natural means of emphatic outlet; rhythmical repetition is the chief means of establishing the meters of poetry. Good writing employs repetition to achieve the emphasis of emotional italics, as in Lear's cry of "Never, never, never, never, never" at the death of Cordelia. Refrain, a formalized poetic repetition, achieves an incremental emphasis like that of Francois Villon's "Where are the snows of yesteryear?"

Clausal Constructions. Through clausal constructions, emphasis in writing is maintained by subordinating one idea to another, on the basis of relative importance. Independent clauses should carry the more important ideas; dependent clauses, the less important.

Syntactical Positioning. Syntactical positioning is a stylistic device to achieve emphasis by placing the most important idea last and the next most important first. In establishing proper periodicity, syntactical positioning tucks away all empty-word transitions somewhere in the middle of the sentence. Scholarly writing in general is a notorious violator of this emphatic device.

Shift in Word Order. The two major principles of word order in Modern English syntax are these: the normal subject-predicate sentence occurs as subject, verb, inner complement, and outer complement; single word modifiers usually precede and word-group modifiers usually follow their substantives. Any departure from these two principles is an act of emphasis. Several means of achieving word-order emphasis are: *a)* *inversion of complement(s):* a shift of either the inner or the outer complement or both to the syntactical position of the subject in order to maintain continuity, establish enumeration, or underline the importance of a construction (as in Dickens' famous "Talent, Mr. Micawber has; money, Mr. Micawber has not."); *b)* *use of introductory formulae:* making expletive constructions in order to shift a special emphasis to the subject ("There's a *man* at the door!"); *c)* *shift to passive voice:* using the passive voice to emphasize either the inner or the outer complement ("*She* was given a kiss by the young man!" or "A *kiss* was given her?"); *d)* *use of prepositional word groups:* by turning a noun group of the inner complement into a prepositional group, an author can reduce the emphasis of that complement and shift it to the outer position ("The young man gave a *kiss* to the lady."); *e)* *reversal of single word modifiers:* the placing of single word modifiers *after* their substantives in order to achieve stress and emphasis on the modifier ("Do you have water *enough?*").

Special Emphatic Devices. Whenever an author calls special attention to a word, phrase, clause, or sentence, he is emphasizing it. He can call special attention to his language by tricks of typography such as italics, boldface, capitalization, lower case; by sound-pattern controls such as alliteration, assonance, consonance, rhyme, rhythmical groupings, and distinctive-features control; by stress markings, stage directions, and editorial comments. Whatever the means, these special emphatic devices form the borderline union between communication and communion: that moment when action becomes act and language is thereby lifted to the level of art.

Even if a writer has mastered unity, coherence, and emphasis, he still of course has no guarantee that his work will achieve art, particularly if he is laboring in the vineyard of academic prose. One of the chief writing problems of contemporary Modern English is that its scholarly prose is stylistically way below its creative prose. The main reason for this difference between the two kinds of prose is *the divorce between the spoken and the written word*. This divorce took place under the authoritarianism of the eighteenth-century grammarians; it has since been widened by a Puritan heritage and a tradition of the literary genteel in both Britain and America, further aided and abetted by the snobbery of cultural insecurity. It is the central writing problem of today. Yet the artistic use of English is often most eloquent when it is "incorrect" or substandard. To communicate is one thing, but to enthrall is another. And great literary art enthralls most often when it is dominated by the *speaking voice* of the author or one of his projected characters in moments of passionate conviction. Shakespeare is uproariously effective when illogical, the condemned Bartolomeo Vanzetti brings tears into court with his beautiful "broken" English, and the slangy Holden Caulfield has captivated a generation of Americans. Holden, as a matter of stylistic fact, is a literary descendant of Huck Finn—that democratic master of the spoken word and the private voice become universal. Both Huck and Holden prove that functional efficiency is preferable to refinement; indeed, refinement usually kills by rendering bloodless. The evolution of the language, in the mouths of the people rather than in the textbooks of scholars, has consistently been opposed to the sterility of proscriptive rules and a nonexistent ideal. That evolution begins with the history of Old English.

QUESTIONS FOR RESEARCH AND DISCUSSION

1. Write a phonemic transcription of Lincoln's Gettysburg Address as you would pronounce it and then as you think Lincoln might have pronounced it. Now compare your transcriptions with those of your classmates. What do the differences tell you about regional and dialect variants on both a contemporary and a historical basis? Is there only one right way to actualize the phonology of Modern English? Prove your answer by detailed argument.

2. Analyze the Gettysburg Address according to its word-group cadences; indicate its stress and pitch peaks and its major close junctures. Do you now see any basis for calling this speech a poem of "parallel structures" and "kindred thought-rhymes"? What is the normal range of syllables to each cadence? Does the speech indicate Lincoln's saturation with the syntax and style of the Bible? Use the Lord's Prayer as a basis for comparison and defend your answer with detailed illustration and example.

3. The critic Kenneth Burke maintains that the phoneme /p/ in English indicates *rejection*. Either defend or attack Mr. Burke's theory; illustrate your argument with specific examples.

4. Organize a class project of analyzing Dylan Thomas's "Vision and Prayer" according to its distinctive acoustic features. What are the outstanding sound-pattern attributes of this poem? How well do they support the sight-pattern symbols of diamond and chalice and the metaphysical significance of the symbols themselves? Does Thomas demonstrate the mutual interpenetration of artistic form and spiritual value in this poem? Substantiate your answer in critical detail.

5. Draw up a list of ten homophonically parallel statements in which the use of open juncture /+/ discriminates the differences in internal structure and therefore of meaning. Why is this task more difficult than it at first seems? Illustrate your answer with some "near misses." Now write a brief paper on the importance of the *segmental* phoneme in determining semantic values.

6. The Nazi dictator Adolf Hitler was noted for the immense range of his stress and pitch energy in speaking. Listen to the public utterances of several leading American statesmen and do a comparative analysis on the outstanding attributes of their speech habits. Pay particular attention to stress, pitch, juncture, tempo, and gesture. What do such habits tell about the man behind them? Is man's personal use of language a rather accurate mirror of temperament and character? Defend your answer in detail.

7. Make as many derivative words as you can from the following three bound Latin morpheme bases: *-duct, -ject, -script*. What do these derivatives tell you about the inventive flexibility of Modern English morphology? Be specific.

8. List as many new compounds as you can that have entered the English language as a direct result of the technological advances of the Atomic Age and the Space Age. How important are Anglo-Saxon morphemes in the formation of these compounds? Do directive adverbs play a major role in these fresh coinages? Defend your answers with illustrations and statistics.

9. Get four of your classmates to join you in a study of the use of telescoping by *Time* magazine over the past twenty-five years. Divide the research into five periods of five years each. What is the trend of usage through these five periods? How important a feature is this in the journalistic style of the magazine? What is the ratio of portmanteaus to blends? Is there any correlation petween *Time*'s daring morphology and its immense popularity? Do you detect any contradiction in language usage and official language attitude in this magazine? What cultural lessons have you learned from this project?

10. Write an imaginary dialogue between two American teen-agers on the telephone; use non-declarative sentences as much as possible. What does this dialogue have to say about the importance of *terminal contours* in the expressive communications of everyday speech? Do most people speak in the classically defined *complete* sentence? In the light of your knowledge gained in this exercise, what would you say really constitutes a *sentence fragment?* Answer in detail.

11. Study several official U.S. Government documents and pamphlets. Do these publications abide by the rule of writing so that you cannot possibly be misunderstood? How does the syntax of American bureaucratese differ from that of the artistic prose of fiction? Is it possible to use language to hinder rather than to help communication? Illustrate your answer with detailed argument and example.

12. Prose is basically the language of *discursive progression;* poetry, that of *recursive pattern.* Apply this formula to the work of five American novelists: Sinclair Lewis, Ernest Hemingway, F. Scott Fitzgerald, William Faulkner, and Thomas Wolfe. Now rank these five authors according to the poetic content of their prose. Which is the most journalistic? the most lyric? the most dramatic? the most repetitious? the most convoluted? the most epic? Do these five novelists properly illustrate the widely held belief that "the style is the man"? Defend your answer in detail.

SELECTED BIBLIOGRAPHY

Bryant, Margaret M. *Modern English and Its Heritage.* Second Edition. New York: The Macmillan Company, 1962. A popular *introductory* text: simple, clear, well-organized, fully documented, and provocative of discussion and research.

Francis, W. Nelson. *The English Language: An Introduction.* New York: W. W. Norton & Company, 1965. A scholarly text especially valuable for its adaptation to the needs of college freshmen.

Fries, Charles C. *American English Grammar.* (NCTE Monograph, No. 10). New York: D. Appleton-Century Company, 1940. A pioneer work in the analysis of *spoken* American English.

Fries, Charles C. *The Structure of English.* New York: Harcourt, Brace, and Company, 1952. A key document in the study of Late Modern English, especially useful in the analysis of syntax and sentence construction.

Gleason, H. A., Jr. *An Introduction to Descriptive Linguistics.* Revised Edition. New York: Holt, Rinehart and Winston, 1961. From phonemics to transformations, a mature and scientifically honest study of the current structure and function of English.

Hockett, Charles F. *A Course in Modern Linguistics.* New York: The Macmillan Company, 1958. An excellent complement to Gleason's, offering many valuable insights into the present-day workings of English, with critical emphasis on language, literature, and man's place in nature.

Jespersen, Otto. *Essentials of English Grammar*. University, Alabama: University of Alabama Press, 1964. A recent reprint of a classic study of English grammar from a more traditional point of view. Imaginative and well-informed, Jespersen does not hesitate to make the value judgments shunned by most modern linguists.

Strang, Barbara M. H. *Modern English Structure*. New York: St. Martin's Press, 1963. A subtle blend of traditional grammar and modern structural linguistics, especially valuable for its knowledge of current British usage.

Trager, George L., and Henry Lee Smith, Jr. *An Outline of English Structure*. Fifth Printing. Washington, D.C.: American Council of Learned Societies, 1962. A central work in the current study of Late Modern English phonology, morphemics, and metalinguistics. Scholars support it or attack it; they cannot ignore it.

Whitehall, Harold. *Structural Essentials of English*. New York: Harcourt, Brace and Company, 1956. An excellent brief account of the language, especially valuable for those who plan to teach English at the secondary level.

CHAPTER 3

The History of
Old English
450–1150 A.D.

IMPORTANT DATES

410 The Romans leave Britain, ending the first period of Latin influence.

449 Teutonic Invasions bring the founders of the English nation and language to Britain.

597 St. Augustine introduces the second period of Latin influence into Britain.

725 Approximate date of the oral composition of *Beowulf*, the greatest English poem before the works of Chaucer.

787 Beginning of the Danish Invasions, which influenced basic English in both vocabulary and grammar.

871–899 Reign of King Alfred the Great, who united England in 886, fostered learning, and founded an excellent English prose style.

1000 Approximate date of the flourishing of the monastic revival that preserved Old English poetry in four great codices.

1066 Date of the victory of William the Conqueror at the Battle of Hastings; it marks the beginning of the Norman Conquest, the most important influence on the development of English.

1154   Date of the ending of the *Anglo-Saxon Chronicle;* it officially marks the close of Old English and the beginning of Middle English.

OUTSTANDING PERSONS

Ælfric   English abbot (955–1020) who did much to develop English prose style in the tradition of Alfred the Great.

Aidan   Scottish monk who converted Northumbria to Christianity (635–655), to help make all of Britain Christian by 700.

Alfred the Great   First king of a united England (886–899), patron of scholarship, and father of English prose.

Athelstan   King of England (925–939) who was victorious in celebrated Battle of Brunanburh (937), subject of an Old English heroic poem.

St. Augustine   First Christian missionary to Britain (597), who with the help of Queen Bertha converted all the kingdom of Kent.

The Venerable Bede   Early intellectual leader of the English, who wrote on grammar, prosody, science, chronology, and the Bible; his most famous work is the *Ecclesiastical History of the English People* (731).

Caedmon   First known English poet, who flourished in the monastery at Whitby about 650–675.

Cnut   Danish King of England (1016–1035), who symbolized the merging of the Danes and the English into one race and nation.

Cynewulf   Father of English religious poetry, who flourished about 750.

Harold   The English King who succeeded Edward the Confessor (1042–1066), only to lose his life and crown at the Battle of Hastings (1066).

Olaf Tryggvason   Scandinavian leader who defeated the English at the Battle of Maldon (991), subject of an Old English heroic poem, to further the third phase of the Danish Invasions.

William the Conqueror   Illegitimate Duke of Normandy who defeated Harold at the Battle of Hastings and was then crowned King of England on Christmas Day, 1066; he represents the Norman Conquest, which drove English underground for nearly three centuries to emerge a very different language.

MAJOR ATTRIBUTES OF THE LANGUAGE

Basically West Teutonic in vocabulary.
Participates in the "consonant shift" of Grimm's Law.
Maintains "strong" and "weak" declensions of adjectives.
Supports "strong" (irregular) and "weak" (regular) conjugations of verbs.
Fixes stress on the root syllable.
Is fully inflected and therefore synthetic in syntax, rather than analytic.
Fosters grammatical rather than natural gender.
Is extremely flexible and resourceful in word-formation processes.
Enjoys the aesthetic vitality of an "oral tradition" in literary art.

THE HISTORY OF ANY LANGUAGE is intimately associated with the social, economic, and political evolution of the people who speak it. A study of the development of Old English in its growth, maturation, and decline is a study also in the cultural forces that helped to shape the language. The history of Old English indicates five major periods of evolution, each period dominated by a central social issue and its resultant effect upon the language: first period—Teutonic invasion and settlement (449–597); second period—the Christianizing of Britain (597–700); third period—the creation of a national English culture (700–899); fourth period—Danish and English warfare, political adjustment, and racial assimilation (899–1042); fifth period—the decline and subjection of Old English as a result of the Norman Conquest (1042–1154).

Using these five periods, we can organize the facts concerning the history of Old English. That history begins in 449, when the Angles, Saxons, and Jutes started a series of invasions into Britain that led to the formation of a new nation and its own island language.

FIRST PERIOD
TEUTONIC INVASION
AND SETTLEMENT, 449–597

ABOUT FORTY YEARS AFTER THE withdrawal of Roman troops from Britain, West Teutonic tribes from the general region of Denmark and the Low Countries began a series of invasions into the lowlands of Britain that resulted in the founding of the English nation. The invasions themselves began, as is often the case, upon an invitation of the invaded. In 449, the

Celtic leader Vortigern, hard pressed by the warring Picts and Scots, offered the Jutes of Northern Denmark the Isle of Thanet in exchange for military assistance. Like Caesar before them, the Jutes came and saw

MAP I. THE PEOPLES OF ENGLAND, 550 A.D.

and conquered—not only the Picts and Scots, but also the Celts. And so the Jutes settled in Kent and on the Isle of Wight.

In 477 the Saxons from between the Rhine and the Elbe established themselves in Sussex; by 495 they had also taken over Wessex. A generation or so later, the Angles from Southern Denmark and Schleswig-

Holstein invaded the east coast and the midlands of Britain; by 547 they were in possession of an Anglian kingdom north of the Humber River. The displaced Celts, constantly driven westward, sought their final refuge in Cornwall and Wales. By the middle of the sixth century, the island realm of the English, according to the disposition of the various peoples, looked something like Map 1.

English as the name of a people and their tongue predates *England* as the name of their geographical inhabitance and political identity by about four hundred years. In 601, for example, Pope Gregory called King Æthelbert of Kent *rex Anglorum*. Indeed, early Latin writers used the terms *Angli* and *Anglia* indiscriminately for all West Teutons living in Britain. Writers in the language spoken by the Teutons never referred to it as anything but *Englisc*. The island inhabited by these Teutons was divided tribally until the late ninth century into seven petty kingdoms known as the Anglo-Saxon Heptarchy: Northumbria, Mercia, East Anglia, Kent, Essex, Sussex, and Wessex. When Alfred the Great did finally succeed in becoming king of all the English-speaking tribes in 878, the dominance was Saxon, not Anglian, and the country did not receive the name *England* until about 1000 A.D.

Unity among the tribes, nevertheless, was unavoidable: they all spoke a version of the same language—Old English. Each version was a dialect variant, but the variation was small. Those dialects, in turn, were *Northumbrian*, spoken by Angles living north of the Humber River; *Mercian*, spoken by Angles living between the Humber River and the Thames; *West Saxon*, spoken by Saxons living between Cornwall and Kent, below the Thames River; and *Kentish*, spoken by Jutes living in Kent—the extreme southeastern tip of England—and on the Isle of Wight. As dialects of the same basic tongue, these four versions of Old English sounded much alike. Thus the West Saxon word for "cold" is *ceald*, the very same term used in Kentish, and twin of the Northumbrian and Mercian *cald*. Most of the Old English vocabulary shows variations no greater than in the example above. The speakers of the other three dialects would have had no trouble in understanding the Lord's Prayer in this West Saxon version of *Matthew* 6:9–13:

... Fæder ūre þū þe eart on heofonum, sī þīn nama gehālgod.
Tō becume þīn rīce. Gewurþe ðīn willa on eorðan swā swā on heofonum.
Ūrne gedæghwāmlīcan hlāf syle ūs tō dæg.
And forgyf ūs ūre gyltas, swā swā wē forgyfað ūrum gyltendum.
And ne gelǣd þū ūs on costnunge, ac ālȳs ūs of yfele. Sōþlīce.

OLD ENGLISH AS WEST TEUTONIC.   This West Saxon version of the Lord's Prayer shows that Old English was remarkably like the German of today. And no wonder: both Old English and Modern German are member languages of the *Teutonic* branch of Indo-European. Indo-European, in turn, is the greatest single family of languages on earth, both in geographic distribution and in numbers of speakers. All member languages of this important family are marked by *inflectional usage* and *common word stock*. In contrast to the first attribute, some languages— like Chinese—are *isolating:* they use only invariable monosyllabic roots and indicate their function and meaning by means of syntactical positioning and pitch height; other languages—like Turkish, Hungarian, and Bantu—are *agglutinative:* they affix by juxtaposition and thus form compounds, the components of which undergo little change in either meaning or form; and still other languages—like Eskimo—are *incorporating:* they express the entire syntactical movement of subject, verb, inner and outer complements in one word. But all member languages of the Indo-European family employ inflections—that is to say, they indicate such grammatical features as case, number, gender, tense, and voice by variation of word forms. These same languages, furthermore, share a common word stock: a hard-core vocabulary similar in form and sound, not to be found outside the family. Thus the Modern English *three* has unmistakable cognates in other Indo-European languages: *tri* in Sanskrit, *thri* in Persian, *treis* in Greek, *tres* in Latin, *tri* in Celtic, *tri* in Slavonic, *tri* in Lithuanian, *thri* in Gothic, *drei* in German, *thriu* in Icelandic, *drie* in Dutch, and either ðrīe, ðrīo, or ðrēo in Old English.

To place Old English in the Indo-European family, one may analyze its various language branches in two major groupings: *satem* and *centum*, depending upon which word is used to designate *hundred*. In so doing, the analyst discovers nine leading branches of Indo-European—five in the *satem* group and four in the *centum:*

> *Satem* Group
>> *Indian* Branch. Languages: Sanskrit, Pali, Hindi, Urdu, Hindustani, Bengali, Punjabi, Mahrati, Romany, etc.
>> *Iranian* Branch. Languages: Persian, Avestan, Afghan, Kurdish, etc.
>> *Armenian* Branch. Languages: Old Armenian, Modern Armenian dialects.

Albanian Branch. Languages: Ancient Illyrian dialects, Modern Albanian.

Balto-Slavonic Branch. Languages: Lithuanian, Prussian, Lettic (Baltic); Great Russian, White Russian, Ukrainian (East Slavic); Polish, Czecho-Slovakian, Sorbian (West Slavic); Bulgarian, Serbo-Croatian, Slovenian (South Slavic).

Centum Group

Hellenic Branch. Languages: Ancient Greek dialects (Attic, Ionic, Doric, Aeolic), Modern Greek.

Italic Branch. Languages: Oscan, Umbrian, Latin, Italian, French, Spanish, Portuguese, Rumanian.

Celtic Branch. Languages: Gallic; Irish, Erse, Manx (Gaelic); Cornish, Welsh, Breton (Britannic).

Teutonic Branch. Languages: Old Norse, Icelandic, Norwegian, Swedish, Danish (North Teutonic); Gothic (East Teutonic); Old High German, Modern High German, Old Saxon, Modern Low German, Old Low Franconian, Dutch, Flemish, Old Frisian, Modern Frisian, OLD ENGLISH, MIDDLE ENGLISH, MODERN ENGLISH (West Teutonic).

Old English belongs to the *centum* group and the West section of the Teutonic branch. It thus possesses the following basic traits. 1) It enjoys a highly Germanic vocabulary, almost completely free of foreign terms and generally pure and non-hybrid in nature. 2) Old English participates in the Great Consonant Shift from Indo-European, as originally described by Rasmus Rask and Jacob Grimm and then later slightly modified by Karl Verner. 3) It supports two systems of verb conjugations: one "weak" and regular; the other, "strong" and irregular. 4) Old English maintains a twofold declension of adjectives: one not accompanied by either article, demonstrative, or possessive pronoun; the other, so accompanied by one or the other of these words. 5) As a Germanic tongue, the language of *Beowulf* maintains the principle of fixed stress upon the root syllable, as the direct result of an earlier shift of accent toward the front. 6) Unlike its present-day linguistic offspring, Old English employs a full inflectional system. 7) Gender in the language is determined grammatically, rather than logically or naturally. 8) Though relatively small in vocabulary, Old English is flexible and resourceful in its morphological processes.

One of the most immediately discernible features of Old English is its non-hybrid vocabulary. Apart from the slight influences of Celtic and Latin, Old English is free from the cosmopolitan derivations that constitute so large a portion of the dictionaries of Late Modern English. The texture of this earliest version of English is almost pure Germanic. And even though about 85 percent of this original Germanic vocabulary has dropped from the language, the 15 percent that remains supplies the hard core to English in the twentieth century.

Primitive people have a habit of developing concrete and specialized, rather than abstract and generic, vocabularies; the speakers of Old English were no exception. Consequently, present-day speakers of English find that the Germanic element is fundamental to their language, both in the frequent occurrence of such function words as pronouns, prepositions, conjunctions, and auxiliaries, and in the basic quality of the concepts expressed in the most important and often used nouns and verbs of everyday life—*mann* (man), *wīf* (wife), *cild* (child), *hūs* (house), *lufian* (to love); *mete* (meat, food), *etan* (to eat), *drincan* (to drink), *slæpan* (to sleep), *libban* (to live), *feohtan* (to fight); *dæg* (day), *niht* (night), *sunne* (sun), *mōna* (moon), *mōnað* (month), *gēar* (year); *eorðe* (ground, soil, earth), *heofon* (sky, heaven), *God* (God), *fæder* (father), *mōdor* (mother), *dohtor* (daughter), *sunu* (son), *brōðor* (brother), *sweostor* (sister); *gærs* (grass), *lēaf* (leaf), *bridd* (bird), *wæter* (water), *glædnes* (gladness), *sorg* (sorrow); *ābīdan* (to abide), *beran* (to bear), *licgan* (to lie), *rǣran* (to rear) *restan* (to rest), *sēon* (to see), *singan* (to sing), *stincan* (to stink), *wacan* (to awake), *wilcumian* (to welcome). In short, most matters of *līf* and *dēað* in Modern English are well expressed by the basic Germanic vocabulary inherited from Old English and in a manner that is *gōd, cwic,* and *strang.*

As a West Teutonic language, Old English participates in the *Great Consonant Shift* from Indo-European. This linguistic phenomenon, first systematically formulated in 1822 by the German philologist Jacob Grimm (following up a suggestion supplied by his Danish contemporary Rasmus Rask), took place over a period of centuries and finally resulted in three sets of phonemic displacements: 1) Indo-European voiceless stops lost their stopped quality and became Germanic voiceless fricatives; 2) Indo-European voiced stops then lost their voice and became Germanic voiceless stops; 3) Indo-European voiced aspirated stops finally lost their aspiration and became Germanic voiced stops. From the outcome of this phonemic displacement, it is obvious that the changes occurred in three separate stages, thereby avoiding homophonic confusion. The three steps of phonemic displacement are charted as follows:

Voiceless *stops* become voiceless *fricatives:*

Indo-European	/p/	/t/	/k/
	↓	↓	↓
Germanic	/f/	/þ/	/h/

Voiced stops become *voiceless* stops:

Indo-European	/b/	/d/	/g/
	↓	↓	↓
Germanic	/p/	/t/	/k/

Voiced *aspirated* stops become *voiced only* stops:

Indo-European	/b'/	/d'/	/g'/
	↓	↓	↓
Germanic	/b/	/d/	/g/

As an illustration of what is known as Grimm's Law, the Indo-European /p/ in Latin *piscis* and *pes* becomes Germanic /f/ in English *fish* and *foot*. In similar manner, Indo-European /t/ in Latin *tres* becomes Germanic /þ/ in English *three;* Indo-European /k/ in Latin *centum* becomes Germanic /h/ in English *hundred;* Indo-European /d/ in Latin *dentem* becomes Germanic /t/ in English *tooth;* Indo-European /g/ in Latin *genu* becomes Germanic /k/ in English *knee.* But the law that Leonard Bloomfield called a "dangerous metaphor" has, like all laws, its exceptions. Thus the medial /d/ in *hundred* should be, in accordance with Grimm's Law, the voiceless Germanic /þ/. But as Karl Verner demonstrated in 1875, when the Indo-European accent was not on the vowel immediately preceding the voiceless fricative, the fricative in Germanic becomes voiced. Hence it is that /þ/ changes to /ð/ in Germanic *stressed* positions. In West Teutonic, the tendency is for /ð/ to ultimately become /d/. Such a tendency explains, for example, why the /þ/ of *ic cwæþ* (I said) turns to a /d/ in *we cwædon* (we said) in Old English. As a regular reversal of the Great Consonant Shift, then, Verner's own Law proves the validity of Grimm's; it is also of extreme importance for an understanding of the preterit forms of many "strong" Old English verbs.

Germanic verb inflections are far more simplified than those of Greek and Latin, two languages much closer in cognates to the original Indo-European. As a West Teutonic tongue, Old English offers no exceptions to the general simplicity of the Germanic verbs. Old English verb inflections distinguish only *two simple tenses* (present and past), *three moods* (indicative, subjunctive, and imperative), *two numbers*, and *three persons*. And except for an occasional use of the various forms of *weorðan* (to become, happen, be) with past participles, the language operates almost entirely in the *active voice*. Old English is therefore a lean and economical means of communication, more efficient in the concrete immediacy of poetry than in the abstract discursiveness of prose.

The verb structures within the language divide into two great systems: 1) the *strong irregular* verbs, which indicate a shift in tense by internal phonemic mutation—change of the root vowel; and 2) the *weak regular* verbs, which form their past tense by addition of *-ede*, *-ode*, or *-de* to the infinitive stem and their past participles by addition of *-ed*, *-od*, or *-d*. Representing the basic Indo-European type, the strong verbs of Old English number slightly over three hundred and are very much in the minority. Yet because of their irregularity in formation of the principal parts of the *infinitive, preterit singular* (first and third person), *preterit plural*, and *past participle*, these same strong verbs tax the memory of the student of Old English out of all proportion to their numerical importance. The strong verbs sub-divide into the following seven classes—six general plus a reduplicating seventh:

Class I.   Gradation series: *ī; ā; i; i.*

bītan, *bite*	bāt	biton	biten
grīpan, *grip*	grāp	gripon	gripen
rīdan, *ride*	rād	ridon	riden

Class II.   Gradation series: *ēo, ū; ēa; u; o.*

flēogan, *fly*	flēag	flugon	flogen
lūcan, *lock*	lēac	lucon	locen
scūfan, *shove*	scēaf	scufon	scofen

Class III.   Gradation series: *i, e, ie; a, ea; u; u, o.*

drincan, *drink*	dranc	druncon	druncen
helpan, *help*	healp	hulpon	hulpen
gielpan, *boast*	gealp	gulpon	golpen

Class IV.   Gradation series: *e; æ; ǣ; o.*

beran, *bear*	bær	bǣron	boren
stelan, *steal*	stæl	stǣlon	stolen
teran, *tear*	tær	tǣron	toren

Class V.   Gradation series: *e; æ; ǽ; e.*

metan, *measure*	mæt	mǽton	meten
sp(r)ecan, *speak*	sp(r)æc	sp(r)ǽcon	sp(r)ecen
wegan, *carry*	wæg	wǽgon	wegen

Class VI.   Gradation series: *a; ō; ō; a.*

bacan, *bake*	bōc	bōcon	bacen
hladan, *load*	hlōd	hlōdon	hladen
wascan, *wash*	wōsc	wōscon	wascen

Class VII.   No regular gradation series (*reduplicating*).

Preterits in *ē:*

blandan, *blend*	blēnd	blēndon	blanden
hātan, *be called*	hē(h)t	hēton	hāten
slǽpan, *sleep*	slēp	slēpon	slǽpen

Preterits in *ēo:*

blāwan, *blow*	blēow	blēowon	blāwen
fealdan, *fold*	fēold	fēoldon	fealden
gangan, *go*	gēong	gēongon	gangen
hēawan, *hew*	hēow	hēowon	hēawen
rōwan, *row*	rēow	rēowon	rōwen

There are, of course, minor exceptions and modifications within the seven major classes of strong Old English verbs. But the important point is that these verbs have constantly been reduced by the impact of the weak regular verbs, which constitute *the native Germanic feature* of the language. In other words, verbs like *fremman* (to perform), which shapes its preterit as *fremede* and its past participle as *gefremed*, predominate over verbs like *wēpan* in Old English, even as Modern English verbs like *walk* (*walked, walked*) vastly outnumber verbs like *sing* (*sang, sung*). In the very beginning of the language, then, one can see the eventual triumph of the Germanic verb forms over the Indo-European. Today the remaining strong irregular verbs in English number only a few score, and the work of regularization continues.

As a West Teutonic language, Old English is further characterized by another important Germanic feature: the maintenance of *two declensions for the adjective*, one "strong" and the other "weak." The strong form of the Old English adjective is used when the adjective is *predicate*, is *not* accompanied by either the definite article or a possessive pronoun, and does not belong to any of the weak categories. Bearing in mind, then, the fact that the *instrumental* case in Old English corresponds with the *ablative* in Latin, one may give the following paradigm for the adjective *eald* (old), in the *strong declension:*

	Masculine	Feminine	Neuter
	SINGULAR		
Nom.	eald	eald	eald
Gen.	ealdes	ealdre	ealdes
Dat.	ealdum	ealdre	ealdum
Acc.	ealdne	ealde	eald
Ins.	ealde	ealdre	ealde
	PLURAL		
Nom. Acc.	ealde	ealda, -e	eald
Gen.	ealdra	ealdra	ealdra
Dat. Ins.	ealdum	ealdum	ealdum

In contrast, Old English employs the weak form of the adjective under the following conditions: 1) after the definite article *sē*, the demonstrative *þēs*, or a possessive pronoun; 2) when modifying a vocative noun; 3) in the comparative always and in the superlative often; 4) in the inflection of the ordinals, always with the exception of *ōþer* (second) and often with the exception of *fyrmest, fyr(e)st, ǣrest* (first); 5) when acting as a noun; 6) much more regularly in poetry than in prose. To illustrate further this contrast between the two forms of the Old English adjective, we may give the following paradigm of *ealda* (old), in the *weak declension:*

	Masculine	Feminine	Neuter
	SINGULAR		
Nom.	ealda	ealde	ealde
Gen.	ealdan	ealdan	ealdan
Dat. Ins.	ealdan	ealdan	ealdan
Acc.	ealdan	ealdan	ealde
	PLURAL		
Nom. Acc.	ealdan	ealdan	ealdan
Gen.	ealdra	ealdra	ealdra
	ealdena	ealdena	ealdena
Dat. Ins.	ealdum	ealdum	ealdum

Like the German of today, Old English also fully inflects a definite article to go with its weak adjective.

Old English inherits an important linguistic trait of West Teutonic: *the subsequent stress shift from almost any syllable to that of the root.* Old English thus applies the Germanic principle of fixed stress on the root syllable, a principle that permits Verner's Law (in which *unaccented* postcedent vowels change /þ/ to /d/, /h/ to /g/, and /s/ to /r/) to modify Grimm's. Since almost every unprefixed word in Old English locates its root in the first syllable, the Germanic stress shift is one of *fronting* the stress. The few exceptions to this general rule of maintaining stress on the first syllable may be found in the Old English verbs that are introduced by prefixes of the type found in Modern English *forget, abide,* and *understand.* So important is this principle of fixed stress on the root syllable in Old English that Otto Jespersen calls the earlier Germanic stress shift which brought it into being the greatest phonetic influence in the history of the English language.

The Germanic stress shift is responsible for certain major features of English, whether Old, Middle, or Modern. Since the most important syllables are stressed, the language emphasizes *the essential.* Psychological value stressing, in turn, underlines the key words of English sentences. Because English participates in the great range of stress and unstress of the Germanic system, its vowels and consonants maintain a corresponding sharpness of phonemic clarity. Historically, the principle of fixed stress (fronted on the root) is the chief defender of the native suprasegmental system against the threat of dominance by the Norman French. This principle determines the accentual structures and rhythmical collocations of compounds, word groups, and metrical cadences. To appreciate further the importance of fixed stress as inherited from Old English, we need only to contrast the Germanic steadfastness of

lóver, lóving, lóvingly, lóvely, lóveliness, lóveless, and *lóvelessness*

against the Indo-European fickleness of

fámily, famíliar, familiárity, and *phótograph, photógrapher, photográphic.*

Thus the immovability of stress from the root syllables in Old English is a distinct advantage to that highly concrete and poetic language.

As a synthetic language participating in the major attributes of progenitor Indo-European, Old English supports a full inflectional system, whereby it operates syntactically. With inflectional endings determining function in every word from the definite article to the verb, the position of every word becomes relatively unimportant. This flexibility of positioning is a marked feature of the Old English nouns, which, like those of Modern German, have three genders, two numbers, and four cases (for the instrumental takes the same form as that of the dative). As in both the adjectives and the verbs, the Old English nouns separate into two main classes: strong and weak. The strong nouns are those that originally had their stems ending in a vowel; the weak nouns originally had their stems ending in *n*. A few minor consonantal declensions also exist. But the chief details of the Old English noun inflections may be illustrated in the following three paradigms—two examples of the strong declension (masculine *a*- stem *gār* "spear" and feminine *o*- stem *gūð* "battle") and one of the weak (masculine *n*- stem *cempa* "warrior"):

SINGULAR

Nom.	gār	gūð	cempa
Gen.	gāres	gūðe	cempan
Dat.	gāre	gūðe	cempan
Acc.	gār	gūðe	cempan

PLURAL

Nom.	gāras	gūða, -e	cempan
Gen.	gāra	gūða, -ena	cempena
Dat.	gārum	gūðum	cempum
Acc.	gāras	gūða, -e	cempan

The distinctive inflections of the Old English nouns are therefore three: the *-es* of the genitive singular; the *-um* of the dative plural; and the *-as* of the nominative and accusative plural. Even though they overlap and coincide in many instances, the case endings of Old English permit the language to behave syntactically much in the manner of Modern German. Hence an inversion of subject and verb is a common occurrence in Old English sentences, especially when they begin with an adverb: *Đa hēt se cyning swā dōn* (Then ordered the king it to be so done); *þā ārās hē from þǣm slǣpe* (then arose he from sleep). Similarly, in a subordinate clause, Old English often places the object before the verb: *þā se cyning þā þās word gehȳrde, þā andswarode hē him* (when the king these words heard, then answered he him). Full inflections in the language allow the freedom of a non-analytic syntax.

Full inflections in Old English also support a system of grammatical gender. Old English is like other Indo-European tongues in that it classifies nouns (and therefore all their agreeing modifiers) into masculine, feminine, and neuter categories solely on the basis of the way they form their case endings and consequently without any reference to the natural logic of their sex. The results of this method of determining gender in Old English, as in Modern German, often lack rhyme or reason. *Hand*

(hand) and *heorte* (heart) are feminine, *fōt* (foot) and *earm* (arm) are masculine, and *hēafod* (head), *ēage* (eye), and *ēare* (ear) are neuter. As for the body of which these organs are members, it can act as either neuter (*līc*) or masculine (*līchama*). *Mōna* (moon) and *dæg* (day) are both masculine, whereas *sunne* (sun) and *niht* (night) are both feminine. *Mæden* (maiden) and *wīf* (wife) are both neuter. This unnatural gendering in the Old English nouns is further complicated by the compounds, for they decline in the case endings of their second formant elements. Thus the masculine-neuter *dæg-weorc* (day's work) functions as a neuter and the masculine-feminine *dæg-hwīl* (day, lifetime) as a feminine. A feminine ale-bench (*ealu-benc*) may stand in a masculine beer-hall (*bēor-sele*) for a neuter mankind (*gum-cynn*).

Even though the total vocabulary of Old English never rises beyond fifty to sixty thousand words, the language is completely self-sufficient in both expression and communication. Without the cosmopolitan borrowings that so markedly characterize the immense vocabulary of present-day English, the earliest version of the language relies heavily upon developing its own native morphological resources. These resources, rich in simplicity, concrete meaning, and the flexibility of variation, prove adequate to the tasks demanded of them by poetry and prose.

Variation is the central feature in the literary artistry of Old English. In *Beowulf*, for example, the alliterative demands of the poetry yield a good three dozen synonyms for the terms "hero" and "prince": *æðeling, æscwiga, āglæca, beadorinc, bēaggyfa, bealdor, beorn, brego, bytta, byrnwiga, ceorl, cniht, cyning, dryhten, ealdor, eorl, ēðelweard, fengel, frēa, freca, fruma, hæleð, hlāford, hyse, lēod, mecg, nið, oretta, ræswa, rinc, secg, þegn, þengel, þēoden, wer,* and *wiga.* Throughout the range of Old English poetry, moreover, there are at least thirty synonyms for the "sea": *brim, flōd, flōdweg, flōdwielm, flot, flotweg, gārsecg, hæf, heaðu, holm, holmweg, holmwylm, hronmere, hronrād, lagu, mere, mereflōd, merestræt, merestrēam, sæ, sæflōd, sæholm, sæstrēam, sæweg, seglrād, strēam, wæd, wæg, ȳþ,* and *ȳþmere.* These synonymous variations show not only the flexibility of the Old English vocabulary but also something of its metaphoric quality and its capacity for compounding.

The metaphoric quality of the Old English morphology is most vividly apprehended in its *kennings*, those truncated images that symbolize the names of various things. Through these Old English poems in miniature, a king becomes "the protector of earls" or "the treasure keeper of heroes"; a sword "the leaving of files" or "the light of battle"; a ship, "the wave-goer" or "the foamy-necked bird." The capacity for compounding in Old English is much like that of Modern German: what results in both languages is usually self-explanatory. Dawn is literally *day-red* (*dægred*); geometry, *earthcraft* (*eorþcræft*); epilepsy, *falling-sickness* *fielleseocnes*); lamp, *light-vessel* (*leohtfæt*); creation, *beginning-work* (*frumweorc*); astronomy, *star-law* (*tungol-æ*); medicine, *leech-craft* (*læcecræft*).

In addition to its ability to convey both the simplest and the most difficult meanings by self-explanatory compounds, Old English morphology possesses a wealth of affixes from which to form new words from old or to modify and vary the root idea. Among the most frequently used suffixes of Old English are the following: *-ig, -full, -leas, -lice, -nes, -ung;* *-dom, -end, -ere, -had, -ing, -scipe, -sum,* and *-wis.* The leading prefixes are *a-, be-, for-, fore-, ge-, mis-, of-, ofer-, on-, to-, un-, under-,* and *wiþ-.* As Baugh has indicated, we can take the simple Old English verb *settan* (to set) and modify it into various meanings through the use of these same prefixes: *asettan* (place), *besettan* (appoint), *forsettan* (obstruct), *foresettan* (place before), *gesettan* (garrison), *ofsettan* (afflict), *onsettan* (oppress), *tosettan* (dispose), *unsettan* (put down), and *wiþsettan* (resist). Until overrun by foreign influences, the language developed its native resources to a marvelous degree of expressive efficiency and borrowed only those terms easily assimilated into its Germanic vocabulary.

CELTIC AND LATIN INFLUENCES.   When the invading Teutonic tribesmen settled in Britain, they encountered a language tradition other than their own. The original population on the island was Celtic, and although Celtic was the predominant tongue of Britain, possibly because of the Roman occupation, ended in 410 A.D., some Latin was spoken in the towns. Regardless of how much Latin the Celts had absorbed, it is certain that they had the first opportunity to exercise an influence on the course of the English language. The Celts failed to exert more than an infinitesimal effect upon Old English because as a conquered and subjugated people, they were quickly absorbed by the Angles, Saxons, and Jutes. The Celts lost their civilization and with it their language, and neither the civilization nor the language made a lasting impression upon the mastering English.

The meager survival of a few Celtic terms may be found in the names of some British places (*Kent, Deira, Bernicia, Devonshire, Cornwall, Cumberland, London, York,* etc.), rivers (*Thames, Avon, Exe, Esk, Usk, Dover, Wye*), and hills (*Barr, Bredon, Bryn Mawr, Creech, Pendle, Torr,* etc.). If we add the names based upon Celtic *cumb* (deep valley), *pill* (tidal creek), and *brocc* (badger), we extend the list of terms only slightly. Apart from these place names, Celtic has given the English language only a dozen or so other words of any lasting significance: *binn* (basket, crib), *bratt* (cloak), *brock* (badger), *crag, loch* (lake), *cumb* (valley), *torr* (peak), *dun* (dark), *ass, cross, curse, ancor* (hermit), *clugge* (bell), and the modern loans *slogan, pibroch,* and *clan.* In short, Celtic was the first real influence on Old English—and the least.

If Celtic was the submerged tongue of a conquered people, then Latin was the universal language of a master empire that could teach the more primitive Teutons much about things commercial, military, religious, and intellectual. The three earliest means of influence exerted by Latin upon Old English were Roman contacts upon the European continent *before* the Germanic invasions of Britain, Celtic transmissions of a few Latin words acquired during the Roman occupation of the island, and the cultural impact of the Christian missionaries, mainly Irish, who converted the Old English world to a Latin-dominated religion.

From the several centuries of military, economic, and social traffic between Romans and Teutons on the continent, at least fifty Latin words eventually entered the English language. These words indicate the areas of influence of the higher civilization upon the lower. Thus the Germanic tribes that were to found the English nation adopted Latin military terms: *camp* (battle), *segn* (banner), *pīl* (javelin), *weall* (wall), *pytt* (pit), *stræt* (street, road), and *mīl* (mile). From commercial trade between the Romans and the Teutons came such Latin words as *cēap* (bargain, cheap), *mangere* (trader, monger), *pund* (pound), *wīn* (wine), *flasce* (flask, bottle), *cytel* (kettle), *mēse* (table), *sigel* (brooch, necklace), *līne* (rope, line), and *gimm* (gem). Certain household terms pertaining to the *cycene* (kitchen) and to the foods prepared in it probably entered Old English from Latin while Anglo-Saxon civilization continued to flourish on the continent: *cuppe* (cup), *disc* (dish), *līnen* (flax), *cīese* (cheese), *spelt* (wheat), *pipor* (pepper), *senep* (mustard), *popig* (poppy), *cires* (cherry), *butere* (butter), *plūme* (plum), *pise* (pea), *minte* (mint), and *ynne* (onion). A few other Latin words from the period of continental influence are *cealc* (chalk), *copor* (copper), *pic* (pitch), *tigele* (tile), *mūl* (mule), *draca* (dragon), *pāwa* (peacock), *segne* (seine), *sicor* (safe), *pīpe* (musical instrument), *cirice* (church), *biscop* (bishop), *cāsere* (emperor), *miscian* (to mix), and *ynce* (ounce, inch).

The list of borrowed Latin terms via Celtic transmission is only about 10 percent of the number from the continent: *ceaster* (camp, town), *port* (harbor, gate, town), *munt* (mountain), *torr* (tower, rock), and *wic* (village). The cultural impact of the Christian missionaries upon Old English, on the other hand, was immense and historically important.

SECOND PERIOD
THE CHRISTIANIZING
OF BRITAIN, 597–700

IF THE TRADITIONAL STORY REPORTED by the Venerable Bede may be believed, Gregory the Great wished for the conversion of Britain, even before he became Pope, simply because the blond Angles looked like angels. When Gregory assumed the throne of St. Peter, he commissioned St. Augustine, a personal friend of intense humility and devotion, to lead a missionary band of forty monks in a peaceful invasion of Britain for the purpose of turning the warlike Teutons away from their pagan customs, heathen beliefs, and vengeful practices. Fortunately for the course of Christianity, when he arrived in Britain St. Augustine found an immediate and powerful ally in Queen Bertha of Kent, the Frankish wife of King Æthelberht, who had been allowed by her husband to continue the practice of her New Testament faith. Within three months after his arrival in Kent in 597, St. Augustine had baptized King Æthelberht himself. By the time the Apostle of the English and the first Bishop of Canterbury died in 604, the entire kingdom of Kent had become Christian.

Celtic Christianity and the Welsh clergy rejected St. Augustine's claims for the supremacy of Canterbury and therefore of Roman authority. London continued in its pagan ways, and it was not until after the death of St. Augustine that the next major success for the cause of conversion took place: in 627, Paulinus baptized the powerful King Edwin of Northumbria. But for thirty years Northumbria fought the rising power of Mercia and as a consequence came under the religious sway of the Scottish monk Aidan and the independent Christianity of Iona. Only when the Synod of Whitby was summoned by King Oswy of Northumbria in 664 did Rome receive a full recognition as the orthodox heir of St. Peter's authority. With that recognition, the English Kingdoms not only imitated the superior organization of the Franks, but also rejected the politically incoherent tribalism of the Celts. By 700 Britain had been permanently Christianized under the spiritual leadership of the Papacy. This leadership provided a strong stimulus toward the achievement of national unity under a central kingly government that could wield the powers of systematic administration, legislation, and taxation.

The adoption of Roman Christianity in Britain produced several important cultural forces that were to result in great linguistic effects. The strongest single cultural force was the *fostering of learning*. With the establishment of church schools throughout England and scholarly monasteries at Canterbury, York, Malmesbury, Wearmouth, and Jarrow, the Catholic clergy bestowed the best of Roman civilization upon the Anglo-Saxon world. Within a century a succession of famous teachers like Theodore of Tarsus, Hadrian, Aldhelm, the Venerable Bede, and Alcuin made England the intellectual leader of Europe. These religious men and their academic disciples trained young minds in Greek and Latin, sacred and profane literature, explication of Holy Writ, poetry, astronomy, ecclesiastical arithmetic, grammar, prosody, science, chronology, arts and handicrafts, agriculture, and domestic economy.

The impact of classical learning upon the Old English vernacular was tremendous. Old English poetry, a literary glory of the Western world before the advent of Dante, experienced a rich blending of the secular and the divine. The second period of Latin influx, both in ecclesiastical and in domestic terms, helped to prepare the way for the later hybrid development of English. The monastic introduction of the means to record oral-tradition literature in manuscript form began the history of the *written* English word. With the beginning of English writing (about the year 700), however, the Teutonic purity of the language was no more: a growing minority of Latin imports had already become a part of the original linguistic corporation.

One language borrows from another according to its immediate needs. Since Latin had become the official speaker for the new religion in Britain, it was natural that the Teuton converts to that religion adopt important terms from the foreign tongue. As proved by phonetic tests and literary evidence, a number of Latin imports entered Old English during the period of Christianization or immediately thereafter. These imports, in turn, may be classified as church-related, domestic, and learned.

When Old English did not have a native term to apply to some spiritual or physical feature of the Christian church, it appropriated the Latin one for its use. Thus the following Latin words were incorporated into the English language: *abbot, alms, altar, angel, anthem, ark, Arian, candle, canon, chalice, cleric, cowl, deacon, disciple, epistle, hymn, litany, manna, martyr, mass, minster, noon, nun, offer, organ, pall, palm, pope, priest, provost, psalm, psalter, relic, rule, shrift, shrine, shrive, stole, sub-deacon, synod, temple,* and *tunic.* Since the Christian church dominated much of daily life in the Dark Ages, Latin domestic terminology made itself felt among the household words of the Anglo-Saxons. Thus Old English adopted the following nonclerical terms for everyday use: *aloes, anchor, balsam, beet, box, cap, chest, cook, coulter, doe, fan, fennel, fever, hyssop, lentil, lily, lobster, mallow, marshmallow, mat, millet, mussel, myrrh, oyster, pear, pine, place, plant, purple, radish, rue, savory, silk, sock,* and *sponge.* In addition to these secular terms, the Latin of newly come Christianity also offered the Teuton converts learned and literary words: *calend, circle, consul, elephant, giant, gloss, grammatic(al), legion, mancus, master, meter, notary, phoenix, school, talent,* and *verse.*

THIRD PERIOD
THE CREATION OF A
NATIONAL ENGLISH CULTURE, 700–899

THE TWO CENTURIES DURING WHICH a national English culture was created among the Anglo-Saxons divide into three distinct eras: the era of the composition of great pagan and Christian poetry, 700–787; the era of the Scandinavian invasions of England, 787–878; the era of national unity under Alfred the Great, 878–899. The eighth century was noted for the production of an Old English poetry that showed its lyric intensity, dramatic excitement, stylistic purity, heroic energy, pagan melancholy, and Christian solace. A good prose style is the late development of every language. The major aesthetic achievements of Old English, at least in its earlier stages, are the verse compositions in a special archaic dialect of mixed forms. These great poems may be classified into five important groups: 1) the secular elegies, of which the *Wanderer* and the *Seafarer* are the best; 2) the Cædmonian poems, in which pagan elements blend with Old Testament themes to yield heroic verse of immense power, most strongly executed in *Genesis B;* 3) the Cynewulfian poems of the Christian faith, in which medieval rhetoric predominates; 4) the later imitations of Cynewulf, among which the *Dream of the Rood* stands out as the finest lyrically meditative dream vision in all of Old English; 5) the masterpiece of the language and greatest poem in any European vernacular before the work of Dante—*Beowulf.*

BEOWULF.   As the supreme poetic achievement in Old English, *Beowulf* is a magnificent cultural blend: of folk themes and aristocratic art, of animal brutality and human dignity, of tribal legends and universal symbols, of historical fact and imaginative truth, of pagan *mythos* and Christian *ethos*, of literary substance and musical decoration, of linear progression and circular return. Just as the anger of Achilles is the heartbeat of the *Iliad*, so the monsters in *Beowulf*, symbolizing the forces of evil that every man must battle against in his fallen state of nature, are far more valuable for the energy of the poem than are the historical tragedies alluded to as minor motifs.

The structure of *Beowulf* is the highly sophisticated one of a cyclic-fugal monodrama in three acts: Act I—Beowulf comes to Denmark and vanquishes Grendel (1–1250); Act II—Beowulf kills Grendel's vengeful mother and returns home (1251–2199); Act III—Beowulf destroys the dragon, with the help of Wiglaf, and dies (2200–3182). The recitation time for each of these three acts is about an hour: long enough to provide an evening's entertainment, yet short enough to keep the beer-drinking audience of Teuton warriors from getting restless. Thus *Beowulf* is not an epic in the Homeric sense of the term. The Old English monodrama lacks epic scope and epic tone, for its author is primarily a dramatic lyricist dealing with heroic materials. The dramatic variation of fact and fiction, the lyric insight into states of mind, the impressionistic expression of emotion—all these tasks capture his poetic energies.

By means of variation, recapitulation, cumulative enrichment, and the association of ideas, the *Beowulf* poet interlocks his basic themes throughout the three acts of the monodrama. Such interlocking of themes is the result of at least eight basic intentions, which demonstrate the magnificent cultural blend of the poem: to recount the well-known adventures of the bear's-son hero—the battles with Grendel, Grendel's mother, and the dragon; to portray the details of Beowulf's life in a *pointillist* manner— in keeping with variation, allusion, and cyclic progression; to satisfy the antiquarian interests of the audience in a mirror-of-society per- formance; to point Christian morals to a people not yet far removed from pagan times and heathen customs; to deliver such courtesy-book examples as nobility, generosity, loyalty, and valor to the warrior members of the tribal king's inner court; to provide a kind of epic setting for the major action of the poem; to uphold the relationship between a lord and his *comitatus* (kingly retainers of noble rank) by showing that princeless people are defenseless; and to substantiate the pervadingly somber mood of the poem by the lyric expression that man's life is short and uncertain. All these intentions the *Beowulf* poet achieves with a stylistic mastery of the chief features of Old English poetry.

THE SCANDINAVIAN INVASIONS.   Within half a century after the oral composition of *Beowulf*, what is popularly known as the Viking Age began. From the middle of the eighth century to the early part of the eleventh, North Germanic tribes attacked, plundered, and conquered the peoples living along the North Sea and the Baltic. Russia felt the scourge of the Swedes; the Faroe Islands, Iceland, Greenland, and Labra- dor that of the Norwegians; Normandy and England that of the Danes. For a quarter of a century (1016–1042) a Danish king, in the person of Cnut and his two successors, sat on the throne of England and exercised control over most of the Scandinavian world from his capital of London. Before that culmination of Scandinavian power, a century of raids and battles between Danes and English formed a second era within the period of Old English history that witnessed the creation of a national culture.

As the *Anglo-Saxon Chronicle* indicates, the Danish invasions of Eng- land that began in 787 and ended in 878 with the Treaty of Wedmore divide into two stages. The first stage ran from 787 to 850 and may be called "early raids"; the second stage, which extended from 850 to 878, was a time of "army warfare." In the first stage, small isolated bands plundered towns and monasteries along the English seacoast. What the Danish pirates were after in their raids on such places as Lindisfarne, Jarrow, and the East Anglian settlements were jewels, costly robes, sacred vessels of silver and gold, and slaves. With the arrival of a Danish fleet of three hundred and fifty ships off the Isle of Thanet in 850, however, avarice included the land itself, for the following year saw the beginning of large-scale invasions, pitched battles between armies of major size, and a growing series of Danish settlements on English soil. By 866 a big Danish army had overrun East Anglia; the following year it captured York; two years later it cost King Edmund his life. By 870 most of eastern England was under Scandinavian control.

For the next eight years, the triumphant Danes tried to conquer Wessex. They would have succeeded had it not been for the resourceful courage and military genius of one man—King Alfred, by nature a gentle scholar of precarious health. After suffering an almost disastrous midwinter raid in 878, Alfred—with fresh reinforcements of Saxon thanes from Somerset, Wiltshire, and Hampshire—launched a counteroffensive from his refuge in the Parret fenland (fifty miles from Cornwall and the end of the English world), fell upon the Danish army under Guthurum, and crushed it in the Battle of Ethandun. As a result of that English victory, Wessex was saved, the Danes withdrew behind a line from Chester to London into their own Danelaw, Guthurum accepted baptism, and political adjustment and racial assimilation between the two peoples began. With the securing of London for the English territory a few years later, King Alfred was free to turn his attention to cultural matters.

THE GOLDEN ERA.   During the twenty-one years from the signing of the Treaty of Wedmore in 878 to his death in 899, King Alfred, the English Charlemagne, achieved what history can call the Golden Era of National Unity. Politically, Alfred remodeled the Kingdom of Wessex and founded an efficient administrative system within the local shires. Militarily, he created a navy, garrisoned permanent earthwork fortifications against Danish incursions, and revamped the English army. Sociologically, he encouraged the growth of a city life that ultimately surpassed the highest cultural achievements of monasticism at its best. Religiously, he began the task of educating an ignorant clergy, most of whom did not know the meaning of the Latin they intoned at Mass, and of restoring the sacked monasteries in Mercia and Northumbria. Scholastically, he welcomed intellectual refugees from the North of England, imported foreign scholars to strengthen English learning, and replenished many a ravaged library. Literarily, he founded the prose tradition of the English language by keeping the first historical record in English via the

Anglo-Saxon Chronicle, by compiling a handbook of universal history and geography for the use of his subjects, and above all by translating three important medieval works from the Latin: Pope Gregory's *Pastoral Care*, the Venerable Bede's *Ecclesiastical History of the English People*, and Boethius' famous bridge between the ancient classical world and the Renaissance, *The Consolation of Philosophy*. In addition to all these accomplishments, this remarkable Anglo-Saxon king extended learning to the higher laity, established the first "public schools" to make literate the sons of nobles and thanes, and everywhere championed a mastery of the Old English vernacular. Truly, he was Alfred "the Great."

FOURTH PERIOD
POLITICAL ADJUSTMENT,
AND RACIAL ASSIMILATION, 899–1042

FOR ALMOST A CENTURY AFTER the death of King Alfred, until the year 991, the revitalized Kingdom of Wessex continued its political and military conquest of the Danelaw. The task of the Saxon kings was facilitated because the Viking warriors, once united for offensive warfare, failed in the pursuits of peace to execute a racial unity and coherence. A number of rival settlements, each under the authority and jurisdiction of a petty ruler called either *king* or *earl*, sprang up and flourished. In their rivalry, these settlements were no match for the national might of Alfred's successors: Edward the Elder (900–924) and Athelstan (924–940).

During the reign of Athelstan, the English secured one of their most brilliant victories, for in 937 in the Battle of Brunanburh, fought in Northumbria, the Anglo-Saxon army scored a stunning triumph over a combined force of Danes and Scots. This Battle of Brunanburh is celebrated in an Old English poem of the same name. By the reign of Edgar (959–975), Wessex had absorbed the original Danelaw, only the Celtic Wales and Scotland remained independent, and the English king could honestly consider himself an "Emperor of Britain." The Danes tolerated a light rule, accepted baptism, enjoyed their good farm lands, followed their own customs, obeyed their own laws, and discovered that they had much in common with their West Teutonic cousins. Eventually there was a fusion of the two peoples: a blood union in which the Danes adopted the language of the English and the English learned concepts of freedom higher than their own and legal matters that included the primitive beginnings of the jury system.

Near the end of the tenth century, just at the time when it appeared that the English had completely mastered the Danes at home, a new series of Scandinavian invasions began. In 991, Olaf Tryggvason sailed up the Thames with an allied Danish fleet of ninety-three ships. In the ensuing Battle of Maldon, celebrated in Old English heroic verse, Tryggvason defeated the English forces under the East Saxon earl Byrhtnoth. With the death of their gallant leader, the English decided to bribe the invading Danish host and turn it away from plunder. But the payment of blackmail has a habit of escalating, and such proved the case with Olaf. Three years after his original raid, Tryggvason, soon to become king of Norway, joined forces with King Svein of Denmark and launched a new attack on London.

For the next twenty years, the English bought one temporary truce after another by paying each time a higher price for peace. Enjoying the fruits of bribery, the Danes continued to break every pledge and to march, murder, and rob. Then in 1014, King Svein decided to make himself King of England too. Joining forces with his son Cnut, Svein won a series of victories over English armies throughout Britain and succeeded in driving Ethelred the Unready into exile. After seizing the English throne, Svein died suddenly that same year and was succeeded by his son Cnut (or Canute). For three years Cnut fought to consolidate his claims to the throne and ultimately established a quarter of a century of Danish rule in England in the persons of himself (1016–35), his son Harold I (1035–40), and his half-brother Hardecanute (1040–42).

In the latter half of the tenth century, before the Danes achieved their two-generation mastery in Britain, the intellectual and religious example of Alfred the Great came to a great emulative fruition in the work of three church leaders: Dunstan (d. 988), archbishop of Canterbury; Athelwold (d. 984), bishop of Winchester; and Oswald (d. 992), bishop of Worcester and archbishop of York. With the political blessing of King Edgar (959–975), these three clergymen followed the continental examples of the monasteries at Cluny, Fleury, and Ghent, removed secularism from the abbeys of England, and applied the Benedictine Rule to monks pledged to poverty, chastity, and obedience.

The resultant monastic revival, for which Athelwold's *Concordia Regularis* became the unifying rule in organization and practice, led to a general reformation of morality in England. Religious rehabilitation was responsible for an intellectual improvement that witnessed the growth of scholarly monasteries, the establishment of more church schools, and the encouragement of learning among both the regular and the secular clergy. Before the year 1000, monasticism in England had again become the center of literary activity. From it flowed English popularizations of "universal knowledge" and the preservation of important manuscripts in Latin and in the vernacular, handing down to the present the bulk of Old English poetry in four great codices: *Cotton Vitellius A XV, Junius XI*, the *Exeter Book*, and the *Vercelli Book*. With growing church influence, learning, and literary activity, the Latin language once again made itself felt in the vocabulary of Old English.

LATIN INFLUENCE.   In contrast with the early popular Christian borrowings of Latin into Old English, the later imports from the official religious tongue—from the reign of Alfred the Great through the monastic revival—are religious, literary, learned, and scientific. They have the smell of the library upon them, entering the language of Anglo-Saxon civilization in books rather than in speech.

Among the religious terms that entered Old English, the following are significant: *alb, Antichrist, antiphoner, apostle, cantor, canticle, cell, cloister, collect, creed, chrism, dalmatic, demon, dirge, font, idol, nocturn, prime, prophet, sabbath, synagogue*, and *troper*. Literary borrowings include *aspide* (viper), *camel, history, lamprey, paper, scorpion, tiger*, and *title*. Learned imports, on the other hand, are *accent, brief* (verb), *decline* (act of grammar), *pumice, quatern* (book quire), and *term(inus)*. Scientific specialist terms from Latin consist of such botanical names as *cedar, celandine, centaury, coriander, cucumber, cypress, fig, ginger, hellebore, laurel, lovage, magdala* (almond), *periwinkle, petersili* (parsley), and *verbena;* and of such medical items as *cancer, circuladl* (shingles), *paralysis, plaster*, and *scrofula*.

Unassimilated Latin terms were also borrowed by Old English without becoming a part of the native vocabulary at that time. Such terms remained in their foreign forms and were later reintroduced into the English language; a few of these forms include *absolutionem, acolitus, adamans, apocalipsin, apostata, basilica, bibliothece, catacumbas, cathedra, columne, cometa, confessores, corporale, cristalla, epactas, invitatorium, prologus*, and *unguentum*.

Old English documents show that the Christianizing of Britain introduced at least four hundred and fifty Latin words into the language. About a hundred of them were too refined to receive common coinage into the Anglo-Saxon vocabulary. The remaining three hundred and fifty Latin imports are not a true indication of the extent of the impact of Latin upon Old English, which was extensive and thorough in the intensity with which Latin stimulated Old English to develop its native resources to express new ideas, and in the degree to which Old English assimilated its Latin imports and Anglicized them in new verb forms and noun compounds.

The first feature—that of Latin stimulation of the native resources of Old English—may be seen in the following few Anglo-Saxon terms for Christian ideas: a *hēahfæder* (high father) is a patriarch, a *wītega* (wise one) is a prophet, a *þrōwere* (a pain-sufferer) is a martyr, and a *hālga* (holy one) is a saint; the Latin *eucharist* becomes Old English *hūsl* (housel); *Scriptures, gewritu* (writings); *ēvangelium, gōdspell* (gospel, good news), and *Spiritus Sanctus, Hālig Gāst* (Holy Ghost); Old English synonyms for the idea of God are heroic and concrete in their variation: *scieppend* (creator, maker), *fruma* (founder, beginner), *metod* (measurer), *fæder* (father), *dryhten* (prince), *wealdend* (ruler), *þēoden* (chief), *weard* (protector), and *hlāford* (lord, loaf-guardian); a cross in Old English may be either a *rōd* (rood), a *trēow* (tree), or a *gealga* (gallows); resurrection is *ærist* (arising), moral violation is *synn* (sin), and the world ends on *dōmdæg* (Doomsday, Judgment Day).

The degree to which Latin imports were assimilated into Old English is seen in the formation of verbs from Latin bases, as in *plantian* (to plant) and *crispian* (to curl), *culpian* (to humiliate self), *fersian* (to versify), and *gemartyrian* (to martyr). The use of *martyr* with Old English suffixes to form *martyrdōm, martyrhād*, and *martyrung* is a further indication of assimilation, and the Latin derivation *church* joins with Old English bound and free morphemes to form over forty derivatives and compounds.

SCANDINAVIAN INFLUENCE.   The influence of Latin, like that of Norman French later on, was aristocratic. The impact of Scandinavian upon Old English was democratic. Danes and Anglo-Saxons, as North Teutons and West Teutons, fought and made peace together like members of the same family; they lived side by side, intermarried, and eventually became truly one. Culturally, the two peoples were about equal; linguistically, they shared a common basic vocabulary, for Old English and Old Norse were very much alike—indeed identical in such important words as *man, wife, father, folk, mother, house, thing, life, sorrow, winter, summer; will, can, meet, come, bring, hear, see, think, smile, ride, stand, sit, set, spin; full, wise, well, better, best, mine, thine, over, under*. The Norman Conquest reduced to practically nothing the linguistic penetration of Scandinavian in the one major area where the Danes were superior to the native English: national administration, in which equable division of governmental units, fair taxation, strong criminal law, regulated commerce, and a high sense of personal honor predominated. The Scandinavian influence on Old English was not technical, learned, or literary but rather basic, commonplace, and everyday. The basic is often profound, and such was the impact of Scandinavian upon Old English in vocabulary, phonology, morphology, and grammar.

As with Celtic, the Scandinavian influence may be seen in the Danish place-names throughout England, especially in Yorkshire, Lancashire, Lincolnshire, Cumberland, Westmoreland, and Norfolk. Whereas the Celtic place-names are very small in number, the Scandinavian run to 1500. All English settlements whose names end in the Scandinavian morphemes *-by* (farm, town), *-thorp(e)* (village), *-thwaite* (isolated piece of land), and *-toft* (house and grounds) show the Danish impact on British geography —for example, *Derby, Grimsby, Rugby, Thoresby, Whitby; Althorp, Bishopsthorpe, Gawthorpe, Linthorpe; Applethwaite, Braithwaite, Cowperthwaite, Langthwaite, Satterthwaite; Brimtoft, Eastoft, Langtoft, Lowestoft*, and *Nortoft*.

In even sharper contrast with Celtic, which gave only a dozen words other than place-names to English, Scandinavian is the source of about eighteen hundred entries into the standard vocabulary of the language and of hundreds of others in the various British dialects. The simple everyday quality of the Scandinavian word loans into English is demonstrated in the following basic terms, which are traceable to Old Norse: 1) nouns: *axle-tree, band, bank, birth, boon, booth, brink, bull, calf* (of leg), *crook, dirt, down, dregs, egg, fellow, freckle, gait, gap, girth, guess, hap, keel, kid, law, leg, link, loan, mire, race, reindeer, reef* (of sail), *rift, root, scab, scales, score, scrap, seat, sister, skill, skin, skirt, sky, slaughter, snare, stack, steak, swain, thrift, tidings, trust, want, window;*

2) adjectives: *awkward, flat, ill, loose, low, meek, muggy, odd, rotten, rugged, scant, seemly, sly, tattered, tight, ugly, weak, wrong;* 3) verbs: *to bait, bask, batten, call, cast, clip, cow, crave, crawl, die, droop, drown, egg on, flit, gape, gasp, get, give, glitter, hit, kindle, lift, lug, nag, ransack, raise, rake, rid, rive, scare, scout, scowl, scrape, scream, screech, scrub, skulk, snub, sprint, take, thrive, thrust,* and *want.*

So permeating is the Scandinavian influence on the fundamental concepts of the English vocabulary that even today a household tragedy in Britain or America finds expression in key words from the Danes: a housewife who suffers *anger* from an overdose of wedlock may *take wing* from the marriage *haven,* or *give* her *husband* the *gate* or the *knife,* or crack his *skull.* A few dialect variants include *dag* for *dew, garth* for *yard, kirk* for *church, kirn* for *churn, kist* for *chest, loup* for *leap, lythe* for *listen, may* for *maid, mum* for *mouth, nowt* for *neat* (cattle), and *waur* for *worse.* Such dialect variants are relics of a past linguistic struggle in which native forms often crowded out their imported Old Norse equivalent rivals.

Even though an Anglo-Saxon of the ninth and tenth centuries had no great difficulty in understanding the cognate speech of a Viking, important *phonological differences* did exist between Old Norse and Old English. Both North Teutonic and West Teutonic, for example, had developed the phonemic consonant combination /sk/. Old Norse retained this sound; Old English, except possibly in the graphemic grouping *scr,* palatalized /sk/ to /š/ (written *sc*). The Modern English spelling for /š/ is *sh;* hence words like *ship, shape,* and *fish* show that they are native terms. By way of contrast, the original Teutonic /sk/ in words like *sky, skin, skill, scrape, scrub, bask,* and *whisk* shows that they are all Scandinavian loans. The Old English *scyrte* has become Modern English *shirt;* Old Norse *skyrta,* Modern English *skirt.* In a manner similar to the retention of /sk/, Old Norse maintained a hard, compact, and grave pronunciation of /g/ and /k/. The presence of these sounds in such words as *kid, dike, get, give, gild,* and *egg* indicates their Scandinavian origin.

Consonant differences did not constitute the only phonological divergence between Old Norse and Old English. The original Teutonic *ai* became Old Norse *ei* (*sveinn*) and Old English *ā* (*swān*), or Old Norse *au* (*lauss*) and Old English *ēa* (*lēas*). From their vocalic separation from native English cognates, such words as *nay* (no) and *hale* (whole) show that they come from Scandinavian sources. Phonology reveals that *aye, swain*, and *reindeer* are from these same sources. In the linguistic struggle for the dominance of one pronunciation over another, Old English made modifications and refinements on Old Norse words (*shift*, for example, is an Anglicized form of *skipta*); Old Norse did the same kind of adapting on Old English (thus the English king *Æðelred Eadgares sunu* becomes in a Scandinavian saga *Aðalráðr Játgeirsson*).

The *morphological* impacts of Scandinavian upon Old English were several and of varied degrees of importance. Apart from the first forty Danish words taken into the English language—terms mainly devoted to naval, military, and legal affairs—the earliest morphemic influence of Scandinavian was the impetus to native translations of foreign ideas and concepts, as in *bōtlēas* (not compensable), *hāmsōcn* (attack on an enemy in his house), and *landcēap* (land purchase tax). The Danes revitalized native English expressions that had spent themselves into obsolescence. Thanks to Scandinavian, words like *bairn*, *blend*, *dale*, *rim*, *run*, and *till* gained new life in the English language. In some cases the imported morpheme replaced the native; thus Old Norse won out over Old English in the perseverance of such terms as *anger*, *awe*, *bark*, *boon*, *cut*, *loan*, *sister*, *sky*, *take*, *weak*, and *wing*. In other cases the imported morpheme developed the specially different meaning of the synonym, as in *ill* for native *sick*, *skin* for *hide*, and *skill* for *craft*.

But the most valuable linguistic contributions of Scandinavian were 1) achieving order in the confused pronoun system of Old English with the introduction of Danish *they*, *them*, *their*, *the same*, and (probably) *both* into the language; 2) contributing several Danish "empty" form words to help in the gradual evolution of English syntax from a synthetic to an analytic nature, words like *hence*, *thence*, *whence*, *though*, and *till*; 3) accelerating the reduction of grammatical forms and the leveling of inflections in North England, where the Danes sacrificed stylistic niceties for simple clarity and direct communication—a process soon reinforced by the Norman Conquest.

In addition to the contribution of their plural pronouns, the Danes gave the Anglo-Saxons *are* to replace the West Saxon *syndon* as the non-singular present tense of *to be*. This contribution, beyond its intrinsic value, is a symbol of the intimacy achieved between two tongues that were spoken together in the same area for two centuries. This closeness undoubtedly resulted in mutual practices of phrase and clause construction, shared patterns of intonation and syntactical grouping, and common expressions of idiomatic usage. The Scandinavian habit of strongly stressing the directive element of an idiomatic verb, for instance, is an important feature of the suprasegmental morphology of Modern English. Throughout Old and Middle English, Danish stylistics reinforced the native tendency toward retaining the relative pronoun in relative clauses and using or omitting *that* in other clauses. The Scandinavian rules governing the use of *shall* and *will* very nearly coincided with those of Middle English. Shakespeare's use of verb auxiliaries is more Danish at times than English. The sentence just written is a present-day witness to the Modern English habit of placing the genitive modifier *before* its possessed noun, a grammatical inheritance from Scandinavian in contrast with the practices of Old English and Modern German.

FIFTH PERIOD
THE DECLINE AND SUBJECTION
OF OLD ENGLISH, 1042–1154

WITH THE DISSIPATION OF CNUT's Nordic Empire by his weak and incompetent successors, England had a quarter century to unify her people under a strong monarchy in order to resist nationally any further foreign incursions. That England failed to unite into a powerful state is due in large measure to the temperament of Edward the Confessor (1042–66), inept son of Ethelred the Unready and of Emma, daughter of Richard I, Duke of Normandy. In the depths of his being, Edward was not a Saxon king but a Norman monk. During the long years of his exile, from boyhood to middle age, the Confessor developed a religious sensibility and a pious practice that completely vitiated political ambition and administrative vision.

As a result of his protracted association with Norman monasticism, when Edward became king he was personally something of a saint, but in statesmanship, he was little better than a fool. Through his personal sanctity he maintained the monastic ideal of chastity; hence his unconsummated marriage with Eadgyth, daughter of Earl Godwin, produced no heir to the English throne and left a disputed succession to divide further a disunited country at the moment of its greatest peril. The Confessor did nothing in the course of his reign to improve the laws and institutions of his island realm. Instead of effecting royal control over the great earldoms of England, Edward promoted provincialism and intersectional rivalry so that Northumbria and Mercia stood opposed to the leadership of the south. To make government affairs worse, he packed his own court with Norman secretaries and chaplains, appointed Bishop Robert of Jumièges as Primate of England, and turned over the administration of Herefordshire and the wardship of the Welsh March to the Norman Earl Ralph.

Militarily, the Confessor bent every foolish effort to make Britain almost totally defenseless to a continental invasion: he refused to let the English army learn the advanced techniques of cavalry fighting, he erected no loyalist castles to serve as rallying points and armed centers of resistance, he permitted a series of Sussex ports to fall into Norman hands, and in the heart of London he allowed some Rouen wine merchants to hold their own wharf at the mouth of the Wall Brook. Thus Edward was the first shock wave of the Norman Conquest. His own ingenuous ineptitude weighed heavier in the ultimate subjugation of England than did the cunning efficiency of William the Conqueror.

During the ninth and tenth centuries, while the Danes were settling in the northern and eastern portions of England, other Norse tribesmen invaded northern France via the Seine River and fanned out over a coastal district to the depth of seventy-five miles. The district came to be known as Normandy and its Scandinavian inhabitants as the Normans. These highly adaptable and fiercely energetic Teutons rapidly learned several important lessons from the French civilization they had entered: the value of military tactics for the success of an army, the superior methods of Frankish law and its jury system, the strict necessity of organizing society under a strong central authority (as seen in the example of the Catholic Church), the preferability of avoiding dissipation of public power through private wars, and the great economic advantage of collecting revenue in hard money rather than in awkward and bulky payments in kind. The Normans learned these lessons so well that when they attacked a politically confused and militarily weakened England, they represented the most powerful and efficient state on the European continent.

This Norman state was supported by the blessing of the Pope, whose bishops and abbots served under the secular authority of the Duke, and was led by one of the boldest, bravest, and most resourceful men in history, William, illegitimate son of Robert I by a tanner's daughter from Falaise. Having succeeded to the dukedom of Normandy at the age of eight, subsequently surviving (through the help of regents) several early attempts on his life, and finally triumphing in a series of crucial struggles against rebellious barons and the vague overlordship of the French king, William was eminently schooled for the conquest of an island country that he felt was rightfully his. William had some legal basis for his feelings: as second cousin of Edward the Confessor, he had been led to believe that he would succeed to the English throne. For the price of his freedom, Harold, the Confessor's brother-in-law, once swore neither to stand as a candidate for kingship nor to oppose William's claim. When this same Harold assumed the royal power in January 1066, a day after the death of Edward, the outraged William decided upon the conquest of England.

On October 14, 1066, on an isolated hill six miles northwest of Hastings, near the southern edge of the great forest of Andredsweald in Sussex, was fought one of the most important battles in the history of the world. That the victory finally fell to William of Normandy instead of to Harold of England was due partly to luck. For six weeks during the late summer and early autumn of that year, bad weather kept the Norman invasion ships in their continental port—at the very time when the King of Norway, Harald Hardrada, wanted to try his hand at an English expedition. Thus in the critical last days before the Norman invasion, Harold had to abandon his southern watch and march north to save the battered armies of Earls Edwin and Morcar, near York. On September 28, the crack housecarls of Harold—the finest mounted infantry in all Europe—completely destroyed the Viking host at Stamford Bridge, but with heavy losses. Three days later, William opened his campaign with a landing at Pevensey. And so timing, perhaps the most important item in warfare, was on the side of the Conqueror.

Harold helped fate by returning to London in four hectic days of wild riding and by deciding to engage the invading army in Sussex with only the strong remnant of his housecarls and a levy of southeastern troops. The English king should have waited for reinforcements from the north and the southwest. Flushed with victory at Stamford Bridge and fearing that delay would serve only to strengthen the military cause of William, Harold made his gallant stand on Senlac Hill, just eight days after his return to London. For several hours it looked as if the Conqueror had taken on more than he could handle, for the stout English infantry wielded their long Danish battle-axes, repulsed one Norman charge after another, and kept their great shield wall unbroken at the top of the hill. By mid-afternoon William understood the desperateness of the situation and feigned a retreat, in order to pull the English infantry off the hill. His stratagem worked, and the battle renewed with the odds in favor of the Normans, who enjoyed a superior spear-thrusting and sword-swinging cavalry and a deadly accurate archery.

When a Norman arrow felled King Harold, the English resistance disintegrated and the mass confusion ended in total defeat. As darkness descended upon the Andredsweald, William possessed the field. With an army of no more than twelve thousand well-trained and firmly disciplined troops, he was now in a position to subjugate a disorganized nation of a million and a half.

Shortly after the military disaster at Hastings, the old Wessex capital Winchester submitted to the yoke of the Norman conqueror. A few weeks later, after a futile proclamation in favor of the succession of Edgar Atheling, London capitulated. After this collapse of resistance in the south, William of Normandy was crowned King of England in Westminster on Christmas Day, 1066. His coronation marked the beginning of a Norman dynasty that ran for nearly a century—until 1154, the date of the close of the *Anglo-Saxon Chronicle* and the start of the Plantagenet line. These eighty-eight years of conquest witnessed the confiscation of Saxon estates, the construction of impregnable citadels to house armored cavalry, the reduction of the powerful English earldoms to a system of petty feudal shires, the destruction of northern separatism and the political opposition of the Danelaw, the peaceful penetration of Scottish society and religion, the suppression of Scandinavian liberties, and the ultimate achievement of hammering out a united Anglo-Norman nation on the anvil of brute force.

Brutally forceful the Normans were. William left scarcely a house standing between York and Durham; scores of villages remained uninhabited for almost a generation. But from massacre and mutilation, wholesale slaughter and devastation, emerged a new manner of life that was important for the history of the English language.

As a result of the Norman Conquest, the Old English nobility practically ceased to exist. Within ten years after the Battle of Hastings the twelve earls of England were all Norman. Norman clergy, under the secular authority of William and his successors, took over the highest offices of the Church: archbishop, bishop, and abbot. Since the prestige of a language is determined by the authority and influence of those who speak it, the French of the Norman masters became the tongue of status in England for more than two hundred years. The Norman King of England and his French nobility remained utterly indifferent to the English language until about 1200. During that time the royal court patronized French literature, not English. When the court and its aristocratic supporters did finally pay attention to the native language of the land they dominated, that language was no longer the basically Teutonic and highly inflected Old English but the hybrid-becoming, Romance-importing, and inflection-dropping Middle English.

QUESTIONS FOR RESEARCH AND DISCUSSION

1. Organize a series of reports on the contributions of the following persons to the historical development and aesthetic grace of Old English: Ælfric, Alfred the Great, The Venerable Bede, Cædmon, and Cynewulf.

2. Conduct a round table discussion on the Angles, Saxons, and Jutes: their origin, tribal organizations, political and economic character, religious beliefs, personality and temperament, common language characteristics. In what ways did Northumbrian, Mercian, West Saxon, and Kentish differ from one another?

3. Write a research paper on "The Linguistically Fortunate Invasions of England During the Anglo-Saxon Period." Use your knowledge of Modern German, French, or some other leading European language as a basis for achieving comparisons and critical values.

4. The Battle of Hastings has been called one of the half dozen most important engagements in the history of the Western world. Defend this judgment with as much historical evidence—political, economic, cultural, linguistic—as you can muster.

5. Lead a series of classroom investigations into *Beowulf:* study the history, folklore, mythology, and oral tradition of the poem. From an understanding of the structure and texture of this Old English masterpiece, compare and contrast it with the formal epics of Homer and Virgil. Wherein lies the primitive power and majesty of *Beowulf?*

6. Using Charles W. Kennedy's *The Earliest English Poetry* as a central guide and major source, organize classroom reports on and discussions of the following topics: Germanic Tradition; Continental Backgrounds; The Elegies; The Riddles and Gnomic Verse; The Cædmonian Poems; The Signed Poems of Cynewulf; Poetry in the Cynewulfian Manner; The Religious Heroic Tale; Christian Allegory; Minor Religious Poems; The Historic Battle Poems. From these reports and discussions, write a major essay on the poetic wealth of Old English.

7. Mimeograph copies of the Parable of the Prodigal Son (St. Luke, XV, 11–32) as it appears in the West Saxon Gospels and distribute them to the class. After allowing a week for study, now conduct a discussion on the following items of linguistic concern: vocabulary, syntax, prose rhythm, and general stylistics in the Old English version of the parable. In what important ways does Anglo-Saxon show itself to be a historical progenitor of Modern English? Be specific in your answers.

8. Let two members of the class report on Grimm's Law and on Verner's Law and then challenge the class to illustrate these two laws with extended examples of each in action. Allow a week or two for this project.

9. Pretend that you have been asked by a foreigner to draw up a list of the five hundred most important common words in present-day English. Draw up your list and then compare and contrast it with the other lists drawn up by your classmates. How much repetition is there? how much diversity? Now let everyone in class divide the work equally and check on the origin and etymology of each term assigned him. What does this lesson tell about the relative frequency of Anglo-Saxon loans in the usage of Modern English?

10. Conduct a group investigation into the use of Celtic, Scandinavian, and Norman French in the place names of the United States. Are these sources as important in American English as in British? How do you account for such a drastic difference in the incidence of occurrence? Answer in detail.

11. Collect as long a list as possible of the "strong" irregular verbs of present-day English. How many verbs of the *sing-sang-sung* variety are there on the list? how many of the *think-thought-thought* variety? how many of the *let-let-let* variety? How can you account for so small a composite list in contrast with the immense number of "weak" regular verbs now in the language? Give some examples of spectacular regularization like "I *DDT'd* the apple orchard." Now write a brief article on the linguistic advantages inherent in the Germanic trait of regularizing the verb whenever possible.

12. Discuss the Old English legacy of stressing the root syllable and of forwarding stress whenever possible. How important are these Germanic principles of stress in the current structure and function of the English language? Answer in detail and with illustrative examples.

SELECTED BIBLIOGRAPHY

Anderson, Marjorie, and Blanche Colton Williams. *Old English Handbook.* Cambridge, Massachusetts: Houghton Mifflin Company, 1935. This is a splendid combination of Old English grammar and reader, with ample notes and glossary.

Baugh, Albert C. *A History of the English Language*. Second Edition. New York: Appleton-Century-Crofts, 1957. See especially Chapter 3 ("Old English") and Chapter 4 ("Foreign Influences on Old English") for excellent traditional coverage.

Bloomfield, Morton W., and Leonard Newmark. *A Linguistic Introduction to the History of English*. New York: Alfred A. Knopf, 1963. See Chapter IV ("The Morphology of Old English") for a scholarly treatment of the main morphological features of the language.

Bonjour, Adrien. *Twelve BEOWULF Papers (1940–1960), with Additional Comments*. Geneva, Switzerland: Libraire E. Droz, 1962. A collection of essays filled with sensitive criticism on the various aspects of the greatest poem in Old English.

Jespersen, Otto. *Growth and Structure of the English Language*. Ninth Edition. New York: Doubleday, Anchor Books, 1955. See Chapter III ("Old English") and Chapter IV ("The Scandinavians") for a lively account of the early stages of English.

Kennedy, Charles W. *The Earliest English Poetry*. New York: Oxford University Press, 1948. A critical survey of English poetry written before the Norman Conquest.

Malone, Kemp. "The Old English Period (to 1100)." Part I of *The Middle Ages*, Volume I of *A Literary History of England*, edited by Albert C. Baugh. New York: Appleton-Century-Crofts, 1948. Pp. 3–105. The finest brief general survey of the entire range of Anglo-Saxon literature.

Robertson, Stuart, and Frederic G. Cassidy. *The Development of Modern English*. Second Edition. Englewood Cliffs, New Jersey: Prentice-Hall, 1954. See especially Chapters 2–6 for an excellent account of the leading historical attributes and evolutionary features of Old English.

Trevelyan, G. M. *History of England, Volume One: From the Earliest Times to the Reformation*. Garden City, New York: Doubleday, Anchor Books, 1953. See especially the first six chapters, for a clear and concise narration of Old English history, written with stylistic grace and citing many useful sources for further study.

CHAPTER 4

The Structure of
Old English

PHONOLOGY

IT IS IMPOSSIBLE TO RECONSTRUCT the sounds of Old English with absolute accuracy. A dogmatically certain phonemic solution for the language of *Beowulf*, either as orally composed about the year 700 or as scribally committed to manuscript form about the year 1000, cannot be made. The best that we can do is a phonological analysis that will approximate the historical truth. For this task, fortunately, the Old English alphabet supplies great assistance; it is far more phonemic than that of Modern English. With the Christianizing of Britain, the Anglo-Saxons adapted the Latin alphabet for their own language. In most cases the phonetic correspondence between the two tongues was very close; where major differences appeared, Old English borrowed from the runic, the Old High German, alphabet.

Old English spelling did not include the letters *j*, *q*, *v*, and *z*, but possessed four characters peculiar to its alphabet: the *digraph* (æ), *eth* (ð), *thorn* (þ), and *wen* (Þ). The thorn and the wen (equivalent of the later Latin *w*) were employments of the runic alphabet, whereas the *eth* was formed by crossing the staff of Latin *d*. The use of *k* in Old English writing was very rare. Otherwise the Anglo-Saxons used an alphabet like that of their present-day British and American descendants.

Several sounds peculiar to the pronunciation patterns of Old English have long since vanished. Two of them are those represented by the Old English graphemes *g* and *h:* /ɤ/ and /x/. The voiced velar /ɤ/ is heard in North German *sagen* and Old English *āgan* (own); under conditions of fronting it becomes /ŷ/, as in *gēar* (year); under conditions of hard-palatalizing, it becomes /g/, as in *gār* (spear). The voiceless velar /x/ is in German *ich* and Old English *niht* (night). To complicate pronunciation further, Old English often combined this voiceless velar /x/ with the point consonants /l n r/ to produce the difficult combinations /xl xn xr/ as in *hlūd* (loud), *hraefn* (raven), and *hnutu* (nut). The similar union of /x/ with /w/, even though greatly softened, has all but disappeared from Late Modern English.

In addition to these consonantal sound differences, Old English did not support an independent phonemic status for /ŋ v z ð/; these were merely *positional allophones* of /n f s θ/. As for its vocalic sound structures, Old English had no vowel diphthongs based on the /y/ glide, a phonemic formant so important in Modern English. Length in the rather simple vowel system of Old English was a matter of tension applied by the glide /:/. Perhaps a few complex nuclei made use of the glide /w/, as in *feower* /féwwer/ (four) and *feawa* /fáwwe/ (few). As for the "short" vowels of Old English, they were remarkably like those of present-day usage—with two important exceptions: the rounded /y/, as in *cynn* (kin), and /ö/, as in *oexen* (oxen).

Even with these obvious differences in pronunciation to help organize a phonemic solution of Old English, a few historical difficulties remain. They center in the chronological progress of the language, a progress obscured by the establishment of the West Saxon literary standard at an early date. From early Middle English documents, it is easy to infer the general direction of the Old English phonemic drift, but the literary documents themselves mask the main lines of chronological development. Thus the principal problems in phonemicizing Old English arise from the following points: the phonemic status of the sounds symbolized by *c, cg, g, h,* and *sc;* the allophonic or phonemic status of the two sounds symbolized by *a* and *æ;* the exact nature of length-correlation in Old English; the status of vowels in weak-stressed inflections. To arrive at a reasonable solution, we must make the following inferences from the extant evidence:

1) *c* represents the tense stop /k/ and its fronted contrast /ķ/, a sound much like Modern English /c/.

2) *cg* is the graphemic equivalent of the independent phoneme /ĝ/, a sound very similar to present-day /j/.

3) *g*, dependent upon position and vowel environment, symbolizes the eventual development of two distinct phonemes: the back voiced stop /g/ and the fronted voiced spirant /ŷ/, a sound close to that of modern /y/.

4) *h* is the written form of early phonic variants that become two separate sounds: the localized voiceless spirant /x/, found only in non-initial positions, and the non-localized voiceless fricative /h/, found only in initial positions.

5) *sc*, except in low back environments, ceases to be the phonemic cluster /sķ/ and diphthongizes into the voiceless alveolo-palatal /š/.

6) *a* and *æ*, despite their allographic overlapping, have already attained the status of independent phonemes: *a* (and *ea*) symbolizing either /a/ or /ɔ/ and *æ* simply /æ/.

7) Ten of the eleven vowels of Old English can form complex nuclei by joining with the lengthening glide /:/; the umlauted *o* /ő/ appears to be the only exception.

8) In normal speech, as distinct from the overstressing of alliterative poetry in the bardic tradition, Old English vowels in stressless positions tend to be reduced to either *schwa* (/ə/) or *colorless i* (/ɨ/).

THE OLD ENGLISH PHONEMES.   The phonological structure of Old English may be outlined as follows:

CONSONANTS

Labial

Voiceless:	/p/	*pæð* (path)
Voiced:	/b/	*bæð* (bath)
	/m/	*mæðel* (council)

Labiodental

Voiceless:	/f/	*fæðm* (embrace)
Voiced:	no independent contrasting phoneme	

CONSONANTS

Interdental

Voiceless: /θ/   *ðōð* (though)

Voiced: no independent contrasting phoneme

Alveolar

Voiceless: /t/   *tōð* (tooth)

         /s/   *sōð* (truth)

Voiced: /d/   *dōð* (imperative of *do*)

         no independent contrasting phoneme

         /n/   *nōð* (daring, boldness)

         /l/   *lēap* (basket)

Alveolopalatal

Voiceless: /k̯/   *cēap* (cattle, bargain)

         /š/   *scēap* (sheep)

Voiced: /r/   *rōðer* (rower, sailor)

         /ĝ/   in non-initial positions only: *ecg* (edge, point)

         no independent contrasting phoneme

Palatal

Voiceless: /h/   *heald* (custody, guard)

         /k/   *ceald* (cold)

         /x/   in non-initial positions only: *cniht* (boy, youth)

Voiced: /g/   *gār* (spear)

         /ŷ/   *gēar* (year)

Velar

Voiced: no independent contrasting phoneme

         /w/   *weald* (forest)

VOWELS

Lax

High-Front: /i/   *hlid* (lid)

High-Front Rounded: /y/   *cynn* (kin)

High-Central: /ɨ/   *liornian* (to learn)

High-Back: /u/   *lust* (desire, appetite)

Mid-Front: /e/   *bedd* (bed)

Mid-Front Rounded: /ŏ/   *oexen* (oxen)

Mid-Central: /ə/   *meolcan* (to milk)

Mid-Back: /o/   *crop* (crop)

Low-Front: /æ/   *bæc* (back)

Low-Central: /a/   *healt* (halt)

Low-Back: /ɔ/   *crabba* (crab)

VOWELS

Tense

High-Front:	/i:/	*hīd* (a "hide" of land)
High-Front Rounded:	/y:/	*drȳge* (dry)
High-Central:	/ɨ:/	*līoht* (light)
High-Back:	/u:/	*hūs* (house)
Mid-Front:	/e:/	*spēd* (luck, success)
Mid-Central:	/ə:/	*sēoðan* (to seethe)
Mid-Back:	/o:/	*rōd* (rood, cross)
Low-Front:	/æ:/	*hǣlan* (to heal, cure)
Low-Central:	/a:/	*dēaf* (deaf)
Low-Back:	/ɔ:/	*bān* (bone)

From these we see that the consonant system of Old English suffered from underdevelopment and the lack of clear-cut independent contrasts; the later emergence of the phonemes /v ð z c j ž y ŋ/ constituted a phonological improvement. The Old English vowel system was overdeveloped and unstable. As a matter of linguistic fact, by the year 1000 the Midlands dialect had lost /ɨ ə a/; it never supported the Germanic /ö/. The later diphthongizing of the tense vowels by means of /y/ and /w/ was a vocalic phenomenon of distinct advantage: it permitted sharper pronunciation contrasts, avoided a marked tendency toward glottal stopping, and established a secondary stability in the primary feature of change in the Great Vowel Shift of Early Modern English. Old English operated with more tension, gravity, stress energy, and with a generally lower tongue-height than is employed by its present-day descendant.

DISTINCTIVE ACOUSTIC FEATURES.   Since Old English did not maintain a system of glottal stopping in its phonology, the language, like Modern English, was characterized by seven basic distinctive-feature oppositions:

1) *Vocality vs. Consonantality*. The simple contrast of syllabic/non-syllabic: the eleven lax and ten tense Old English vowels in opposition to the consonants; the phonemes /m n l r ŷ w/, however, represent intermediate terms in this contrast.

2) *Tension vs. Laxness*. In the Old English vowels, an opposition of simple (short) nuclei against complex (long) nuclei, dependent upon the presence or absence of the glide of tension /:/; in the Old English consonants, an automatic distinction of voiceless (tense) vs. voiced (lax).

3) *Interruption vs. Continuance.* The Old English stops /p t ḳ k/ and obstruents /b d ĝ g/ in opposition to the non-impeding other consonants and the vowels.

4) *Gravity vs. Acuteness.* A basic opposition of "muffling," produced by long oral cavity and/or small lip aperture, against a sharp lack of this feature; in Old English, gravity is achieved in the back vowels /u u: o o: ɔ ɔ:/, the labial consonants /p b m f/, and the palatal consonants /h k x g ŷ/; the velar-labial /w/ is also grave.

5) *Compactness vs. Diffuseness.* In Old English, the presence of a central formant region makes the low vowels /æ æ: a a: ɔ ɔ:/ and the back consonants /h k x g ŷ w/ compact; all other vowels and consonants in the language either are or tend to be diffuse.

6) *Nasality vs. Orality.* The presence of the nasal passage as a formant region makes a basic distinction between the nasals /m n/ and the oral obstruents /b d/; since the velar /ŋ/ has not yet achieved independent phonemic status, there is no nasal contrast with the palatal /g/ in Old English.

7) *Stridency vs. Mellowness.* A basic contrast in Old English between the non-muffled fricatives /s/ and /š/ and the mellow interdental /θ/.

From these seven basic oppositions in the language the Old English poets fashioned a verse noted for alliteration, assonance, consonance, and the union of exciting sound patterns with a powerful syncopated rhythm.

As for the relative importance of the six distinctive acoustic features other than that of syllable-formation, an analysis of sixty lines of *Beowulf* establishes the following indices of occurrence:

DISTINCTIVE FEATURE	OCCURRENCES PER LINE
Gravity	10.68
Tension	8.76
Compactness	6.31
Interruption	3.58
Nasality	3.07
Stridency	1.27

Although the figures above cannot be taken as absolute either for *Beowulf* as a whole or for the entire range of Old English poetry, they indicate the predominance of gravity, tension, and compactness in the language. The consonant alliteration of *Beowulf* supports the fact that gravity is the leading feature of the poem: the acute /s/ is the only non-grave consonant among the first seven most frequent alliterators, and grave /m/ outnumbers acute /n/ by a wide margin: 249–54.

OLD ENGLISH SUPRASEGMENTALS.   Modern linguists know little about the intonation system of Old English—there are no Anglo-Saxons alive to speak the language and thereby inform us on stress, pitch, juncture, and internal and terminal contours. The task of recreating the suprasegmentals of Old English is hard but not hopeless. That any language, current or historical, can support more than four degrees of phonemic stress is highly improbable. And stress is the key to juncture, pitch, and the intonational contours of Old English. From an understanding of the Germanic tradition of stress on the root syllable and from the fact that inflections remained undamaged for a relatively long period of time, we can say that Old English supported four degrees of stress. Because of the alliterative tradition of oral poetry and its built-in principle of overstress and the lack of a reliance upon the grapheme, the visual morpheme, and a habit of silent reading—the stress patterns of Old English, like those of Modern German, tend to discriminate morphemic boundaries rather than word boundaries and syntactical units. The result of such discrimination is that Old English achieves more maximum (´) and major (^) stress than Modern English. Present-day readers of the language slur and weaken to minimum stress (˘) syllables that their Anglo-Saxon forefathers would probably maintain at minor (`) energy.

Even now the reinforcement of alliteration in Modern English produces a stress echo from the past, heard, for example, in the different patterns of two compounds: *postman* and *mailman*. The stress disposition of *postman* is that of a normal modern compound:

$$\overset{´\,+\,`}{\text{postman.}}$$

The minor stressing of the second formant element (*man*) is unmistakable: the phonemic weakening to *schwa* (ə) is the clue. In the alliterative compound *mailman*, however, the minor stress becomes major:

$$\overset{´\,+\,^}{\text{mailman.}}$$

This extra energy on the syllable *man* keeps the vowel at its full value of /æ/. Old English supports compounds of the *mailman* variety far more than does Modern English. Hence a fuller intensity of pronunciation in Old English also yields more pitch levels of both the highest (/4/) and the high (/3/) variety than are generally achieved in Modern English. In strong emotional passages in the poetry, the intonation patterns of Old English are extremely musical, even melodramatic. The accompanying junctures are strongly pronounced and more sharply syncopated. Open juncture /+/, for example, occurs more readily in Old English than in Modern. The intonation contours themselves are very similar to those of Modern English, with these slight modifications: more dramatic differences of pitch-level change in the terminal contours of high rising (/3/↗) and high falling (/3/↘); and a marked tendency toward more internal contours of the normal-rising type (/2/↗).

MORPHOLOGY

IN OLD ENGLISH THE MORPHEME takes functional precedence over syntactical positioning and stress modification. Such precedence is the result of a system of full inflections. By analogy with the relatively fixed word order of Modern English, the following nonsense sentence reveals its surface structure and the specialist functions of its constituents: *The cuddy floke strimmered tollily John's willywog flump.* No speaker of Modern English will have difficulty in identifying *cuddy* as an adjective modifying the noun subject *floke* or in understanding *tollily* to be an adverb describing the action of the past tense verb *strimmered,* which takes *flump* for its noun object modified by the adjectival noun compound *willywog.* In Old English, however, such a nonsensical statement could not be grammatically accurate; there are not enough inflectional clues, for *paradigmatic* form is far more important than *word-order function.*

In Old English the paradigm itself—the set of inflectional forms—defines a word in class and function. Thus in Old English a *noun* is an inflected form with a fixed grammatical *gender* and a variable *number* and *case;* its adjective has a variable *gender, number, case,* and *definity;* its substituting pronoun, a fixed *person* and a variable *number, gender,* and *case.* The Old English verb is an inflectional form that undergoes a paradigm of variable *mood, tense, person,* and *number.* To return to the nonsensical statement *The cuddy floke strimmered tollily John's willy-wog flump* for a moment, the speaker of Old English could not fully understand it because the sentence contains too many uninflected *root syllables.*

THE OLD ENGLISH ROOT SYLLABLE.   As a West Teutonic language, Old English maintains its maximum stress on the *root syllable.* The root syllable is a *morphological base* to which thematic vowels and affixes may be added to form words. Etymologically, the root syllable is the minimum irreducible base common to all cognate forms. Among the Old English nouns, the root is the *nominative* case (citational form) *directly* if that case ends in a consonant: *stān* and *scip,* and *by reduction* if that case ends in a *thematic vowel: cear*-u and *luf*-u. Thus in the Old English words for *stone, ship, care,* and *love,* the inflectional endings that determine their grammatical functions and meanings in sentences are added to these roots: *stān-, scip-, cear-,* and *luf-.*

The inflectional endings themselves are, obviously, *bound morphemes* of a syllabic nature: either *-es* or *-e* for the genitive singular, *-e* completely for the dative and instrumental singular, either *-e* or zero for the accusative singular, *-as* or *-u* or *-a* for the nominative plural, either *-a* or *-ena* for the genitive plural, *-um* entirely for the dative and instrumental plural, and *-as* or *-u* or *-a* for the accusative plural. The root syllables themselves are *free* morphemes that can combine with other free morphemes to form compounds like *stānæx* (stoneworker's axe), *stānbæð* (vapor bath made by water on hot stones), *stānboga* (rocky arch), *stānbrycg* (stone bridge), *scipāc* (shipbuilding oak), *scipgyld* (ship-tax), *sciphlæder* (ship's ladder), *scipwered* (ship-host, crew), *ceargealdor* (sorrowful song), *ceargēst* (sad spirit, devil), *cearseld* (home of care), *cearsorg* (sad anxiety), *lufestice* (the "love-stitch" plant), and *luftācen* (love-token).

The Old English verbs achieve their root syllables by reducing the infinitive form back to the first consonant before the *-an* or *-ian* inflection. In the so-called weak or regular Old English verbs, this root syllable remains constant throughout all the various forms of its complete paradigm. Thus *dēman* (to judge) has *dēm-* as its root syllable, to which the present tense adds *-e, -(e)st, -(e)ð; -að* in the indicative singular and plural, and *-e* in the subjunctive singular and *-en* in the subjunctive plural. As a regular weak root syllable, in the past tense *dēm-* forms a stem of *dēmd-* by the addition of *-d,* to which the indicative joins *-e* and *-es(t)* in the singular and *-on* in the plural, and the subjunctive appends *-e* in the singular and *-en* in the plural. The third mood in Old English, the non-finite imperative, employs only the zeroless root *dēm* in the singular and adds *-að* in the plural. With the prefixing of *ge-* and the affixing of *-ed,* the root *dēm-* forms its past participle: *gedēmed;* the affixing of *-ende* yields the present participle *dēmende;* following the purposive preposition *tō,* the root syllable *dēm-* may add either *-enne* or *-anne* to form its gerund: *tō dēmenne.* Although the strong irregular verbs of Old English undergo basically the same paradigmatic sets as do the weak regular verbs, there are notable differences: 1) the root syllables of the strong verbs experience *vowel mutation* in the past tense and often shift their vowels even in the present tense; 2) the strong verbs form their past participle in *-en* rather than in *-ed.*

Even if the root syllable of Old English nouns, adjectives, and verbs remains fairly constant, the morphology of the inflections is wastefully complicated and redundant. With no less than seven classes of strong verbs and three of weak, with from eight to twenty noun declensions and from six to nine adjectival declensions, depending upon how much emphasis the analyst wishes to give to variations, and with considerable morphemic overlapping and suppression—the Old English inflections were historically doomed from the beginning. With the stress located on the root syllable, the inflections have no means whereby to maintain and enforce their functionalism. In short, an evolving analytic syntax needs stressed roots to help fashion its word-group cadences and interdependent semantic relationships; it has little or no use for the synthetic markers known as inflections.

Old English morphology modifies the root syllable with three basic types of *inflections:* initial, internal, and final. The one initial inflection of Old English is *ge-,* a bound syllabic morpheme that conveys this minimum unit of meaning: *perfective force.* It is therefore a frequent companion of the past participle. The internal inflections of Old English, in contrast, are all bound phonemic morphemes; they do not constitute independent syllables in themselves. Analogous to the vocalic shifts in present-day *sing/sang/sung,* these internal inflections are intimately associated with the strong verbs of the language; such inner changes in the root syllable basically denote *non-present* tense. Thus the *i* of the present infinitive *gilpan* (to boast) becomes *ea* in the third person preterit singular *gealp* (he boasted). But the most important in function and use are the final inflections of Old English. These bound syllabic morphemes dominate the entire range of paradigmatic sets in the language, in both the declensions and the conjugations. Hence it is that *-on* in the verbs conveys the meaning of *third person plural preterit*, whereas *-um* in the nouns indicates the *dative plural*.

By placing only the inflections in morphemic braces ({ }), we can illustrate these basic units of Old English meaning in the three opening lines of *Beowulf:*

> Hwæt! wē Gār-Den{a}   in geār-dag{um}
> þēod-cyning{a} þrym   {ge}fr{ū}n {on},
> hū ð{ā} æþeling{as}   ellen frem{ed} {on}.

Inflectionally, the {a} in *Gār-Dena* and *þēod-cyninga* indicates *genitive plural;* the {um} of *geār-dagum, dative plural;* the {ge} of *gefrūnon, past participle;* the {ū} of that same word, *perfect tense;* its {on} and that of *fremedon, third person plural;* the {ā} of *ðā* and the {as} of *æþelingas, nominative plural,* and the {ed} of *fremedon, past tense.* Thus the heroic exordium may be translated as follows:

> Lo! we of the Spear-Danes   in yore-days
> Have heard the glory   of the clansmen-kings,
> How the noble warriors   performed valor-deeds.

The sense of this Modern English passage is very much that of the Old English original, but its morphology and syntax are different. To see the difference is to know historical evolution in miniature.

MORPHOLOGICAL CONTRASTS.   The morphological contrasts between Old and Modern English are many. A brief study of the bound morphemes of Old English reveals their lack of development in the phonemic category. Apart from the limited use of internal inflections, the language employs almost no phonemic bound morphemes. An exception is the *n* in *nolde,* a procliticized equivalent of *ne wolde* (he willed or wished not). But the general rule holds true—because Old English is not *contractional* by nature. Modern English, however, is contractional: centuries of demanding stress upon the root syllable and the resultant evolution into an analytic syntax produce many encliticized morphemes of a bound phonemic nature. To illustrate, *John/z/ stop/t/* is a morphemic impossibility in Old English; it is an example of the structural economy and semantic flexibility of Modern English.

If the present-day language is almost completely free of bound syllabic inflectional morphemes, its progenitor is almost entirely enslaved by them. Old English maintains a grammatical gender not only for nouns and pronouns, but also for adjectives and demonstratives. Thus the *unchanging* forms of *this good* in

> this good champion
> this good maiden
> this good woman

are out of the question in their Old English equivalents:

> ðēs gōda cempa (masculine)
> ðēos gōde mægð (feminine)
> ðis gōde wīf (neuter)

With grammatical gender to complicate further the inflectional system of Old English, *case government* in that language becomes a morphemic nightmare. Yet what is overdone on the *nominal* side remains underdeveloped on the *actional*. The verb system of Old English, that is, is complex in its relatively unimportant classes and simple in its failure to express adequately voice, tense, and aspect.

Most of Old English literature occurs in the active voice, in either the present or the preterit tense, and in some definite aspect. With *hātte* (is/was called) as the only example of the archaic medial-passive voice, Old English forms its passive voice either by combining some part of the auxiliaries *bēon, wesan* (to be), or *weorðan* (to become) with the past participle or by using the general active introduced by an equivalent to Modern German *man* and Modern French *on*. The Anglo-Saxons knew nothing of the progressive tenses, which use the present participle, or of the emphatic present and past; furthermore, they were hazy in handling the perfect and pluperfect. Old English does not have the imperfect, the iterative imperfect, and the inceptive imperfect. Morphologically, Modern English is far more specialized in its use of modal and timer auxiliaries; its empty function terms constitute a more expressive verb system than that of Old English.

In addition to the complex morphology of its inflected verbs, nouns, and adjectives, Old English supports other peculiar linguistic features. Among the personal pronouns, for example, there is the complication of *dual* number for the first and second persons. With the later syncretizing of the accusative with the dative, the first person pronouns *ic* (I), *mīn* (my), *mē* (me), *wē* (we), *ūre* (our), and *ūs* (us) are joined by *wit* (we two), *uncer* (of us two), and *unc* (us two); similarly, the second person pronouns *ðū* (thou), *ðīn* (thy), *ðē* (thee), *gē* (ye), *ēower* (your), and *ēow* (you) are supplemented by the dual forms of *git* (ye two), *incer* (of you two), and *inc* (you two). In the third person pronouns, however, Old English shows morphological chaos. Thus *his* and *him* may be either masculine or neuter forms of the genitive and dative singular; the nominative masculine singular *hē* coincides at times with the feminine; the plural accusative for all genders is the same as the feminine accusative singular: *hīe;* the dative plural *him* blurs with the masculine and neuter singular of the same form; and the genitive plural *hiera* or *heora* remains too close to (indeed later blends into) the feminine genitive and dative singular *hire*. The later introduction of *she, her, it, its,* and the Scandinavian plurals *they, their,* and *them* into the pronoun system of Late Middle and Early Modern English is a distinct morphemic improvement.

The Old English pronoun system suffers further from the lack of a well-developed relative pronoun; the interrogative indefinites *hwā* and *hwilc* do not assume their role of syntactical linkage until the eighteenth century. The demonstratives (and their accompanying definite article) undergo the greatest inflectional reduction—from eighteen separate case forms to four, plus the invariable *the: this/these, that/those*. In like manner, the Old English adjective reduces itself from ten inflections to none, except for the degrees of comparison, in which comparative *-ra* and superlative *-ost* evolve into *-er* and *-est* respectively. Also inflected for comparison, the Old English adverb achieves its form by the following morphological devices: adding the instrumental *-e* of the adjective to the root syllable; adding the genitive *-es* or the dative *-um* of nouns to the root syllable of the adjective; or adding the suffix *-līce* (eventually modern *-ly*) or the suffix *-mǣlum* (Chaucer's *-mele*, existent today only in *piecemeal*) to the adjectival root. The fact that a *lovely* woman may drive *slow* in Modern English indicates the morphological flexibility and the functional shifts possible with the analytic method, in which stress and syntactical positioning determine meaning.

CHIEF MORPHOLOGICAL PROCESSES.   Old English, like Modern, supports three kinds of word-forms:

 Morpheme Words, as in *æfen* (evening), *eorl* (warrior, leader), and *sōð* (truth).

 Compounds, as in *æfenlēoht* (evening light), *eorlriht* (earl's right), and *sōðlufu* (loving kindness).

 Derivatives, as in *eorlisc* (of noble rank), *sōðfæst* (trustworthy), and *sōðfæstnes* (fidelity, justice).

The base of an Old English derivative is like that of a Modern English one in that it may be either a morpheme word (*eorl* in *eorlisc*), a compound (*geār-dag* in *geār-dagum*), or another derivative (*sōðfæst* in *sōðfæstnes*); it is unlike, however, in that the Old English derivative does not employ a bound morpheme as its base. The morphological processes of Old English are far more restricted and less flexible than those of Modern English. Whereas the present version of the language maintains at least fifteen major methods of word formation, its historical progenitor operates by means of the following five:

 1) *Compounding.* Combining free morphemes with a falling stress pattern, usually from maximum (ˊ) to major (ˆ); this process is characteristically Germanic and is a mainstay of Old English poetry and prose. Reduction of the stress energy on the second formant element to minor (ˋ) is a feature of Modern English.

 2) *Affixing.* Combining bound morphemes with either free morphemes, compounds, or derivative bases to form derivative words: *mānful* (wicked) and *unmihtig* (weak).

 3) *Internal Modification.* Replacing phonemes within a word by other phonemes in order to change meaning and/or function. This process is extremely important for the use of internal inflections in Old English, especially in the non-present tense of verbs.

 4) *Use of Full Inflections.* Though most often coincident with affixing, this process is the characteristic one of Old English to express syntactical relationships: *meodo-scencum* (with mead vessels). Modern English substitutes a highly specialized empty-word system to do the equivalent work.

 5) *Use of Kennings.* The Old English equivalent of imagery as a major morphological process in Modern English. A *kenning*

is the metaphorical naming of a person, place, or thing. Thus Grendel is the *sceadu-genga* (shadow-stalker, walker in darkness); the hall Heorot, the *horn-gēap* (wide-gabled) place; any ship, the *fāmig-heals* (foamy-necked) floater.

Old English occasionally experiences *stress modification, replacement,* and *zeroing* as morphological processes, and it borrows sparingly. As for lengthening, the language often strives for a kind of *syllabic equality* by employing phonemic doubling of consonants in medial positions; Modern English, by way of contrast, economizes against such lengthenings as these: /pp/, /tt/, /ḳḳ/, /kk/, /bb/, /dd/, /ĝĝ/, /gg/, /ss/, /xx/, /θθ/, /mm/, /nn/, /ll/, and /rr/. Old English knows little or nothing of such useful morphological processes as *reduplication, onomatopoeia, acronyming, clipping, back formation, telescoping, idea naming,* and above all *functional shift.* The failure of Old English morphology to respond to functional shift is a salient sign of the rigidity of the language.

SYNTAX

THE SYNTAX OF OLD ENGLISH is inseparable from its morphology, because the syntax is immediately dependent upon the morphology. *Synthetic* rather than *analytic,* Old English syntax is the result of a full inflectional system. When inflections indicate grammatical relationships, syntactical positioning becomes secondary. In a synthetic language like Old English, therefore, word order has little or no influence upon meaning: the inflectional morphemes do the work of communication. Old English does not have a fixed word order against which to project the grace of a non-standard performance; deviation from the norm means very little, because the norm is not clearly defined.

In the following sentence from the *Colloquy* of Ælfric, the synthetic syntax is responsible for clumsy phrasing and an unemphatic *hypotaxis* (syntactical subordination):

> Sōþ þū segst, ac ic ne geþrīstge for mōdes mīnes nytenyssæ.

Translated literally and in the same awkward syntax, this Old English sentence reads as follows:

> Truth you speak, but I not dare because of mind's my ignorance.

Transposed into an analytic syntax and with proper hypotaxis for the sake of emphasis, the translation then reads like this:

> You tell the truth, but because of my mind's ignorance I do not dare.

The advantage of the second version over the first is apparent. Applying its syntactical order to the Old English original yields this analytic improvement:

> Ðū segst sōþ, ac for mīnes mōdes nytenyssæ ic ne geþrīstge.

But this analytic improvement, if allowed to stand as a norm, makes the inflections superfluous and nonfunctional. Such morphological redundancy, as a result of a syntactical evolution from synthetic to analytic, is a key factor in the leveling of inflections in English.

The sentence quoted from the *Colloquy* of Ælfric is synthetic partly because it is from an Old English interlinear gloss on a Latin text. Thus the inflectional word order of one language reinforces that of another. Had Ælfric himself written such tortuous prose, he could not rightfully be called a founder of English prose style. But this disciple of King Alfred, except for a few idiomatic failures happily writes in a word order much like that of Late Modern English prose. The following passages from his *Homilies* stand as proof:

> Wē habbað oft gehȳred þæt men hātað þysne dæg gēares dæg. . . .
> We have often heard that men call this day New Year's Day. . . .
>
> Uton besettan ūrne hiht and ūre gesælða on þæs ælmihtigan Scyppendes foresceāwunge. . . .
> Let us place our hope and our happiness in the almighty Creator's providence. . . .
>
> Hieronimus, sē wīsa mæssepreōst, āwrāt on ðǣre bēc ðe wē hātað "Ecclesiastica Historia" þæt sum Rōmānisc cāsere wæs Constantīnus gehāten. . . .
> Jerome, the wise mass-priest, wrote in that book which we call *Ecclesiastica Historia* that a certain Roman Emperor was Constantine named. . . .

These examples of analytic word order in Old English syntax show that its prose style had achieved many modern overtones by the year 1000. By that time the great heroic verse of an older tradition had become mere collection pieces for the scribal monks, and the far more synthetic syntax of poetic license could be looked upon as an archaic oddity. Such a syntax exerted little direct influence upon the prose style of The West Saxon Gospels. One may see this lack of influence in the syntactical evolution achieved between the following almost agglutinative lines of *Beowulf* and the ensuing modernesque opening of the parable of the Prodigal Son:

Wīglāf wæs hāten,   Wēoxstānes sunu,
lēoflīc lind-wiga,   lēod Scylfinga,
mæg Ælfheres;   geseah his mon-dryhten
under here-grīman   hāt þrōwian.
Gemunde ðā ðā āre   þē hē him ær forgeaf,
wīc-stede weligne   Wægmundinga,
folc-rihta gehwylc,   swā his fæder āhte;
ne mihte ðā forhabban,   hond rond gefēng,
geolwe linde;   gomel swyrd getēah,
þæt wæs mid eldum   Ēanmundes lāf,
suna Ōhteres. . . .

Wiglaf was he named,   Weoxstan's son,
precious shield-warrior,   prince of the Scylfings,
kinsman of Ælfhere;   he saw his liege-lord
under the battle-mask   hotly to suffer.
He remembered then those honors   which he him earlier gave,
a dwelling-place wealthy   of the Waegmundings,
of folk-rights each,   such as his father had owned;
nor might he then hold back,   hand the shield seized,
the yellow linden;   the old sword he drew,
that was among men   Eanmund's heirloom,
the son of Ohtere's. . . .

11. Hē cwæð, Sōðlīce sum man hæfde twēgen suna.
12. Ðā cwæð sē gingra tō his fæder, "Fæder, syle mē mīnne dæl mīnre æhte þe mē tō gebyreþ." Ðā dælde hē him his æhte.
13. Ðā æfter fēawum dagum ealle his þing gegaderude sē gingra sunu, and fērde wræclīce on feorlen rīce, and forspilde þār his æhta, lybbende on his gælsan.
14. Ðā hē hig hæfde ealle āmyrrede, þā wearð mycel hunger on þām rīce, and hē wearð wædla.
15. Ðā fērde hē and folgude ānum burhsittendan men þæs rīces; ðā sende hē hine tō his tūne þæt hē hēolde his swȳn. . . .

11. He said, Verily a certain man had two sons.
12. Then said the younger to his father, "Father, grant me my portion of my property which to me belongs." Then dealt he him his possessions.

13. Then after a few days all his things gathered together the younger son, and he traveled abroad into a distant kingdom, and he squandered there his possessions, living in his luxury.
14. When he them had all wasted, then was there much hunger in that kingdom, and he was destitute.
15. Then went he and served one of the city-dwellers of that kingdom; then sent he him to his farm where he kept his swine. . . .

The poetry moves by means of rhythmical appositions and cadential equivalents; the prose, by means of syntactical flow. The poetry is primarily substantive, variational, and elevated; the prose, primarily active, direct, and humble. Thus by the Norman Conquest, Old English had become something of an anomaly: its synthetic inflection system was already being contradicted and subverted by its growing analytic syntax.

IDIOMATIC CONSTRUCTIONS.   Apart from the confusion of pronoun references—a habit of Old English—the frequent inversions of word order in the above passages reflect a difference in syntactical idioms. It is neither illiterate nor aesthetic in Old English for the verb to precede the subject in a two-one word order. The syntax of the language is flexible enough, thanks to its synthetic inflection system, to permit a three-one-two positioning (*Ðā hē hig hæfde ealle āmyrrede*) or a three-two-one (*ealle his þing gegaderude sē gingra sunu*) without any sense of word-order violation. Such constructions are idiomatic with the language (although probably more given to the written word than to the spoken) and point to other constructions that help distinguish Old English syntactical usage from that of Modern English, constructions like the following:

1) *The Nominative.* The case for both the subject and for its predicate noun, pronoun, or adjective: *Bēowulf is mīn nama.* (Beowulf is my name.)

2) *The Vocative.* The case of direct address, the vocative is like the nominative; it carries a weak adjective modifier: *Mīne brōþor, mīne þā lēofan* . . . (My brother, my dear ones . . .)

3) *Possessive Genitive.* The most frequently used construction for possession in Old English, the genitive may be either subjective, as in *Higelāces bēod-genēatas* (Higelac's table-companions), or objective, as in *wið Grendles gryre* (against the

terror of Grendel). Occasionally the genitive plural acts as a singular: *heofona rīce* (the kingdom of heaven).

4) *Partitive Genitive*. This construction is used with noun numerals and words that express quantity: *hund missera* (a hundred of half years); *landes tō fela* (too much of land).

5) *Objective Genitive*. Certain verbs in Old English take their direct objects in the genitive case; among these verbs are *bīdan* (to await), *biddan* (to ask), *brūcan* (to use, enjoy), *fandian* (to (try), *lettan* (to hinder), and *truwian* (to trust).

6) *Adverbial Genitive*. The genitive may also be employed adverbially: *singāles* (continually) and *gēara* (long since).

7) *Objective Dative*. The most common use of the dative case in Old English is that of the indirect object: *Efne, ic forgeaf ēow eall gærs and wyrta sǣd-berende ofer eorðan* . . . (Lo, I have given you every grass and seed-bearing plant upon the earth . . .)

8) *Possessive Dative*. Sometimes called the referential or ethical dative, this construction is a frequently used form of possession in Old English: *him on bearme læg* (it lay to him on lap—i.e., it lay in his lap).

9) *Adjectival Dative*. A few Old English adjectives are accompanied by a dative construction: *þēah hē him lēof wǣre* (although he was dear to them).

10) *Prepositional Dative*. Many Old English prepositions govern the dative case; among them are *æfter* (after), *æt* (at), *be, bī, big* (by), *būtan* (except), *for* (for), *fore* (before), *from* (from), *in* (in), *mid* (with), *of* (from), *ofer* (over), *on* (on), *tō* (to), *under* (under), and *wið* (against). If the preposition conveys the idea of motion, it may very well govern the accusative. Sometimes the preposition follows its object with the stress energy of an adverb (and thereby begins an idiomatic construction very popular in Modern English): *ne wæs him Fitela mid* (Fitela was not with him).

11) *Verb-Governed Dative*. A few Old English verbs govern the dative case as direct object—for example, *beorgan* (to protect), *fōn* (to seize), *hȳran* (to obey), *līcian* (to please), *oftēon* (to deprive), *trēowan* (to trust), and *wealdan* (to rule).

12) *Impersonal Dative.* Impersonal verbs in Old English are accompanied by a dative construction: *mē þæt riht ne þinceð* (that does not seem right to me).

13) *Adverbial Dative.* Sometimes the dative case is used to create Old English adverbs, as in *hwīlum* (at times), *miclum* (very), and *wundrum* (wonderfully).

14) *Dative-Instrumental.* In Old English the dative and the instrumental coincide completely, except for the masculine and the neuter singular of adjectives, demonstratives, and interrogatives; corresponding to the Latin ablative, the resultant dative-instrumental conveys the sense of means or instrument.

15) *The Instrumental.* In Old English the instrumental construction is used in expressions of time: *þȳ ylcan mōnðe ond dæge* (in the same month and day); in statements of comparison: *sē eorl wæs þē blīþra* (the earl was the happier); in noun absolutes: *ūp sprungenre sunnan* (the sun having risen).

16) *Objective Accusative.* The case of the direct object in Old English, the accusative is also often used as a cognate construction for the indirect object: *lc þæs Hrōðgar mæg . . . ræd gelæran* (I can give Hrothgar advice).

17) *Subjective Accusative.* In Old English the subject of an infinitive is in the accusative case: *Hī lēton þā of folman fēolhearde speru, gegrundene gāras flēogan.* (They let the file-hard spears, the grinded spears fly from the hand.)

18) *Prepositional Accusative.* Some Old English prepositions always dictate the accusative case in their objects—for example, *geond* (throughout), *oþ* (until), *þurh* (through), and *ymb* (around).

19) *Subjunctive Mood.* As in Latin practice, idiomatic use of the subjunctive mood in Old English verbs is demanded by four basic semantic situations: a) a clause of purpose or result: *þæt þū sīe þȳ leng libbende on eorþan* (that you may be living longer on earth); b) a conditional clause: *nemne him heaðobyrne helpe gefremede* (unless the battle-byrnie had helped him); c) a statement of indirect discourse: *Wulfstān sæde þæt hē gefōre of Hæþum* (Wulfstan said that he departed from Haddeby); d) a

command: *Bēon gegaderode þā wæteru þe sind under þære heofenan* (Let the waters be gathered that are under the heavens).

20) *Command Infinitive.* In Old English a command—apart from use of either the imperative or the subjunctive mood—may be constructed by means of *wuton* or *uton* plus the infinitive: *Ac utan dōn swā ūs þearf is . . .* (But let us act as we must . . .)

21) *Motion Infinitive.* As a substitute for the present participle of Modern English, in Old English the infinitive often accompanies verbs of motion:

Ðā cōm of mōre   under mist-hleoþum
Grendel gongan . . .

Then came from the moor   under the misty slopes
Grendel to go . . .

The *connective* system of Old English is another underdeveloped feature of the language. The synthetic syntax largely accounts for the underdevelopment of the grammatical terms of linkage in Old English: there is no great need to specialize the connectives in order to be explicit. Thus the relative pronouns are practically nonexistent; the definite article and its coinciding demonstrative pronoun do the work of joining clauses. Time and again the reader of Old English confronts such idiomatic connectives as *sē þe* (he who), *þā þe* (those who), and *þāra þe* (of those who). The neuter demonstrative *þæt* (that) introduces noun clauses into syntactical relationships such as direct object, purpose or result, and indirect discourse.

The prepositional connectives of Old English, in contrast, are fairly well developed to state *simple* relations of location, direction, association, and time. Since case endings often do the work of absent prepositions, however, Old English does not have a developed system of these word-group connectives. Old English is deficient in the complex, compound, and group prepositions that help to make Modern English syntax so explicit. Such also is the case with conjunctions. Sentence after sentence in Old English prose is built upon Hemingway's favorite clausal coordinator: *and*. For the modern American writer, this joiner is part of a carefully cultivated style to achieve an immediacy of presentation; for the Old English chroniclers, *and* is used because the deficiencies of the conjunction system do not permit proper subordination.

Matters of time and place are well handled in Old English with the use of *þā* (then, when), *oðþæt* (until), *þǣr* (there, where), and *þenden* (while, as long as). A few more commonly used conjunctions like *swā* (so, as), *swā swā* (so that, just as), and *þēah* (although) contribute to the growing hypotaxis of the language. Transitional words are practically nonexistent. True, *þēah* can carry the idiomatic equivalence of *however*, but Old English has nothing to match the means of paragraph welding found in the Modern English connectives *furthermore, moreover, nevertheless,* and others of their explicit nature.

OLD ENGLISH WORD GROUPS.   Because Old English is basically a morphemic language, it does not depend upon *word-group structures* to develop syntactical relationships nearly so much as Modern English. The word group in Old English, therefore, is not so clearly defined as in Modern English. But even as early as 700, an approximate date for the oral composition of *Beowulf*, the suprasegmental forces of stress and juncture were at work to delineate the boundaries of the various word groups. The great poem itself operates on half-line cadences that often coincide with the rhythmical extensions of the word groups of the language. Such cadences, close to the accent patterns of the spoken word, no doubt influenced the ultimate shaping of the word groups, with at least one maximum stress as a nucleus of the speech material that operates as a unit between two major junctures.

Some of the half-line cadences in *Beowulf* illustrate the evolving syntactical units of Old English as follows:

Noun Word Group:
> *lēof lēod-cyning* (the dear people-king)
> *mistige mōras* (the misty moors)
> *scearp scyld-wiga* (the sharp shield-warrior)

Subject-Predicate Word Group:
> *Weard maþelode* (the watchman spoke)
> *Strǣt wæs stān-fāh* (the street was paved)
> *Godes yrre bær* (he bore God's wrath)

Verbal Word Group:
> *Wealhþēo sēcan* (to look for Wealhtheow)
> *rinc sīðian* (the warrior going)
> *on geflit faran* (to run in a race)

Prepositional Word Group:
> *under mist-hleoþum* (under the misty slopes)
> *on grames grāpum* (in the claws of the hostile one)
> *sweartum nihtum* (on dark nights)

Conjunctional Modifier Word Group:
> *gamol ond gūð-rēouw* (old and fierce in battle)
> *hēah ond horn-gēap* (high and wide-gabled)
> *lāþ ond longsum* (loathsome and long-lasting)

Conjunctional Verb Word Group:
> *seomade ond syrede* (lurked about and ambushed)
> *swefeð ond snēdeþ* (kills and devours)
> *wīston ond ne wēndon* (wished and did not expect)

Clearly the language, even in its early stages, is developing the basic constructions of an analytic syntax. In contrast with the practices of Modern English, however, Old English is weak in complex verb groups and in verbals based on the present participle. Its prepositional phrases, moreover, may exist without the prepositions—thanks to the morphology of inflectional endings. Yet despite the differences in word order and idiomatic collocations, Old English supports the same general principles of phrasing and rhythm that govern the syntactical operations of present-day English.

In the evolution from a synthetic syntax to an analytic, several Old English constructions have fallen by the wayside: duality in the pronouns; every distinction of strong and weak classes in the adjectives; number, gender, and case in both adjectives and articles; gender and case in the demonstratives. As only the genitive case remains in Late Modern English nouns, so only the third person singular present indicative carries over in the verbs. In the pronouns, natural or logical gender applies to the third person, and the dative and accusative cases have combined into one oblique, the objective. The second person today undergoes no form change from singular to plural. Present-day English expresses relationships that are non-existent in Old English: a fully developed system of the passive voice; function-word expressions of the future, perfect, and progressive tenses; function-word constructions to indicate case-relationships and comparisons; word-order groupings to convey such meanings as case-relationships, modification, and agreement.

FORMAL STYLISTICS

OLD ENGLISH POETRY.   The glory of Old English is its heroic poetry. This poetry is *stichic* (linear) rather than *strophic* (stanzaic). It operates within an alliterative accentual line, unrhymed, of four maximum stresses and varying collocations of major, minor, and minimum stresses. The closest Modern English equivalent to the rhythm of *Beowulf* is to be found in the jazz cadences of Vachel Lindsay's poem *The Congo*. We can construct metrical analogues to the rhythmical possibilities of the Old English heroic line, as in the following nonsense examples:

> honeysuckle honeysuckle   typewriter black
> typewriter typewriter   honeysuckle black
> blackbird honeysuckle   typewriter black
> blackbird blackbird   blackbird black

Each of these four lines has two approximately *isochronous* half-line measures; cadential anacruses (completion of metrical time *between* lines) may follow the last maximum stress (*black*). Reinforcing this principle of isochroneity is a principle of *juncture substitution*—that is to say, open juncture /+/ may take the place of absent minimum stress /ᵕ/. Hence Kipling's

> Camped before the citadel and summoned it to siege.

and Lindsay's

> Boomlay, boomlay, boomlay, boom.

are variant versions of the same dipodic (two feet to a half line) rhythm expressed in this line from *Beowulf:*

> Oft Scyld Scēfing   sceaþena þrēatum ...

Reinforcing the syncopation of Old English poetry is the harp, struck as a percussion instrument by the bard in his chanted recital at points in the lines *where either major or minor stresses are missing.* In other words, the harp chords (H) of the Old English *scop* parallel the substitution of open junctures /+/ in order to maintain the isochroneity of the cadences. Such harp chords appear between contiguous maximum stresses, as in

> H
> Oft Scyld Scēfing ...

and between a maximum stress and a minimum, as in

H

þrym gefrūnon . . .

Thus Old English poetry operates within an alliterative accentual line that is constantly reinforced by the syncopation junctures of chanted overstresses and the accompanying chords of a percussion harp. It is rich in variational formulas, in sound-patterns based upon assonance, consonance, decorative internal rhyme, distinctive-features control, and in the imaginative use of kennings, heroic epithets, self-explanatory compounds, and the art of understatement known as *litotes*.

The styles of Old English poetry vary with subject matter and the genius of the author. The earlier the work, the shorter the line and the more original the formulas and images. Despite brilliant exceptions to the rule, as in *The Dream of the Rood*, the later Old English poetry tends toward religiosity, bombast, and empty imitation. The best poetry within the language is undoubtedly pagan. With the influence of Christianity, the spoken word yields place to the written, invention gives way to convention, the harp eventually falls silent, the line expands in speech material, and sentiment chokes out emotion. Something of this evolution of Old English poetry may be ascertained in the following four examples of style:

The Sublime Grotesque, from *Beowulf* (739–745).

Nē þæt se āglǣca   yldan þōhte,
ac hē gefēng hraðe   forman sīðe
slǣpendne rinc,   slāt unwearnum,
bāt bān-locan,   blōd ēdrum dranc,
synsnǣdum swealh;   sōna hæfde
unlyfigendes   eal gefeormod,
fēt ond folma.

Indeed that fiend   thought not to delay,
but he seized immediately   in the first rush
a sleeping warrior,   slit him open irresistibly,
bit his bone-locker,   drank blood from his veins,
gulped him down in chunks;   soon he had
of the unliving one   everything devoured,
even feet and hands.

Contrast Lyrical, from *The Wanderer* (41–48).

þinceð him on mōde   þæt hē his mondryhten

clyppe and cysse,   and on cnēo lecge
honda and hēafod   swā hē whīlum ǣr
in gēardagum   giefstōles brēac.
Ðonne onwæcneð eft   winelēas guma,
gesihð him biforan   fealwe wēgas,
baþian brimfuglas,   brǣdan feþra,
hrēosan hrīm and snāw   hagle gemenged.

he thinks in his mind   that he his liege-lord
embraces and kisses,   and lays on his knees
his hands and head   as he used to do
in former days when   he enjoyed the gift-stool.
Then awakens again   that miserable man,
he sees before him   the fallow waves,
the seabirds bathing,   spreading their feathers,
the hoarfrost and snow falling   mingled with hail.

The Religiously Ecstatic, from *The Dream of the Rood* (18–23).

Hwæðre ic þurh þæt gold   ongytan meahte
earmra ǣrgewin,   þæt hit ǣrest ongan
swǣtan on þā swīðran healfe.   Eall ic wæs mid sorgum gedrēfed.
Forht ic wæs for þǣre fǣgran gesyhðe.   Geseah ic þæt fūse bēacen
wendan wǣdum and blēom: hwīlum hit wæs mid wǣtan bestēmed,
besylwed mid swātes gange,   hwīlum mid since gegyrwed.

Yet sight through that gold might I get
of that wretched original wrong when first on the right
it began to sweat blood. And all sorrow-sick was I,
afraid before that fair sight. Saw I that bright beacon
change clothing and colors: at times it was sweat-swept,
sullied with sweat-blood—at times with gems bejeweled.

Bombast Imitative, from *Exodus* (161–169).

On hwæl hrēopon   herefugolas
hilde grǣdige;   hræfen gōl,
dēawigfeðere,   ofer drihtnēum,
wonn wælcēasega.   Wulfas sungon
atol æfenlēoð   ǣtes on wēnan,
carlēasan dēor   cwyldrōf beodan
on lāðra lāst   lēodmægnes ful:
hrēopon mearcweardas   middum nihtum,
flēah fǣge gāst,   folc wæs gehǣged.

While circling screamed   the carrion birds
greedy for battle;   the raven cried,
dewy-feathered one,   dark lover of death,
over the corpses.   The wolves sang

> a terrible evening song   in expectation of food,
> those unscrupulous beasts   savage in announcing
> on the track of the enemy   the fall of the host:
> the borderguards howled   in the middle of night,
> the doomed ghost fled,   the people were hedged in.

The emphasis on decorative description and the consequent lack of narrative thrust in this last passage reflect the literary decadence of late Old English poetry.

OLD ENGLISH PROSE.   Generally, the prose of the Anglo-Saxons is not nearly so distinguished as their poetry. Often gnarled in syntax and clumsy in idiomatic constructions, Old English prose tends to be dense and chaotic in its references. In the hands of the imitative Ciceronians, language and style suffer from redundancy and periphrasis. With a master wielding the pen, however, Old English prose can be simple, clear, eloquent, and moving:

Historical Reportage, from *The Anglo-Saxon Chronicle.*

Hēr gefōr Ælfrēd Aþulfing, syx nihtum ǣr ealra hāligra mæssan. Sē wæs cyning ofer eall Ongelcyn būtan ðǣm dæle þe under Dena onwalde wæs, and hē hēold þæt rīce ōþrum healfum lǣs þe xxx wintra. And þā fēng Ēadweard his sunu tō rīce. (901)

In this year died Alfred, son of Athulf, six nights before the Mass of All Saints. He was king over all of England, except for that portion which was under the jurisdiction of the Danes, and he had ruled the kingdom for twenty-eight and one-half years. And then his son Edward succeeded to the throne.

Overblown Eloquence, from Wulfstan's *Sermon to the English.*

Lēofan men, gecnāwað þæt sōð is: ðēos woruld is on ofste, and hit nēalǣcð þām ende; and ðȳ hit is on worulde ā swā leng swā wyrse, and swā hit sceal nȳde for folces synnan from dæge tō dæge ǣr Antecrīstes tōcyme yfelian swȳðe; and hūru hit wyrð þænne egeslīc and grimlīc wīde on worulde.

Dear men, recognize what the truth is: this world is in haste, and it approaches the end; and therefore with the world it is always the longer the worse, and so before the coming of Antichrist, from day to day, because of the sins of the people it shall necessarily grow very evil; and then widely throughout the world things shall indeed be terrible and fierce.

Clear Narrative, from King Alfred's translations of Orosius' *His-*

tory—"Voyages of Ohthere and Wulfstan."

And of Scīringeshēale hē cwæð ðæt hē seglode on fīf dagen tō þæm porte þe mon hēt æt Hæþum; sē stent betuh Winedum, and Seaxum, and Angle, and hȳrð in on Dene. Ðā hē þiderweard seglode from Scīringeshēale, pā wæs him on þæt bæcbord Denamearc and on þæt stēorbord wīdsǣ þrȳ dagas; and þā, twēgen dagas ǣr hē tō Hæþum cōme, him wæs on þæt stēorbord Gotland, and Sillende, and īglanda fela. On þǣm landum eardodon Engle, ǣr hī hider on land cōman. And hym wæs ðā twēgen dagas on ðæt bæcbord þā īgland þe in tō Denemearce hȳrað.

And he said that from Sciringssal he sailed in five days to the port which men call Haddeby; it stands among the Wends, the Saxons, and the Angles, and it belongs to the Danes. When he sailed thence from Sciringssal, then for three days was Denmark on his larboard and the open sea on his starboard; and then, two days before he came to Haddeby, on his starboard were Jutland, Zealand, and many islands. On those territories dwelt the Angles, before they came to this land. And for two days then on his larboard were the islands which belong to Denmark.

Rhythmical Elevation, from King Alfred's translations of The Venerable Bede's *History*—"The Conversion of Edwin."

Ðyslīc mē is gesewen, þū cyning, ðis andwearde līf manna on eorðan tō wiðmetenesse þǣre tīde þe ūs uncūð is, swā līc swā ðū æt swǣsendum sitte mid þīnum ealdormannum ond þegnum on wintertīde, ond sīe fȳr onǣlæd ond þīn heall gewyrmed, on hit rīne ond snīwe ond styrme ūte; cume ān spearwa and hrædlīce þæt hūs ðurhflēo, cume þurh ōþre duru in, þurh ōþre ūt gewīte. Hwæt hē on þā tīd þe hē inne bið, ne bið hrinen mid þȳ storme ðæs wintres; ac þæt bið ān ēagen bryhtm ond þæt lǣsste fæc, ac hē sōna of wintra on þone winter eft cymeð. Swā þonne þis monna līf tō medmiclum fæce ætȳweð; hwæt þǣr foregange, oððe hwæt þǣr eftfylge, wē ne cunnun. Forþon gif þēos nīwe lār ōwiht cūðlīcre ond gerisenlīcre brenge, þæs weorþe is þæt wē þǣre fylgen.

Thus it seems to me, you king, that this present life of men on earth is like unto that time which is unknown to us: it is exactly as if you were sitting at a banquet in the wintertime with your counselors and warriors, and the fire is kindled and the hall warmed, and it rains and snows and storms outside; comes a sparrow and quickly he flies through the hall, he comes in by one door and goes out at the other. That time during which he is inside he is not touched by the storm of the winter; but that is the twinkling of an eye and the briefest interval, for he soon from the winter must return to the winter. Even so small a time as that appears to be this life of men; what precedes it, or what shall follow it, we do not know. Therefore if this new doctrine makes anything clearer and more fitting, then it is well that we follow it.

With sensuous imagery and poetic cadence, this last passage shows how communication can transcend itself into the exalted substance of art.

QUESTIONS FOR RESEARCH AND DISCUSSION

1. Using Clark Hall's *A Concise Anglo-Saxon Dictionary* as a source book, conduct an investigation into the occurrence of /xl xn xr xw/ in the vocabulary of Old English. How would you account for the evolution of /x/ to /h/ in initial positions? What factors would favor the eventual dropping of /h/ before /l n r/? Be specific in your answers.

2. Organize a class project of research into the use of /h/ before /w/ in present-day American English. Listen to the speech habits of at least five-hundred members of your academic community, dividing the number equally among your classmates. Pay close attention to common words like *what*, *where*, and *why*. What are the percentages of /hw/ as against those of /w/? Is the use of /hw/ on the decline? Can you foresee its eventual total displacement by /w/ in American English? Are factors of social class, education, and geography significant in the maintenance of /hw/? What are some of the valuable linguistic lessons learned from this project?

3. A linguist has just made the statement that /p/ is the most sparsely distributed phoneme in the entire range of Old English literature. Conduct an investigation, involving all the members of the class, into this assertion. Is it true or false? Defend your answer with statistics based on a wide sampling of literary material.

4. Let five members of the class gather information and enter into a round table discussion of the following phonological features of Old English poetry: alliteration—patterns and function; assonance, consonance, and internal rhyme; stress and chant; rhythm and meter; possible uses of the harp.

5. Leading linguistic authorities believe that every language is adequate to its task at any given moment in its cultural history. Evolution therefore is merely change, not necessarily progress. Organize a debate on the following subject: *That Modern English represents a morphological improvement upon Old English.* Let at least two students take the affirmative and two the negative of this question. From the debate itself, now write a brief essay on the subject of *linguistic snobbery in reverse, or how a language cannot better itself.*

6. Someone has just told you that Old English is more like Modern German than Modern English in its use of inflections. Lead a research project to prove this assertion either right or wrong and write up the results.

7. Gather a parallel list of twenty-one idiomatic constructions in Modern English to go with those of Old English, as outlined in this chapter. Now comment in detail on the syntactical differences between the two languages.

8. Contrast the high degree of specialization in the function words of Modern English grammar with the lack of this specialization in Old English. How do you account for so dramatic a difference between the two languages? What is the correlation, if any, between inflectional morphology and the presence of grammatical function words? Be specific in your answer.

9. Compare and contrast the word-group structures of *Beowulf* with those of the *Anglo-Saxon Chronicle*. What are the chief differences between the word groups of the poetry and those of the prose? Pay careful attention to such features as number of syllables between major junctures, stress patterns, regularity of rhythm, and control of phonology. Do the syntax and style of these two documents illustrate the basic oppositions between *recursive* and *discursive*? Defend your answer in detail.

10. Gather together several leading translations of *Beowulf* and compare them in diction, rhythm, liveliness of style, and faithfulness to the spirit of the original. Then write a critical paper on the major problems of translating from Old English into Modern English. What are the chief æsthetic pitfalls of translation?

SELECTED BIBLIOGRAPHY

Bloomfield, Morton W., and Leonard Newmark. *A Linguistic Introduction to the History of English.* New York: Alfred A. Knopf, 1963. See especially pp. 132–171 for a discussion of Old English morphology and dialects.

Bright, James W. *An Anglo-Saxon Reader.* Revised and enlarged by James R. Hulbert. New York: Henry Holt and Company, 1935. See especially pp. ix–cxxxii for an outline of both the grammar and the literature of Old English.

Brodeur, Arthur G. *The Art of BEOWULF.* Berkeley and Los Angeles: University of California Press, 1959. A systematic study of the greatest piece of literary art in Old English.

Bryant, Margaret M. *Modern English and Its Heritage.* Second Edition. New York: The Macmillan Company, 1962. See especially pp. 31–51, 182–190, and 211–218 for graphic discussions of Old English heritage and phonology and the development of the English alphabet.

Greenfield, Stanley B. *A Critical History of Old English Literature.* New York: New York University Press, 1965. Reflects the most recent developments in our knowledge of Anglo-Saxon life and literature.

Hall, John R. Clark. *A Concise Anglo-Saxon Dictionary.* Fourth Edition, with a supplement by Herbert D. Meritt. Cambridge University Press, 1960. An indispensable one-volume study of the lexical content of Old English.

Hockett, Charles F. *A Course in Modern Linguistics.* New York: The Macmillan Company, 1958. See especially pp. 375–377 for a description of the phonemes of Old English.

Hodgkin, R. H. *A History of the Anglo-Saxons.* Two volumes. Third Edition. New York: Oxford University Press, 1953. The best general study of the Old English period available.

Kennedy, Charles W. *The Earliest English Poetry.* New York: Oxford University Press, 1948. A critical survey of English poetry written before the Norman Conquest.

Klaeber, Fr., ed. *Beowulf and the Fight at Finnsburg.* Third Edition, with supplement. New York: D. C. Heath and Company, 1941. See especially pp. v–clxxxvii. This is considered the best edition of the Old English masterpiece.

Robertson, Stuart, and Frederick G. Cassidy. *The Development of Modern English.* Second Edition. Englewood Cliffs, New Jersey: Prentice-Hall, 1954. See especially pp. 87–145 for a discussion of the evolution of English phonology and inflectional usage, with insights into the structures of Old English.

CHAPTER 5

The History of
Middle English
1150-1500 A.D.

IMPORTANT DATES

1204 Loss of Normandy as the property of the English king; it marks the beginning of the rise of English nationalism.

1250 The double allegiance of the English nobility ends; thus the most valid reason for the use of the French language in England is gone.

1258–1265 Barons' War, in which the English upper and middle classes unite against the "foreign element" to strengthen the doctrine of "England for the English."

1300 The English language once again becomes the native tongue of the nobility.

1337–1453 Hundred Years' War strengthens English patriotism, which ultimately leads to the total disuse of French in England.

1344–1400 Lifetime of Geoffrey Chaucer, champion of the vernacular and father of mainstream English poetry.

1348–1350   The Black Death (bubonic plague) causes a serious shortage of labor and therefore strengthens the role of the lower classes and the importance of the language they speak: English.

1356   The Sheriff's Court in London and Middlesex is conducted in English.

1362   Parliament opens with a speech in English. *The Statute of Pleading* demands that the King's Court and all other courts be henceforth conducted in English. This act constitutes the official and legal recognition of the language.

1381   The Peasants' Revolt further strengthens the role of the laborers and the importance of their language, English.

1385   Date by which the English language is in general use throughout the schools.

1400   Date by which English is used in the writing of wills.

1415   Battle of Agincourt, in which Henry V, with his English longbowmen, establishes a pride in all things English.

1423   The records of Parliament begin to be written in English.

1425   English is adopted as the language of writing.

1450   English becomes the language of written town laws.

1476   William Caxton introduces printing into England, hastening the end of Middle English and the commencement of the Early Modern English of the Renaissance.

1489   All statutes in England are written in English.

1500   Approximate date of the end of Middle English.

OUTSTANDING PERSONS

William Caxton   Father of English printing (1476), champion of middle-class literacy, and hastener of Modern English.

Geoffrey Chaucer   Author of Middle English masterpieces *The Canterbury Tales* (1387–95) and *Troilus and Criseyde* (1382–86), champion of the vernacular, literary supporter of the London dialect, importer of the European Renaissance, and father of English poetry.

Edward I   The monarch who during his reign (1272–1307) develops a national consciousness and unity and demands the preservation of the English language against the incursions of French.

Eleanor of Provence   Wife of Henry III, Eleanor symbolizes the dominance of French—in language, literature, and general culture—both in England and on the Continent.

John Gower   Leading literary contemporary (1325?–1408) of Chaucer, who epitomizes in his poetry the three levels of language usage in medieval England: Latin, French, and English.

Henry III   His long reign (1216–72) opens the gates for the great influx of French and Latin that ultimately changes English from a one-tradition language to a hybrid of several heritages. His French favoritism leads to the strengthening of English nationalism.

Henry V   Great English king (1413–22) who ends the military dominance of France at the Battle of Agincourt (1415), strongly influences the ascendancy of English in Britain, and leads the way for its general adoption as the language of writing.

King John   The monarch who loses England's Norman estates (1204) and signs the Magna Carta (1215), granting greater political and civil liberties to his subjects.

William Langland   Most important literary figure in the Alliterative Revival (1350–1400), Langland writes one of the poetic masterpieces of Middle English and the greatest social document of its kind: *Piers Plowman* (1362–87).

Simon de Montfort   Norman-born baron who leads the coalition of barons and the middle class, which produces the Provisions of Oxford (1258) and the Barons' War (1258–65), thereby curtailing the foreign element in England, strengthening English nationalism, and preparing the way for the predominantly English government of Edward I.

Wat Tyler   Leader of the Peasants' Revolt (1381), which strengthens the role of the laboring class and therefore the importance of the English tongue; the subsequent rise of trade unions and guilds hastens the advent of Early Modern English.

John Wycliffe   Leading writer of English prose in the fourteenth century, Wycliffe (1328?–84) champions the first English translation of the Bible.

MAJOR ATTRIBUTES OF THE LANGUAGE

Undergoes great changes in vocabulary and grammar.

Receives immense influx of Norman, French, and Latin words to become a hybrid language, flexible and resourceful.

Experiences a gradual leveling of inflections.

Develops a dominant system of "weak" (regular) verbs.

Transforms old grammatical gender into new natural (logical) gender.

Suppresses much of the older West Teutonic vocabulary and weakens the Old English morphological processes.

Evolves a more analytic and hypotactic syntax, in which word order determines function: a major basis of Modern English.

Distills a Standard Spoken and Literary English by 1450 out of four major dialects: Northern, East Midland, West Midland, and Southern.

Specializes into three levels of expression: *Popular* (native English), *Literary* (assimilated French), and *Learned* (reintroduced Latin and its cognate Greek).

Disseminates its final achievements in London version via printing after 1476 to hasten the entrance of Early Modern (Renaissance) English.

THE HISTORY OF MIDDLE ENGLISH is the history of the rise of English nationalism and the fall of medieval chivalry, of growing restrictions on the monarchy and the expanding influence of the middle class. Within the three and a half centuries of this history, three distinct phases of the language stand out in bold relief. Phase one is Early Middle English; it extends from the end of *The Anglo-Saxon Chronicle* (1154) to the close of the reign of Edward I (1307). The outstanding historical characteristic of Early Middle English is the struggle for the survival of the language. Phase two constitutes Mature Middle English; this period runs from the death of Edward I (1307) to the death of Henry V (1422). The slow ascendancy of the language is the major historical attribute of Mature Middle English. Phase three is the brief history of Late Middle English, which spans the time from the death of Henry V (1422) to the commencement of the Tudor dynasty in the coronation of Henry VII (1485). Late Middle English is the language triumphant.

So impressive is the change wrought in the native tongue of Britain during these three and a half centuries that even a schoolboy can detect the vast differences between what was and what became the English language. At the start of phase one, the language sounds a good deal like present-day German. After a dozen generations of refinement in a French finishing academy run by Latin professors, the language graduates at the end of phase three with hybrid honors and talks very much like Modern

English. During the evolution from Old English to Early Modern, the linguistic emphasis shifts from the auditory morpheme to the visual, from the spoken word to the written.

EARLY MIDDLE ENGLISH
THE STRUGGLE FOR SURVIVAL,
1154–1307

HENRY PLANTAGENET, COUNT OF ANJOU, assumed the English throne in 1154, the year in which *The Anglo-Saxon Chronicle* comes to an end. England was exhausted from twenty years of anarchy and her people were sick of the excesses of Norman brutality. Duke of Normandy and ruler of all western France, Henry II crushed his baronial opposition in Britain, developed an efficient judicial and administrative system, established a habit of obedience to government, and prepared the way for subsequent constitutional reforms. What he could not do was put a halt to the aristocratic neglect of the English language. For almost a century and a half—from William the Conqueror's victory at Hastings in 1066 to the loss of the Norman estates by King John in 1204—the French-speaking upper class remained indifferent to the English language.

In twelfth-century England, the symbol of the vast social separation between manor lord and serf was a simple matter of not speaking the same language. Dependence upon bailiffs and men-at-arms to act as interpreters merely complicated an already bad situation. Celtic prevailed in Wales and Cornwall; Latin dominated the conservative clergy; French controlled the thought patterns of the king and his court, the nobility, the high churchmen, the knights, and the merchants. As for the common people, only 1 percent of whom understood the language of their masters, they were divided into various dialects of Middle English and archaic carry-overs from Old. It is no wonder that the French lyrics and epic romances that were sweeping Europe should implant a foreign literary tradition on the soil of England, for English was out of favor, its literature in decay, and there was no means of reviving an earlier heroic age by importing the great Icelandic sagas.

The English nationalism that demanded the universal use of the language of the people instead of the aristocratic tongue of their Norman masters is rooted in the reigns of the two Plantagenet brothers, Richard the Lion-Heart (1189–99) and King John (1199–1216). During the decade of absenteeism of Richard, his efficient Archbishop of Canterbury and Justiciar of the Crown, Hubert Walter, governed England well and instituted several policies of immense social and political significance. Through charters, Hubert granted to the towns the privilege of self-government by elected officials. By entrusting municipal independence to the middle class, he strengthened the democratic role of London against the authority of the throne. In extending self-government to the shires by placing power in the hands of the local gentry, Hubert Walter permitted the election of coroners from the suitors of the Shire Court and the selection of juries by those coroners. Thus to self-government was added the principle of representation, both indispensable for the future development of a national Parliament. Before such a development could take place, of course, the King of England would have to concentrate upon affairs at home and submit his person to the obedience of a common law considered higher than the exercise of regal will.

When King John lost Normandy to Philip of France in 1204, he ensured the ultimate disuse of French in Britain. Gradually relinquishing their continental estates, the English nobility cultivated a rivalry with France that culminated in the Hundred Years' War. Thanks to the selfish bungling of John, the English kings who succeeded him—even while still speaking a caricature of the French tongue—had to deal with questions peculiar to the country they governed: relations with Wales and Scotland, the development of a legal code, and the establishment of a Parliament. Once the barons of Runnymede had forced John to sign the Magna Carta in 1215, the English nobility saw to it that class alliances should prevent "taxation without representation" and the return of feudal anarchy. No longer would the life of the nation be the instrument of one man's desires. Although protection against the officers of the king and the right to a fair and legal trial originally applied only to "freemen," as guaranteed by Magna Carta, three hundred years later all Englishmen were "freemen" before the law.

During the reign of Henry III (1216–72), the impulse to English nationalism gradually gained momentum in reaction to foreign abuses at home and the French favoritism of the English court. The double allegiance of the Norman-English barons to Henry III and Louis IX had to end, and Louis himself told these barons, convoked at Paris, that they must make up their minds as to which properties they preferred: Eng-

lish or French. By 1250, the double allegiance was over. But such a termination did not stop the immense influx of foreigners into Britain. Beginning in the reign of John and continuing into that of Henry III, the
French invasion of the island kingdom took place in three distinct stages:
from Poitou, from Provence, and again from Poitou.

Completely French in taste, education, and association, Henry III in
1233 dismissed all native-born officers from his court and filled the va-
cancies with lackeys from Poitou. Under the dominating advice of Peter
des Roches, the Poitevin clerk whom he made bishop of Winchester, the
king flooded England with two thousand knights from Poitou and Brit-
tany and put them in charge of the castles that controlled the various
baronies and counties of the country. In 1236 he married Eleanor of
Provence, who prevailed upon him to fatten the fortunes of her many
relatives with lands and money. For at least ten years after the wedding,
Provençals poured into England. At times to reward favorites, at times to
please the Pope, Henry III dispensed ecclesiastical dignities to foreigners.
Before long the French clergy in England had a combined income three
times their patron king's.

As a result of the abuses of Henry III, the English barons and middle
class united to drive the foreign element out of office and even out of the
country. Struggling to extend the political guarantees of Magna Carta,
the self-seeking barons forced the Provisions of Oxford (1258) upon the
throne. The rising class of knights and gentry, the "bachelors" accustomed to a measure of self-government as coroners and jurymen, extracted
the same rights and privileges of vassalage and tenantship from the barons.
Thus a third power, of great democratic possibilities, came into being,
and it demanded an "England for the English." Led by Simon de Montfort, this power joined with liberal-minded barons, a band of rebellious
clergy, a hard core of free-thinking Oxford University students, and a
popular front of the poor to fight for reforms in the bloody seven years
of the Barons' War (1258–65).

A disciple of Grossetête, Bishop of Lincoln (d. 1253), Simon de Montfort stood unalterably opposed to royal and papal self-indulgence in England. Considering reforms as the will of God, Simon looked upon the law
as an authority higher than that of the king. With his victory at the Battle
of Lewes in 1264, Simon became the *de facto* monarch of England.
Though he died in defeat a year later at the Battle of Evesham, Simon

was a conqueror: he dominated the thinking of Henry III's son and heir Edward I.

During the reign of Edward I (1272–1307), a growing sense of national consciousness dictated an ever widening use of the English language. Though French continued to be the official language of Parliament, law court, and contractual negotiation, upper-class knowledge of it in England was diminishing. The gradual wane of French is unmistakable from two important pieces of evidence: the translation of polite society French literature into English, and the vastly quickened pace of the adoption of French words into English. So long as people read a foreign language with native ease, there is no need for translations; when those same people abandon the foreign language in a return to their own, they take a fund of familiar and useful expressions from the foreign language with them.

Despite the influence of his Provençal mother, Edward I spoke English as his first language. His anti-French attitude resulted in the appointment of government officials who were English. They in turn encouraged the use of their native tongue among the upper classes. Espousing English thus became a matter of patriotism. By 1300 the English nobility looked upon French as a foreign language, to be learned for purposes of cultural refinement and with some degree of difficulty.

THE LANGUAGE.   By the time the upper classes of England had to come to terms with the language of the common people, the language had undergone vast changes from Old English. Early Middle English is a record of those changes, and it says that the most important single influence of the Norman Conquest upon English was the removal of the conservative pressures that tended to impede its evolution. As the tongue of a subjugated country, Old English immediately lost prestige. West Saxon was no longer the literary standard of the conquered Britons, and the Anglo-Saxon scribal tradition was suppressed. Neither church nor state had much time to give to the language of the English peasants, and the socially and intellectually elite could not be bothered with it.

Under such conditions of *laissez faire*, the language benefited from a return to oral primacy: colloquial ease determined usage and variant dialect forms competed for acceptance. Unhindered by rules of prescription and proscription, the English peasants demanded stress on the root syllable and remodeled the language with tongue and palate. After two centuries of such uninhibited remodeling, by the end of the reign of

Edward I the English language had begun its evolution toward a cosmopolitan vocabulary and had initiated several processes of great linguistic change: inflectional leveling and the loss of grammatical gender, a simple morphology for the plural, clarity and order among the pronouns and the demonstratives, a reduction of irregular verbs, and a fixing of word order for the development of an analytic syntax.

The most significant change wrought in the grammar, as distinct from the vocabulary, of Early Middle English was the *general reduction of inflections*. Three factors were responsible for the gradual phonetic transmutations that resulted in the loss of almost all inflectional endings in the English language: 1) the Old English habit of stressing the root syllable, an intonation pattern that guaranteed the forward positioning of accent and a phonemic weakening of syllables in unstressed positions; 2) a morphological simplification, due to the speech interference of Scandinavian and French, for the sake of an easier communication; 3) the suppression of West Saxon as a standard dialect, thereby permitting variant forms of the language to compete for ascendancy.

The inflectional leveling of Early Middle English followed this general scheme. First, the final -*m* in dative constructions of the strong declensions shifted to -*n;* in other words, a grave labial nasal became an acute apical nasal. Second, this dative -*n* then fell away from the inflection, influencing similar constructions (as in the infinitive form of the verb, for example) into dropping the -*n* also. Third, unsupported by any final consonant and standing in the non-accented position of the inflectional vestige, the remaining vowels (*a, o, u, e*) lost their phonemic coloring and became the "indeterminate" *schwa* (ə). Graphemically equated with the letter *e* (or occasionally *i, y,* or *u*), this *schwa* eventually fell silent. The unpronounced final *e* of Modern English, therefore, is a visual morphemic relic of inflectional leveling.

The inflectional leveling produced immediate effects. The morphological simplification resulted in the establishment of -*s* as the distinctive form of the possessive singular and the nominative and accusative plural in the noun. With -*es* as an alternate form of the plural in the strong declension and -*en* in the weak, the noun case endings were vastly reduced. In some instances the inflections for both case and number were completely destroyed. The adjective too changed, for the nominative singular soon dominated all cases in the singular and the nominative plural all cases in the plural. In the weak declension of the adjective, both singular and plural ended in -*e* and hence number no longer made a distinction. Since the strong declension of the adjective often supported the same -*e* ending, by 1250 the only remaining distinctions between singular and plural in the adjective were in strong monosyllabic forms that had terminated in a consonant in Old English.

A corresponding loss of pronominal inflections led to an immense streamlining of the demonstratives. Although a plural *tho* (those) persisted into Shakespeare's day, the demonstrative forms contracted from a confusing eighteen to a manageable five: *the, that, this, those, these.* In addition to the loss of their entire dual system, the personal pronouns combined their accusatives and datives into one form: *him, her,* and *them. It* became the oblique as well as the nominative form in the neuter. With the Scandinavian introduction of the third person plurals *they, their,* and *them,* the pronoun system of the language was greatly clarified. By 1500, through a gradual penetration southward, these Scandinavian forms became the normal English plurals.

By that time, a linguistic phenomenon of far greater importance had taken place—the establishment of a fixed word order as the chief determinant of function in an analytic syntax. With the leveling of inflections, the language had to resort to some other means of indicating function and therefore meaning. Through the evolution of a fixed word order, the use of juxtaposition, prepositions, and other function words, Middle English achieved the bases of Modern English syntax by the reign of Henry VII. Within such a syntax, grammatical gender gave way to natural gender when the gender-distinguishing modifiers—the strong adjectives and the demonstratives—were reduced to one uninflected form.

Inflectional leveling in the Early Middle English verbs was less spectacular than in the nouns, pronouns, and adjectives. The strong or irregular verbs had always been a minority, even in the earliest days of Old English. After the Norman Conquest two factors united to reduce the strong verbs to a minimum: the loss of native words and the conversion of newly formed verbs into the weak or regular conjugation. At least one-third of the Old English strong verbs disappeared during the period of Early Middle English—more than a hundred key words. In the evolution of the language, nearly another hundred strong verbs have died out, and a sizable number have been regularized. The habit of regularizing newly adopted verbs and functionally shifted nouns and adjectives in Modern English is the natural outcome of a process started in Early

Middle English. With the removal of conservative pressures for "correct" usage, the English peasants acted on analogy and changed the patterns of some strong verbs to those of the weak. In the thirteenth century verbs such as *burn, brew, bow, climb, flee, flow, help, mourn, row, step, walk,* and *weep* were being regularized. Had not the prestige of English risen at the time when printing stabilized a revived conservatism, the language might have been rid of all irregular verbs. Even though the past participles of some regularized verbs have survived in their strong forms (*cloven, graven, hewn, laden, molten, mown, shaven, sodden, swollen*) as adjectives, today the strong verbs themselves have been reduced to a few score.

INFLUX OF NORMAN FRENCH. The great changes that took place in the grammar of Early Middle English were accompanied by an immense influx of Norman French into its vocabulary. At least 10,000 French terms entered English before the onset of the Tudor dynasty; about 7,500 of these Middle English borrowings are still in use. The period of largest French influx began late in Early Middle English, around 1250, and extended for a century and a half, to 1400. Approximately 40 percent of the entire English appropriation of French words occurred in this span of one hundred fifty years. But the precedent for such linguistic acquisition had been set in the century between 1150 and 1250, when some nine hundred Norman terms entered the English vocabulary.

The Normans assumed a different role than the Scandinavians, who had mingled with the English more or less on a basis of equality. The Normans formed the upper class; their language was consequently aristocratic. Norman cultural leadership is evident in the terminology of church, government, military establishment, legal system, master-servant relationship, cuisine, fashion, leisure-time activity, commerce, and the arts. So strong was the need for these early Norman loans to a more impoverished culture that most of the French words that entered the English language before 1350 have not only remained in use but have also achieved the force of native stock.

The borrowed Norman words tended to be functional and essential rather than decorative and refining. These early linguistic appropriations began with the church; in matters of doctrine and faith, the French clergy had to reach their English communicants as soon as possible. With French as the official vernacular of monastery and convent, the following words soon entered the English language: *religion, theology, sermon, homily, sacrament, baptism, communion, confession, penance, prayer, orison, lesson, passion, psalmody, clergy, clerk, prelate, cardinal, legate, dean, chaplain, parson, pastor, vicar, sexton, abbess, novice, friar, hermit, crucifix, crosier, miter, surplice, censer, incense, lectern, image, chancel, chantry, chapter, abbey, convent, priory, hermitage, cloister, sanctuary, creator, saviour, trinity, virgin, saint, miracle, mystery, faith, heresy, schism, reverence, devotion, sacrilege, simony, temptation, damnation, penitence, contrition, remission, absolution, redemption, salvation, immortality, piety, sanctity, charity, mercy, pity, obedience, virtue, solemnity, solemn, divine, reverend, devout, preach, pray, chant, repent, confess, adore, sacrifice, convert, anoint,* and *ordain.*

The church was not the only institution that channeled Norman French into the English language; government was hard at work borrowing, and so were the army, the navy, the law courts, the fashion salons, and the kitchens. The following selective lists indicate the extent of the Norman influx into Early Middle English:

1) Government Terms: *government, govern, administer, crown, state, empire, realm, reign, royal, prerogative, authority, sovereign, majesty, scepter, tyrant, usurp, oppress, court, council, parliament, assembly, statute, treaty, alliance, record, repeal, adjourn, tax, subsidy, revenue, tally, exchequer, subject, allegiance, rebel, traitor, treason, exile, public, liberty, office, chancellor, treasurer, chamberlain, marshal, governor, councilor, minister, viscount, warden, castellan, mayor, constable, coroner, crier, noble, nobility, peer, prince, princess, duke, duchess, count, countess, marquis, baron, squire, page, courtier, retinue, sir, madam, mistress, manor, demesne, bailiff, vassal, homage, peasant, bondman, slave,* and *caitiff.*

2) Military Terms: *army, navy, peace, enemy, arms, battle, combat, skirmish, siege, defense, ambush, stratagem, retreat, soldier, garrison, guard, spy, captain, lieutenant, sergeant, dart, lance, banner, mail, buckler, hauberk, archer, chieftain, portcullis, moat, havoc, array, harness, brandish, vanquish, besiege,* and *defend.*

3) Legal Terms: *justice, equity, judgment, crime, bar, assize, plea, suit, plaintiff, defendant, judge, advocate, attorney, bill, petition, complaint, inquest, summons, indictment, jury, juror, panel, felon, evidence, proof,*

bail, ransom, verdict, sentence, decree, award, fine, forfeit, punishment, prison, gaol, pillory, pardon, trespass, assault, arson, larceny, fraud, property, estate, tenant, dower, legacy, patrimony, heritage, heir, executor, entail, just, innocent, and *culpable.*

4) Fashion Terms: *fashion, dress, apparel, habit, gown, robe, garment, attire, cape, cloak, coat, frock, collar, veil, train, chemise, petticoat, lace, embroidery, pleat, gusset, buckle, button, tassel, plume, kerchief, mitten, garter, boots, satin, taffeta, fur, sable, beaver, ermine, blue, brown, vermilion, scarlet, saffron, russet, tawny, jewel, ornament, brooch, chaplet, ivory, enamel, turquoise, amethyst, topaz, garnet, ruby, emerald, sapphire, pearl, diamond,* and *crystal.*

5) Culinary Terms: *dinner, supper, feast, repast, collation, mess, appetite, taste, victuals, viand, sustenance, mackerel, sole, perch, bream, sturgeon, salmon, sardine, oyster, porpoise, venison, beef, veal, mutton, pork, bacon, sausage, tripe, loin, chine, haunch, brawn, gravy, poultry, pullet, pigeon, mallard, partridge, pheasant, quail, plover, squirrel, pottage, gruel, toast, biscuit, cream, sugar, olives, salad, lettuce, endive, almond, fruit, raisin, fig, grape, orange, lemon, pomegranate, cherry, peach, confection, pastry, tart, jelly, treacle, spice, clove, thyme, herb, mustard, vinegar, marjoram, cinnamon, nutmeg, goblet, saucer, cruet, plate, platter, roast, boil, parboil, stew, fry, broach, blanch, grate,* and *mince.*

6) Domestic and Social Terms: *arras, curtain, couch, chair, cushion, screen, lamp, lantern, sconce, chandelier, blanket, quilt, coverlet, counterpane, towel, basin, dais, parlor, wardrobe, closet, pantry, scullery, garner, recreation, solace, jollity, leisure, dance, carol, revel, minstrel, juggler, fool, ribald, lute, tabor, melody, music, chess, checkers, dalliance, conversation, ambler, courser, hackney, palfrey, rouncy, stallion, rein, curb, crupper, rowel, curry, trot, stable, harness, mastiff, terrier, spaniel, leash, kennel, scent, retrieve, forest, park, covert, warren, joust, tournament,* and *pavilion.*

7) High Cultural Terms: *art, painting, sculpture, beauty, color, figure, image, tone, cathedral, palace, mansion, chamber, ceiling, joist, cellar, garret, chimney, lintel, latch, lattice, wicket, tower, pinnacle, turret, porch, bay, choir, cloister, baptistry, column, pillar, base, poet, rime, prose, romance, lay, story, chronicle, tragedy, prologue, preface, title, volume, chapter, quire, parchment, vellum, paper, pen, treatise, compila-*

tion, study, logic, geometry, grammar, noun, clause, gender, copy, expound, and *compile.*

8) Medical Terms: *medicine, chirurgy, physician, surgeon, apothecary, malady, debility, distemper, pain, ague, palsy, pleurisy, gout, jaundice, leper, paralytic, plague, pestilence, contagion, anatomy, stomach, pulse, remedy, ointment, balm, pellet, alum, arsenic, niter, sulphur, alkali,* and *poison.*

MAP 2. MAJOR MIDDLE ENGLISH DIALECT AREAS

MIDDLE ENGLISH DIALECTS.   With the eventual rise of the London dialect as the standard version of the language, regional variants lost some of their distinctive differences. From the four dialects of Old English, five major dialects of Middle English evolved: West Saxon became Southern; Kentish remained the speech in the Southeast; Mercian divided into East Midland and West Midland; Northumbrian remained Northern. Since the Middle English dialects developed within geographic barriers, they may be delineated graphically, as in Map 2.

The five major versions of Middle English all had linguistic features peculiar to themselves. Southern and Kentish, for example, were more conservative in the retention of Old English inflections; thus they maintained a decayed use of the past participle prefix (original *ge-* transmuted to either *y-* or *i-*) into the fourteenth century. Northern, on the other hand, had liberal flavor and a high density of Scandinavian terms in its vocabulary, and exerted immense influence on East Midland when the London version of that dialect was becoming Received British Standard. Both East Midland and West Midland developed a spirit of linguistic compromise that made use of Northern and Southern elements and eventually led to a general convergence of dialects.

Before such convergence took place, however, the major five Middle English dialects could be briefly characterized as follows:

> *Northern*. Spoken north of the Humber River and including Early Scottish and such provincial variants as that of Yorkshire, Northern Middle English 1) retained Old English *ā* as an unrounded vowel /a:/ or /æ:/ (*stane* for *stone*, *ham* for *home*), 2) employed *-and* for the ending of the present participle, 3) spelled Old English *hw* and Middle English *wh* as *qu*, 4) used *-es* as the final inflection of the present indicative plural of the verb, 5) substituted *them* for *him* and *their* for *here* in the third person plural of the pronoun, 6) preferred the phoneme /s/ to the phoneme /š/ in the equivalents of Modern *shall* (*sal*) and *should* (*solde*), 7) made *are* predominate as the present plural of the verb *to be*, 8) did not soften Old English /k/ to /c/ before front vowels (thus *kirk* instead of *church*), and 9) kept *at* in general use for *to*.
>
> *West Midland*. Spoken south of the Humber, north of the Severn, and east of Wales, West Midland Middle English 1)

changed Old English *a* before *m* and *n* (except *ng, nd, mb*) to o (thus *mon* for *man, nome* for *name, ronk* for *rank*), 2) maintained two forms of present indicative third person singular for the verb (*-eth* in southern part and *-es* in northern), 3) substituted *v* for initial *f* in southern part, 4) used both *-and* and *-end* as the ending of the present participle, 5) retained Old English *y, ȳ, eo,* and *ēo* as front rounded vowels (*u, ui, eo, o, oe, u, ue*), and 6) employed the distinctive forms *ho* and *ha* for the feminine third person singular pronoun.

Southern. Spoken west of Kent, Surrey, and Sussex and south of the Severn and the Thames, Southern Middle English 1) substituted *v* for initial *f*, 2) behaved exactly like West Midland in the retention of Old English *y, ȳ, eo,* and *ēo,* 3) used both *-ing* and *-ind* as the ending of the present participle, 4) preferred *-eth* as the inflection for the present plural indicative of the verb, and 5) retained Old English *i, y, ī,* and *ȳ* so that *u* or *i* substituted for the *e* in other dialects (for example, *huren* or *hiren* instead of *heren*, "hear").

Kentish. Spoken in the extreme southeastern tip of England (Kent, Surrey and Sussex), Kentish Middle English 1) substituted *v* for initial *f*, 2) used both *-ing* and *-ind* as the ending of the present participle, 3) preferred *-en* as the inflection for the present plural indicative of the verb, 4) interjected a semi-vowel before *o* when preceded by *b* or *g* (for example, *guod* instead of *god*, "good"), and 5) occasionally lowered high-front *i* to mid-front *e* in words like *pet* for *pit* and *fer* for *fire*.

East Midland. Spoken between the Thames and the Humber in the eastern section of the Midlands, East Midland Middle English 1) did not support most of the distinguishing features of the other dialects, 2) eventually borrowed functional items from other dialects (for example, plural pronouns from Northern and the *-ing* form of the present participle from Kentish), 3) preferred *-en* as the inflection for the present plural indicative of verbs, and 4) used *-end* as the ending of the present participle.

In the general convergence of these five major dialects, East Midland acted as the gathering magnet. The primary reason for this attractive power, of course, was the city of London.

EARLY MIDDLE ENGLISH LITERATURE.   The impact of Norman French upon Early Middle English was not confined to linguistic matters *per se:* it extended to the artistic use of language as well. Under this Norman French influence, English storytelling softened its earlier heroic tone. Enjoying the fresh technique of full description, detailed setting, psychological characterization, and exploitation of crisis, the romance became the central form of narrative art, courtly in manner and worldly wise in outlook. The forerunner of the modern novel and a literary equivalent of the present-day Western, the medieval romance abounded in number, subject matter, spies, battles, conversions of the heathen, intrigues, and love affairs. Although drawing on material from ancient Greece and Rome, from Spain and France, the medieval English romance chose King Arthur as its hero par excellence. From Geoffrey of Monmouth, a Welsh chronicler of the mid-twelfth century, to Malory, who published his *Morte Darthur* in 1485, English patriotism and mysticism combined to make the little finger of Arthur stronger than the back of Charlemagne or Alexander.

The courtly love depicted in the medieval romance was supported by the sentiments developed in ballad and lyric, as imported from Provence via Normandy. Nor could the church stamp out the religion of courtly love, for the church was engaged in advancing a Mariolatry that sanctified the courtly love of religion. Despite the labored dullness of such long homilies and treatises as the *Ormulum* (c. 1215), the *Ancren Riwle* (c. 1220), and *Cursor Mundi* (c. 1300), the hand of the church on Early Middle English literature was not altogether detrimental. On the contrary, it was in the church that the great secular and democratic art form of England got its start: the drama.

Even before the Norman Conquest, the Mass of Easter contained the rudimentary play of a simple colloquy known as the *Quem quaeritis* ("Whom seek ye?"). This question the angel asks the three Marys, who answer: "Jesus of Nazareth." Then the angel replies, "He is not here, he is risen." From such a bare beginning evolved the greatest dramatic literature of the Western world. Mainly in the hands of the clergy for some three hundred years, Early Middle English drama finally emerged from the church, secularized itself with non-Biblical figures (clowns and native types), and performed beyond the churchyard in pageant carts drawn through the town. With the trade guilds undertaking their production, the plays evolved into three basic types: mystery, miracle, and morality. Mystery plays dealt with Biblical subjects (Creation, the Slaughter of the Innocents, the Sacrifice of Isaac); miracle plays portrayed the lives of the saints; morality plays dramatized the conflict of good and evil in the soul of man. If *Everyman* (c. 1500) is the only undisputed masterpiece among the cycles of medieval drama, they are still extremely important for the development of English literature: they prepared the cultural setting for Shakespeare.

MATURE MIDDLE ENGLISH THE SLOW ASCENDANCY OF THE LANGUAGE, 1307–1422

DURING THE THIRTY YEARS BETWEEN the death of Edward I and the outbreak of the Hundred Years' War (1307–1337), French continued to decline in importance in England. English had become so much the viable tongue of all classes in the early fourteenth century that both the church and the universities undertook measures to sustain an artificial use of French. French was the speech of conversation in the Benedictine monasteries at Canterbury and Westminster. Students at Oxford University were required to make grammatical analyses of French and translate their Latin studies into that language. Statutes of several of the Oxford colleges demanded that students converse in either Latin or French. In 1332 the English Parliament felt compelled to bolster the sagging use of French by decreeing that all members of the nobility and the gentry should see to it that their children were properly instructed in that language. This political preferment of French joined with a scholarly abuse of English in a vain attempt to maintain the linguistic supremacy of an aristocratic conservatism. But the grammatical treatises after 1250 indicate that by this time French was considered a foreign language in England. The political rise of Paris assured the dominance of Central French upon the continent, and in comparison with the refinements of that tongue the artificial French of England sounded somewhat ridiculous.

From the beginning of the Hundred Years' War in 1337 to the

Peasants' Revolt in 1381, the growing prestige of English was supported by the nationalism induced through open conflict with France and by the rise of a substantial English middle class. The military victories over the French at Crécy (1346) and Poitiers (1356) injected a new sense of patriotism in the British people, who quite naturally nurtured feelings of animosity toward the enemy and his language. This hostility toward all things French contributed in large measure to the ultimate disuse of the language in England. In support of this patriotic tendency, a middle class growing in size, wealth, and political strength sanctioned the importance of the English language.

A general improvement of the status of the English villeins and in the standard of living among the free laborers contributed to the rising prestige of the language they spoke. A sharp reduction of the labor market, brought about by the terrible bubonic plague of 1348–50, resulted in an immediate escalation of wages. The serious shortage of labor that produced monetary gains for the English workers also enhanced the value of their native tongue, for the importance of a language is directly related to the importance of its speakers. The expanding economic strength of the middle class led to the development of trade unions and guilds, which reinforced the power of the craftsmen and merchants. The Peasants' Revolt of 1381 showed that in time every area of England would have to acknowledge the growing dignity and importance of labor. The final triumph of English, therefore, was a direct outcome of the enlarged role of the common man in the political, economic, and military affairs of his country.

The four decades between the Peasants' Revolt and the death of Henry V (1381–1422) mark the official recognition and the general use of English in Britain. A generation earlier, the language had been accorded certain legal advantages over French: in the Sheriff's Court of London and Middlesex (1356) and in the King's Court and others (1362). Although court records were still to be written in Latin, the Statute of Pleading—enacted by Parliament in 1362—demanded that the pleading of all cases be conducted in English. Parliament itself opened that year with the chancellor giving an address in the native tongue. By 1385 English had become the classroom language of the British schools.

At the start of the fifteenth century, then, French had been reduced to a linguistic luxury for culture and fashion. Meanwhile, English was becoming the official written word, as well as spoken. The beginning of this elevation took place in legal documents, especially in wills. After 1400 the growth of English usage in private correspondence was also remarkable. Extremely influential, the reign of Henry V (1413–22) served as the turning point in the establishment of the written English word. Not only did Henry V defeat the French forces at Agincourt (1415), strike a death blow at medieval chivalry and the use of cumbersome armor, and revive a pride in all things English, but he also promoted by example the adoption of his language as the means of written communication in Britain.

Mature Middle English covered about 115 years in the history of the language. This linguistic era was a time in which the greatest influx of French words into English took place, an influx marked by two signs of profound penetration: assimilation and hybrid formation. It was a time that witnessed the continued loss of native words from the Anglo-Saxon. An intensified differentiation of meaning nurtured a tri-level vocabulary, rich in synonyms and adequate for any language situation. Mature Middle English also experienced a reduction in the morphological processes inherited from Old English and a corresponding growth in a Latinic system of affixing.

While all these changes were happening, the London version of the East Midland dialect kept gaining linguistic ascendancy until it finally became the Spoken Standard. Soon the Spoken Standard became the Written Standard. Meanwhile, a sprinkling of Low Countries vocabulary (from Flemish, Dutch, and Low German) seasoned Mature Middle English. During this period of the language, moreover, several important literary efforts transpired: the Biblical translations of John Wycliffe, a pioneer in the refinement of English prose; the Alliterative Revival, as led by the *Pearl* poet and William Langland; and above all the creation of a new verse tradition in the works of Geoffrey Chaucer, the artistic fountainhead of the English Renaissance.

FRENCH INFLUENCE.   During Mature Middle English the entrance rate of French words into the language was at its highest. The peak of the invasion was reached in the half century between 1350 and 1400, during the full flower of Chaucer's literary career and at a time when a patriotic nationalism was reorienting every class of British society back to the uses of the native tongue. In the return to English, the carry-over from French was enormous.

A sampling of French loan words active in the English language by the fourteenth century reads as follows: *action, adventure, affection, age, air, bucket, bushel, business, calendar, carpenter, cheer, city, coast, comfort, cost, country, courage, courtesy, coward, cruelty, damage, debt, deceit, dozen, ease, envy, error, face, faggot, fame, fault, flower, folly, force, gibbet, glutton, grain, grief, gum, harlot, honor, hour, jest, joy, labor, malice, manner, marriage, mason, metal, mischief, mountain, noise, number, ocean, odor, opinion, order, pair, people, peril, person, pewter, piece, point, poverty, powder, power, quality, quart, rage, rancor, reason, river, scandal, seal, season, sign, sound, sphere, spirit, square, strife, stubble, substance, sum, tailor, task, tavern, tempest, unity, use, vision,* and *waste; able, abundant, active, actual, amiable, amorous, barren, blank, brief, calm, certain, chaste, chief, clear, common, contrary, courageous, courteous, covetous, coy, cruel, curious, debonair, double, eager, easy, faint, feeble, fierce, final, firm, foreign, frail, frank, gay, gentle, gracious, hardy, hasty, honest, horrible, innocent, jolly, large, liberal, luxurious, malicious, mean, moist, natural, nice, obedient, original, perfect, pertinent, plain, pliant, poor, precious, principal, probable, proper, pure, quaint, real, rude, safe, sage, savage, scarce, second, secret, simple, single, sober, solid, special, stable, stout, strange, sturdy, subtle, sudden, supple, sure, tender, treacherous, universal,* and *usual; advance, advise, aim, allow, apply, approach, arrange, arrive, betray, butt, carry, chafe, change, chase, close, comfort, commence, complain, conceal, consider, continue, count, cover, covet, cry, cull, deceive, declare, defeat, defer, defy, delay, desire, destroy, embrace, enclose, endure, enjoy, enter, err, excuse, flatter, flourish, force, forge, form, furnish, grant, increase, inform, inquire, join, languish, launch, marry, mount, move, murmur, muse, nourish, obey, oblige, observe, pass, pay, pierce, pinch, please, practice, praise, prefer, proceed, propose, prove, purify, pursue, push, quash, quit, receive, refuse, rejoice, relieve, remember, reply, rinse, rob, satisfy, save, scald, serve, strangle, strive, stun, succeed, summon, suppose, surprise, tax, tempt, trace, travel, tremble, trip, wait, waive, waste,* and *wince.*

This selective list indicates the breadth and depth of the French influence upon Mature Middle English. It extends to phrases as well: *plenty of, to the contrary, if need be, because of, to make peace, tender age, to take leave, to draw near, to hold one's peace, to come to a head, to make believe, hand to hand, on the point of, according to, subject to, at large, by heart, in vain, without fail.* All these expressions are English versions of original French models.

During the fourteenth century the English language borrowed French words and phrases in their Anglo-Norman forms. In the fifteenth century, however, French had become a completely artificial tongue in Britain; consequently, a large portion of the English borrowing from French during this period was from the Central or Parisian dialect of that language. Since most French loans before 1350 tended to develop a native force in English, this general observation seems to hold true: Norman French influence upon English is basically popular and reflects the intimacy of the spoken word; Central French influence, on the other hand, is basically literary and reflects the formal elegance of the written word. Before the close of the fifteenth century, Caxton was locking into print such literary borrowings from Central French as *adolescence, affability, aggravation, appellation, cohort, combustion, destitution, diversify, furtive, harangue, immensity, ingenious, pacification, prolongation, ravishment, representation,* and *sumptuous.*

Apart from the fundamental difference between spoken and written attributes, Norman loans are distinguished from Central or Parisian by the simple means of phonology. The outstanding phonological criteria for such discrimination are as follows:

1) Central French dropped the Norman *s* before *t* at the end of the twelfth century; thus Norman *feast* and *hostel* contrast with Parisian *fete* and *hotel.*

2) Central French softened Norman /j/ and /c/ to /ž/ and /š/ sometime in the thirteenth century; hence Norman *charge, change, chamber, chase, chair, chimney, just, jewel, journey, majesty,* and *gentle* contrast with Parisian *chamois, chaperon, chiffon, chevron, jabot,* and *rouge.*

3) Central French forwarded and broke Norman /k/ to /c/ early in the Middle English period; thus Norman *cattle* contrasts with Parisian *chattel.*

4) Norman French maintained an initial /w/ in place of Central /g/; hence Norman *warden* contrasts with Parisian *guardian.*

5) Central French dropped the /w/ from Norman /kw/ in initial positions on stressed syllables; thus the Modern English pronunciation of words like *quit, quarter, quality, question,* and *require* shows that they were early Anglo-Norman entrants into the language.

6) Central French shifted the Anglo-Norman diphthong *ei* to *oi* early in the twelfth century; *ei* evolved to phonemic /iy/, whereas *oi* became /ɔy/; hence Norman *real* contrasts with Parisian *royal.*

7) Central French changed Anglo-Norman *-arie* and *-orie* to *-aire* and *-oire;* thus Modern English words like *salary* and *victory* show that they are relatively early borrowings from Norman French rather than from Parisian.

In addition to these seven criteria, other less general phonological differences between Central and Norman French existed.

Far more important than the influx of French words into the English vocabulary was the rapid assimilation of these foreign words. As Jespersen remarked, the juxtaposition of French synonyms with their English equivalents helped to quicken the process of assimilation. Taking such assimilation for granted, Chaucer employed double expressions—one native and one foreign—to heighten his style: *make* and *endyte, faire* and *fetisly, swynken* and *laboure, cure* and *hede, poynaunt* and *sharp, lord* and *sire.* What was elevated style in Chaucer, however, became a mannerism of learned redundancy in Caxton: *awreke* and *avenge, honour* and *worship, olde* and *auncyent, feblest* and *wekest, glasse* and *mirrour, fowle* and *dishonestly.* A greater indication of assimilation is the union of French roots with English words and affixes to form hybrid compounds and derivatives. The use of *gentle* in such words as *gentlewoman, gentleman, gentleness,* and *gently,* therefore, constitutes a clear portrait of the progress of assimilation in the century between 1230 and 1330.

In a similar manner, *faith* soon combined with Middle English elements of the thirteenth and fourteenth centuries to produce such derivatives as *faithless, faithful, faithfully,* and *faithfulness.* Many borrowed French adjectives combined with the native adverbial morpheme *-ly* to form such hybrid contributions as *commonly, courteously, eagerly, faintly, feebly, fiercely, justly,* and *peacefully.* Quick assimilation did not always guarantee survival of the derivative term; archaic combinations like *chasthed* (chastity), *lecherness, debonairship, poorness, spusbruche* (adultery, spouse-breach), and *becatch* have long since fallen into disuse. Other derivatives and compounds of early formation, on the other hand, have remained viable to the present-day: *ungracious, overpraising, commonweal*, and *battle-ax*.

The influx and assimilation of French words into English produced quite a few duplications of meaning, which inevitably led to either a synonymic differentiation or a suppression and loss of one of the duplicates. Many times the suppression applied to the challenging French term itself; more often, however, it was the native Old English word that fell into complete disuse. Though Chaucer uses *em* (from Old English *ēam*) in his *Troilus and Criseyde*, for example, it is the French equivalent *uncle* which has survived into modern times—a result predictable from the frequency of appearance of *uncle* in that same poem: it vastly predominates over *em*. In like manner, *anda* gave way to *envy*, *andig* to *envious*.

The following list of French replacements and English losses makes a graphic demonstration of this process of linguistic suppression:

FRENCH REPLACEMENTS	ENGLISH LOSSES	FRENCH REPLACEMENTS	ENGLISH LOSSES
noble	æþele	gracious	hold
people	lēode	glory	wuldor
crime	firen	cruel	slīþe
army	here	beauty	wlite
peace	sibb	confess	andettan
flower	blǣd	compose	dihtan
disease	ādl	improve	gōdian
age	ieldu	pity	miltsian
praise	lof	reward	lēanian
air	lyft		

French replacements were not always responsible for the loss of a native English term. Now and then another native word took the ascendancy and suppressed its own English equivalent. Thus *lord* overcame both *dryhten* and *frēa*. Similarly, *guilty* purged the language of *scyldig*, and *warrior* got rid of *cempa*.

If French replacements did not succeed in suppressing native English terms, then the duplicates usually separated into synonyms of differentiated meaning. The result for the language was increased flexibility of expression and enriched diction in the vocabulary. Synonyms permit the avoidance of a trite repetition of morphemes; they also allow for a greater differentiation of styles—in both formal and informal usage. Synonyms are also a basis for subtle shades of meaning, the leisurely processes of philosophical reflection, and the scientific accuracies inherent in specialized vocabularies.

The differentiation of meaning in Mature Middle English, therefore, was of distinct advantage; from the very outset of this development, the language can speak from either heart or head in terms appropriate to each and without confusion. Thus the native English vocabulary is more emotional and informal, whereas the imported French synonyms are more intellectual and formal. The warmth and force of the former contrast with the coolness and clarity of the latter. If a speaker can be intimate, blunt, and direct in basic English, he can also be discreet, polite, and courteously elegant in the diction of borrowed French. The central features of both linguistic methods are apparent in the following list of synonyms developed in the period of Mature Middle English:

NATIVE ENGLISH	FRENCH EQUIVALENT	NATIVE ENGLISH	FRENCH EQUIVALENT
hearty	cordial	might	power
friendship	amity	ask	demand
loving	amorous	shun	avoid
help	aid	seethe	boil
stench	odor	wish	desire
house	mansion		

One of the strongest examples of this differentiation between warm force and cool clarity may be seen in the later opposition between the synonyms *God* and the *Deity*. Many French loans, however, carry native force with them; *boil* is an example. Regardless of their intimacy or detachment, special French entries like *beef, mutton, pork,* and *veal* are indispensable linguistic commodities.

DECLINE OF NATIVE MORPHOLOGICAL PROCESSES.   With the vast influx and profound assimilation of French into English, several native methods of word formation declined. Reduced in importance were the morphological processes of internal modification and terminal inflectionalizing. At the same time the linguistic habit of combining free morphemes into self-explanatory compounds was curtailed. Basically Germanic modes of language behavior gave way to Latinic—a surrender which may be seen in the loss of vitality in the affixes inherited from Old English.

The intensifying prefix *for-* (like German *ver-*) maintained a dim life in Middle English, but such combinations as *forhang* (kill by hanging), *forcleave* (cut to pieces), and *forshake* (shake off) did not survive. Although *for-* persists into Modern English in such words as *forbear, forbid, forget, forgive, forgo, forsake, forswear*, and *forlorn*, it is an obsolete relic. The prefix *to-*, similar to *for-* in intensifying destructive or prejudicial meaning, was once used with the force of German *zer-*; today it is extinct. The prefix *with-* (against) has all but disappeared; it survives in such words as *withdraw, withhold*, and *withstand*, but no new derivatives are being formed with it. Suffering from the same disuse after the Norman Conquest, such viable prefixes as *over-, under-*, and *un-* owe their life to a revival in Modern English: thus *overkill, undersell*, and *unzip*.

Several Old English suffixes met a similar decline: *-lock, -red, -dom, -hood* and *-ship*. Despite the appearance of these suffixes in such words as *wedlock, hatred, wisdom, falsehood*, and *kinship*, they are seldom utilized. Modern English uses *-ness*, the most viable of the Old English suffixes, as its noun formant: thus *bookishness* and *togetherness*. The adjective endings *-ful, -less, -some*, and *-ish* have remained vital.

RENEWED LATIN INFLUENCE.   During the period of Mature Middle English, Latin reasserted its invasion rights. With the influx of French terms after the Norman Conquest, Latin cognates and progenitors filtered directly into English via literature at an impressive rate. Although spoken among ecclesiastics and scholars, medieval Latin was for practical purposes a dead language confined to the literature of the written word. The Latin terms that entered English during the fourteenth and fifteenth centuries, therefore, were less popular than the French.

In the monumental work of translating the Bible into English, John Wycliffe and his associates probably let in more than a thousand Latin words that have passed into common use. Through the work of Wycliffe and other writers, many Latin terms became permanent additions to the English language. Coming from such diverse fields as law, medicine, theology, science, and literature, these Latin additions often began as professional specialist and ended up by being widely accepted as general learned. According to the *New English Dictionary*, some of the direct borrowings from Latin during this period are *abject, adjacent, allegory, conspiracy, contempt, custody, distract, frustrate, genius, gesture, history, homicide, immune, incarnate, include, incredible, incubus, incumbent, index, individual, infancy, inferior, infinite, innate, innumerable, intellect, interrupt, juniper, lapidary, legal, limbo, lucrative, lunatic, magnify, malefactor, mechanical, minor, missal, moderate, necessary, nervous, notary, ornate, picture, polite, popular, prevent, private, project, promote, prosecute, prosody, pulpit, quiet, rational, reject, remit, reprehend, rosary, script, scripture, scrutiny, secular, solar, solitary, spacious, stupor, subdivide, subjugate, submit, subordinate, subscribe, substitute, summary, superabundance, supplicate, suppress, temperate, temporal, testify, testimony, tincture, tract, tributary, ulcer, zenith,* and *zephyr.*

A larger Latin influence than that of vocabulary enrichment was the development of a new system of derivative formation. With the decline of the native morphological processes, English experienced an accompanying growth in the use of Latin, often reinforced by French, affixes. With the entrance of such prefixes as *counter-, dis-, re-, trans-, sub-, super-, pre-, pro-, de-* and of such suffixes as *-able, -ible, -ent, -al, -ous,* and *-ive,* the evolutionary history of English derivatives was forever changed. So linguistically rich was the contribution of Latin affixes to the word-formation methods of English that Shakespeare could make poetry out of a bound morpheme: *melt* becomes *discandy*.

LONDON DIALECT: STANDARD ENGLISH.   In the period of Mature Middle English, the London dialect rose to the eminence of Received British Standard, both in the spoken and in the written word. Considering the economic, political, and military importance of London, such linguistic conquest was inevitable. But the admixture of Mercian (East End of London), West Saxon (West End of London) and Kentish (South London) contributed largely to the development of the Standard, even as it had previously helped to create the poetic dialect. With the influx of Northern laborers, tradesmen, and seamen into the city, moreover, a mixing of radical and conservative elements of the language took place. London English maintained an intermediate position that could draw upon the best features of the extremes of Southern conservatism and Northern radicalism. Sharing characteristics with each of the other dialects, London English found little trouble in gaining adherents.

Of the several reasons for the rise of the London dialect to Standard English, three predominate: 1) the national importance of the city itself as the political capital, commercial center, and cultural heart of Britain; 2) the numerical superiority and social status of the speakers of the London dialect, and 3) the intelligently utilitarian evolution of the dialect itself. A secondary factor in the rise of the London dialect is the prominence of the East Midland region in the political life of the country. Within this region operated two mighty forces in favor of learning, Oxford and Cambridge, and both helped support the development and the dissemination of the London dialect. In like manner, though he was aristocratically somewhat Southern and conservative, Chaucer became a powerful artistic ally of the emerging Standard English. Within a half century after his death in 1400, Standard had grown from Spoken to Written to Literary. And Caxton was soon to spread it throughout the island kingdom.

LINGUISTIC SEASONING FROM THE LOW COUNTRIES.   In the half century between 1327 and 1377, scores of words from Flemish, Dutch, and Low German entered English. They were the advance scouts for a steady invasion that has accounted for at least 2500 Low Dutch verbal immigrants into the language. The major impetus to such language entrance in the Middle Ages was commercial—the woolen industry. Exported English wool supplied looms in Flanders, Holland, and northern Germany. Superior weavers from the continent took up residence in England in considerable numbers, and with them they brought further sources to enrich the English vocabulary. Subsequent trade and travel among English, Flemish, Dutch, and German merchants strengthened the trend of linguistic borrowing from the Low Countries. Such words as *nap, deck, bowsprit, lighter, dock, freight, rover, mart, groat,* and *guilder* were in English usage before the advent of the Renaissance. Later loans include *cambric, boom, beleaguer, furlough, commodore, gin, gherkin, dollar, easel, etching, landscape, cruller, cookie, cranberry, bowery, boodle,* and the like.

LITERARY ACHIEVEMENT.   Great literary efforts in the vernacular during Mature Middle English constituted the dawn of both prose and poetry in the language. The three outstanding cultural events during this period were John Wycliffe's translation of the Bible, the Alliterative Revival, and the career of Geoffrey Chaucer.

One of the most influential of all English preachers, John Wycliffe (1328?–84) bent his energies to the task of achieving social and ecclesiastical reform. Believing that the church should have no concern with temporal matters, that the clergy should minister to the people and not be allowed to own property, and that the Bible is its own absolute authority, Wycliffe was a master of moderate treatment, Biblical precept, and good common sense. With the help of such scholars as Nicholas of Hereford and John Purvey, Wycliffe made the entire Bible available to the people of England for the first time—and in their common idiom. With his faith in the superiority of personal piety over external form and ritual, Wycliffe helped give religion back to the individual. In so doing, he influenced the sentence structure and turn of phrase in the Authorized Version of 1611. He was thus a pioneer in the perfecting of a simple, direct, yet eloquent and dignified English prose style.

About midway in Wycliffe's life there was a return to the earlier tradition of alliterative poetry in the accentual rhythms of Old English. This poetic revival concentrated in the North and in the Northwest Midlands, although the most famous work of the movement, *Piers Plowman*, originated in the West Midlands. The two outstanding figures of the Alliterative Revival were the *Pearl* poet and William Langland. The *Pearl* poet gave English literature dream-vision allegory, personal elegy, and dramatic debate noted for sensuousness, metrical versatility, and control. The purity of his method was extremely rare in Middle English literature. In *Sir Gawain and the Green Knight,* this unknown genius (if the same author) fashioned the finest Arthurian romance in the language, masterful in plot, background description and local color, narrative thrust, suspense, and dialogue. In the masterpiece of Langland, on the other hand, social criticism asserted itself as a major force in the literary life of the nation. With deadly accuracy and sometimes blunt vulgarity, Langland castigated the miserable conditions of the working man, the basic dishonesty of the English courts, the material greed of the church, and the ignorance and stupidity of the clergy. In the great A and B versions, *The Vision of William Concerning Piers the Plowman* was the massed cry of suffering humanity for a redress of injuries. As a means of democratic protest, the poem stands as one of the most intense social documents of the Western world.

THE CONTRIBUTIONS OF CHAUCER.   The literary contributions of Geoffrey Chaucer (1344–1400) to the cultural life of Britain were the supreme artistic achievement of Mature Middle English. Chaucer passed through three phases of creative growth. In the first two he was imitative, derivative, and translated from continental sources: the Latin of Ovid; the French of the *Roman de la Rose* and the poetry of Machaut, Descamps, and Froissart; the Italian of Boccaccio, Petrarch, and Dante. In the mature phase of his English period, Chaucer wrote two masterpieces: *Troilus and Criseyde* (1382–86) and *The Canterbury Tales* (1387–95). Through Chaucer, European literary conventions, epic machinery, romantic motifs, verse forms, and stylistics made a new fountainhead of English poetry and hastened the Renaissance in the island kingdom. He gave an artistic refinement to dream-vision, allegory, and elegy, and he launched English poetry into a new metrical tradition: the classical foot, in which stress and syllable counting still play a major role.

Chaucer was not only the chief introducer of "iambic pentameter" into English poetry but also the adopting father of such foreign strophic modes as the "heroic couplet" and the *terza rima* immortalized by Dante in his *Commedia*. Chaucer invented his own stanzaic unit, the seven-lined verse paragraph (ababbcc) known as rhyme royal. Using this verse form to tell the tragicomic love affair between mysterious Criseyde and transparent Troilus is a stroke of genius. Rhyme royal permits Chaucer to exploit a stanzaic pattern that can constantly threaten the action of high tragedy with the superb language of high comedy. Chaucer thus capitalizes on the tension between these aesthetic oppositions—by dissipating true pathos with the emotional excesses of apostrophic melodrama. The result is the first psychological novel in the English language, a novel enjoying an economy of poetry and built upon the quiet humor of the intellectual laugh.

In *The Canterbury Tales*, courtly love is only one of several primary bases for Chaucer's insight into human nature. The characterization of the pilgrims themselves becomes Chaucer's great literary gift to the spirit of modernity, for the intrigues, rivalries, and passions among the travelers to the shrine of St. Thomas à Becket constitute a *comédie humaine* of more intrinsic interest and formal value than are generated by the stories they tell. As a medieval anthology in which courtly romances, parodies, lays, classical legends, folk-tales, fabliaux, saints' lives, miracles, tragic stories, exempla, sermons, beast fables, and short lyrics appear, *The*

Canterbury Tales remains an artistic panorama of the fourteenth century in England. From the dirty joke to the battle of the sexes, from the criticism of a corrupt clergy to the affirmation of human goodness, from the use of dream psychology to the abuse of astrology, from a mastery of the four elements to a submission to the Trinity, Chaucer has created in this incomplete work a vivid, fascinating, and credible world in which sanity, tolerance, whimsical humor, and gentle satire act for the imagination rather than for the moral will. In this world where the Wife of Bath is an earth-goddess progenitor of James Joyce's Molly Bloom, *to make* is *to mean*. From his making as supreme comic poet of the Middle Ages, Chaucer is a worthy companion of Dante and the English narrative harbinger of a vaster literary universe to come in the dramas of Shakespeare.

LATE MIDDLE ENGLISH
THE LANGUAGE TRIUMPHANT,
1422–1489

THE MOST OUTSTANDING HISTORICAL FEATURE of Late Middle English is the growing importance of the written word. From the death of Henry V in 1422 to the final abolition of French from the legal statutes of England in 1489, the position of English as the language of writing in Britain constantly improved. After 1423 the records of Parliament were kept in the native tongue of Chaucer. By 1425 the language of correspondence, private and public, informal and formal, was English. By 1450 the town laws of the country had been translated into the language of the people, and a Literary Standard English, based upon the Received Spoken Standard of the London dialect, had been established.

In 1476 William Caxton introduced printing into England, to spread the Literary Standard and a popular literacy, with vast implications for both the language and its literature. In 1489, four years after his accession, Henry VII put an absolute end to the use of French in the statutes of England. With that act the language that had gone underground in 1066 emerged completely triumphant over foreign domination. What came out on top, however, was a far cry from what had gone under: the changes wrought in the English language during the four intervening centuries were enormous.

As a transition period between the age of Chaucer and the age of

Shakespeare, Late Middle English was a time of literary imitations. This era of the written word produced the writers Lydgate, Hoccleve, Skelton, Hawes, Malory, and Caxton, and witnessed the emergence of the Scottish Chaucerians: Henryson, Dunbar, Gavin Douglas, and Lindsay. The renewed influx of exotic Latin terms into Late Middle English gave the language a rash of *aureate diction*, a kind of Latin gilding that resulted in artificial and stilted elegance. Moderate with his own use of aureate diction, Chaucer introduced such words as *laureate, mediation, oriental*, and *prolixity* into the vocabulary of the language. Later and lesser poets rioted with *abusion, dispone, diurne, equipolent, palestral, sempitern* and *tenebrous*.

Far more valuable than aureate diction was the further development of the rich tri-level structure of synonyms during Late Middle English. In the specializations of vocabulary, popular, literary, and learned expressions graced the language with accuracy and flexibility. If basic English during this period was strong and simple, it was also not wholly basic *English*—that is to say, many French adoptions struck with the same native force: *bar, beak, cell, cry, fool, frown, fury, glory, guile, gullet, horror, humor, isle, pity, river, rock, ruin, stain, stuff, touch*, and *wreck; calm, clear, cruel, eager, fierce, gay, mean, rude, safe*, and *tender*. But as a general rule, the three levels of synonymous statement achieved in Late Middle English follow the pattern of popular English, literary French, and learned Latin. This pattern for synonyms may be seen in the following few examples:

ENGLISH	FRENCH	LATIN
rise	mount	ascend
ask	question	interrogate
goodness	virtue	probity
fear	terror	trepidation
holy	sacred	consecrated

In addition to aureate diction, literary imitation, and the development of a tri-level system of synonyms, Late Middle English was marked by four general attributes attendant upon a Written Standard. First, during this period the leveling of inflections begun in the closing stages of Old English was completed. Second, dialect differences were further reduced so that the future history of London English became that of British English as a whole. Third, in this evolutionary state of the language the principles of word order put the final touches upon a functionally analytic syntax; future developments were merely stylistic refinements. Fourth, Late Middle English supported a phonetic instability that led to the Great Vowel Shift, the silencing of certain consonants, and the phonemic transmutation of others. This phonetic instability was the progenitor of Early Modern English.

QUESTIONS FOR RESEARCH AND DISCUSSION

1. Organize a series of reports on the importance of the following historical figures in the development of Middle English: William Caxton, Geoffrey Chaucer, Henry V, William Langland, and John Wycliffe.

2. Let four members of the class engage in a round table discussion of the major attributes of the four leading dialects of Middle English: Northern, East Midland, West Midland, and Southern. What are some of the outstanding literary productions of these various dialects? What chief features of each did the London Standard come to use in its linguistic compromise? Now let the entire class write a brief critical paper on the advantages inherent in dialect rivalry.

3. Make a study of the 85 percent of the Old English vocabulary that was suppressed in the evolution of Middle English. Are there any apparent patterns in the dropping of these thousands of terms from the active vocabulary of the language? Give some examples of words and phrases you think it would have been well for the language to have retained in common use. Defend your choices.

4. Draw up two lists of loans into Middle English—one Norman, one Central French—that you think have achieved the status of native force. What are the chief characteristics of these terms? In what ways do they resemble the original Anglo-Saxon stock? Be specific in your answers.

5. Let three members of the class organize a dramatization of the three levels of expression that came into specialization during the period of Middle English: *Popular* (native English), *Literary* (assimilated French), and *Learned* (reintroduced Latin and its cognate Greek). Dramatize these three levels by translating the Twenty-third Psalm into the terminology appropriate to each of these levels. Now engage the class in a discussion of the values and the dangers inherent in such a specialization of vocabulary. Is literary grace in the English language dependent upon maintaining a purity of diction on one level or another? or does it consist in mixing the various levels? or is there no direct correlation at all? Defend your answer in detail.

6. Using Middle English as a starting point, investigate the correlation between use of a native tongue and the development of patriotic nationalism. Now extend your research to encompass the current political-linguistic problems in India, Ireland, Union of South Africa, Russia, the Spanish-speaking republics of Latin America, the Philippines, Israel, Canada, and Puerto Rico. From this study, would you say that there is any hope for one language to dominate the world in the foreseeable future? Defend your answer in detail.

7. Discuss the liberal and the conservative forces behind the evolution of Middle English. Now let the class choose four of its members—two to represent the liberal forces, two the conservative—to debate the following proposition: *That the rise of a democratic spirit in England was beneficial to the progress of the language.*

8. Organize a series of reports on the aesthetic achievements of Middle English in the following areas of literary endeavor: the medieval romance, the dream allegory, the social satire, the religious lyric, the folk ballad, and the cycles of mystery, miracle, and morality plays.

9. Write a major research paper on the importance of the morphological process of affixing in Middle English. Pay particular attention to the use of French and Latin imports in this process.

10. Illustrate the literary genius of Chaucer by comparing his poetry with that of his leading contemporary John Gower. What major advantages does Chaucer enjoy over his rival? In what ways is Chaucer the English Dante? Develop your answers with detailed examples.

SELECTED BIBLIOGRAPHY

Baugh, Albert C. *A History of the English Language.* Second Edition. New York: Appleton-Century-Crofts, 1957. See especially Chapters 5–7, pp. 127–237, for "The Norman Conquest and the Subjection of English, 1066–1200"; "The Re-establishment of English, 1200–1500"; and "Middle English."

Baugh, Albert C. "The Middle English Period (1100–1500)." Part II of *The Middle Ages,* Volume I of *A Literary History of England,* edited by Albert C. Baugh. New York: Appleton-Century-Crofts, 1948. Pp. 109–312. A fine brief survey of the entire range of Middle English literature.

Bloomfield, Morton W., and Leonard Newmark. *A Linguistic Introduction to the History of English.* New York: Alfred A. Knopf, 1963. See especially Chapter V for a scholarly study of the various Middle English dialects.

Bryant, Margaret M. *Modern English and Its Heritage.* Second Edition. New York: The Macmillan Company, 1962. See especially pp. 55–80 for a concise discussion of "Middle English Heritage."

Emerson, Oliver Farrar. *A Middle English Reader*. New and Revised Edition. New York: The Macmillan Company, 1948. See especially the "Grammatical Introduction." Probably the best one-volume textbook on Middle English language and literature, with an anthology of illustrations of the various dialects and ample notes and glossary.

Jespersen, Otto. *Growth and Structure of the English Language*. Ninth Edition. New York: Doubleday, Anchor Books, 1955. See especially Chapter V for an account of the French influence on Middle English.

Moore, Samuel, Sanford B. Meech, and Harold Whitehall. "Middle English Dialect Characteristics and Dialect Boundaries." *Essays and Studies in English and Comparative Literature*, University of Michigan Publication, Language and Literature XIII. Ann Arbor: University of Michigan Press, 1935. Pp. 1–60. A pioneer work in the field of Middle English dialects.

Robertson, Stuart, and Frederic G. Cassidy. *The Development of Modern English*. Second Edition. Englewood Cliffs, New Jersey: Prentice-Hall, 1954. See especially Chapter 6 for a discussion of the evolution of Middle English into a word-group language with the gradual leveling of its inflections.

Trevelyan, G. M. *History of England, Volume I: From the Earliest Times to the Reformation*. New York: Doubleday, Anchor Books, 1953. See especially pp. 141–350 for a succinct history of medieval England, from the Norman Conquest to the accession to the throne by Henry VII.

CHAPTER 6

The Structure of Middle English

—◆—

PHONOLOGY

MIDDLE ENGLISH ORTHOGRAPHY.　　Because Middle English escapes the Great Vowel Shift and the attendant changes in the pronunciation of certain consonants, it spells remarkably well—it looks like it sounds. Thus the Middle English alphabet, like the Old English, is highly phonetic; it supports a strong correspondence between the grapheme and the phoneme. Several phonological principles underlie this correspondence. Consonants are not silenced; each one receives its full measure of pronunciation. Middle English orthography indicates the tension and therefore length of a vowel by either doubling it or positioning it before a single consonant followed by another vowel. Hence the central vocalic cluster in both *reed* and *rede* is the tense diphthong /ey/. Middle English shows the laxness and therefore shortness of a vowel by doubling a following consonant. The absence of a final vowel after a single consonant usually means that the antecedent vowel is lax and short. Thus the stressed vocalic cluster in both *adrad* and *mannes* is the simple and lax low-central /a/.

In addition to these phonological principles, the alphabet of Middle English is phonemically revealing. The loss of the Old English digraph (æ) from the spelling habits of the Middle Ages testifies to the suppression of the simple and lax low-front phoneme /æ/. The disappearance of *thorn* (þ) and *eth* (ð) bears witness to the fact that voiceless *th* /θ/ and voiced *th* /ð/ have become independent phonemes in Middle English and are no longer mere allophonic variants. The *yogh* (ʒ) grapheme gives way to *y* for /y/ and *g* for /g/ and eventually disappears from the alphabet. The impact of French upon the phonology of English is seen in the addition of three new graphemic symbols: *v*, *z*, and *q*. The *v* indicates that /v/ has become a phoneme completely independent of /f/, whereas the *z* shows that /z/ is no longer just an allophone of /s/. As for *q*, it contains the possibilities of both /k/ and /kw/, depending upon phonemic environment.

Before attempting a phonemic solution for the orthography of Middle English (and here we must rely on the written record), we need to consider certain sound features of the language, for the problems contained in these features are central to that solution. Most Middle English consonants offer no trouble in their phonological interpretation. The consonants, taken as a whole, are less bothersome than the vowels. Beyond the emergence of the phonemes /v/, /ð/, and /z/, however, Middle English presents further evolutions from Old English. From all evidence available, it appears that the diphthongal opening forced by /š/ into the consonantal system of Old English has been followed in Middle English by the entrance of /c/ for /ḳ/ and /j/ for /ĝ/; that the relatively unstable phoneme /ŷ/ becomes /y/; that the Old English voiceless palatal /x/ remains fairly constant in Middle English, as represented by the consonantal graphemic cluster *gh*; that the voiced velar /ŋ/ achieves independent phonemic status and is no longer a positional allophone of simple /n/.

As for the Middle English vowels, the biggest linguistic assumption deals with the development of a complex system of tense vowels built upon three glides: the palatal /y/, the labial rounding /w/, and the lengthening and centering /ˇ/. Thus the tension of the Old English vocals has been fully diphthongized in Middle English. The central problem within this diphthongizing, in turn, is the development of "heavy" versions of tense vocalic clusters introduced by /e/ and /o/. Thus *meat* is distinguished from *meet* by the lower quality of the diphthong /eˇ/ as against the diphthong /ey/; in like manner, *boat* /boˇt/ contrasts with *boot* /bowt/. The so-called tense *a* is achieved by adding /ˇ/ to yield

/aˇ/, as in *blame* /blaˇmə/. To develop this system of contrasts further, the linguist has to accept a fundamental difference between the quality of tension in double *o* and *o* plus consonant plus vowel. Hence, *soon* /sown/ sounds lighter than *stone* /stoˇn/. Similarly, with double *e* as contrasted with *e* plus consonant plus vowel: *sweet* /sweyt/ is not so heavy as *swete* /sweˇt/. The introduction of the vocalic triphthong /yuw/ into the language occurs during Middle English.

THE PHONEMES OF MIDDLE ENGLISH.   Starting with the twenty-four consonants and then proceeding to the six lax and the eleven tense vowels, we may demonstrate the segmental phonemes of Middle English as follows:

CONSONANTS

Labial
    Voiceless: /p/   *peyne* (pain)
    Voiced: /b/   *bene* (bean)
                /m/   *mene* (mean)

Labiodental
    Voiceless: /f/   *feynen* (to pretend)
    Voiced: /v/   *veyne* (vein)

Interdental
    Voiceless: /θ/   *theen* (thrive)
    Voiced: /ð/   *they* (they)

Alveolar
    Voiceless: /t/   *tene* (grief)
                /s/   *seen* (to see)
    Voiced: /d/   *dele* (part)
                /z/   *zele* (zeal)
                /n/   *ney* (near)
                /l/   *lene* (lean)

Alveolopalatal
    Voiceless: /c/   *chesen* (to choose)
                /š/   *shene* (bright)
    Voiced: /r/   *reysen* (to raise)
                /j/   occurs mainly in non-initial positions:
                      egge (sword)
        no independent contrasting phoneme

Palatal
    Voiceless: /h/   *hele* (health)
                /k/   *kene* (sharp)
                /x/   in non-initial positions only:
                      night /nixt/ (night /nayt/)

CONSONANTS

	Voiced:	/g/	*geyn* (profit)
		/y/	*yere* (year)
Velar			
	Voiced:	/ŋ/	in non-initial positions only: *thencen* (to think)
		/w/	*were* (doubt)

VOWELS

Lax			
	High-Front:	/i/	*bidden* (to ask)
	High-Back:	/u/	*buk* (buck)
	Mid-Front:	/e/	*bed* (bed)
	Mid-Central:	/ə/	in unstressed positions only, usually final: *bedde* /bedə/
	Mid-Back:	/o/	*box* (box)
	Low-Central:	/a/	*badde* (bad)
Tense			
	High-Front:	/iy/	*ryden* (to ride)
	High-Front Rounded:	/iw/	*rude* (rude)
	High-Back Rounded:	/uw/	*route* (company)
	Mid-Front:	/ey/	*beten* (to heal)
	Mid-Front Centered:	/eˇ/	*beaten* (to smite)
	Mid-Back:	/oy/	*boy* (knave)
	Mid-Back Rounded:	/ow/	*boot* (boot)
	Mid-Back Centered:	/oˇ/	*boat* (boat)
	Low-Central:	/ay/	*lay* (song)
	Low-Central Rounded	/aw/	*laude* (praise)
	Low-Central Centered:	/aˇ/	*lame* (feeble)

The triphthong /yuw/ introduced during Middle English occurs quite readily in labial environments—for example, in words like *pewe, beautee, musen,* and *furye.* The interjection of the glide /y/ is a native English corruption of the pronunciation of French imports and is primary evidence in support of the more abrupt onset and greater explosiveness of English stress.

From the phonemic solution above, we can see that the consonants of Middle English are very much like those of Modern. Only these few changes need occur to make them exactly alike: the loss of voiceless palatal /x/; the addition of voiced alveolopalatal /ž/; the systematic initial positioning of voiced alveolopalatal /j/; the silencing of voiceless palatal /k/ and voiced palatal /g/ in initial positions before the alveolar nasal /n/, as in *kneel* and *gnaw;* the silencing of voiced velar /w/ before voiced alveolopalatal /r/, as in *wring;* the silencing of voiced alveolar

/l/ before voiceless labiodental /f/, voiceless palatal /k/, and voiced labial nasal /m/, as in *half*, *folk*, and *palmer*. Although as a general rule all Middle English consonants are pronounced, two exceptions are models for the development of further silencing: initial *h* in French imports like *honour* and medial *g* in the *gn* cluster in French imports like *resigne*. The *h* is zeroed; the *g*, of course, tends to become the glide /y/, which puts tension on the vowel.

The vocalic phonemes of Middle English are like some chemical solution in a state of suspended saturation: the least jolt will lead to a remarkable precipitation. The demands of English stress placed on imported sounds serve as the series of taps to bring about the changes. For there must be change. The lax vowels are oversimplified and therefore incapable of sufficient differentiation. The tense vowels, on the other hand, are overly complex and cannot long maintain their subtle distinctions. Once the lengthening and centering glide /˘/ gives way to /h/, then this new offset glide tends to become /y/ after front vowels and /w/ after back vowels. Under the impact of *schwa* in stressless positions and its eventual silencing in many situations, before /y/ and /w/ the low vowels tend to become mid, the mid vowels tend to become high, and the high vowels tend to drop through /ə/ to /a/. When that phonemic movement begins, the Great Vowel Shift is on.

DISTINCTIVE ACOUSTIC FEATURES.   Like Old English before it and Modern English after it, Middle English supports seven basic distinctive-feature oppositions:

1) *Vocality vs. Consonantality*. The simple contrast of syllabic/non-syllabic: the six lax and eleven tense Middle English vowels in opposition to the consonants; the intermediate terms of this contrast are the phonemes /m n l r y w/ and the glide /˘/.

2) *Tension vs. Laxness*. In the Middle English vowels, an opposition of simple (short) nuclei against complex (long) nuclei, dependent upon the presence or absence of the glides of tension: /y/, /w/, and /˘/; in the Middle English consonants, an automatic distinction of voiceless (tense) vs. voiced (lax).

3) *Interruption vs. Continuance*. The Middle English stops /p t c k/ and obstruents /b d j g/ in opposition to the non-impeding other consonants and the vowels.

4) *Gravity vs. Acuteness*. In Middle English the "muffling" of gravity, produced by long oral cavity and/or small lip aperture, is achieved in the back vowels /u o uw ow oˇ/, the labial consonants /p b m f v/, the back consonants /h k x g ɴ/, and the velar-labial /w/; all other phonemes tend toward acuteness.

5) *Compactness vs. Diffuseness*. In Middle English the presence of a central formant region makes the low vowels /a aw aˇ/ and the back consonants /h k x g ɴ w/ compact; all other Middle English phonemes either are or tend to be diffuse.

6) *Nasality vs. Orality*. In Middle English the presence of the nasal passage as a formant region makes a basic distinction between the nasals /m n ɴ/ and the oral obstruents /b d g/.

7) *Stridency vs. Mellowness*. A basic contrast in Middle English between the non-muffled fricatives /s z š/ and the mellow interdentals /θ ð/.

In phonological features Old and Middle English are much alike, but there are important differences: Middle English sustains a fuller system of contrasts in every category except compactness/diffuseness. The younger version of the language is also noted for greater differentiation in the consonants, sharper articulation of tension in the vowels, more voicing among the consonants, a fuller use of palatal softening, and a slightly deeper commitment to gravity, nasality, and the strident-mellow distinction. Old English is more guttural, hard, tense, and compact.

A brief study of the mellifluous poetry of Chaucer demonstrates the sound-pattern features and advantages of Middle English. In the new artistic tradition adopted from the French, alliteration ceases to be functional and becomes a form of decorative embellishment of the lines. The lines themselves, rich in assonance and consonance, are grouped in *strophic* units rather than in *stichic*. The *rhyme* is now the organizational thing, and Middle English is relatively easy to rhyme in. Again as a result of direct French influence, Middle English poetry is more liquid and languidly musical than that of either Old English or Modern. But what Middle English gains in sweetness and light it loses in dark stormy power, for it is no match for the syncopated explosiveness of Anglo-Saxon heroic verse or for the rhetorical thunder of Modern English poetry, as seen in the work of Shakespeare and Milton.

Upon occasion, in the hands of a great poet like Chaucer, Middle English can achieve impressive cacophony and onomatopoeia—as in the following passage from "The Nun's Priest's Tale":

> And cryden, "Out! harrow! and weylaway!
> Ha! ha! the fox!" and after hym they ran,
> And eek with staves many another man.
> Ran Colle oure dogge, and Talbot and Gerland,
> And Malkyn, with a dystaf in hir hand;
> Ran cow and calf, and eek the verray hogges,
> So fered for the berkyng of the dogges
> And shoutyng of the men and wommen eeke,
> They ronne so hem thoughte hir herte breeke.
> They yolleden as feendes doon in helle;
> The dokes cryden as men wolde hem quelle;
> The gees for feere flowen over the trees;
> Out of the hyve cam the swarm of bees.
> So hydous was the noyse, a, *benedicitee!*
> Certes, he Jakke Straw and his meynee
> Ne made nevere shoutes half so shrille
> Whan that they wolden any Flemyng kille,
> As thilke day was maad upon the fox.
> Of bras they broghten bemes, and of box,
> Of horn, of boon, in whiche they blewe and powped,
> And therwithal they skriked and they howped.
> It semed as that hevene sholde falle.   (3381–4001)

The swift movement and lather-dither noise of this passage unite to create a chicken-licken impression that the sky *is* falling. Besides the interesting use of a foreign term (metrically incorporated into the passage with impeccable skill) and of the Northern form *skriked*, these quoted lines reveal the non-fronting influence of French stress patterns (as in *meynée*) and the fluid state of final *e* as the remnant of dead inflections. Chaucer pronounces this *e* when it serves his metrical purpose, as in *feere*, where it separates two stresses. When Chaucer has no metrical need of this final *e*, he silences it, as in *thoughte* and *wolde*. As a general rule of Mature Middle English poetry, whenever this final *e* can be elided with a following stressed vowel, it is so elided. By Late Middle English, this final *e* has for the most part fallen silent.

MIDDLE ENGLISH SUPRASEGMENTALS.   As is the case in Old English, the Middle English suprasegmental phonemes cannot be discussed with absolute assurance. There is no certain way of determining the superfixes of a language that has not been spoken for centuries. But we can make some educated guesses. To begin, from the record of forwarded stress on French imports it can be seen that Middle English continues the Germanic tradition of emphasizing the root syllable. Morphologically, then, major stress (ˆ) maintains its native strength. Inflectional *schwa* (ə) in the language furnishes primary evidence in support of the existence of minimum stress (˅) in weakened positions. With the gradual loss of the inflections, syntactical stressing becomes a superfix of great semantic importance; syntax in Middle English is therefore a primary determinant of maximum stress (ˊ). In such contrasts as *wolde* and *wolden*, furthermore, we can hear a minor stress (ˋ) in the inflectional ending of *wolden*. This stress is stronger than the minimum stress ending of *wolde*. Hence Middle English supports four degrees of stress: maximum, major, minor, and minimum. Perhaps the big difference between the stress patterns of Old and Middle English is this: minor stress in Old English tends to be an allostress of major; in Middle English, of minimum.

In direct relation with these four degrees of Middle English stress, the language (more likely than not) employs four levels of intonation or pitch: highest /4/, high /3/, normal /2/, and low /1/. The principles that govern these four levels of phonemic pitch are probably the same in Middle English as in Modern. Thus four basic contours prevail: two internal and two terminal. The two internal contours are normal steady (/2/–/2/) and normal rising (/2/↗/2/); the two terminal contours are high rising (/3/↗) and high falling (/3/–/1/). Abrupt voice cutoff accompanies the high-rising pattern; gradual voice fade, the high-falling.

As for the Middle English system of junctures, it is much like that of Modern English—that is, in Middle English, open juncture /+/ defines morphemic and word boundaries on stressed elements; optional internal close juncture /|/ defines word group boundaries without the written need for punctuation; obligatory internal close juncture /‖/ defines phrasal and clausal boundaries with the written need for punctuation; and obligatory terminal close juncture /#/ defines sentence boundaries with the need for written punctuation. Because of the morphological reduction of compounding in Middle English, the use of open juncture /+/ in this version of the language is considerably less than in either Old or Modern. In Middle English poetry, open juncture is practically nonexistent because of the constant rhythmical contrast achieved by avoiding contiguous stresses. As a result of French suprasegmental influences upon the rhythmical demands of the Middle English poetic line, an aristocratic non-forwarding of stress permits pronounced modifications on both internal and terminal pitch contours: a slight exaggeration to the rise and a brief delay in the fall.

SUMMARY.   There is a high degree of correlation between Middle English orthography and phonology. Middle English phonology indicates twenty-four consonantal phonemes, remarkably like those of Modern English. The six lax vocalic phonemes, though much like those of Modern English, are underdeveloped and insufficiently specialized. The eleven tense vocalic phonemes further intensify the instability of Middle English, for they rely upon subtle distinctions that cannot be maintained against the constant pressures of tongue-heightening. The continual demand of forwarding the stress not only results in the eventual reduction of most inflections to zero but also initiates a motion in the first formant elements of the Middle English vocalic diphthongs, a motion that eventually produces the Great Vowel Shift of Early Modern English. The four-part structuring of the Middle English suprasegmentals (stress, pitch, juncture, and contour), moreover, allows for a further refinement of syntax to assume the abandoned functions of the leveled inflections. The entire phonological spectrum of Middle English reveals the language in a period of transition.

MORPHOLOGY

THE MOST IMPORTANT CHARACTERISTIC OF Middle English is the *morphemic simplification* that takes place, a simplification due primarily to the leveling of inflections: initial, internal, and above all final. In Middle English the Old English inflectional prefix *ge-*, an indicator of the past participle, evolves to *y-* or *i-*, then to an ultimate zeroing that obliterates the form. With the reduction of the strong irregular verbs, the morphemes of internal modification assume a much smaller role in the language. The four principal parts of the strong verbs tend to become three; often the preterit singular prevails over the plural, and at other times the preterit plural coincides with the past participle and therefore dominates the singular. The weakening of unstressed inflectional *m* to *n* in late Old English, as seen in the dative plural of nouns, adjectives, and disyllabic pronouns, is accompanied in Middle English by the phonetic change of *a, o, u* in unstressed endings to *e* (pronounced /ə/). Since *e* is already a prevalent form in the inflectional endings of Middle English, the resultant confusion of forms results in the abolition of the distinctions of grammatical gender in the nouns, adjectives, and pronouns. By the time of Mature Middle English the final *e* is syncopated before words beginning with a vowel or with an *h;* parallel with this morphemic feature is the frequent loss of inflectional *n.* By Late Middle English this inflectional *n* and the final unstressed *e* have both been silenced: the *e* in pronunciation and the *n* from the orthography as well. Eventually this inflectional vestige *e* drops from the spelling also.

Operating by *analogy*, the more common form generally substitutes for the less common. Thus the accusative case comes to ascendancy in the Middle English noun. With the loss of grammatical gender, the neuter form in both the adjective and the adjectival pronoun prevails over the masculine and the neuter. In the personal pronouns, the accusative case gives way to the dative. As for the Middle English verbs, the third person present indicative supplies the root form. The disappearance of feminine forms from the Middle English adjective and the non-personal pronoun joins with the almost complete suppression of feminine and neuter inflections inherited from Old English to establish natural gender. Even the occasional inflectional vestiges of older feminine and neuter forms are divorced from grammatical gender, and it is interesting that no noun of foreign derivation assumes the outmoded morphology of grammatical gender. This phenomenon is further proof of the pervasive quality of morphemic simplification in Middle English.

THE NOUN. Most Middle English nouns fall into either one of two declensions: first, those which do not end upon a weak *e* in the nominative singular; second, those which do end upon this weak *e*. We may illustrate these two major declensions by running the following Middle English words through the nominative, accusative, vocative, genitive, and dative cases, both singular and plural—*dōm* (doom), *dai* (day), *trē* (tree), *tǭken* (token), *ēnde* (end), *helpe* (help), *soule* (soul), and *þewe* (habit):

DECLENSION I.

SINGULAR

N.A.V.	dōm	dai	trē	tǫken
G.	dōmes	daies	trees	tǫknes
D.	dōm	dai	trē	tǫken

PLURAL

N.A.G.D	dōmes	daies	trees	tǫknes

DECLENSION II.

SINGULAR

N.A.V.	ēnde	helpe	soule	þewe
G.	ēndes	helpes	soules	þewes
D.	ēnde	helpe	soule	þewe

PLURAL

N.A.G.D.	ēndes	helpes	soules	þewes

The two major inflectional morphemes of the Middle English noun are the *-es* of the genitive singular and the *-es* of the plural in all cases. The weak *-e* of Declension II in the nominative, accusative, vocative, and dative singular is doomed to extinction. And once all nouns agree in their morphemic inflections, nature and logic determine their gender. Despite the substitution of *-is* or *-ys* for standard *-es* in the Northern dialect, the occasional use of an uninflected plural in a neuter long stem inherited from Old English, and the retension of *-en* as a weak declension plural in such Middle English relics as *oxen, brethren, eyen,* and *children,* the morphemic simplification in the language is regular and clear. A genitive singular in *-e* is extremely rare, and the internal mutations of such nouns as *fōt* (foot) and *man* (man) do not blur the main outlines of the simplification:

	SINGULAR		PLURAL	
N.A.	fōt	man	fēt	men
G.	fōtes	mannes	fētes (fōte)	mennes (manne)
D.	fōt(e)	man, manne	fēt	men

Such simplification gives Middle English a distinct morphological advantage over the ponderous forms in Old English.

THE ADJECTIVE.   Morphemic simplification in the Middle English adjective is even more dramatic than in the noun, for the adjective generally maintains only one inflectional vestige from Old English: final *e*. This morphemic relic is added to the adjective that ends other than on *e* in order to form the plural, the weak form after a demonstrative or possessive pronoun, or a rarely used dative case. Like the Middle English nouns, the adjectives are grouped in two declensions: those which do not end upon an unstressed *e*, and those which do so end upon this *e*. The weak form of the adjective appears after a possessive or a demonstrative pronoun or the definite article, and in the vocative case. If the adjective *follows* the noun without the repetition of the demonstrative or the definite article, it is then uninflected. A look at the adjectives *wīs* (wise), *manī* (many), *lītel* (little), *frē* (free), and *grēne* (green) as they appear, both weak and strong, in the two declensions will illustrate the inflectional simplicity of these modifiers:

DECLENSION I.

		Strong			DECLENSION II. Strong
Singular	wīs	manī	litel	frē	grēne
Plural	wīse	manī (manīʒe) (manīe)	lītel (lītle)	frē	grēne

		Weak			Weak
Singular⎫ *Plural* ⎭	wīse	manī (manīe)	lītel	frē	grēne

Although the Southern dialect reveals an archaic *-es* genitive singular and maintains a rather rigid distinction between strong and weak forms of the adjective, the Northern dialect tends to drop even the final *e* and achieve a merger of the two declensions. Loan words from Old French enter into the same classes as corresponding Middle English adjectives and receive similar inflection—that is, borrowed adjectives not ending in a vowel form their plurals on weak *e*, whereas polysyllabic adjectives that have experienced the shift of Germanic accent to the first syllable stay uninflected. A similar morphemic simplicity prevails in both the comparative and the superlative forms: *-re* or *-er*, and *-est*. During Middle English the adverbs *mǭre* and *mǭst* emerge as the comparative and superlative modifiers of polysyllabic adjectives.

THE VERB.   The Middle English verbs belong to two major classes, as in Old English: the weak and the strong. In the weak verbs a dental suffix indicates preterit tense; in the strong verbs, the mutation of the root vowel. The outstanding change in the strong verbs during Middle English is the analogical reduction of many of them to the weak class.

The strong verbs also undergo a general compression of principal parts, from four to three. As in Old English, the Middle English strong verbs divide into six sub-classes, according to the graduation of their stem vowels in the present, preterit singular, preterit plural, and past participle:

1) ī – ǭ – i (ǭ) – i
   drīven – drǭf – driven (drǭf) – driven

2) ē (ū) – ę̄ – ǭ (ę̄) – ǭ
   chēsen – chę̄s – chǭsen (chę̄s) – chǭsen

3) i (e) – a (ǭ̧) – u (ou, ǭ̧) – ǭ, u (ou)
   helpen – halp (holp) – holpen – holpen
   drinken – drank – dronken – dronken

4) ę̄ – a – ē, ę̄ (ǭ) – ǭ (u)
   stę̄len – stal – stēlen – stǭlen

5) ę̄ (i) – a (ē, ę̄) – ē, ę̄ – e (i)
   ę̄ten – ēt (at) – ēten – eten
   sitten – sat – sēten – seten

6) ā̧ (ę̄, o) – ō – ō – a (ā, ę̄, o)
   tāken – tōk – tōken – tāken

As these examples show, often two of the principal parts are identical in form.

The weak verbs in Middle English divide into two subclasses: the first with a preterit ending of *-ed(e)*, and the second with a preterit ending in *-de* or *-te*. To the first subclass of weak verbs belong verbs of the Old English first weak class with original short stems not ending on either *d* or *t*, verbs of the Old English second weak class whose preterit morpheme *-ode* has weakened to *-ede*, weakened strong verbs with short stems, and borrowed verbs of similar formation. All other Middle English weak verbs belong to the second subclass: polysyllabic verbs of the Old English first weak class, original long stems, original short stems ending in *d* or *t*, verbs of the Old English third weak class, weakened strong verbs with long stems, and borrowed verbs of similar formation. Both subclasses of the Middle English weak verb generally end their past participles upon *-ed*. With very few exceptions, borrowed verbs from both Old Norse and Old French assume the morphological characteristics of the weak sub-classes, in accordance with their own phonological details.

As in Old English, the Middle English verb supports both inflected and compound forms. The compound forms employ originally independent verbs that have been weakened to the function of auxiliaries. The growth of functional auxiliaries is a major step in the morphological transition from Middle English to Modern, insofar as the verb system is concerned. The compound verb forms of Middle English have four indicative tenses: future, present perfect, past perfect, and future perfect; two optative or potential tenses with the use of such auxiliaries as *may* and *can:* present and past; a present perfect infinitive and participle; and a passive voice in all the modes and tenses of the active, inflected and compound. Middle English is also noteworthy for its refinements on the passive voice and for the range and flexibility of its compound verb and verbal constructions.

As for the inflected forms of the Middle English verb, they all belong to the active voice and are of two tenses, present and preterit. These inflected forms also occur in two moods, indicative and subjunctive; and they support an infinitive and a present and a past participle. The overlapping of morphemic endings that leads to a great simplification of the Middle English verb system may be seen in the following scheme:

INFLECTIONS OF THE MIDDLE ENGLISH VERB

		Weak	*Strong*
PRESENT INDICATIVE			
Singular	*1st*	e	e
	2nd	est	est
	3rd	eþ (eth)	eþ (eth)
Plural	*1st*	e(n)	e(n)
	2nd	e(n)	e(n)
	3rd	e(n)	e(n)
PRETERIT INDICATIVE			
Singular	*1st*	ede, de (te)	—
	2nd	edest, dest (test)	e (—)
	3rd	ede, de (te)	—
Plural	*1st*	ed(en), de(n), te(n)	e(n)
	2nd	ed(en), de(n), te(n)	e(n)
	3rd	ed(en), de(n), te(n)	e(n)
PRESENT SUBJUNCTIVE			
Singular	*1st*	e	e
	2nd	e	e
	3rd	e	e
Plural	*1st*	e(n)	e(n)
	2nd	e(n)	e(n)
	3rd	e(n)	e(n)

INFLECTIONS OF THE MIDDLE ENGLISH VERB

		Weak	Strong
PRETERIT SUBJUNCTIVE			
Singular	1st	ede, de (te)	e
	2nd	ede, de (te)	e
	3rd	ede, de (te)	e
Plural	1st	ede(n), de(n), te(n)	e(n)
	2nd	ede(n), de(n), te(n)	e(n)
	3rd	ede(n), de(n), te(n)	e(n)
PRESENT IMPERATIVE			
Singular	2nd	e	—
Plural	2nd	eþ (eth), e	eþ (th), e, —
PRESENT INFINITIVE			
		e(n)	e(n)
PRESENT PARTICIPLE			
		ende (ande), inge	ende (ande), inge
PAST PARTICIPLE			
		ed (d, t)	e(n), (e)n

There is a constantly increasing rate of loss of final *n* in all -*en* forms and of final *e* in the preterit tense of the strong class. Where this final *e* remains in Late Middle English, it has fallen silent. Except for some slight differences in the imperative, both the strong and weak verbs agree in their inflections of the present tense. The imperative plural ending is gradually reduced to *e* or lost completely. Three classes of weak verbs in Old English have become but one inflectional group. This streamlining of the verb system constitutes a major morphological advantage for Middle English.

THE ADVERB.   The general morphemic simplification of Middle English extends to its adverbs. Old accusative and dative forms to indicate adverbial function are gradually curtailed. A corresponding reduction of mutational monosyllables and of forms ending in -*inga*, -*enga*, -*unga* further refines the adverb, and the loss of final *e* from simple Middle English adverbs results in their assuming the same form as the adjectives on which they are based. The extension of the genitive -*es* adverbial form in Middle English leads to an invasion of the -*en* morphology of adverbs of place. The two outstanding developments are the rise of -*ly* as the morpheme of adverbial indication and the growth of compound and complex adverbs to achieve more specialized modifications. Adverbs that ended in -*līce* in Old English experience a slow and steady weakening of their terminal morpheme; the outcome of this phonetic change is the confusion of the Middle English adverbial ending *-līke* with the adjectival *-lī* (*-lȳ*), from Old English *-līc*. The resultant *-ly* form for the adverb becomes the distinctive ending and greatly expands its usage in both native and foreign words. The growth of such compound and complex adverbs as *upward, sūþward, dropmēle* (drop by drop), *besīde, away, adūne, forþi* (because), *þerin, þerof, alway, sumtime, sumwhīle, within,* and *withoute* enlarges the scale of explicit meaning.

THE PRONOUNS.   Nowhere is the morphemic simplification of Middle English more evident than in the pronouns. First of all, the Middle English pronouns that are adjectival in function (possessives, demonstratives, indefinites) undergo a reduction to two forms, one singular and one plural. In contrast, the Middle English pronouns that are substantive in function (personal, interrogative, inflected relative) maintain an accusative-dative case, derived from an original dative, distinctly different from the nominative. The genitives of the personal pronouns become the possessive pronouns, and in that form they operate also as possessive adjectives. Although the dual forms of the personal pronouns fall away in Early Middle English, this loss is minor in comparison with the vast reduction of overlapping, redundant, and confusing pronominal morphemes. At the beginning of the Middle English period, there are at least sixty-six inflected personal pronouns; by the end of Late Middle English, there are only twenty-two.

In like manner, the demonstrative pronouns, with only singular and plural forms without any distinction of gender, simplify to the following seven major Middle English forms: *þē, þat, þis, þǭ, þise, þēse,* and *þǭs.* With the addition of *s* in Late Middle English to form possessive substantives, the possessive pronouns take on a modern look: *mȳ, mīn, thȳ, þīn, his, her, heres, ōur, ūres, yōur, yūres, their.* As in Old English, Middle English personal pronouns operate reflexively alone and when combined with *self;* forms like *mīself* and *þȳself* occur as early as the fourteenth century. In this century of Mature Middle English, however, a more important morphological emergence takes place: that of the relative pronoun forms *which/whiche, whōs/whōse, whōm,* and the compound relatives *þat hē, þat his, þē which, which þat,* and *þē which þat.* This morphemic specialization, parallel with a corresponding simplification elsewhere in the language, is significant in the development of a connective system adequate for the increased demands of a syntax in transition from synthetic to analytic. Further refinements among the interrogative-indefinite pronouns *whō*, *which* and *whether* strengthen the central principles of that syntax.

FOREIGN ASSIMILATIONS.   If the morphemic simplification of native elements is the general rule of Middle English, then an important corollary is a vast extension of the morphological process of forming derivatives. This process receives impetus from the foreign assimilations based on French stems and Latin affixes. As for French words taken directly into Middle English, the substantives and adjectives usually enter in the Old French accusative case, simply because it differs from the nominative by having terminal *s* in the plural and none in the singular. The stem of the French present plural verb serves as the basis for the Middle English verb form. The French infinitive, on the other hand, enters Middle English as a substantive: *dinner, remainder, attainder, rejoinder, merger, user*, and *misnomer*.

Interesting as these examples of assimilation are, hybridism is the most striking feature of linguistic union. Adding any English inflection or other bound morpheme to a French base results in a hybrid derivative. Using braces ({}) to enclose the bound English morphemes, various gradations of the hybrid derivative may be shown as follows:

1) *Simple possession:* Duke{s}
2) *Superlative degree:* nobl{est}
3) *Verbal noun:* serv{ing}
4) *Adjective noun:* close{ness}
5) *Noun adjective:* court{ly}
6) *Noun adverb:* nob{ly}
7) *Noun noun:* court{ship}

The list may be extended to show constructions using native English suffixes *-ful*, *-less*, and *-dom*, but the point is clear: whether it be a native past tense made from an imported French verb (survive{d}) or an English abstraction derived from a Greek concretion (martyr{dom}), the entire process of morphological derivation in the language undergoes an immense change and revitalization in the Middle English period. Nor does English supply only the bound morphemes for the assimilation; from medieval times on, countless native stems join with such suffixes as

-ess, -ment, -age, -ance, -ous, -ry, -ty, -fy, -fication, -ability, and the omnipresent *-able*. The introduction of Latin prefixes and suffixes into the language dates mainly from Middle English. So important is their entrance that they eventually work a major change in the morphological processes of English.

MORPHEMES AND WORDS.   As in Old and Modern English, Middle English morphemes are of two classes: bound and free. The bound morphemes, in turn, subdivide into phonemic and syllabic. Because Middle English is not fully synthetic in its syntax and therefore does not support a full complement of function words, it is not contractional by nature; consequently it does not support many bound phonemic morphemes. In this respect, Middle English resembles Old. With the enormous influx of foreign affixes, Middle English enjoys a wealth of bound syllabic morphemes. As for the free morphemes of Middle English, they more readily form derivatives than compounds. In this respect, the language suffers a diminution in an important native morphological process.

The following list shows the three basic morphemes of Middle English in action:

> 1) *Bound phonemic:* This morpheme occurs initially in a contraction like *nolde* for *ne wolde* and internally as a vowel mutation within the past and participial forms of the strong irregular verbs—for example, the /a/ in *drank*. Terminally, the bound phonemic morpheme does not exist in Middle English until the silencing of weak inflectional *e*.

> 2) *Bound syllabic:* This morpheme occurs, native and foreign, both initially and terminally, as in the intensive *to-* of *tobroke* and the noun formant *-dom* of *wisdom*. With the advent of French and Latin morphology, the bound syllabic morpheme expands its *medial* function in English, as seen for example in the *-ambula-* of Chaucer's *preambulacioun.*

> 3) *Free word:* This morpheme is the irreducible unit of autonomous meaning; it may be *lexical*, as in *man*, *grammatical* as in *the*, or both as in *wood* (mad) in the sentence *The man is wood.*

The free word forms of Middle English, like those of Old and Modern, exist in three basic categories: morpheme words—*ship* and *man;* compounds—*shipman;* and derivatives—*companionship* and *manfully.*

With the reduction of the native habit of compounding, affixing becomes the chief morphological process in Middle English. The shrinkage of the strong verb system in the language results in a marked weakening of internal modification as a means of word formation. The leveling of inflections throughout the Middle English period places more emphasis on syntactical positioning and therefore results in a growth in stress modification and functional shift—two morphological processes that take on a central role in the development of Modern English. Middle English shows an extension of zeroing and a regularizing of replacement; it borrows infinitely more than Old English. Two new morphological processes emerge: reduplication and onomatopoeia. Both these methods of word making may be seen in Chaucer's *ha! ha! tehee! wehee!* and *weylawey!*

SYNTAX

WITH THE GRADUAL LEVELING OF inflections in Middle English, the language slowly develops a new principle for the determination of function, beyond that of form: syntactical positioning. Where a word appears in the sentence is more important in Middle English than in Old. As a language of transition, however, Middle English is neither wholly synthetic nor wholly analytic.

Clausal word order exists in three major types: 1) *common:* the normal 1–2–3–4 syntax of Modern English, in which subject, verb, inner complement, and outer complement appear in that exact order; 2) *inverted:* a reversal of subject and verb positioning so that the word order reads 2–1–3–4; 3) *transposed:* a forwarding of the inner complement to the position of the subject, by which the syntax becomes 3–1–2–4. Within these major types, of course, certain variations may take place. Thus the literary word order of Old English employs a transposed-inverted construction, in Genesis 271, that results in a 3–2–1 syntax: *Fela worda gesprǣc sē engel* (Many words spoke the angel). As a general rule, the earlier the Middle English prose the more likely it is to depart from the common clausal order. Especially in the verb position does Middle English syntax most resemble the habits of Old English—that is, the Middle English verb often appears at the end of the clause, whether principal or subordinate, and therefore after the complement(s): *oc Crīst it ne wolde* (but Christ it not willed); *and tē Lundenisce folc him underfēng* (and the London people him received); *ðat hē mīlde man was* (that he a mild man was). Even more frequently than it ends a clause, the Middle English verb precedes its subject: *warth þē kīng dẹd* (was the king dead); *and forþī him luveden God and gōd men* (and because him loved God and good men); *þā wiste þē kīng* (when knew the king).

Metrical inversion abounds in Middle English poetry, but Chaucer's lines show an amazing modernity of syntax. As for the dialects, Southern is very conservative and tends to preserve the word order of Old English; Northern, on the other hand, is radical and evolves rapidly toward the principles of present-day English syntax. The Mature Northern Middle English (c. 1340) of Richard Rolle of Hampole illustrates a syntactical evolution well advanced toward analytic—as seen in this passage from "On the Nature of the Bee":

> Thē bee has thrē kӯndis. Āne es þat scho es never ӯdill, and scho es noghte with thaym þat will noghte wyrke, bot castys thaym ōwte and puttes thaym awaye. Anothīre es þat, when scho flӯes, scho tākes ērthe in hyr fēte þat scho bē noghte lyghtlӯ ǫverheghede in the ayere of wӯnde. Thē thyrde es that scho kēpes clẹn and bryghte hire winges.

> The bee has three natures. One is that she is never idle, and she is naughty with them that will not work, but casts them out and puts them away. Another is that, when she flies, she takes earth in her feet so that she may not be lightly raised too high in the air from the wind. The third is that she keeps clean and bright her wings.

Apart from positioning objective complements before the direct object, this Middle English syntax is much like Modern. A quaint flavor of archaic constructions permeates the passage, but like the Northern *-es* of the present indicative third-person singular (later to become the dominant English verb inflection, as simple *-s*), such constructions are a matter of idiom.

SYNTACTICAL IDIOMS.   Several peculiarities of word order and grammatical construction are distinct in Middle English and may rightly be called syntactical idioms:

1) *Appositive.* The Middle English appositive, as both word and phrase, often follows its noun: *Henrī abbot* (the abbot Henry); *þē kīnges suster of France* (sister of the King of France).

2) *Predicate modifier.* The predicate modifier in Middle English often precedes both subject and verb: *gōdman hē wes* (he was a good man).

3) *Adjective modifier*. The Middle English adjective, strong and uninflected, frequently follows its substantive: *þē hert sorowful and mēke* (the sorrowful and meek heart); in indefinite adjectival constructions like *alle hī* (they all), the word order is the reverse of that of Modern English.

4) *Separated relative*. In Middle English, the relative pronoun is generally separated from its antecedent.

5) *Terminal adverb*. In relative constructions, the Middle English adverb, later to become a preposition, usually appears in the terminal position: *hē þat al his trīst is tō* (he in whom is all his trust).

6) *Adjectival noun*. The Middle English adjectival form frequently occurs in syntactical constructions that function as noun makers: *for hēvīe* (for heaviness).

7) *Redundant subject*. Loose Middle English syntax often permits an unnecessary repetition of the subject: *þē bodī it seide* (the body it said).

8) *Oblique cases*. The Middle English noun retains a few idiomatic constructions from Old English, in the oblique cases: the objective, inanimate, and adverbial genitive; the prepositional, adverbial, instrumental, and temporal dative; the durational and cognate accusative.

9) *Pronoun features*. The Middle English pronouns differ from those of Modern English: the Middle English pronoun is often omitted as subject and object; it frequently serves as a redundant subject; it need not agree with its antecedent, and the personal occasionally acts as the reflexive.

10) *Demonstrative-possessive*. In Middle English, the demonstrative pronoun sometimes acts as a possessive: *alle þē limes* (all their limbs).

11) *Verb features*. A few of the outstanding features of the Middle English verb are idiomatic: the frequent lack of agreement with the subject, the omission of the linking verb with the dative case, the common use of the impersonal, the general interchangeability of direct and indirect discourse, the regular employment of present for future tense and of the preterit for all past

time, the universal substitution of the subjunctive for the optative and of the preterit for the present tense in clauses of non-reality, and the customary use of various forms of the verb *to be* as auxiliaries of the passive for intransitive verbs.

12) *Verbal idioms.* In Middle English, the infinitive commonly appears without *to* and continues to function as a verbal complement; the Middle English participle occasionally acts as a noun.

A few minor syntactical idioms, such as the frequent omission of the definite article and the relative pronoun and the division of the preposition *toward*, also exist.

MIDDLE ENGLISH CONNECTIVES.   The connective system of Middle English shows a marked development upon that of Old English. In addition to the emergence of the relative pronouns *which/whiche, whōs/whōse, whōm, þat hē, þat his, þē which, which þat,* and *þē which þat* in the fourteenth century, Middle English prepostions and conjunctions also grow in number and function. Most Old English prepositions are preserved in Middle English; *frǫ* (from) is a derivation from Old Norse *frā*. Old French supplies simple adoptions such as *par, rūnd, except, maugrē* (in spite of), *sāve,* and *acordaunt* (according). Old English *wiþ* ceases to mean *against* and assumes the modern significance *with*. Most important of all, Middle English develops compound and phrasal prepositions that are of great help in furthering specialization and explicitness in the later stages of the language. A few of these compound and phrasal prepositions are: *aȝein* (again), *aȝeines* (against), *alǫng, amǫng, arōund, besīde, nēȝhǫnd/nērhǫnd* (near at hand), *tōward, ūttāken* (except), *according tō, be rǫson of, bi cause of,* and *in regard of.*

As for the conjunctions of Middle English, most of them are phonetic evolutions from those of Old English: *eiþer/eiȝþer* (either), *ouþer/ōþer/or* (or), *siþen/siþenes/siþe* (since), *þē . . . þē* (that which, he who etc.). Among the correlatives, the older form *swā . . . swā* gives way to the transitional *alswǫ . . . ase* and finally to the modern *as . . . as*. In the emergence of the Middle English correlatives *eiþer . . . or* and *neiþer . . . nor* the language best shows its syntactical maturation. Despite the fact that Middle English remains rather impoverished in transitional adverbs and phrases, in its relative pronouns, interrogative indefinites (*whō, which,* and *whether*), prepositions, and conjunctions, the language achieves word-group, phrasal, and clausal linkage without the stiffness that characterizes Old English syntax.

MIDDLE ENGLISH WORD GROUPS.   Throughout its three and a half centuries of change, Middle English slowly ceases to be a morphemic language like Old English and gradually becomes a word-group language like Modern English. This evolution is a direct result of inflectional leveling and the accompanying rise of an analytic word order. A close correlation of syntactical positioning with the superfixes of stress, juncture, and pitch, make the emerging word groups of Middle English remarkably like those of Modern.

So advanced is the syntax of Chaucer that even his poetry offers excellent examples of the various Middle English word groups, the structural and rhythmical building blocks of the language:

> *Endocentric*
>> Noun Word Group.
>>> *The tendre croppes* (the tender crops)
>>> *This ilke worthy knyght* (this same excellent knight)
>>> *Hir mouth ful smal* (her very small mouth)
>> Verb Word Group.
>>> *hath perced* (has pierced)
>>> *weren esed* (were made comfortable)
>>> *hadde maad* (had made)
>> Modifier Word Group.
>>> *honoured for his worthynesse* (honored for his excellence)
>>> *as meeke as is a mayde* (as meek as a maiden)
>>> *greye as glas* (gray as glass)
>> Verbal Word Group.
>>> *To riden out* (to ride out)
>>> *for to doon his pilgrimage* (to make his pilgrimage)
>>> *To speke of phisik and of surgerye*
>>>> (to speak of medicine and of surgery)
>> Conjunctional Word Group.
>>> *A lovyere and a lusty bacheler*
>>>> (a lover and a lusty bachelor)

so charitable and so pitous (so loving and so merciful)
Thanne wolde he speke and crie
 (then he would speak and cry)
Exocentric
 Subject-Predicate Word Group.
  Me thynketh it (it seems to me)
  A YEMAN hadde he (he had a yeoman)
  she raughte (she reached)
 Prepositional Word Group.
  Of which vertu (from which power)
  for oure feith (for our faith)
  With scalled browes blake and piled berd
   (with scabby black eyebrows and mangy beard)

From these examples, it is evident that the boundaries of Modern English word groups are already set in Middle English. What remains to be done within these boundaries is a more analytic rearrangement of the exact word order. The verb word group still lacks modal auxiliaries and aspect indicators, the modifier word group needs some refinement and an independence from the linking verb, the verbal word group will profit from a strong emergence of the gerund, and the prepositional word group will benefit from more specific and explicit compound and phrasal linkers.

MIDDLE ENGLISH SENTENCES. Middle English employs several familiar sentence types. Although the local idioms may sound strange and the word order of constructions may differ, the three basic types of a *simple* sentence in Middle English are like those of Modern: with no complement, with one complement, and with two complements. These basic types may be illustrated as follows:

 With No Complement
  My tale is not bigonne. (My story hasn't started.)
  Thou lixt! (You lie!)
  Moot I thryve! (May I prosper!)
 With One Complement
  The revers shaltou se. (You will see the opposite.)
  God it woot. (God knows it.)
  She nolde do that synne. (She would not commit that sin.)

With Two Complements

    He yaf me mete and drynke. (He gave me food and drink.)

    He wex a litel reed for shame.

        (He grew a little red because of shame.)

    Men loven wommen al biside hire leve.

        (Men love women completely without their permission.)

Middle English further makes use of both the *compound* and the *complex* sentence. The compound sentence has more than one independent clause; it may be seen in the following statement from Psalm XCI of *The West Midland Prose Psalter:*

    And hē shal shadow þē wyþ hys shulderis, and þōu shalt hǭpe under hys feþers.

    (And He will shade you with his shoulders, and you will hope under His feathers.)

The complex sentence in Middle English has at least one subordinate clause accompanying the independent statement. Chaucer's delightfully gabby and meddlesome Pandar demonstrates this sentence type:

    But if ye late hym deyen, I wol sterve . . .

    (But if you let him die, I will perish . . .)

Pandar is an excellent example of the gain in informality of Middle English over Old. As the language evolves syntactically, it loses much of its heroic elevation. The spoken word is more readily heard within the written. The sound of the human voice, moreover, indicates that Middle English is much more like Modern in the sentence-determining possibilities of the terminal contours. Thus Middle English has a far greater flexibility than Old English in the support of such non-declarative sentence types as the completional, equational, exclamational, and interjectional.

FORMAL STYLISTICS

POETRY.   One of the two major schools of poetry in Middle English is the Alliterative Revival. The medieval return to the native metrical tradition finds that the accentual line has expanded in speech material, a fact demonstrated in the following brief chart:

POEM	DATE	MEAN OF SYLLABLES PER LINE
Beowulf	ca. 725	10.217
Andreas	ca. 850	10.38
Maldon	ca. 1000	10.98
Gawain	ca. 1375	13.7
Piers Plowman	ca. 1387	14.4

With the lengthening alliterative line, the bardic harp ceases to be a percussion instrument of functional metrical accompaniment and becomes a *melodic* instrument of musical *decoration*. Eventually the harp falls silent and passes from the literary scene in England.

Under the pressures of evolution, the alliterative line loses several key features of the earlier tradition: 1) the principle of overstress in a highly morphemic language; 2) the dramatic sense of heavy juncturing induced by the high occurrence of contiguity of major stresses within the line; 3) the primitive delight in syncopation as developed in oral chant, with the percussional harp filling in the juncture rests of truncated measures. Yet medieval alliterative poetry compensates for these losses with artistic gains of its own. Thus the poetry of the Alliterative Revival boasts rich sound patterning and fecund use of dream allegory, social satire, religious mysticism, upon occasion earthy diction, and expansive imagery. Most of these qualities may be seen in the opening passage and closing lines of Passus V of *Piers Plowman*, where the rhythm shifts to staccato and the diction changes to the colloquial:

> In a somer seson   whan soft was the sonne,
> I shope me in shroudes   as I a shepe were,
> In habite as an heremite   vnholy of workes,
> Went wyde in þis world   wondres to here.
> Ac on a May mornynge   on Maluerne hulles,
> Me byfel a ferly   of fairy, me thouȝte;
> I was wery forwandred   and went me to reste
> Under a brode banke   bi a bornes side,
> And as I lay and lened   and loked in þe wateres,
> I slombred in a slepyng   it sweyued so merye.
>
> (Prol. 1–10)

> In a summer season   when soft was the sun,
> I clothed me in garments   just like a shepherd,

In the habit of a hermit   sinful in deeds,
Who'd gone wide in this world   wonders to hear.
Yet on a May morning   on Malvern Hill,
I met with a marvel   of enchantment, it seemed;
I was worn out from wandering   and went to my rest
Under a broad bank   by the side of a brook,
And as I lay and leaned   and looked into the water,
I slept in a slumber   it murmured so smoothly.

"Now, bi cryst," quod a cutpurs,   "I have no kyne þere!"
"Ne I," quod an apewarde,   "bi auȝte þat I knowe!"
"Wite god," quod a wafrestre,   "wist I þis for sothe,
Shulde I neuere ferthere a fote   for no freres prechynge."

(V, 639–642)

"Now, by Christ," said a pickpocket,   "I have no relatives there!"
"Nor I," said an ape-keeper,   "by anything I know!"
"God defend us," said a cooky-seller,   "if I knew this for certain,
I'd never move a foot further   for no friar's preaching."

The second major school of poetry in Middle English is the new main-stream tradition, the Chaucerian. It abandons the alliterative accentual line of the Anglo-Saxons and adopts the syllabic (misthought classical-footed) line of the French. Stichic verse gives way to strophic, in which rhymed stanzas become the dominant unit of organization. Chaucer himself introduces into Middle English literature verse forms such as the couplet, *terza rima*, his own rhyme royal, the octet, and decasyllabic and the hendecasyllabic line; as a master of borrowed French forms, he also uses the alba, the aubade, the ballade, and the roundel to good advantage.

If the Chaucerian line seems less metrically exciting than the syncopation and overstressed verse of Old English, the Middle English method of poetic formation is far more flexible for a mature and subtle narration which develops speaker verisimilitude, psychological realism, three-dimensional characterization, humor, and the natural pace of dramatic suspense. In *Troilus and Criseyde*, the supreme piece of finished poetry in Middle English, a masterful tension between the hyperbolic and the litotic, between apostrophic madness and literal sanity, between the transcendent ideal and the earthly real, demonstrates the important artistic advances of the new tradition. Indeed, the greatness of Chaucer depends in large measure upon that tradition. From it come several rich literary veins—in technique, subject matter, architectonics, imagery, symbol, and mythic projection—later mined by the English Renaissance. As a direct heir of and contributor to that tradition, Chaucer becomes the broad medieval base for the towering edifice of poetry that is Shakespeare. Something of the humane humor and earthy modernity of Chaucer's art may be seen in the following passages from *Troilus and Criseyde* and "The Miller's Tale":

> And Lord! so he gan goodly on her se,
> That nevere his look ne bleynte from hire face,
> And seyde, "O deere herte, may it be
> That it be soth, that ye ben in this place?"
> "Yee, herte myn, God thank I of his grace,"
> Quod tho Criseyde, and therwithal hym kiste,
> That where his spirit was, for joie he nyste.   (V, 1345–1351)

> And Lord! he began to look on her so kind,
> That never did his gaze turn from her face,
> And said, "Dear heart, O can it be I find
> That you are with me truly in this place?"
> "Yes, my heart, I thank God for His grace,"
> Said then Criseyde—and kissed him on the spot,
> That where his soul was then, for joy he knew not.

> Of gooth the skyn an hande-brede aboute,
> The hoote kultour brende so his toute,
> And for the smert he wende for to dye.
> As he were wood, for wo he gan to crye,
> "Help! water! water! help, for Goddes herte!"
>
> This carpenter out of his slomber sterte,
> And herde oon crien "water" as he were wood,
> And thoughte, "Allas, now comth Nowelis flood!"
> He sit hym up withouten wordes mo,
> And with his ax he smoot the corde atwo.
> And doun gooth al; he foond neither to selle,
> Ne breed ne ale, til he came to the celle
> Upon the floor, and ther aswowne he lay.   (3811–3823)

> Off goes the skin a hand's breadth about,
> The hot plow-blade has so burnt his butt,
> And from the sting he thought that he would die.
> Like a man gone mad, he woefully began to cry,
> "Help! water! water! help, for God's heart!"
>
> This carpenter then out of his sleep did start,
> And heard somebody cry "water" like mad,
> And thought, "Alas, now comes that Noah's flood!"

Then he sat up without another word,
And with his ax in two he cut the cord.
And down goes all; he found nothing for sale
Till he came to the sill—neither bread nor ale—
And there on the floor unconscious he lay.

PROSE.   Although Chaucer's poetry is the literary summit of Middle
English, his prose is undistinguished—an image of the ineptitude of the
language itself. As in Old English, Middle English poetry is far more
artistically mature, refined, and eloquent. Part of this supremacy of
poetry can be attributed to the aristocratic tradition; in English, prose is
the method of democracy and the popular art forms of the masses. Middle English prose is often gnarled in syntax, clumsy of idiom, dense and
chaotic in its references, and redundant and periphrastic in expression, although on great occasions it can be simple and moving. In word order,
it shows a steady progression away from the inverted and transposed
toward the modernesque common. Through a gradual reduction of
dialect variants, Middle English prose finally achieves the Written Standard of London. The following six passages, chosen on the bases of time
and locale, constitute a miniature history of this literary form:

Historical Reportage (Early East Midland), from *The Peterborough Chronicle:*

1132. Ðis gēar cōm Henrī Kīng tō þis lānd. Ðā cōm Henrī abbot and
wreide þē muneces of Burch tō þē kīng forþi ðat hē wolde under-
þēden ðat mynstre tō Clunīe, swā ðat tē kīng was wēl nēh bepaht and
sende efter þē muneces. And þurh Godes milce and þurh þē Biscop of
Seresberī and tē Biscop of Lincoln and tē ōþre rīce men þe þēr wæron,
þā wiste þē kīng ðat hē fēorde mid swīcdōm.

1132. During this year King Henry came to this district. Then the
abbot Henry came and accused the monks of Peterborough before the
king because he wanted to make that cathedral subject to Cluny, so
that the king was very nearly deceived and he sent for the monks.
And through the mercy of God and through the Bishop of Salisbury
and the Bishop of Lincoln and the other powerful men who were
there, then the king knew that he was dealing with fraud.

Monastic Guide in the Tradition of Ælfric (Early Southern),
from *The Ancren Riwle:*

SPELLUNGE and smecchunge bēoð ine mūðe bōðe, ase sihðe is ī þēn
eien; auh wē schullen lēten smecchunge vort tet wē spēken of ōwer

mēte, and spēken nū of spellunge and tẹrefter of herrunge, of bọ imẹne sume cherre ase gọ̄ð tōgederes.

Both conversation and tasting are in the mouth, as sight is in the eyes; but we shall by-pass tasting until we talk about your food, and shall speak now of conversation and thereafter of hearing, of both together for a while—because they go together.

Biblical Translation (Mature West Midland), from *The West Midland Prose Psalter*, Psalm I:

Blesced bē þē man þat ȝēde nouȝt in þē cōūnseil of wicked, ne stōde nouȝt in þē waie of sinȝẹres, ne sat nauȝt in fals jugement. 2. Ac his wylle was þē wylle of ōūre Lọrd, and hē schal þenche in his lawe bọþe daye and nyȝt. 3. And hē schal bē as þē trē þat is sett bȳ þē ērnynges of waters, þat schal ȝeve his frut in his tȳme. 4. And his lẹf schal nouȝt fallwen, and alle þynges þat þē ryȝtful dōþ schal multiplīen. 5. Nouȝt sọ bēn þē wicked, nouȝt sọ; as a pōūdre þat þē wȳnde casteþ fram þē fāce of þē ērþe. 6. Forþi ne schal nouȝt þē wicked arīse in jugement, ne þē sinniẹrs in þē cōnseyl of þē ryȝtful. 7. For ōūre Lọrd knew þē waie of þē ryȝtful, and þē waye of synnẹrs schal perissen.

Blessed is the man who walks not in the counsel of the wicked, who stands not in the path of sinners, who sits not in false judgment. 2. But his will has been in the will of our Lord, and he shall be mindful of His law both day and night. 3. And he shall be like the tree that is set by the running stream, which shall give of its fruit in due season. 4. And its leaf shall not wither, and all things that the righteous do shall increase and prosper. 5. Not so are the wicked, not so; but like a puff of dust that the wind whirls from the face of the earth. 6. Therefore the wicked shall not stand tall in the judgment, or the sinners in the congregation of the righteous. 7. For our Lord knows the way of the righteous, and the path of the sinners shall perish.

Mystical Essay (Mature Northern), from the *Treatises of Richard Rolle of Hampole:*

The fyrste comandement es, "Thȳ Lọrde God þōū sall lōūte and til hym ānelȳ þōū sall serve." In this comandement es forbọden all mawmetrȳse, all wychecrafte and charemynge, thē wylke may dō nā remedȳ till ānȳ sēknes of mane, woman, or bēste, for þay erre þē snarrys of þē dēvelle bȳ þē whilke hē afforces hym tō dyssayve manekȳnde. Alswā in þis comandement es forbọdyn to gyffe trouthe till sorcerȳe or till dyvȳnynges bȳ stērnys, or bȳ drẹmys, or bȳ anȳ swylke thynges.

The First Commandment is, "You shall worship your Lord God and Him only shall you serve." In this commandment is forbidden all idolatry, all witchcraft and enchantment, which can work no cure for any sickness of man, woman, or beast, because they are the snares of the devil by which he himself tries to deceive mankind. In this commandment it is also forbidden to place any trust in sorcery or in divinations by means of stars, or dreams, or any such things.

Political Petition (Mature London), from *The First English Petition to Parliament,* 1386:

Tō thē mǫǫst nǫble and worthīest lǫrdes, mǫǫst ryghtful and wȳsest Cōnseille tō ōwre lige Lōrde thē Kyng, compleynen, if it lȳke tō yōw, thē folk of thē Mercerȳe of London as a membreof thē sāme citee, of manȳ wrōnges subtiles and alsǫ ǫpen oppressions ydō tō him bȳ lǫnge tȳme hēre bifōre passed. . . . For in thē sāme yēre thē forsaid Nicholus, withōūten nēde, ayein the pęęs māde dȳverse enarmynges bī day and eke bī nyght, and destruyd thē Kynges trewe lȳges, som with ǫpen slaughtre, somme bī false emprisonementz; and some fledde thē citee for fęęre, as it is ǫpenlīch knowen.

To the noblest and most honorable lords, the wisest and most righteous Counsel to your Liege Lord the King, if it pleases you, the cloth merchants of London complain as a member of the same city about many subtle wrongs and also open oppressions done to them for a long time past. . . . For in the same year, the forenamed Nicholas [Brember, unlawful Mayor of London], without any cause, made several different armed uprisings against the peace, both by day and by night, and destroyed the King's true servants, some by open slaughter, some with false emprisonments; and others fled the city out of fear, as it is plainly known.

Critical Preface (Late Literary Standard), from William Caxton's "Preface" to *Eneydos,* 1490:

And also my lorde abbot of westmynster ded do shewe to me late, certayn evydences writon in olde englysshe, for to reduce it in-to our englysshe now usid. And certaynly it was wreton in such wyse that it was more lyke to dutche than englysshe; I coude not reduce ne brynge it to be understonden. And certaynly our langage now used varyeth ferr from that whiche was used and spoken whan I was borne. For we englysshe men ben borne under the domynacyon of the mone, whiche is never stedfaste, but ever waverynge, wexynge one season, and waneth & dyscreaseth another season. And that comyn englysshe that is spoken in one shyre varyeth from a nother.

From these examples of the literary evolution of Middle English, two points are clear: the language starts out as late Old English and ends up as Early Modern (there is no need to translate from Caxton's "Preface");

and the poetic maturity of Middle English, contrasted with the immaturity of its prose, can be readily seen in the direct and simple eloquence of *The West Midland Prose Psalter*, where the parallel structures and kindred-thought rhythms of Hebraic poetry match the aesthetic capabilities of the language.

QUESTIONS FOR RESEARCH AND DISCUSSION

1. Conduct an investigation into the silencing of Middle English consonants in Modern English. Are there any regular patterns in this process of silencing? If so, do the patterns indicate any linguistic laws? If not, how can you account for the silencings that do occur? Be specific in your answers.

2. How accurate is Modern English spelling in indicating the tension and therefore the length of a vowel? Correlate this current spelling with the Middle English practices of doubling the following consonant to indicate a short vowel and of either doubling the vowel or following it with a single consonant and then another vowel to indicate length. What are the major differences between Middle English and Modern English in the relationship between spelling and the phonemic quality of the vowels? Develop your answer in detail.

3. Write a brief essay on the emergence of phonemic diphthongs in Middle English, both consonantal and vocalic. Be comparative in your essay and make direct references to the scarcity of diphthongs in Old English.

4. Assume that you have just read the following linguistic value judgment about Middle English: "The language of Chaucer represents a softening—under direct Norman and Central French influence—of the Germanic tension and explosive strength of Old English. Middle English is therefore more musical, languid, and liquid than its Anglo-Saxon ancestor." Then listen to expert readings—either in person or on record—of Old English and Middle English. Now write a major critical paper in which you either defend or attack the value judgment quoted. What is the consensus of the class?

5. Organize a panel discussion on the importance of rhyme in Middle English poetry. Let four members of the class participate in the discussion and deal with the following major topics: a) continental origins of rhyme, b) medieval strophic verse patterns, c) literary genres governed by rhyme, d) Middle English innovations.

6. Investigate the role of dialect rivalry in the achievement of inflectional leveling in Middle English. What other historical factors aided in this process of morphological reduction? Do either German or French show a similar development in their morphology at this time? At a later date?

Now write a brief essay on the importance of inflectional leveling in the history of the English language.

7. Engage in a doubly comparative discussion: contrast the chief morphological processes of Middle English with those of Old English and of present-day Modern English. What are the peculiar morphological advantages in each of the three historical versions of the language? Be specific.

8. Let six members of the class organize a group investigation into the relative importance of *common, inverted,* and *transposed* word order in Middle English syntax. Divide the work into two groups of three students each, with one group studying the syntax of the "General Prologue" to Chaucer's *Canterbury Tales* and the other group studying a passage of comparable length in Wycliffe's translation of the Bible. What are the major syntactical differences between the poetry and the prose of Middle English?

9. Now let six more members of the class organize a similar investigation into the relative importance of *common, inverted,* and *transposed* word order in Modern English syntax. Divide the work into two groups of three students each, with one group studying the syntax of a thousand lines of Walt Whitman's *Song of Myself* and the other group studying a passage of comparable length from Hemingway's novel *The Old Man and the Sea*. What are the major syntactical differences between the poetry and the prose of Modern English?

10. With the results of both investigations available to the class, write a critical paper on the apparent syntactical differences between the prose and poetry of Middle English and the prose and poetry of Modern English. Pay close attention to idiomatic structures.

11. Organize a panel discussion among four students on the stylistic merits of *Piers Plowman, Troilus and Criseyde, The Pearl,* and *Everyman*. Concentrate on such items as euphony, rhythm, imagery, symbolism, dramatic propriety, artistic variety, and moral relevance.

SELECTED BIBLIOGRAPHY

Bryant, Margaret M. *Modern English and Its Heritage*. Second Edition. New York: The Macmillan Company, 1962. See especially Chapter 18, for a study of the phonology of both Middle and Early Modern English.

Emerson, Oliver Farrar. *A Middle English Reader*. New and Revised Edition. New York: The Macmillan Company, 1948. This book covers the entire range of Middle English language and literature.

Hockett, Charles F. *A Course in Modern Linguistics*. New York: The Macmillan Company, 1958. See especially pp. 377–379 for a brief description of the phonemes of Middle English.

Kurath, Hans, and Sherman M. Kuhn, eds. *Middle English Dictionary*. Ann Arbor: University of Michigan Press, 1952—, in progress. This will become the definitive work on the lexical range of Middle English.

Pyles, Thomas. *The Origins and Development of the English Language*. New York: Harcourt, Brace & World, 1964. See Chapter VI for a good brief account of "The Middle English Period (1100–1500)."

Robinson, F. N., ed. *The Works of Geoffrey Chaucer*. Second Edition. Boston: Houghton Mifflin Company, 1957. An excellent one-volume edition.

Skeat, Rev. Walter W., ed. *The Vision of William Concerning Piers The Plowman, by William Langland (or Langley)*. Tenth Edition, Revised. Oxford: The Clarendon Press, 1948. Perhaps the best one-volume edition.

Wagenknecht, Edward, ed. *Chaucer: Modern Essays in Criticism*. New York: Oxford University Press, Galaxy Book, 1959. This is a collection of twenty-six scholarly essays by various authorities who demonstrate the vast range and broad humanity of Chaucer.

Zesmer, David M. *Guide to English Literature: From Beowulf through Chaucer and Medieval Drama*. New York: Barnes & Noble, 1961. See especially Part II, pp. 81–286, for a well-organized survey of the entire range of Middle English literature. The annotated bibliographies, pp. 322–381, by Stanley B. Greenfield are extensive.

CHAPTER 7

The History of
Early Modern English
1500-1650

———————◆———————

IMPORTANT DATES

1460–1529 Life of John Skelton, clergyman, satirist, and poet, who typifies the enormous growth in the English vocabulary, for Skelton introduces about 1500 new words into the language.

1485–1509 Reign of Henry VII, first of the Tudor Dynasty, which marks the end of Middle English.

1509–1547 Reign of Henry VIII, during which the Protestant Reformation reduces the dominance of Latin in England.

1531 Publication of Sir Thomas Elyot's *The Governour*, first book on education printed in England and symbol of the conscious effort to enrich the vocabulary of Early Modern English with foreign loans.

1536–1547 Introduction of the European Renaissance into English poetry by Sir Thomas Wyatt and Henry Howard, Earl of Surrey, who develop the Tudor lyric, sonnet, and blank verse.

1550 Approximate date of a nucleus of common spelling practices in Early Modern English.

1553 Publication of Thomas Wilson's *Art of Rhetorique*, a popular text of Renaissance England, used by Shakespeare, which defends plainness in writing and opposes the use of "inkhorn" (learned foreign) terms.

1558–1603   Reign of Elizabeth I, period of the most spectacular growth of British power and of immense language development and literary achievement.

1564–1616   Life of William Shakespeare, greatest dramatic poet of England, whose artistic impact on English remains tremendous.

1579   Publication of Sir Thomas North's translation of Plutarch's *Lives of the Noble Grecians and Romans,* source for Shakespeare's Roman plays and epitome of the popular demand to share in the riches of the European Renaissance.

1582   Publication of Richard Mulcaster's *Elementarie,* the finest treatise on English spelling in the sixteenth century.

1588   Defeat of the Spanish Armada leads to the European supremacy of Britain and to the global importance of English.

1604   Publication of Robert Cawdrey's *The Table Alphabeticall of Hard Words,* which marks the beginning of English lexicography.

1607   Captain John Smith founds Jamestown, Virginia, symbol of the transplanting of English to the colonies of the growing British Empire.

1611   Publication of the King James or Authorized Version of the Bible, one of the greatest literary influences on the subsequent development of English.

1623   Publication of the First Folio of Shakespeare's plays.

1642   Closing of the English theaters by a Puritan-dominated Parliament marks the end of Renaissance drama and prepares the way for authoritarianism in art and language.

1649   Charles I is beheaded.

OUTSTANDING PERSONS

Sir Francis Bacon (1561–1626)   Father of the English essay and a key figure in developing a clear, economical, and precise English prose style.

Miles Coverdale (1488–1569) and William Tyndale (1492–1536) Originators of the great prose style of the Early Modern English Bible.

John Donne (1573–1631)   Master of metaphysical poetry and the eloquent sermon.

Robert Greene (1560–1592)   One of the perfecters of Early Modern English prose, first great pamphleteer, master of social realism, and forerunner of Daniel Defoe.

Henry Howard, Earl of Surrey (1517–1547)   Father of blank verse, soon to become the great dramatic vehicle of Renaissance England.

Ben Jonson (1573–1637)   Chief dramatic rival of Shakespeare, master of comic realism, and forerunner of the Neoclassical Age and its Authoritarian English.

John Lyly (1554–1606)   Father of the euphuistic style in Renaissance English prose, noted for its poetic sound patterns, elaborate conceits, and syntactical balance.

Christopher Marlowe (1564–1593)   Forerunner of Shakespeare, Marlowe helps perfect blank verse as the aesthetic vehicle of Elizabethan drama.

John Milton (1608–1674)   Last of the great Elizabethans and first of the great Puritans, Milton is a transitional figure in Early Modern English.

Sir Thomas More (1478–1535)   One of the "Makers of English," even though his most famous work (*Utopia*, 1517) is written in Latin, the international language of Renaissance scholars.

Richard Mulcaster (1530–1611)   Teacher of Edmund Spenser, father of English orthography, and champion of the scholarly use of Early Modern English.

William Shakespeare (1564–1616)   The supreme literary artist of Early Modern English.

Sir Philip Sidney (1554–1586)   Epitome of the English Renaissance: man of letters and man of action, a perfecter of the Elizabethan sonnet and of Early Modern English prose.

John Skelton (1460–1529)   One of the "Makers of English" and the greatest single contributor of new words to the vocabulary of Early Modern English.

Edmund Spenser (1552–1599)   Greatest narrative poet of the English Renaissance (*The Fairie Queene*, 1580–99) and a reviver of archaic morphology.

Sir Thomas Wyatt (1503–1542)   Father of the Tudor lyric and an importer of European verse forms into English literature.

MAJOR ATTRIBUTES OF THE LANGUAGE

Undergoes a stabilization of orthography.

Experiences an immense enrichment of vocabulary from different sources.

Shares in the growing prestige for the vernacular tongues of Europe.

Undergoes much experimentation with its morphology.

Supports a phonemic instability that leads to the beginning of the Great Vowel Shift.

Refines the word order within the various word groups of its analytic and hypotactic syntax.

Tolerates a variety in usage and form.

Witnesses an almost complete loss of the old inflectional system.

Maintains idiomatic constructions different from those of present-day English.

Is morphologically and syntactically more free, flexible, and daring than present-day English.

DURING THE CENTURY AND A half of the English Renaissance, the printing press became the indispensable disseminator of the written word, and its use was accompanied by a corresponding spread of popular education and literacy. The growing prestige of the vernacular languages of Europe, initiated by the Florentine poet Dante Alighieri (1265–1321), supported national pride in English and helped reduce Latin as the language of scholarship. The Protestant Reformation, moreover, dealt a death blow to the dominance of Latin in the church and the schools. With its vastly increased use Early Modern English was open to the cultural penetration of the multifarious European Renaissance. What it could not borrow from foreign tongues it invented. Thus the entire period of Early Modern English was one of linguistic innovation and experiment.

When William Caxton introduced printing into England in 1476, Early Modern English had the means to promote a written standard and to spread it throughout the island kingdom. Along with extending literacy and expanding popular education, the printing press became a powerful cultural force that put back into the language what had been lost with the Norman Conquest—the conservative pressures of self-awareness and social snobbery. At the same time, it also fostered a radical spirit of appropriation from other tongues. In that tension between conservative grammar and ultra-liberal vocabulary Early Modern English evolved with enormous energy. On the side of conservatism, the grapheme and the visual morpheme took command of the printers, who locked into type a premature orthography. Hence unpronounced final *e* and such silent consonant clusters as *gh, kn,* and *gn* in words like *bought, knife,* and *gnat* have become part of the inconsistent present-day English spelling. But in visualizing the "long" and "short" vowels, Early Modern English fared better: the long vowel was printed as either a double vowel (*sweet*) or a vowel-consonant-vowel (*fate*), and the short vowel appeared singly before a doubling of the consonant before another vowel (*ridding* as contrasted with *riding*). As for the phonemic content of the visualized vowels, the result was chaotic—for the graphemes invariably corresponded to Middle English, whereas the Great Vowel Shift of Early Modern English was to make enormous displacements in phonology.

More important than either the orthographic conservatism or the phonological inconsistency wrought by the printing press was the mistaken notion that English is primarily the written word. The grapheme and the visual morpheme began to dominate the literate imagination, and the raw power of the oral tradition gradually gave way to the elegant refinement of the silent literary. In time, the divorce between the spoken and the written was legalized by the authoritarian grammarians of the eighteenth century and their heirs. Had William Shakespeare cast his lot with the snobbish new literary tradition rather than with the democratic oral tradition of the spoken word upon the stage, the world might have had a series of well-polished narrative poems like *Venus and Adonis* and *The Rape of Lucrece* instead of such towering masterpieces as *Othello* and *King Lear.* Yet printing—the champion of conservatism—was also the great linguistic catalyst for the doubling of the English vocabulary in the short span of a hundred and fifty years. To this lexical fact Shakespeare's plays bear artistic witness.

LINGUISTIC ACHIEVEMENTS. As a European vernacular, Early Modern English faced several major problems at its outset: how to replace Latin as the language of scholarly writing; how to stabilize a widely variant orthography; how to enable its vocabulary to meet the demands of growing commercial power and cultural prestige; how to develop stylistically to support great literary expression. Much of the history of Early Modern English is the record of how the language solved these problems.

The revival of learning fostered by the Renaissance allowed Englishmen to share in the cultural riches of the European continent and the ancient world. With human attention fixed on the things of this life, ironically enough spiritual matters became a grave issue—especially where language was involved. With the scriptures too long kept from the people, the Protestant Reformation championed the translation of the Bible into the vernaculars of Europe. Early Modern English produced at least seven major versions of the Bible in the brief span of the seventy-five years between the martyrdom of William Tyndale in 1536 and the publication of the classic Authorized Version in 1611: the Tyndale New Testament (1536), the Coverdale Bible (1537), the Great Bible (1539), the Geneva Bible (1560), the Bishops' Bible (1568), the Douai (Catholic version) Bible (1610), and the world-famous King James Bible (1611).

Continuing the work of John Wycliffe, William Tyndale established the literary character of the translations of the Bible into English—both Early Modern and present-day. Choosing the spoken language of the people, Tyndale deliberately avoided abstract diction and stilted phraseology. In his translation, Miles Coverdale (1488–1569) sought rhythmical beauty, ease of reading, oral-tradition immediacy, and simple clarity. The Prayer-book Psalter shows the stylistic genius of Coverdale, who must be regarded with Tyndale as one of the great refiners of Early Modern English. Over 90 percent of the Tyndale–Coverdale language entered directly into the King James Version, the supreme religious translation of the entire Renaissance.

During the sixteenth century the ancient historians Thucydides, Xenophon, Herodotus, Caesar himself, Livy, Sallust, and Tacitus were introduced to the English people in their own tongue. Classical philosophers such as Plato, Aristotle, Cicero, Seneca, Epictetus, and Marcus Aurelius appeared in Early Modern English editions. Virgil, Ovid, Horace, Terence, Theocritus, and a host of minor names received the honor of translation. The two greatest English renditions of the Renaissance in the field of secular masterpieces were Sir Thomas North's version of Plutarch's *Lives of the Noble Grecians and Romans* (1579), an important source for Shakespeare's plays, and George Chapman's fourteen-syllables-to-the-line translation of seven books from Homer's *Iliad* (1598).

Other Early Modern English translations included the works of St. Augustine, Boethius, Peter Martyr, Erasmus, John Calvin, and Martin Luther. All these translations enhanced the prestige of Early Modern English and helped to develop a simple and eloquent prose style. They also contributed much to the vocabulary of the language.

Another way in which Early Modern English solved the problems confronting it was through experimentation and innovation. By their use of English in serious scholarship and formal writing, Sir Thomas More and Sir Thomas Elyot have been called "Makers of Early Modern English." The greatest contributions to the language were made by the fecund mind and facile pen of John Skelton (1460–1529), a clergyman satirist who epitomized the enormous expansion of the English language during the Renaissance. Father of Skeltonic verse, short doggerel lines that rhyme in groups of variable length, Skelton was unconventional, undignified, wittily vulgar, and cynically realistic—of perfect temperament to tamper and play with language. As a consequence of his receptivity to the new and the different in speech, Skelton introduced at least fifteen hundred new words into Early Modern English, according to F. M. Salter.

The following list of workaday English words is a brief sample of Skelton's lexical contribution to the language: *abbreviated, accomplished, accumulate, administer, admiration, advance, advantage, allude, ambiguous, ample, antiquity, aptitude, attempt, attribute, base, beneficial, brevity, bruited, celebrate, concern, congruency, contriver, cowardliness, custody, dastard, decay, deduce, demeanour, derivation, describe, devilish, drowsy, drudge, drunkard, economy, embitter, enormity, enure, exceeding, expiatory, extol, fervency, formidable, fortified, furnish, gall* (to harass), *gravity, habituate, imaginative, imitation, immolation, impetuosity, inaccessible, inclusive, indelible, inebriate, informed, intemperate, intended, intuitive, laboriously, lucky, mandatory, miserable, monstrously, native* (adjective), *obfuscate, obtusively, operative, penalty, people* (verb), *persuade, pretence, prodigious, prognosticate, ram* (verb), *rare, reasoned* (adjective), *recompense, repair, requisite, satiate, seriousness, shorten, situated, stagger, steadily, succinct, suffocate, sumptuously, tempestuous, tolerate, urgent,* and *variety.*

Books in English came to command a sales market far greater than those in Latin. Desire to reach the largest possible audience combined with simple economics to warrant scholarly experimentation in Early Modern English. In 1534, Sir Thomas Elyot prefaced his *Doctrinal of Princes* by saying that he had translated it from the Greek to see whether "our English tongue mought receive the quicke and proper sentences pronounced by the greekes." In his *Castle of Health,* published in the same year, Elyot defended his having written about so important a subject as medicine in his own vernacular by pointing out the fact that the entire history of medicine was one of the written vernacular, for "the grekes wrate in greke, the Romains in latine, Avicenna, and the other in Arabike, which were their own proper and maternall tongues." Later in the century, Richard Mulcaster wrote in his native language because he wanted to be of scholarly service to the unlearned, who understood only English. But he could not resist shooting at snobbery, for he reminded the conservative champions of Latin that "he that understands Latin very well, can understand English farre better, if he will confesse the trueth, though he thinks he have the habite and can Latin it exceeding well."

The growing patriotism in Renaissance England produced a healthy pride in the use of English. Tired of the reactionary accusations that his language was crude, barbarous, barren, vulgar, and unworthy, in 1586 George Pettie boasted in his *Civile Conversation* that he could write in English "as copiouslye for varietie, as compendiously for brevitie, as choycely for woordes, as pithily for sentences, as pleasauntly for figures, and every way as eloquently, as any writer should do in any vulgar tongue whatsoever." Pettie was not congratulating his own private talent; he was praising the public genius of Early Modern English. Sir Philip Sidney, the well-rounded Renaissance gentleman, had done the same thing three years earlier, when he said that "for the uttering sweetly and properly the conceit of the minde, which is the end of speech, that English hath it equally with any other tongue in the world."

Mulcaster honestly believed that "the English tung cannot prove fairer, then it is at this daie, if it maie please our learned sort to esteme so of it, and to bestow their travell upon such a subject, so capable of ornament, so proper to themselves, and the more to be honored, bycause it is their own." The scholarly displacement of Latin by Early Modern English, therefore, was an extension of the process that revived the language in Middle English and resulted in the ousting of Norman and Parisian French from the circles of power, authority, and prestige.

ORTHOGRAPHIC PRACTICES.   From the quotations in the foregoing section, we can see that the spelling habits of Early Modern English were anything but phonetic or fixed. The poor correspondence between orthography and phonology in Early Modern English was inherited from Norman scribes, who wrote quite a bit of confusion into a language they did not fully understand. The confusion deepened when evolving pronunciations shifted further away from the approximations of Middle

English spelling conventions. As Baugh said, "the average man of education in Shakespeare's day did not spell by mere whim or caprice, but had formed fairly constant spelling habits." The trouble was that gentlemen of learning had their own habits, based upon personal linguistic insight and idiosyncratic logic. With the importance of the grapheme and the visual morpheme in printing, variant systems of Renaissance English spelling had to be reduced to a standard convention. The standard that emerged was somewhat irrational and certainly non-phonemic, but it was preferable to no standard at all.

Individual attempts to be consistent and systematic in spelling by Sir John Cheke and Richard Stanyhurst, for example, though historically interesting, were not sufficiently conventional to meet the orthographic needs of the time. Cheke doubled tense vowels (as in *taak, haat, maad, mijn,* and *thijn* for *take, hate, made, mine,* and *thine*), discarded final *e* (as in *giv* and *belev*), and substituted *i* for *y* (as in *mighti* and *dai*). The use of final *e* to indicate vowel tension (and therefore length) militated against Cheke's personal spelling habits. In addition, he was inconsistent in one method by being consistent in another—thus, *belev* should have read *beleev*, but the dropping of final *e* got in the way of doubling the vowel. The vowel doubling would have locked into permanency the phonemics of Middle English, the structure of which was changing rapidly under the pressures of the Renaissance. Stanyhurst, on the other hand, spelled to equate English syllables with the quantitative demands of his verse translation of Virgil (1582). Hence he got such odd orthography as *mee, neere, coonning, woorde, yeet,* and *thee* for *the* and *too* for *to.* Had he known that Latin was an accentual rather than a quantitative language, perhaps Stanyhurst could have avoided his inconsistencies on the adverbial ending: *-lye, -lie,* and *-ly.* At any rate, neither Cheke nor Stanyhurst was linguistically advanced enough to bring about a serious fixing of the spelling habits of Early Modern English.

Attempts at phonetic reform by the early lexicographers Thomas Smith, John Hart, and Charles Butler were failures, simply because logical prescription attempted to do away with psychological usage. The printers themselves, quick to justify a line with the use of additional letters, contributed to the general confusion. In Robert Greene's pamphlet *A Notable Discovery of Coosnage* (1591), to cite an instance, the printer spelled *coney* in nine variant forms: *cony, conny, conye, conie, connie, coni, cuny, cunny,* and *cunnie.*

Richard Mulcaster, who honored Latin but worshipped English, was the earliest major exponent of the linguistic doctrine that correctness is a matter of usage plus social acceptability. He was primarily interested in finding out what was going on in Early Modern English rather than in dictating, no matter how learnedly or brilliantly, to the language. Mulcaster saw clearly that a living language is in constant flux, and thus he could say that "when the age of our peple, which now use the tung so well, is dead and departed there will another succeede, and with the peple the tung will alter and change." Aware of the historical evolution of his native language, Mulcaster understood that spelling could never perfectly represent phonology, because "letters can expresse sounds withall their joynts & properties no fuller then the pencill can the form & lineaments of the face." In other words, Mulcaster saw that graphemes are but the abstract portraits of the concrete phonemes; there is bound to be functional overlapping. That is, the same letter or combination of letters can convey the sense of several different sounds. This graphemic instability coupled with changes in pronunciation made it impossible for Mulcaster to fix an absolutely phonetic system of spelling Early Modern English. He was wise enough to accept the limitations that custom and convention placed upon his efforts to refine and stabilize the orthography of his language. That is precisely why his *Elementarie*, published in 1582, "which entreateth chefelie of the right writing of our English tung," was the finest treatise on English spelling in the sixteenth century.

Rather than try to substitute a new system of spelling for the old, Mulcaster worked from usage, admitted popular approval as the final authority, and consequently standardized many current spellings, justified them, and advocated their consistent use. More interested in establishing a common practice in spelling than in promulgating phonetic correlations with the graphemes themselves, Mulcaster included in the latter part of his *Elementarie* a "General Table," in which he recommended an orthography for seven thousand of the most common words in Early Modern English. Some of the outstanding principles underlying his list of spellings were: 1) the riddance of superfluous letters, as in *put* for *putt*, *grub* for *grubb*, and *led* for *ledd*; 2) the inclusion of all necessary letters, such as the heard phonetic *t* in *scratch* and *fetch*; 3) the use of final *e* to indicate a preceding tense vowel, as in the distinction between *made* and *mad*; 4) a consistent differentiation between stressed -*y* and stressless -*ie* in terminal positions; 5) the employment of analogy to make words like *fear* and *dear* correspond graphemically with *hear*; 6) a respect for the "prerogative" of custom so that traditional spellings might finally stabilize analogously, as in *where, here,* and *there.* Despite a few idiosyncrasies that did not prevail in the spelling habits of the language—such as the *-sse* for simple *-ss* on stressed endings, the dropping of the *u* in words like *guise, guide,* and *guest,* and the indication of lax vowels by placing a short superfix over them—Richard Mulcaster did more than any other Englishman to help stabilize the orthography of the language.

Ben Jonson quoted Mulcaster as an authority so universally acknowledged as to need no citation of name. Even Milton's peculiarities in employing a final *e* where convention has dropped it (as in *kinde*), in doubling the final *l* (as in *gratefull*), in substituting *sse* for terminal *ss* (as in *harshnesse*), in adding *k* to *-ic* (as in *logick*), and in contracting the past participle (as in *authoriz'd* and *chanc't*) were not sufficiently weighty to tilt the balance of orthographic authority against Mulcaster's basic outline of spelling practices. By codifying the customs of Early Modern English orthography, Mulcaster kept the spelling of the language from ever becoming phonetic in nature, and asserted this basic principle: as a language, English is primarily psychological rather than logical.

Since every system of orthography is arbitrary and conventional, the traditional spelling of English is not so bad as some critics claim. Thanks to Mulcaster and the impact of the printing press upon its early orthographic codification, the non-phonetic spelling of English has distinct advantages. First of all, such a system of spelling perpetuates tradition and permits the gradual accumulation of *metaphysical pathos* that canonizes the visual value of the time-honored written form. Second, non-phonetic spelling maintains the lines of etymological derivation and evolution, important in so hybrid and cosmopolitan a language as English; its inheritance is easy to trace, thanks to the conventions of non-phonetic spelling. A third advantage in such a system of spelling is its enormous flexibility— that is, the English orthography codified by Mulcaster allows for a wide latitude of graphemic and phonological correlation. Hence one sound may be spelled in several different ways and one letter may have more than one sound value. This orthographic flexibility of English runs parallel with its morphological vitality and metaphoric dynamism. The very look of the language, equated with its pronunciation, indicates its cultural sophistication, unrigid strength, and nonliteral imagination.

All these attributes add up to a fourth advantage: the psychological challenge of inventiveness. By escaping a simple this-for-that equation of spelling and sound, the language has avoided hardening into a surface-level efficiency that may lead to mathematical abstraction and scientific naiveté. The language has been free to communicate and commune beyond the literalism of the conscious, self-conscious mind. Finally, the economy of English orthography is undeniable. Any system of graphemes that can represent at least sixty phonemic units, together with a dozen suprasegmental phonemes and many allophonic variants, without any recourse to the diacritical marks that are the plague of so many languages, has to be judged economical.

THE GREAT VOWEL SHIFT.   At the very time when the orthography of Early Modern English was stabilizing, the sound patterns of the language were undergoing a remarkable displacement. This displacement was rather minor in the consonants and the lax vowels. In the tense vowels, however, it amounted to a general change in tongue positioning and a tighter closing of the mouth, so that the first formant elements of the diphthongs moved either from high-back to low-front or from high-front to low-central, through a clockwise motion in the mouth that often made use of the mid-central *schwa* /ə/ as the intermediate phonemic step of a transverse and diagonal shortcut. The changes in the pronunciation from the Mature Middle English of Chaucer to the Early Modern English of Shakespeare, insofar as these tense vowels were concerned, were so dramatic that Jespersen has named their phonemic displacement the Great Vowel Shift.

To illustrate the basic features of this shift, we may take several words common to Chaucer, Shakespeare, and the Late Modern English of T. S. Eliot, and phonemicize their stressed vowel clusters:

WORD	TENSE VOWEL PRONUNCIATION		
	Chaucer	*Shakespeare*	*Eliot*
bide	/iy/	/əy/	/ay/
rude	/iw/	/ɨw/	/uw/
house	/uw/	/əw/	/aw/
beet	/ey/	/ih/	/iy/
clean	/eˇ/	/ey/	/iy/
boy	/oy/	/ɔy/	/ɔy/
boot	/ow/	/uh/	/uw/
boat	/oˇ/	/ow/	/ow/
lay	/ay/	/ey/	/ey/
laugh	/aw/	/a/	/ae/ or /a/
laud	/aw/	/ɔ/	/ɔ/
lame	/aˇ/	/eh/	/ey/

It is clear that most of the phonemic change from the tense vowels of Middle English to those of Early Modern English occurred on the first formant element of the diphthongs. When it did not so occur, then the lengthening and centering Middle English glide /ˇ/—the rough equivalent of present-day /h/—was changing to either /y/ or /w/, the second formant elements in the narrow diphthongs of Modern English. If the pronunciation displacement was not too great, it took effect in one stage so that the phonemes of Early Modern English agree with those of present-day. If the displacement was relatively large, however, it took effect in two stages so that some phonemes of Early Modern English represent a transition step between Late Middle English and Late Modern. One of the most interesting features of the Great Vowel Shift is the behavior of Middle English /aw/, which became lax: forwarding to /æ/ or remaining simple /a/ when accompanied by consonant transmutation, as in *laughter* (where /x/ changed to /f/), or backing to /ɔ/ when accompanied by consonant stability or silencing, as in *laud* and *slaughter*. As for the phonemic displacements themselves, they may be charted on the first formant elements as follows:

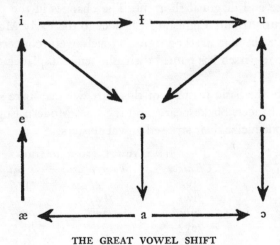

THE GREAT VOWEL SHIFT

From this movement also came three simple vowels: /ɨ æ ɔ/.

OTHER SOUND CHANGES.   More stable than the tense vowels, the lax vowels and the consonants of Early Modern English nevertheless also changed in pronunciation; these changes further helped to distinguish the language from its Middle English progenitor. In Early Modern English the *schwa* (/ə/) and the *colorless i* (/ɨ/) came to be the standard lax vowel sounds of most unaccented syllables. A gradual change took place in Middle English /u/ and /a/ (as heard in present-day *good* and *father*) during the sixteenth century, so that these two sounds eventually became /ə/ and /æ/, respectively. Whereas Chaucer pronounced *but* /but/ to rhyme with present-day *foot* /fut/ and *cat* /kat/ to rhyme with present-day *not* /nat/, Shakespeare's *but* /bət/ rhymed with present-day *tut* /tət/ and his *cat* /kæt/ with present-day *hat* /hæt/. In addition to the tense vocalization of *oo* /uw/ as in *food*, Early Modern English developed two lax pronunciations for this graphemic cluster: /u/ as in *good* and /ə/ as in *blood*.

What changes occurred in the Early Modern English consonants involve either silencing or transmutation. Hence the velar fricative quality of *gh* /x/ shifted to that of the labiodental fricative /f/. In the Renaissance version of the language, the *b* fell silent in the final sequence *-mb* and *d* intruded where it normally did not belong, as in *sound* and *lend*. The Early Modern English *l* of post-consonant *al* on stressed syllables generally ceased to be pronounced; when pronounced, as in *vault* and *fault*, the *l* has usually been inserted. The *h* in French loans like *author* and *throne* converted the original /t/ to /θ/. The Early Modern English loss of *r* before sibilants led to such reductions as *bass* for *barse* and *ass* for *arse*. The initial consonant clusters *gn-* and *kn-* had silenced their first formant elements by the time that Shakespeare took command of the Elizabethan stage. Stressless reduction of /iŋ/ to /ɪn/ began in Early Modern English. During this period of the language the voiced alveolopalatal /ž/—the soft sibilant sound heard in such words as *azure* and *pleasure*—made its entrance into English. With that entrance the consonantal system of the language was completed.

VOCABULARY ENRICHMENT.   Because the spelling practices of Early Modern English codified at a time when the Great Vowel Shift was radically modifying its phonology, the language has achieved a cultural solidarity of the written word. Pronunciations of English vary, but a non-phonetic orthography keeps the visual morphology constant. Renaissance translations of the Bible and secular masterpieces into the "vulgar tongue" of the English people stimulated the Early Modern English vocabulary, and its consequent growth could meet the demands of Britain's expanding commercial and cultural power. Beyond the prerequisite of

genius, it is no accident that Shakespeare has the largest working vocabulary of any major English writer: he came to aesthetic flower at the
moment in the history of his language when the magic of new words
was most strongly felt.

Vocabulary enrichment was a primary task of Early Modern English—
a task represented as early as 1531 by Sir Thomas Elyot in his book *The
Governour*, the first treatise on education printed in English. In the
dedication to his king, Henry the Eighth, Elyot used the following new
terms: *devulgate, describe, attemptate, education, dedicate, esteme,* and
dispraise. As a champion of the revival of learning, Elyot symbolized the
conscious effort to make the English language use its resources in science,
religion, the arts, and exploration.

As in every age, linguistic purists opposed the wholesale entrance of
foreign terms into Early Modern English. Fine classical scholars like Sir
John Cheke, Roger Ascham, Sir Thomas Chaloner, and Thomas Wilson
objected to adulterating the native tongue by the admixture of non-in-
digenous words. In a letter preface to Sir Thomas Hoby's *The Courtier*
(1561), Cheke stated "that our own tung shold be written cleane and pure,
unmixt and unmangeled with borowing of other tunges, wherein if we
take not heed by tijm, ever borowing and never payeng, she shall be fain
to keep her house as bankrupt." The logic of banking is not applicable
to the psychological behavior of language; had Early Modern English
failed to borrow what it needed, it would have truly become bankrupt.
Yet Ascham, for one, agreed with Cheke and ridiculed what he considered the pedantry of "inkhorn" writing. Sir Thomas Chaloner, the
translater of Erasmus' *Praise of Folly* (1549), called "inkhorn" writers
"archdoltes" and "foolelosophers." The greatest scourge of "inkhorn"
borrowing and usage was Thomas Wilson, whose *Art of Rhetorique*
(1553) went through several editions in the course of the sixteenth century and was undoubtedly used as a textbook by young William Shakespeare.

Wilson excoriated "inkhorn" terms on the ground that they were obscure and given to intellectual burlesque. As an exponent of "plainnesse"
in writing, Wilson satirized words like *expending* (mentally weighing),
ingent (huge), *adepted* (attained), *ingenie* (mind or intellect), *accersited*
(brought), *adjuvate* (to aid), *adnichilate* (reduced to nothing), *condis-
ciples* (fellow students), *panion* (companion), *obtestate* (to call upon),
impetrate (to procure), *collaude* (to recommend), *invigilate* (to be watch-

ful), and *Dome* (house). In refusing these words visas, however, Wilson also tried to shut out such accepted loans as *affability, ingenious, capacity, mundane, celebrate, extol, dexterity, superiority, fertile, antique, sublimity, native, contemplate, pastoral, confidence, compendious, relinquish, frivolous*, and *verbosity*. Well-intentioned as he was, Wilson failed to reduce the vocabulary growth of Early Modern English.

A man should not try to dictate terms to his language simply because he objects to a few momentary abuses which the language will rid itself of anyway, because if the language refuses to rid itself of them they cease to be abuses. As T. S. Eliot has reminded the literary critics of the twentieth century, mature poets plagiarize; even more important for the poets is that a language in the process of vocabulary growth *steals* from other tongues.

Not only did Richard Mulcaster codify the spelling habits of Early Modern English; he also defended its right to borrow the foreign terms it needed. He understood that borrowing would introduce strangeness into the native tongue, but he predicted a swift process of assimilation: "Familiaritie and acquaintance will cause facilitie, both in matter and in words." Mulcaster's opinion was shared by many innovators in Early Modern English, who saw with DuBellay in France that both Greek and Latin had imported foreign words in order to develop their full linguistic potential. Against the charge that lexical creations based upon alien morphology were usually obscure, in *The Governour* Sir Thomas Elyot made the proud boast that "there was no terme new made by me of a latine or frenche worde, but it is there declared so playnly by one mene or other to a diligent reder that no sentence is therby made derke or harde to be understande."

George Pettie's apology for using foreign loans in his translation of Guazzo's *Civile Conversation* claimed such use "in deed the ready way to inrich our tongue, and make it copious, and it is the way which all tongues have taken to inrich them selves." Granted that enthusiasts could abuse the right to borrow from other languages and thereby create affectations, nevertheless by 1600 most literary Englishmen condemned only the abuse in borrowing, not the borrowing per se. Ben Jonson observed in *Discoveries* that "a man coins not a new word without some peril and less fruit; for if it happen to be received, the praise is but moderate; if refused, the scorn is assured." It was, therefore, not the principle of "inkhorn" terms that came to be attacked, but their obscurity from too much lexical strain. In *Pierce's Supererogation* (1593), Gabriel Harvey accused Thomas Nash of the verbal extravaganzas of *interfuseth, finicallitie, sillogistrie, disputative, hermaphrodite, declamatorie, censoriall, moralizers, unlineall usurpers of judgement, infringement to destitute the inditement.* In the subsequent "War of the Theatres," Ben Jonson blasted John Marston for his use of *retrograde, reciprocal, incubus, lubrical, defunct, magnificate, spurious, inflate, turgidous, ventosity, strenuous,* and *obstupefact.*

Since only time and the language can tell what is borrowed well, the immense borrowing that did occur proved a great advantage in developing a cosmopolitan vocabulary. John Dryden, an important figure in the creation of Modern English prose, closed out the seventeenth century with this approval of judicious importation, as stated in the dedication of his translation of the *Aeneid* (1697): "I trade both with the living and the dead, for the enrichment of our native tongue. We have enough in England to supply our necessity, but if we will have things of magnificence and splendour, we must get them by commerce." The rich vocabulary of Shakespeare was living defense of the right to borrow from other tongues.

Enrichments of the vocabulary of Early Modern English took place at an ever increasing rate during the Elizabethan Age. Nouns, adjectives, and adverbs entered the language from Latin and formed such important acquisitions as the following: *anachronism, allurement, allusion, atmosphere, autograph, capsule, denunciation, dexterity, disability, disrespect, emanation, excrescence, excursion, expectation, halo, inclemency, jurisprudence; abject, agile, appropriate, conspicuous, dexterous, expensive, external, habitual, hereditary, impersonal, insane, jocular, malignant; adapt, alienate, assassinate, benefit, consolidate, disregard, emancipate, eradicate, erupt, excavate, exert, exist, exhilarate, extinguish, harass,* and *meditate.* As with words like *anachronism, atmosphere,* and *autograph,* the borrowing was from Greek via Latin. This cognate type of appropriation included other significant additions like *antipathy, antithesis, caustic, chaos, chronology, climax, crisis, critic, dogma, emphasis, enthusiasm, epitome, parasite, parenthesis, pathetic, pneumonia, scheme, skeleton, system,* and *tactics.* Other entries into Early Modern English, from a renewed interest in and study of Greek, came direct: *acme, anonymous, catastrophe, criterion, ephemeral, heterodox, idiosyncrasy, lexicon, misanthrope, ostracize, polemic, tantalize, thermometer,* and *tonic.*

More important than the lexical penetration of Latin and Greek terms into Early Modern English were the special morphological features and semantic alterations that accompanied them. These features and alterations may be called the "peculiarities of borrowing."

Although certain Latin words entered Early Modern English in their original forms—*climax, appendix, epitome, exterior, delirium,* and *axis*—others lost their terminal morphology by a simple process of clipping. One major peculiarity of Elizabethan borrowing was the reduction of Latin endings in the adapted English word; thus *conjectural* came from *conjecturalis, consult* from *consultare, exclusion* from *exclusionem,* and *exotic* from *exoticus.* More often than not, however, the English adaptation of a Latin term involved either a modification of an ending or the direct substitution of one final cluster for another. The change of Latin *-us* to *-ous,* as in *conspicuous* is an instance of modification; the replacement of this same Latin *-us* with *-al,* as in *external,* is an example of direct substitution. In the borrowed Latin nouns, modifications prevailed: *-tas* became *-ty, -antia* became *-ance* or *-ancy,* and *-entia* became *-ence* or *-ency,* as in *celerity, consonance, concurrence, constancy,* and *frequency.* The adjective loans from Latin, on the other hand, underwent a streamlining of *-bilis* to *-ble,* in words like *considerable* and *susceptible.* Many Early Modern English verbs patterned themselves on an *-ate* remodeling of the past participle in the original Latin, for example in *create, consolidate, eradicate,* and *exterminate.*

The reintroduction of foreign terms led to semantic alterations as well. Thus *bishop* and *dish,* active Latin loans in Old English, changed to *episcopal* and *disc, dais, desk* and *discus* in Early Modern English, because they entered the language once again on the basis of their Latin morphology: *episcopus* and *discus.* In other reintroductions of Latin words into Early Modern English, the morphology remained constant but the meaning shifted. Hence it was that *intelligence* for Sir Thomas Elyot could mean an official notification, whereas for John Gower it signified the human mind. In like manner, Chaucer's astrological terms *artificial, declination,* and *hemisphere* came back into the language during the sixteenth century with their present-day meanings.

Acceptance of foreign terms develops a necessary corollary: rejection. Words that fight for currency win out over others, which ultimately drop from the language. Hence in Early Modern English the Latin *recapitulate,* for example, consigned the Greek *anacephalize* to oblivion. Similarly, *eradicate* weeded out *deruncinate.* The disappearance of *uncounsellable* is an instance of the overly intellectual word tending to die out, whereas the easier similar terms usually prevail.

Among the too learned loans that perished from Early Modern English were *adminiculation* (aid), *illecebrous* (delicately attractive), *expede* (to accomplish), *cohibit* (to restrain), and *demit* (to send away). Cognate ease, perhaps, was responsible for the replacement of *exsiccate* by *desiccate* (to dry), of *emacerate* by *emaciate*, of *discongruity* by *incongruity*, and of *appendance* by *appendage*. Clipping often made modifications that killed off the original forms; thus *caution* did away with *cautionate*, *console* got rid of *consolate*, *attempt* eliminated *attemptate*, and *denounce* replaced *denunciate*. Shakespeare's use of the poetic innovation *disquantity* in *King Lear* calls attention to the survival of such *dis-* forms as *disabuse*, *disaffect*, and *disagree*—and to the extinction of such similar morphological combinations as *disaccustom*, *disacquaint*, and *disadorn*.

Not needing an imported word often led to its ultimate loss from the language. Examples of the rejection of the unnecessary may be had in the following dropouts of the language: *exorbitate*, *approbate*, *consternate*, *aspectable* (visible), *assate* (to roast), *exolete* (faded), *suppediate* (to supply), and *temulent* (intoxicated). In the experimentation of Early Modern English several forms of the same expression often vied for supremacy. Thus the eventual emergence of *effective* and *effectual* doomed such variants as *effectuous*, *effectful*, and *effectuating*. Exactly why some words should have survived the linguistic competition while others died is one of the mysteries of English and of the psychological, rather than logical, nature of language.

During the Renaissance, the French language was experiencing a marked growth in vocabulary comparable to that taking place in Early Modern English. As a consequence, English and French adopted identical classical words, although usually in slightly different forms, at roughly the same time. Early Modern English often took from both Latin and French. In other words, French offered cognates like *prejudge* for Latin *prejudicate* and thus strengthened the English habit of borrowing from Latin. That borrowing was either direct or indirect, depending on whether French served as a linguistic intermediary. Words like *fact*, *confiscate*, *congratulate*, and *exonerate* came into Early Modern English in an immediate transfusion from Latin. Words like *consist*, *explore*, *conformation*, *conflagration*, *fidelity*, *ingenuity*, and *proclivity* may very well have entered the language intermediately via French. Other Early Modern English borrowings like *affable*, *audible*, *jovial*, *consequent*, *modest*, and *sublime* were probably from French. Since a word like *obtuse* appeared in English earlier than in French, however, similar loans obviously had to come directly from Latin.

Beyond acting as a linguistic middleman, French also set precedents. In this role, French reinforced the tendency toward vocabulary expansion, refinement, and specialization that so characterized Early Modern English. Thus the following diagram shows what was going on in Elizabethan England with regard to Latinic loans, direct and indirect:

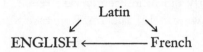

Latin

ENGLISH ←——————— French

Early Modern English borrowed words from more than fifty languages. The major sources, beyond Latin and Greek, were three Romance vernaculars, French, Italian, and Spanish. Travel on the European continent by Englishmen led to importing into Britain what objecting purists labeled as *oversea language*, a cosmopolitan trend helped along by a spirit of adventure, exploration, trade, and an eventual colonization of the New World. During the Renaissance, French adoptions poured into Early Modern English rapidly, words like *alloy, ambuscade, baluster, bigot, bizarre, bombast, chocolate, comrade, detail, duel, entrance, equip, equipage, essay, explore, genteel, mustache, naturalize, probability, progress, retrenchment, shock, surpass, talisman, ticket, tomato, vogue,* and *volunteer.*

The great cultural leadership of Italy during the Renaissance was reflected in the quality of the linguistic loans it made to Early Modern English: *algebra, argosy, balcony, cameo, caprice, cupola, design, granite, grotto, piazza, portico, stanza, stucco, trill, violin,* and *volcano.* Just as it acted as a kind of clearing house for importing Latin, so French also served as an intermediary for Italian loans into Elizabethan England: *battalion, bankrupt, bastion, brusque, brigade, carat, cavalcade, charlatan, frigate, gala, gazette, grotesque, infantry, parakeet,* and *rebuff.*

As a result of England's direct rivalry with Spain and Portugal for control of the seas and mastery of the Americas, Early Modern English brought the following Spanish and Portuguese terms into its vocabulary: *alligator, anchovy, apricot, armada, armadillo, banana, bastiment, bastinado, bilbo, bravado, brocade, barricade, cannibal, canoe, cedilla, cocoa, corral, desperado, embargo, hammock, hurricane, maize, mosquito, mulatto, negro, peccadillo, potato, renegade, rusk, sarsaparilla, sombrero, tobacco,* and *yam.* As with Italian, so with Spanish: often the Spanish loans filtered into Early Modern English via French, as seen in *grenade, palisade, escalade,* and *cavalier.*

Once in a while all three major Romance forms were enough alike that the English borrowing could have come from any or all: words like *galleon, gallery, pistol,* and *cochineal.* For the most part, however, French was importing Italian and Spanish words at an enormous rate during the Renaissance, and such Italian and Spanish terms as did not enter Early Modern English directly did so indirectly via French. Thus the main feature of Latinic borrowing held true for Romance also, as illustrated in this diagram:

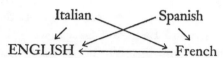

Much of the vocabulary enrichment of Early Modern English, from both classical and Romance languages, grew out of a vast dissemination of the written word. The linguistic formula for the period would be this: scholars and learned clergy plus books yields new English expressions during the Renaissance. As dignified disciples of the irrepressible John Skelton, such "Makers of English" as Sir Thomas More and Sir Thomas Elyot were responsible for many innovations in the language of the Elizabethans. It is fairly certain, for example, that More contributed the following new words to English: *absurdity, acceptance, anticipate, combustible, compatible, comprehensible, concomitance, congratulatory, contradictory, damnability, denunciation, detector, dissipate, endurable, eruditely, exact, exaggerate, exasperate, explain, extenuate, fact, frivolous, impenitent, implacable, incorporeal, indifference, insinuate, inveigh, inviolable, irrefragable, monopoly, monosyllable, necessitate, obstruction, paradox,* and *pretext.* Elyot gave Early Modern English such terms as *accommodate, adumbrate, adumbration, analogy, animate, beneficence, encyclopedia, excerpt, excogitate, excogitation, excrement, exhaust, exordium, experience* (verb), *exterminate, frugality, implacability, infrequent, inimitable, irritate, modesty,* and *placability.* But More and Elyot were only two of many scholars who were busy building the English vocabulary during the Renaissance.

Despite the lexical advantages of the enriched vocabulary of Early Modern English—the avoidance of trite morphemic repetition, the development of philosophic discourse, scientific accuracy of description, and the refinement of specialist nomenclature—the immense linguistic borrowing of the Renaissance had inherent dangers for the language. As Jespersen has demonstrated, the real psychological wealth of a language is in ideas and not in mere names. An overuse of Latinisms in the English language has fostered a mental laziness in those who pride themselves on their big and elegant diction. Academic prose is noted for the stilted and abstract quality of its classical imports; poets avoid such use of these imports, for they weaken style.

The temptation to "show off" in Latinisms is always present in Modern English, simply because the proliferation of classical adjectives in the language has led to both literary and learned stylistic usage beyond the popular. Dickens' delightful Mr. Micawber illustrates the comic tension between the upper levels and the lower when he says, "It is not an avocation of a remunerative description—in other words, it does not pay." The formation of Latinic adjectives in the language was an unnatural process that led to many morphological variants, which permit a superfluity of modifiers, as in Swinburne's "manifold multiform flower."

Vulgar misuse of the riches of the English vocabulary tends to blur the distinctions of the synonyms. The slurring of English pronunciation, on the other hand, confuses different classical forms like *emerge* and *immerge*, *illusion* and *elusion*. Such confusion on *in-* as a negative finally demanded that American gasoline trucks be labeled *flammable* so that motorists would not think them free from the possibilities of fire. Frequently difficult to interpret and undemocratic in usage, many of the classical imports that have continued to enter the language since Early Modern English are for the eye only—they have no fixed pronunciation. Seldom spoken by anyone, words like *diatribist*, *phonotypy*, *photochromy*, and *phthisis* are almost entirely literary. A flood of these classical imports has impeded the normal progress of native English morphology and washed a good deal of harmony out of the language. They accentuate class distinctions, complicate the language, hinder the spread of education to the masses, foster obscuration of statement, and encourage an overblown, turgid style.

Within a century of the period during which foreign loans were expanding the English vocabulary at such an enormous rate, the sensibility of the Age of Reason had become blind to the natural poetry of earth—primarily because its diction had got in the way of its vision. Even the Wordsworth who later inveighed against the poetic violation of the language of men was corrupted enough to let "The fragrant beverage drawn from China's herb" substitute for *tea*. This is the inherent danger of the vocabulary enrichment of Early Modern English: the language can now be used to muddy thought, conceal meaning, and separate men from one another.

Not every literary or scholarly figure in Renaissance England was eager to import foreign terms into his national language. The purist Sir John Cheke was eager to develop English equivalents for Greek and Latin loans. In his enthusiasm for native morphology, he resembled the great nineteenth-century poet-priest, Gerard Manley Hopkins. So passionately was Cheke committed to the development of basic Anglo-Saxon resources that he "improved" upon the Authorized Version of the Bible by replacing *lunatic* with *mooned, publican* with *toller, centurion* with *hundreder, prophet* with *foresayer, parable* with *byword, proselyte* with *freshman, crucified* with *crossed*, and *resurrection* with *gainrising*.

Edmund Spenser returned to the example of Chaucer and revived old words by means of poetical innovation. Under his pen, such antiquities as *astound, blameful,* and *doom* came alive again, and new terms were brought into being: *askew, filch, flout,* and *freak*. Among Spenser's coinages and fresh adaptations that have survived are *baneful, blatant, braggadocio, briny, changeful, chirrup, hapless, oaten, squall, sunshiny,* and *wolfish*. Although most of Spenser's innovations were of a rustic literary flavor and have died out, his practice helped to revive native English processes of word formation, which added such useful terms to the vocabulary as *belt, bevy, craggy, dapper, forthright, glen, glee, glance, surly, blandishment, birthright, changeling, elfin, endear, disrobe, don, enshrine, drizzling, fleecy, grovel, gaudy, gloomy, merriment, rancorous, shady, verdant, wakeful, wary,* and *witless*. Of special interest was Spenser's apparent telescoping of *screw* and *squeeze* to get *scruze*.

The growth of Early Modern English vocabulary can be seen most spectacularly, of course, in the rich energetic language of William Shakespeare. Part of Shakespeare's art is due to the lexical dynamism of the age in which it was produced. Had he been born forty or fifty years later—at the time of Milton—he would have run into the death of the Elizabethan theater and the dominance of a Puritan sensibility, and an authoritarian reason and logic would have reduced his creative powers considerably. As it was, Shakespeare enjoyed the freedom of the Renaissance, in language and in the thought that informed it. With a working vocabulary of from 20,000 to 25,000 words, roughly 10 percent of the entire lexical range of Early Modern English, Shakespeare had, proportionally, the greatest selection of words in the history of English literature. He added such new terms as *agile, allurement, antipathy, catastrophe, consonancy, critical, demonstrate, dire, discountenance, emphasis, emulate, expostulation, extract, hereditary, horrid, impertinency, meditate, modest, pathetical, prodigious, vast, ambuscado, armada, barricade, bastinado, cavalier, mutiny, palisado, pell-mell, renegade, accommodation, apostrophe, assassination, dexterously, dislocate, frugal, indistinguishable, misanthrope, obscene, pedant, premeditated, reliance,* and *submerged* to the increasing wealth of his native tongue.

Most important was Shakespeare's use of his vocabulary. He demonstrated beyond any possibility of contradiction that *poetry is idiom.* In other words, poetry is grammatical rather than lexical, for it depends more upon the combination of terms than upon the terms themselves. Syntactic is stylistic, and Shakespeare was linguistically breathtaking in his daring use of syntax to determine function. By means of functional shift, he would turn nouns into verbs and verbs into nouns, reorganize the morphological spectra of adjectives and adverbs, and make statements that even present-day transformational grammarians, for all their so-called permissiveness, tend to prescribe and proscribe as *ungrammatical.* Thus the brilliance of such imagic combinations as these:

> He childed as I father'd!   (*King Lear*, III, vii)
> And all our yesterdays have lighted fools
> The way to dusty death.   (*Macbeth*, V, v)
>   and o'er green Neptune's back
> With ships made cities. . . .   (*Antony and Cleopatra*, IV, xiv)

Such a modern prohibition as the following—*The table is today*—Shakespeare would turn into a piece of beauty, like this: *The table is today; the grave is tomorrow.*

THE RISE OF LEXICOGRAPHY.   The tremendous expansion of Early Modern English vocabulary required a lexicography that would properly list it, define it, and illustrate it. As early as 1582 Richard Mulcaster had called for the services of a master lexicographer: "It were a thing verie praiseworthie in my opinion, and no lesse profitable than praise worthie, if som one well learned and as laborious a man, wold gather all the words which we use in our English tung, whether naturall or incorporate, out of all professions, as well learned as not, into one dictionarie, and besides the right writing, which is incident to the alphabete, wold open unto us therein both their naturall force and their proper use." Mulcaster's plea was not answered until 1721, almost a century and a half later, when Nathaniel Bailey's *Universal Etymological English Dictionary* was published.

Less ambitious dictionaries, however, were produced before Bailey's exhaustive work. With Robert Cawdrey's *The Table Alphabeticall of Hard Words* in 1604, a one-hundred-twenty-page book that defined some three thousand difficult items, Early Modern English made its first serious contribution to a native lexicography. In 1616, the year of Shakespeare's death, John Bullokar, a "Doctor of Physick," published his explication of hard words in *An English Expositour*. Seven years later, when the First Folio of Shakespeare's plays appeared, Henry Cockeram brought out his *English Dictionarie*. Both Bullokar's and Cockeram's dictionaries enjoyed the popularity of several editions. By the end of Early Modern English, the field of lexicography had been joined by Thomas Blount's *Glossographia* (1656) and Edward Phillips' *New World of English Words* (1658).

GRAMMATICAL FEATURES.   In addition to replacing Latin as the language of scholarship, stabilizing orthography, and enriching vocabulary, Early Modern English achieved a refinement of style to develop a great literary heritage. Certain features of its evolution from Middle English form a sharp contrast with present-day English usage. Early Modern English was somewhat impoverished by a lack of the progressive aspect in its verb system. Thus Lady Macbeth asks her husband when *goes* Duncan hence rather than when *is* he *going* hence. Very few were the constructions like *having considered the event* and *having analyzed the outcome* in the language of the Elizabethans. On the other hand, it abounded with the impersonal use of the verb. They often said such things as *it likes me not* for *I am not pleased with*, or *it yearns me not* for *I am not eager*. Early Modern English also maintained archaic past-tense forms of the verb; Shakespeare could use *holp* for *helped* in his plays, while *brent* and *brast* often did the work of *burnt* and *burst*. The Elizabethans omitted an article where present-day English calls for one and interjected the definite article where current usage omits it. Because of this grammatical feature, Shakespeare's expressions sound odd today: *creeping like snail, with as big heart, in number of our friends, within this mile and half, in table of my heart, at the length*, and *at the last*.

Use of the negative in Early Modern English occasioned two interesting deviations from present-day idiom: syntactical positioning *before* the verb, as in *she not denies it*, and doubling the negative for psychological intensification, as in *this is not my nose neither*, or even trebling or quad-rupling it, as in *Nor never none shall mistress be of it* and *Thou hast spoken no word all this while—nor understood none neither*. Analogously, Shakespearean English made much of the double comparative and the double superlative and was consequently *more happier* with the *most un-kindest* cut of all than is twentieth-century grammar. The prepositions of Early Modern English also had a different idiomatic flavor than ours. The Elizabethans often used *in* for *at*, *of* for *from*, *on*, *upon*, *about*, *dur-ing*, *by*, *at*, *with*, *for*, and *as*. The catch-all use of *of* in Early Modern English is a symbol of the need for more explicitness in the connective system of the language.

During the Elizabethan Renaissance, English experienced grammatical refinements that were of major importance in the development of a polished literary style. In the noun, for example, the *-s* of plurality be-came the standard morphology. A few archaic weak plurals in *-n* sur-vived, as in *oxen* and the mixed forms *brethren* and *children*, some inde-terminate plurals like *sheep* and *deer* remained, and a small number of vowel-mutation plurals like *mice* and *feet* continued in use, but for the most part *-s* became the universal sign of the plural. The Early Modern English noun achieved possession by use of *-'s* in terminal positions. The apostrophe, misthought to substitute for the missing *hi* of *his*, indicated the omission of either *e*, *i*, or *y* of the Middle English genitives: *-es*, *-is*, *-ys*. The group possessive was established during the age of Shakespeare; thus *the man on the flying trapeze's dog* has come to mean *the man's* and not the *trapeze's*.

The pronouns of Early Modern English underwent three major changes: the abandoning of the terms *thou*, *thy*, and *thee*, except in formal prayer and Quaker usage; the replacement of *ye* by *you* in the nominative case; and the gradual acceptance of *its* as the genitive case of *it*. The struggle for *its* to gain universal favor in English was a long and drawn-out affair: both Shakespeare and the King James Bible used *his* as a neuter possessive, and the apostrophe'd form *it's* maintained currency until about 1800.

The emergence of *who/whom* as a relative pronoun further evolved the hypotactic syntax of Early Modern English. When Shakespeare's Iago says, "Who steals my purse steals trash," he is using *who* as an in-definite pronoun, a new construction. Using *whom* as an interrogative of an indirect question was another grammatical innovation. More important was the eventual domination of *-s* over *-eth* as the morpheme of the third person singular in the present indicative mood of the verb. During the

Elizabethan Age the *-eth* form became a literary archaism, for the *-s* form prevailed constantly in spoken discourse. Although the third-person plural form of the present indicative tolerated *-s* into the eighteenth century, the predominant morphology of this version of the verb was the zero ending. A further reduction of strong verbs to weak verbs occurred in the language of Shakespeare; verbs like *bide, crow, crowd, flay, mow, dread, sprout,* and *wade* joined the great process of regularization.

RENAISSANCE ENGLISH LITERATURE.   The chief glory of Early Modern English was the quantity and the quality of its literary production. Immediate heirs to the European Renaissance, the Protestant Reformation, the scholarship of humanism, the excitement of geographic exploration and astronomic discovery, and the democratic impact of the printing press—the Elizabethans wrote with an artistic passion that remains unexcelled in the history of the language. The contemporaries of Shakespeare were above all else imaginative, experimental, and versatile. During the six decades between the publication of *Tottel's Miscellany* (1557), one year before the accession of Elizabeth to the throne, and the appearance of the First Folio of Shakespeare's plays (1623), twenty years after the death of the "Virgin Queen," there was a flood of literary forms: songs, lyrics, sonnet sequences, long narrative poems, short stories, novels, romances, histories, theological dissertations, political tracts and pamphlets, sociological exposés, literary criticisms, and dramas.

The Elizabethan Age was an era in which the commoner became a professional writer and aristocratic arts gave way to democratic. With the national unity and harmony achieved by 1580, the second half of the reign of Elizabeth was marked by peace and stability, which nourished aesthetic accomplishment. The age thus experienced a multifarious literary development: 1) concrete realism in its narrative poetry; 2) the perfection of the lyric as a major art form; 3) the adoption of a pastoral attitude in song, prose fiction, and drama; 4) the refinement of blank verse as an instrument to convey thought and feeling in the natural rhythms of both comedy and tragedy; 5) the experimentation with the quantitative meters of the classical world; 6) the beginnings of the novel in episodic and picaresque tales; 7) a serious prose style purged of euphuistic excesses; 8) the emphasis on inductive reasoning and scientific method in the essays of Sir Francis Bacon; 9) the elevation of the common man to the role of hero; 10) the critical defense of art against the attacks of the Puritans, and of native English writing against the stifling examples of the overpraised ancients; and 11) the flourishing of the greatest drama since the Golden Age of Greece.

SUMMARY.   Early Modern English began Chaucerian and ended up Shakespearean. The language developed under the influence of the printing press, popular education, improved communications, and the growing prestige of the European vernaculars. As a recipient of the riches of the Renaissance, Early Modern English rapidly imported foreign words, experimented and innovated with its native morphology, and gradually replaced Latin as the language of scholarship in Britain. By means of both religious and secular translations, the tongue that Shakespeare spoke enhanced its cultural status, extended its vocabulary, and developed a prose style noted for simplicity and eloquence. Early Modern English fostered the rise of professional writers who, as commoners, helped to establish the literature of their country on a more democratic basis. That basis supported the finest poetry and drama in the history of the language. With the stabilization of its orthography, Early Modern English experienced a vast series of changes in pronunciation. The consonantal silencing and transmutation and the Great Vowel Shift involved in these changes assured a sharp separation between phonology and spelling. But this divorce between sound and sight maintains more advantages than liabilities.

QUESTIONS FOR RESEARCH AND DISCUSSION

1. Organize a series of reports on the various cultural impacts of the Renaissance on the development of the Early Modern English vocabulary. Concentrate on such topics as politics, religion, exploration and trade, translations, aesthetic imports, and the rise of the drama. Now write an essay on Early Modern English as the linguistic mirror of a nation in cultural ferment.

2. Conduct a panel discussion among five members of the class on the historical importance of the following Renaissance figures in the evolution of Early Modern English: John Skelton, Sir Thomas Elyot, Thomas Wilson, Richard Mulcaster, and Robert Cawdrey. What problems in the language do these men typify? Let the other members of the class write a critique on the discussion.

3. Let four members of the class do detailed research into the whole problem of "inkhorn" terms in Early Modern English. Now organize a debate on the following subject: *Learned foreign imports—to use or not to use*. With two students taking the affirmative and two the negative on this question, let the other members of the class write a summary essay

on the advantages and disadvantages inherent in the use of "inkhorn" terms in the literature of Early Modern English.

4. Organize a panel discussion among three members of the class on the development of the lyric, the sonnet, and blank verse during the evolution of Early Modern English. What are the chief characteristics in the various expressions of these three literary art forms? Who are the leading Renaissance masters of these forms? From the comparative examples in the discussion, let the other members of the class write a brief critical paper on the poetic vitality of Early Modern English.

5. Examine the same representative passage from the following translations of the Bible: the Wycliffe Bible, the Tyndale New Testament, the Coverdale Bible, the Bishops' Bible, and the King James Bible. Now write a critique on the various stylistic merits of the five versions, paying particular attention to the evolution of syntax and the refinement of stylistics in the change from Middle English to Early Modern.

6. Let three members of the class organize a panel discussion on the orthographic idiosyncracies of some of the leading cultural figures in Early Modern English. Do such peculiar spelling habits have parallels in the substandard practices of today? Be specific in your answer.

7. Organize a series of reports on the prose styles of the following masters of Early Modern English: Sir Francis Bacon, Robert Greene, John Lyly, John Milton, and Sir Philip Sidney. Now let each member of the class choose any two of the five authors mentioned and do a detailed critical comparison of their prose styles.

8. From both a knowledge of the Great Vowel Shift and a mastery of the phonemes of Early Modern English, let the entire class join in a collective project of studying the sound-pattern beauties of Shakespeare's dramatic poetry. Pay careful attention to ease of rhyme, facility for homophonic puns, and control of metaphysical values through a creative use of distinctive acoustic features. What are the chief *function* devices of Shakespeare's poetry on the phonological level? the chief *decoration* devices? Does Shakespeare seem to have any phonemic predilections or aversions? If so, what are they? From a study of representative passages from his plays, does Shakespeare's poetry support or negate the following linguistic assertion: "Early Modern English is primarily a language of intermediate compactness in the vowels, with the *schwa* serving as its most important single phoneme"? Defend your answer in detail.

9. Write a major critical essay on the outstanding attributes of Early Modern English, contrasting it with both Old and Middle English. How do you account for the enormous vitality and exuberance in the language of the Renaissance? Draw your answer from as many cultural disciplines as possible.

10. Conduct an investigation into the question of the peculiar idioms of Early Modern English. In what major ways do these Renaissance idioms differ from those of the Modern English of today? Be both specific and extensive in your answers.

SELECTED BIBLIOGRAPHY

Baugh, Albert C. *A History of the English Language.* Second Edition. New York: Appleton-Century-Crofts, 1957. See especially Chapter 8, for a study of the historical evolution and the cultural development of Early Modern English in the Renaissance (1500–1650).

Brooke, Tucker. *The Renaissance (1500–1660).* Volume II of *A Literary History of England,* edited by Albert C. Baugh. New York: Appleton-Century-Crofts, 1948. The best one-volume critical survey of the literature written in Early Modern English.

Chute, Marchette. *Shakespeare of London.* New York: E. P. Dutton Co., Everyman Paperback, 1957. A biography of England's greatest dramatist, with an account of the cultural milieu of the Renaissance.

Granville-Barker, Harley, and G. B. Harrison, eds. *A Companion to Shakespeare Studies.* New York: Doubleday, Anchor Books, 1960. A collection of fifteen essays by leading Shakespearean scholars and critics on a variety of important subjects, accompanied by a suggested reading list.

Jespersen, Otto. *Growth and Structure of the English Language.* Ninth Edition. New York: Doubleday, Anchor Books, 1955. See especially Chapter VI for a discussion of the impact of Greek and Latin upon Early Modern English; and Chapter X for a study of Shakespeare's mastery of the language of poetry.

Parrott, Thomas Marc, and Robert Hamilton Ball. *A Short View of Elizabethan Drama.* New York: Charles Scribner's Sons, Scribner Library, 1958. A critical study of the rise, development, and decline of Elizabethan drama, from its Church beginnings to the closing of the theatres in 1642, including scholarly appraisals of all the major dramatists exclusive of Shakespeare.

Pyles, Thomas. *The Origins and Development of the English Language.* New York: Harcourt, Brace & World, 1964. See Chapters VII and VIII for a discussion of the sounds and spellings, forms and syntax of Early Modern English.

Trevelyan, G. M. *History of England, Volume II: The Tudors and the Stuart Era.* New York: Doubleday, Anchor Books, 1953. See especially pp. 11–236 for an account of the political history behind Early Modern English, written in a graceful style.

CHAPTER **8**

The Structure of Early Modern English

—————⟡—————

PHONOLOGY

DURING THE RENAISSANCE RICHARD MULCASTER and the early lexicographers of the language finally stabilized the spelling practices of English. Those practices were codified when the language was undergoing changes in its pronunciation, bequeathing a non-phonetic orthography. With the addition of *j* in the seventeenth century, the English alphabet was completed. The *j* grew out of the calligraphic practice of carrying initial *i*, usually phonemically a consonant, below the line as well as above it. In addition to this graphemic refinement, *u* and *v* in Early Modern English were generally interchangeable. Derived from the Phoenician *vau* and the Greek *upsilon*, the English *u* was originally the uncial or cursive form of *v*. In the Roman alphabet, the *u* was written as *v*. The gradual preference for *v* at the beginning of a word combined with the fact that in this position the letter normally had a consonantal value to force the phonemic separation of the two symbols, wherein *u* was restricted solely to vocalic use. Before that separation, the printing practices of Early Modern English committed the *double u* to its present graphemic form of *double v: w*. As a ligature of *vv*, the *w* was an eleventh century replacement of the runic *wen*.

CONSONANTAL PHONEMES.   With the loss of /x/ in final positions, the use of /j/ in initial positions, and the introduction of /ž/, Early Modern English assumes the same consonantal phonemic system as present-day English. Far more stable than the vowels and still the backbone of the language, the twenty-four phonemic consonants of Early Modern English are as follows:

Labial
Voiceless:	/p/	pan, pie
Voiced:	/b/	ban, buy
	/m/	man, my

Labiodental
Voiceless:	/f/	fan, fie
Voiced:	/v/	van, vie

Interdental
Voiceless:	/θ/	thigh, thank
Voiced:	/ð/	than, thy

Alveolar
Voiceless:	/t/	tan, tie
	/s/	sigh, sank
Voiced:	/d/	die, dank
	/z/	zed, zeal
	/n/	Ned, nigh
	/l/	led, lank

Alveolopalatal
Voiceless:	/c/	chin, chop
	/š/	shin, shop
Voiced:	/r/	red, real
	/j/	Jed, Jo
	/ž/	Jacques, rouge

Palatal
Voiceless:	/h/	head, ho
	/k/	can, cock
Voiced:	/g/	go, get
	/y/	yank, yet

Velar
Voiced:	/ɒ/	ring, rank (thus non-initial)
	/w/	wed, wing

In isolating the consonantal phonemes listed above, we should remember that *voiceless* means *tense; voiced, lax.* We should also be cautioned about the pronunciation of the vowels in the illustrations, for they are Shakespearean in quality: "conservative" as a current Anglo-Irish brogue or the British dialects of present-day Somersetshire or Dorsetshire. Speak-

ing of things Shakespearean, note that in *King Lear*, II, ii, Kent insults
Oswald with this line:

> Thou whoreson zed! thou unnecessary letter!

Obviously Shakespeare felt the grapheme z to be virtually useless in Early
Modern English. It occurs rather sparingly even in the orthography of
today. But the phoneme /z/ continues to be indispensable in English to
express possession, plurality, and the third person singular of the indicative
mood.

VOCALIC PHONEMES.   Because of the Great Vowel Shift, the vocalic
phonemes of Early Modern English tend to be unstable and represent a
transition stage between Middle English and the language of today. This
instability and transition is maintained on the first formant element of the
tense vowels. If we interpret the Old English glide of tension /:/ as the
rough equivalent of /h/, then the exact placing of the tense vowels of
Early Modern English in the evolution of the language would look something like this:

OLD	MIDDLE	EARLY MODERN	LATE MODERN	SAMPLE WORD
/ih/	/iy/	/əy/	/ay/	I
/eh/	/ey/	/ih/	/iy/	we
/æh/	/eh/	/ey/	/iy/	clean
/uh/	/uw/	/əw/	/aw/	house
/oh/	/ow/	/uh/	/uw/	tooth
/ah/	/oh/	/ow/	/ow/	stone
/ah/	/ah/	/eh/	/ey/	name

The lax vowels of Early Modern English, on the other hand, are stable
and much like those today.

A phonemic solution for the vowels of Early Modern English, let it
be stressed, is approximate, based on a general average for the period; it
does not account for the various dialects and archaic vestiges from Middle
English. With these limitations in mind, then, we can list the vocalic
phonemes of Early Modern English as follows:

SIMPLE VOWELS		
High-Front	/i/	fit, fear
High-Central	/ɨ/	fur, sir
High-Back	/u/	foot, put
Mid-Front	/e/	pet, pear
Mid-Central	/ə/	butt, cup

SIMPLE VOWELS

Mid-Back	/o/	boat, ford (Southern England)
Low-Front	/æ/	fat, pat
Low-Central	/a/	pot, cot
Low-Back	/ɔ/	call, pall

COMPLEX VOWELS

High-Front	/ih/	reed, see
High-Central	/ɨw/	rude, sue
High-Back	/uh/	food, tooth
Mid-Front	/ey/	clean, rain
Mid-Front	/eh/	lady, name
Mid-Central	/əy/	ride, sight
Mid-Central	/əw/	house, rout
Mid-Back	/ow/	road, sow
Low-Back	/ɔy/	coin, toy

Thus Early Modern English supports seven complex vowels that must change in order to achieve the pronunciation patterns of today: /ih ɨw uh ey eh əy əw/. From these seven transitional clusters will evolve the following five current tense vowels: /iy uw ey ay aw/, all of which are narrow in articulation. Apart from these future shifts in phonology, however, Early Modern English sounds as if it were a Dublin version of its twentieth-century offspring. This strong resemblance to present-day English goes far beyond phonemics to include morphology, syntax, and grammatical transforms.

DISTINCTIVE ACOUSTIC FEATURES.   Like Old English and Middle English, Early Modern English is characterized phonologically by seven basic distinctive-feature oppositions:

1) *Vocality vs. Consonantality.* The basic contrast of syllabic/non-syllabic nuclei: the nine simple and the nine complex Early Modern English vowels in opposition to the consonants; the intermediate terms of this contrast are the nasals /m n/, the liquids /l r/, and the semivowel glides of tension /y w h/.

2) *Tension vs. Laxness.* In the Early Modern English vowels, an opposition of simple (short) phonemes against complex (long) phonemes, dependent upon the presence or absence of the glides of tension: /y w h/; in the Early Modern English consonants, an automatic distinction of voiceless (tense) vs. voiced (lax).

3) *Interruption vs. Continuance.* The Early Modern English

stops /p t c k/ and obstruents /b d j g/ in opposition to the non-impeding other consonants and the vowels.

4) *Gravity vs. Acuteness.* In Early Modern English the "muffling" of gravity, produced by long oral cavity and/or small lip aperture, is achieved in the back vowels /u uh o ow ɔ/, the labial consonants /p b m f v/, the palatal consonants /h k g ŋ/, and the velar-labial /w/; all other phonemes tend to be acute.

5) *Compactness vs. Diffuseness.* In Early Modern English the presence of a central formant region makes the low vowels /æ a ɔ/ and the back consonants /h k g ŋ w/ compact; all other phonemes in the language either are or tend to be diffuse.

6) *Nasality vs. Orality.* In Early Modern English the presence of the nasal passage as a formant region makes a basic distinction between the nasals /m n ŋ/ and the oral obstruents /b d g/.

7) *Stridency vs. Mellowness.* A simple contrast in Early Modern English between the non-muffled fricatives /s z š ž/ and the mellow interdentals /θ ð/.

From these seven fundamental oppositions, we can see that Early Modern English experiences far more centering than either Old or Middle English. The Renaissance version of the language presents greater opportunities for consonantal stridency than does either of its predecessors. Supporting more voicing than Old English, in its consonants it is less tense, hard, and guttural than its Anglo-Saxon progenitor. In contrast with Middle English, the language of Shakespeare is slightly more acute and maintains a more developed vocalic system. The following phonemic transcription (punctuated for easier reading) of Shakespeare's Sonnet 116 illustrates the sound patterns of Early Modern English:

/let mih nat tə ðə marłj əv truh məyndz
ədmit impedłmənts.   luhv iz nat luhv
hwic ɔltłrz hwen łt ɔltłrehšłn fəyndz,

łr bendz włð ðə rəmuhvłr tə rəmuhv.
ow now, łt iz ən evłr-fiksłd mark
ðət luks ən tempłsts ənd iz nevłr šehkłn;
łt iz ðə star tə evri wandrłn bark,

huwz wərθs unnown, ɔlðow łz həyt bi tehkłn.
luhvz not təymz fuhl, ðow rowzi lips ənd cihks
włðin łz bendłn silklz cumpłs cuhm;
luhv ɔltłrz nat włð łz brihf əwrz ənd wihks,

bət berz ɫt əwt ehvn tə ðə ej əv duhm.
if ðis bi erɫr ənd əpan mih pruhvd,
əy nevɫr rit, nɫr now mæn evɫr luhvd./

SOUND FEATURES OF THE POETRY.   Early Modern English poetry, so rich in mid-vowel and central-vowel assonance, returns to alliteration as a major means of decoration. In Shakespeare's work especially, alliteration is also a key to diction, as the following passage from *Othello* (IV, ii) indicates:

> Had it pleas'd Heaven
> To try me with affliction; had they rain'd
> All kinds of sores and shames on my bare head,
> Steep'd me in poverty to the very lips,
> Given to captivity me and my utmost hopes,
> I should have found in some place of my soul
> A drop of patience; but alas, to make me
> A fixed figure for the time of scorn
> To point his slow unmoving finger at!
> Yet could I bear that too, well, very well;
> But there, where I have garner'd up my heart,
> Where either I must live, or bear no life;
> The fountain from the which my current runs,
> Or else dries up; to be discarded thence!
> Or keep it as a cistern for foul toads
> To knot and gender in! Turn thy complexion there,
> Patience, thou young and rose-lipp'd cherubin,
> Ay, there look grim as hell! (47–64)

So effective is Shakespeare's decorative alliteration that each word it dictates to the poet's mind is charged with electric life; a constantly increasing current of thought and feeling flows until it creates a universe of passion between the two poles of *Heaven* and *hell*.

At least sixteen significant systems of alliteration are responsible for the overall sense of the passage: on *h, p, t, f, r, k, s, m, b, l, g, dr, w, th, n,* and all vowels and semivowels. The tension between *heart* and *head* in Othello leads him, like a serpent, into one flashing coil of language after another—until he ends up where he began, on *h:* from *Heaven* to *hell.* Note also the perfect gesture of language in *well:* from its secondary and echo meaning (a source of water) flows the superb tension and opposition between two of the most important words in the passage— *fountain* and *cistern.* At first reading, no one would predict the tremendous control of language which Shakespeare's alliteration finally indicates.

Because of the growing importance of *schwa* (ə) and *colorless i* (ɨ) and the attendant phonemic weakening in unstressed positions, a series of pronunciation changes makes Shakespeare's English easier to rhyme in than Chaucer's. English has had four major periods of rhyme: 1) Old English, with rhyme rather difficult, possible upon stressed monosyllables, and usually limited by allophonic variants; 2) Middle English, in which meaningless tags like *I gesse* pad out the lines and prove the comparative difficulty of rhyming; 3) Early Modern English, in which great rhyming ease produces a flood of strophic experiments (sonnet, sestina, *terza rima*) marked by sound-pattern decorations such as internal rhyme, alliteration, assonance, and consonance; 4) Late Modern English, in which rhyming difficulty dictates eye correspondences and terminal assonance or consonance. Early Modern English creates more exciting cadence patterns than either Old or Middle English. Nothing in *Beowulf* or the works of Chaucer can match the majestic power and flexible strength of Shakespeare's blank-verse rhythms. Thanks to an analytic syntax, the word groups of Early Modern English are sharply defined and their accompanying junctures are more clear-cut than those of Old and Middle English.

THE SUPRASEGMENTAL PHONEMES.   In the matter of superfixes, Early Modern English is like present-day English. The suprasegmental system of Shakespearean English has four degrees of stress, four heights of pitch, and four kinds of juncture—one open and three close. The language operates orally via four major contours, two terminal and two internal. The suprasegmental features of Early Modern English may be illustrated from the works of Shakespeare:

1) Stress. The four degrees of stress in Early Modern English are *maximum* (loudest): / /; *major* (next to loudest): /ʌ/; *minor* (next to softest): /ˎ/; and *minimum* (softest): /ˇ/. These four degrees of stress can be heard in Shakespeare's line:

Patience, thou young and rose-lipp'd cherubin. . . .

2) *Pitch.* The four levels of pitch in Early Modern English are *highest* (highest attention demanded): /4/; *high* (high attention demanded): /3/; *normal* (normal attention demanded): /2/; and

low (low attention demanded): /1/. These four levels of pitch operate throughout Shakespeare's plays: /3/ at most instances of maximum stress before close juncture; /2/ at the start of each new utterance and at internal close juncture bridges; /1/ as the finale of a terminal contour of the high-falling type; and /4/ at every rhetorical crescendo where maximum stress and syllabic prolongation demand the highest pitch possible, as in the following line from Henry V's St. Crispian's Day speech:

/4/
From this day to the ending of the world. . . .

3) *Juncture.* The four kinds of juncture in Early Modern English are *open* (defining morphemic and word boundaries on stressed elements): /+/; *optional internal close* (defining word-group boundaries without the written need for punctuation): /|/; *obligatory internal close* (defining phrasal and clausal boundaries with the written need for punctuation): /||/; and *obligatory terminal close* (defining sentence boundaries with the written need for punctuation): /#/. These four kinds of juncture are actualized in the following Shakespearean statements:

rose + lipp'd + cherubin ||
From this day | to the ending of the world ||
But we in it | shall be remembered ||
We few || we happy few || we band of brothers #

4) *Intonational Contours.* The four major intonational contours of Early Modern English are two terminal and two internal. The two terminal contours are *high rising* /3/ ↗ and *high falling* /3/-/1/. The high-rising contour indicates either the need to pay attention, or the registering of surprise, or the demand for an answer. This contour may be heard in Gertrude's shocked reply to Hamlet's accusation of murder:

/3/ ↗
As kill a king!

The high-falling contour, on the other hand, is the normal intonational terminal for most statements in Shakespeare's English. It marks the conclusion of Hamlet's response to his mother's stunned surprise:

/3/-/1/
Ay, lady, it was my word.

The two internal contours of Early Modern English are *normal steady* /2/-/2/ and *normal rising* /2/↗/2/. Normal steady occurs regularly with optional /|/; normal rising, with obligatory /|||/. In Renaissance English, as well as in present-day, the slight rise of the pitch at a place of internal close juncture indicates the need for some non-terminal mark of punctuation.

PHONOLOGICAL DIFFERENCES.   Despite the resemblance that Early Modern English has to the phonology of the language today, certain differences call for brief attention. The flavor of an Irish brogue in Renaissance English is unmistakable. If an Elizabethan says, "I will serve the purposes of the Queen," his speech will sound about like this:

/əy wil sarv ðə parpəsłz əv ðə kwihn/

Early Modern English is also characterized by less tension than Old or Middle English. Beyond the phonemic instability that silences some consonants, transmutes others, and completely rearranges the first formant elements of the tense vowels, the language continues the process of fronting the stress on foreign loans. The incompletion of that process in Renaissance England accounts for such accentual differences as the following: *perSEVer, deMONstrate, asPECT, charACTer, enVY,* and *welCOME.* Dynamic and uninhibited, the Elizabethans probably spoke with more rhetorical stressing, at greater pitch heights, and therefore with more syllabic prolongation, than we do.

MORPHOLOGY

EARLY MODERN ENGLISH IS PRIMARILY a word-group language. In keeping with the evolution of its analytic syntax, a further simplification of Middle English inflectional morphology occurs in four ways: the almost total disappearance of verb inflections; the reduction in the number of distinctive vowels in the principal parts of verbs; the abolition of the consonant changes that occurred earlier in many verbs; and the simple regularization of adjectives so that eleven forms in Old English become only one in Early Modern. Although *-s* and *-(e)th* are the interchangeable morphemes that indicate the third person singular of the present indicative of the verb, the *-s* is the more colloquial of the two and gradually dominates the somewhat archaic and certainly literary form -(*e*)*th*. The morphemic simplification of Early Modern English is seen in the following contrast of Chaucer's verb forms with Shakespeare's:

CHAUCER	SHAKESPEARE
I falle	I fall
he falleth	he falls
we fallen (falle)	we fall

A more dramatic instance of morphological streamlining in the verb exists in the contrast between Chaucer's *hath yronne* and Shakespeare's *has run*. But the one significant verb inflection of Early Modern English, as *spoken* in the streets of London, is -(*e*)*s*.

The reduction of distinctive vowels in the principal parts of verbs can be demonstrated in the contrast between the older forms *beran, birep, bær, bæron, boren* and the modern *bear, bears, bore, bore born;* between *bindan, band, bunden* and *bind, bound, bound;* between *berstan, bærst, burston, borsten,* and *burst, burst, burst, burst.* The abolition of the consonant changes in such older forms as *ceas/curon, snap/snidon,* and *teah/ tugon* is so universal in Early Modern English as to have only one exception, in the verb *to be: am/are, is/are,* and *was/were.* The inflectional regularization of the adjective constitutes an enormous morphological advantage for Early Modern English over Middle.

FUNCTIONAL SHIFT. Because of the great reduction in noun forms, *functional shift* is the chief contribution of Renaissance English to the morphological processes of the language. The nouns of Early Modern English achieve a similar ending for both plurality and possession: -(*e*)*s* and -'*s*. The analogy of -*s* genitives and -*s* plurals permits swift development of the group possessive. From it, the archaic construction *the kinges power of England* becomes the modern *the King of England's power.* More important is the reduction of both noun and verb forms to the same general morphology, seen in the following list of homophonic nouns and verbs:

NOUN	VERB
arm/arms	arm/arms
care/cares	care/cares
drink/drinks	drink/drinks
fire/fires	fire/fires
love/loves	love/loves
ring/rings	ring/rings

Whenever the need for a verb arises during the Renaissance and after, English usually responds by making one out of an already existing noun. Hence such verbs as *ape, awe, cook, husband, silence, time,* and *worship* enter the language. Shakespeare converts *eye, nose, lip, beard, tongue, brain, fist, breast,* and *stomach* into verbs. Other examples of this modern process include *jaw, ear, chin, shoulder, elbow, hand, finger, thumb, skin, limb, knee,* and *foot.* Similarly, Early Modern English turns a verb into a noun, a conversion made possible by dropping final -*e* from the morphology of the verb. A few of these nouns include *glance, bend, cut, fetch, hearsay, blemish, gaze, reach, drain, gather, burn, lend, dislike, frown, dissent, fawn, dismay, embrace, hatch, dip,* and *dress.* So vital is this process of functional shift in Early Modern English that it continues to this day, as the following words attest: *flutter, divide, build, haul, dive, go, hobble, lean, bid, hang, dig, find, crave, kill, blast, walk, run, lift, hop,* and *wrap.*

Many times in Early Modern English the noun and the verb are similar but not homophonic. In these instances, the noun is usually distinguished by a voiceless consonant and the verb by a voiced:

NOUN	VERB
calf /kæf/	calve /kæv/
grief /grihf/	grieve /grihv/
house /həws/	house /həwz/
use /yɫws/	use /yɫwz/

In some cases the vowel also may differ between the two forms:

NOUN	VERB
cloth /klaθ/	clothe /klowð/
life /ləyf/	live /liv/

For the most part, the voiceless-voiced distinction prevails in the morphology of Early Modern English and accounts for such later noun-verb oppositions as *bath/bathe, glass/glaze,* and *grass/graze.*

Another morphemic difference between noun and verb in Elizabethan English is that of *ch/k.* The noun is characterized by the *ch* termination and the verb by the *k:*

NOUN	VERB
speech	speak
batch	bake
stitch	stick
stench	stink
ache	ake

By the process of functional shift, the new nouns *bake, stick,* and *stink* are introduced into the language. The visual morpheme *ache* comes to dominate in both noun and verb, but the phonology of *ake* determines the pronunciation. The noun *stitch* soon gets converted to a verb.

In Early Modern English *its* emerges as the pronoun reference for the neuter, with two morphological variants, *his* and *it's.* A language of innovation and experimentation, Renaissance English is tolerant of different morphemic forms. This may be seen in the following variants from the prose passages in Shakespeare's plays, where the demands of meter do not enforce a poetic license: *thou liest/you lie, he hath/he has, thou shalt/you shall, prithee/pray you, shoon/shoes, thou desirest/you desire, methinks/I think, have wrote/have written, spoke/spoken, waked/woke.*

In company with this morphemic tolerance, the use of Latinic affixes expands greatly in Early Modern English. Shakespeare uses *disjoins, discandy, disponge, multitudinous, incarnadine, probation, impartment, celestial, beautified,* and the like. Lexical meaning tends to follow etymological derivation; thus *prevent,* even as late as the Authoritarian English of Milton, may signify its original intent: *præ* (before) + *venire* (to come). An Elizabethan can say, "My friend *prevents* me by a fortnight" and mean that his friend will precede him by two weeks. Hence we must be careful in reading the Elizabethans. Shakespeare's *rival* means *companion;* his *approve, confirm.* A brief list of Elizabethan words, together with their present meanings, demonstrates this feature of Early Modern English:

ELIZABETHAN WORD	PRESENT EQUIVALENT
avouch	proof
climatures	country
extravagant	vagrant
erring	wandering
advantage	superiority
merely	entirely
admiration	astonishment
suppliance	diversion
buttons	buds
entreatments	interviews
eager	acid
pressures	impressions

Contraction is an outstanding morphemic device in Early Modern English; in Shakespeare's plays we hear the sounds of present-day English in colloquial shortenings:

What's the matter?
Who's within!
Here's a skull now.
'Tis for the head.

Thus Early Modern English has far more bound phonemic morphemes than either Old or Middle English. Encliticizing verb auxiliaries to stressed bases is a major feature. Nor do Elizabethan contractions cease upon verb helpers. When Edgar says of Lear, "Safe scape the King," he frontally clips *escape* to a neat contraction used consistently by Shakespeare. Forms such as *e'er, e'en, o'er, 'tween, 'gainst, ha', th',* and *an'* indicate the morphemic economy in Renaissance English.

Shakespeare's use of *I'd* and *I'll* constitutes a morphological advantage for Early Modern English in both flexibility and informality. The rise of the democratic art form of the drama in Elizabethan England coincides with the *popular deformalization* of the language to achieve a *verisimilitude of expression* upon the stage. That verisimilitude shows why *'tis* is preferred to *it's* as the contraction for *it is: it's* is an acceptable possessive of *it*, even as *it* itself is.

Besides the scarcity of the progressive aspect and the compound participle, Early Modern English is characterized by special features in its morphology: double comparatives and superlatives for the adjectives and multiple negation in adverbial modification; archaic forms of the past tense and the odd omission or interjection of the definite article; the impersonal verb and strange idioms with prepositions. The emergence of *who/whom* as a new morphology for syntactical linkage is also important. When Shakespeare writes such things as *Grace me no Grace, nor Uncle me no Uncle*, he initiates a morphological process whereby nouns become *nonce* words that are converted into new verbs. This process is still active today and may be heard in the echoic accents of Thomas Wolfe's "For God's sake thimble me no thimble and spool me no spools!" in the three-o'clock revery of young George Webber. It is a dramatic means of supporting functional shift.

When the three witches in *Macbeth* decide to meet again

When the hurlyburly's done,
When the battle's lost and won

they join morphemic contraction with reduplication. The word *hurlyburly* is another sign of the morphological development of Early Modern

English. In reduplications such as *heigh ho! holla holla! ding-dong, hey-day! tirra-lyra, hey nonino, handy-dandy, hugger-mugger, how now, tut-tut, tilly-fally, rah-tah-tah, do de*, and *sessa!* Shakespeare demonstrates the inventiveness and morphological gusto of Early Modern English. In using onomatopoeia in the conventional *cock-a-diddle-dow* and the original *Come hither, come hither, come hither!* he shows why such inventiveness and gusto are responsible for an age of poetry. If Early Modern English is deficient in such later clippings as *visit* for *visitation* and is ignorant—as Jespersen indicates—of morphological refinements such as *worries, kicks*, and *moves*, its special features nevertheless support the greatest outpouring of song in the history of the language.

MORPHEMIC TYPES.   Like its predecessors, Early Modern English operates by means of three types of morphemes: *bound phonemic, bound syllabic*, and *free word simple*. The bound phonemic morphemes of the language occur as substantival and verbal inflections or as contractions attached to stressed bases. Examples of these bound phonemic morphemes of Early Modern English are:

There/z/ for thy pains.

/t/is but fortune.

I/l/ not stay a jot longer.

The warrant/s/ for yourself.

I/d/ make thee care.

Shake hand/z/.

He call/z/ to horse.

They are heretic/s/.

Falstaff sweat/s/ to death.

And my father die/d/.

I have sen/t/ to seek him.

O, I am slai/n/!

As woman/z/ love.

The wine is Jack/s/.

Early Modern English is richer in bound phonemic morphemes than is either Old or Middle English. They express such important meanings as empty verb and expletive contractions, plurality, possession, past tense, and perfective aspect.

The bound syllabic morphemes go beyond inflectional usage. As affixes of stressed bases, they form *derivatives*, and express past tense, perfective aspect, comparative and superlative form, present participle, plurality, and possession:

The ghost haunt/ɨd/ him.

He has complet/ɨd/ the work.

Something is rott/ɨn/ in the state of Denmark.

I'll go no furth/ɪr/.
The bright/ɪst/ heaven of invention.
Sleep/ɪŋ/ within mine orchard. (variant of /ɪn/)
Your Grac/ɪz/ are right welcome.
Billy Shanks/ɪz/ dog is sick.

These examples cover the bound syllabic morphemes in their inflectional usage. As formants of derivatives, bound morphemes take on lexical meaning, function in an almost unlimited range, and may act as *prefixes, suffixes,* and *bases: ab-, ad-, con-, dis-, pre-, pro-, re-, trans-; -ation, -ition, -ance, -ence, -ability, -dom, -ship; -ceive, -duce, -duct, -ject, -pel, -sist, -tort, -tract.* The few samples of these derivative formants are only an indication of the vast importance of the bound syllabic morpheme in affixing in Early Modern English.

As the minimum unit of non-bound meaning, the free word simple may appear by itself, unite with other simple words to form compounds, or serve as the base of a derivative: *man, horseman, manly.* Since compounds in Early Modern English may also attach bound syllabic morphemes to themselves, the derivatives in the language may employ any of the following as their bases:

1) A morpheme word: *girl* in *girlish.*
2) A compound: *gentleman* in *gentlemanly.*
3) Another derivative: *scornful* in *scornfulness.*
4) A bound morpheme: *-duce* in *traduce.*

Thus the various morphemic types of Early Modern English are similar to those of Late Modern.

MORPHOLOGICAL PROCESSES.   The word-formation methods in Early Modern English are more extensive, flexible, and varied than those in either Old or Middle English. Although affixing is the central morphological process of Early Modern English, the Anglo-Saxon habit of compounding revives during this period of the language and spawns such modifiers as *sharp-tooth'd, fen-suck'd, tender-hefted, dog-hearted,* and *easy-borrowed.* Such adjectival combinations give Shakespeare a distinct morphological advantage over Chaucer.

Uniting with an analytic syntax, functional shift transforms nouns into verbs, adjectives, and adverbs; verbs into nouns and verbals into adjectives; adjectives into nouns and adverbs; adverbs into adjectives, verbs, and nouns. *King Lear* boasts many shifts:

> Necessity's sharp *pinch.* (verb to noun)
> The wheel is come *full circle.* (adjective-noun to adverb)
> *Peace,* thou fiend! (noun to verb)
> *Off, off,* you lendings! (adverb to verb)

Early Modern English also employs stress modification in which homographic constructions may be distinguished as to function: *ABsent/abSENT, ACcent/acCENT, CONduct/conDUCT, FREquent/freQUENT, OBject/obJECT, PRESent/preSENT, RECord/reCORD* etc. By this process Hamlet turns an adjective into a verb and makes a piece of supreme poetry:

> Absent thee from felicity a while . . .

If Early Modern English is deficient in acronyming, clipping, back formation, telescoping, and idea naming, it is nevertheless responsible for strengthening reduplication and onomatopoeia as future methods of word-formation. Both of these processes are evident in Shakespeare's *Fie, foh,* and *fum;* "*Tu-whit, tu-who!*" In addition to the undramatic morphological processes of replacement, zeroing, internal modification, borrowing, and lengthening, most of which are inherited from Old and Middle English, in Early Modern English the idiomatic preposition emerges as directive adverb in verb phrases and noun constructions. Instances of this idiomatic usage—a direct result of functional syntax—are heard time and again in Shakespeare:

> Come *on*
> Take *up,* take *up*
> And make nothing *of*
> To spend *upon* his haters
> I am bound *to*
> As dreams are made *on*
> O Hamlet, what a falling-*off* was there!

Idiomatic usage will undergo refinement and expansion during the centuries following the Elizabethan Age, but the process is so well established in Shakespeare's day that Othello falls into a trance over the terrible difference of meaning between *with* and *on* in the context of Iago's malicious accusations:

Lie with her! lie on her! We say lie on her, when they belie her. Lie with her! 'Zounds, that's fulsome!

SYNTAX

THE SYNTAX OF EARLY MODERN English has certain major characteristics that make it operate much like the language of today. Syntactical positioning determines function: where a word appears is more important in an Elizabethan statement than in a medieval one. Early Modern English communicates via common 1–2–3–4 word order to a far greater degree than does either Old or Middle English. A reduction in inverted 2–1–3–4 word order keeps the Renaissance verb out of the opening positions in the language. In like manner, a lessening of transposed 3–1–2–4 and of transposed-inverted 3–2–1–4 removes a synthetic clumsiness from the syntax of Early Modern English. In the gradual divorce from Germanic syntax, Early Modern English ends clauses upon the verb much less than either Old or Middle English.

With further additions to the connective system of the language, Early Modern English moves from the partial parataxis of its immediate predecessor to a complete hypotaxis. In other words, subordinate relationships are shown far more clearly in the language of Shakespeare than they are in the language of Chaucer. Renaissance English enjoys a sharper defining of the word group as the basic unit of both syntax and rhythm. Within the word groups themselves, the exact disposition of various modifiers sounds archaic and out of focus to twentieth-century ears. The general features of the syntax of Early Modern English, that is, are the same as those of the present-day language, but the specific details are somewhat different.

When a gentleman in *King Lear* says of Cordelia that

> patience and sorrow strove
> Who should express her goodliest

he reveals an archaic strain in the behavior of Elizabethan syntax, for present-day usage would insert an idiomatic preposition after *strove* (probably *over*), change *Who* to *Which*, convert *goodliest* to *best*, and probably place *best* before *express*. These modifications emphasize that Early Modern English is not so rich in idiomatic verb phrases, that it uses *who* for impersonal linkage, that it retains inflectional comparatives and superlatives in the adverbial form, and that it supports different local details of syntactical positioning with the nonessentials. A critic need not object that this example is from poetry: the dramatic lines of Shakespeare are, as C. Alphonso Smith has pointed out, "unfettered by bookish impositions." The syntax of the great dramatist is natural and unstudied, "familiar, conversational, spontaneous." It is the syntax of the speaker, under the emotional pressures of the moment, not that of the formal literary essayist.

But the syntax of Shakespeare shows idiomatic differences between Early Modern English usage and the present. When Portia says to her husband,

> Dear my lord,
> Make me acquainted with your cause of grief

she demonstrates that noun word groups in Early Modern English often have an internal arrangement that appears strange by current standards. The Portia of today would address her Brutus thus: *My dear lord.* In the next scene, Caesar begins a speech with this line:

> Nor heaven nor earth have been at peace tonight.

The lack of selective concordance between subject and verb in this statement, as reflected in *have*, is not poetic license. In the *Areopagitica*, an essay scarcely noted for its poetry, Milton says: "Our faith and knowledge thrives by exercise." In the King James Bible itself, a singular verb may precede or follow a compound and plural subject: "Now abideth faith, hope, and charity, these three," "Out of the same mouth proceedeth blessing and cursing," "To comprehend what is the breadth, and length, and depth, and height," "Thine is the kingdom, and the power, and the glory," "Where moth and rust doth corrupt."

Early Modern English manifests most clearly its idiomatic differences of syntax in the archaic and literary flavor of the King James Version. The Lord's Prayer furnishes a demonstration:

> Our Father which art in heaven, Hallowed be thy name.
> Thy kingdom come. Thy will be done in earth, as it is in heaven.
> Give us this day our daily bread.
> And forgive us our debts, as we forgive our debtors.
> And lead us not into temptation, but deliver us from evil: For thine is the kingdom, and the power, and the glory, for ever. Amen.

So familiar and dear has this passage become to the average speaker of English today that its syntactical peculiarities are masked. A modern version of the prayer, faithful to the meaning of the Renaissance original, casts light upon the idiomatic differences of the King James translation:

> Our Father in heaven, may your name be made holy.
> May your kingdom come. May your will prevail on earth as it does in heaven.
> Give us our daily bread today.
> And forgive our debts, as we forgive those of our debtors.
> And do not lead us into temptation, but deliver us from evil: For the kingdom, and the power, and the glory are yours, forever. Amen.

But the eloquence—thanks to the metaphysical pathos of tradition—is on the side of the King James Version. Further evidence that language is basically psychological rather than logical.

THE WORD GROUPS.   The word groups of Early Modern English are identical with those in the present-day version. Using the plays of Shakespeare to furnish examples, the major word groups of his Renaissance English may be listed as follows:

ENDOCENTRIC

1) *Nucleus Back*
   a) Noun Word Group.
      A dull and muddy-mettled *rascal.*
      That noble and most sovereign *reason.*
      The primal eldest *curse.*
   b) Verb Word Group.
      Would *speak.*
      Will *ship.*
      Doth *hedge.*

2) *Nucleus Front*
   a) Modifier Word Group.
      As *flush* as May.
      Gross as earth.
      Incapable of her own distress.
   b) Verbal Word Group.
      To calm his rage!
      To show yourself in deed your father's son.
      Losing his wits.

ENDOCENTRIC

3) *Compound Nucleus*
   a) Noun Word Group.
      Bread and *clothes*.
      The *devil* and his *dam*.
      So high and plenteous *wit* and *invention*.
   b) Verb Word Group.
      So *shakes* and *pulls* me.
      May *live* and *be*.
      Serves and *seeks* for gain.
   c) Modifier Word Group.
      Whelk'd and *waved* like the enridged sea.
      Dower'd with our curse and *stranger'd* with our oath.
      Old and *foolish*.
   d) Verbal Word Group.
      To be or not *to be*.
      To feed and *clothe* thee.
      Bragging and *telling* her fantastical lies.

EXOCENTRIC

1) *Subject-Predicate Word Group*
   That's strange.
   He speaks well.
   I cry you mercy.

2) *Prepositional Word Group*
   On the tree.
   For them all.
   By an idiot.

SENTENCE TYPES.   The simple sentences of Early Modern English, like those of the language today, are those with no complement, those with one complement, and those with two complements. Examples of these three kinds of simple sentence are as follows:

He wakes. (no complement)

They hit us. (one complement)

She will sing the savageness out of a bear. (two complements)

The normal word order of these sentences is subject-verb, subject-verb-complement, and subject-verb-inner-complement-outer-complement. If there is an indirect object, it appears in the position of the inner complement, with the direct object in that of the outer.

Early Modern English also communicates via the complex and the compound sentences. The complex sentence supports at least one independent and one dependent clause; the compound sentence, at least two independent clauses. The following quotations from *Othello* illustrate these sentence types:

> I strike it, and it hurts my hand. (compound)
>
> If you are so fond over her iniquity, give her
>   patent to offend . . . (complex)

A union of the two types produces the compound-complex sentence:

> The King is mad; how stiff is my vile sense
> That I stand up and have ingenious feeling
> Of my huge sorrows!

The voice of blind Gloucester in *King Lear* indicates the importance of the spoken word in the greatest art form of Early Modern English. That art form thrives upon the *stichomythia* (line-for-line dialogue) of various non-declarative sentences, as determined by the terminal contours of intonation. Sentence types such as the completional, questional, equational, exclamational, interjectional, and imperitival demonstrate the syntactical maturation and the word-group flexibility of Early Modern English. When these two features join with modern suprasegmentals, they produce the breathless give-and-take of this passage from *Hamlet* (I, ii):

> HAM.   Arm'd say you?
> ALL.   Arm'd, my lord.
> HAM.   From top to toe?
> ALL.   My lord, from head to foot.
> HAM.   Then saw you not his face?
> HOR.   O, yes, my lord; he wore his beaver up.
> HAM.   What, look'd he frowningly?
> HOR.   A countenance more in sorrow than in anger.
> HAM.   Pale, or red?
> HOR.   Nay, very pale.
> HAM.   And fix'd his eyes upon you?
> HOR.   Most constantly.
> HAM.   I would I had been there.

HOR.   It would have much amaz'd you.
HAM.   Very like, very like. Stay'd it long?
HOR.   While one with moderate haste might tell a hundred.

MAR.⎱
BER. ⎰ Longer, longer.

HOR.   Not when I saw 't.

Such elliptical expressions, often misnamed incomplete sentences, are rare in the literature of Old and Middle English. They abound upon the Elizabethan stage, witnesses to the syntactical modernity of Renaissance English.

FORMAL STYLISTICS

POETRY.   With the importation of foreign subjects and techniques, the Early Modern English lyric feeds upon new strophic verse forms and a great variety of rhythmical patterns. Love sonnets, pastoral lays, street ballads, rhyming epistles, satires, and dramatic songs flourish in the Elizabethan Age. When the Italian form of the sonnet (rhyming *abbaabba cdcdcd* or *cdecde*), with its octave-and-sestet construction, is converted to the Shakespearean form (rhyming *abab cdcd efef gg*), with its three-quatrains-and-a-couplet construction, the pioneering rhymes, new scansion, and fresh accentual harmony between morphology and syntax in Sir Thomas Wyatt culminate in the verse mastery of Sir Philip Sidney and his contemporaries. In the hands of a master like John Donne, the lyric thrust of Renaissance English is changed from the simple physical to the complex metaphysical.

In the narrative, the romance gradually declines until it is taken over completely by prose and becomes the forerunner of the native English novel. At the same time, elaborate allegory rises to epic height in the *Fairie Queene* of Edmund Spenser. Spenser invents the verse form that bears his name, a nine-line stanza of iambic pentameter, rhyming *ababbcbcc*, with the ninth line a six-accented alexandrine that is used to advantage by the Romantics in the early nineteenth century. The narrative also supplies another poetic form to the aesthetic resources of Early Modern English: the blank verse of Henry Howard, Earl of Surrey, as introduced by his translations from the *Aeneid*. Reaching three or four peaks of intensity with Christopher Marlowe, the blank-verse line becomes the supreme artistic vehicle for the genius of both Shakespeare and Milton.

As distinct from the dramatic, both the lyric and the narrative poetry of Renaissance English are aristocratic in content and tone—a fact seen in the following examples:

LYRIC

a) Lush Conventional Love Sonnet. From *Astrophel and Stella* by Sir Philip Sidney (c. 1580), 3:

Let dainty wits cry on the Sisters nine,
That, bravely masked, their fancies may be told;
Or Pindar's apes flaunt in their phrases fine,
Enam'ling with pied flowers their thoughts of gold;
Or else let them in stately glory shine,
Ennobling new-found tropes with problems old;
Or with strange similes enrich each line,
Of herbs or beasts which Inde or Afric hold.
For me, in sooth, no Muse but one I know;
Phrases and problems from my reach do grow
And strange things cost too dear for my poor sprites:
How then? even thus,—in Stella's face I read
What Love and Beauty be; then all my deed
But copying is, what in her Nature writes.

b) Agonized Original Sonnet. From *Holy Sonnets,* by John Donne (c. 1615), 14:

Batter my heart, three person'd God; for, you
As yet but knocke, breathe, shine, and seeke to mend;
That I may rise, and stand, o'erthrow mee, and bend
Your force, to breake, blowe, burn, and make me new.
I, like an usurpt towne, to another due,
Labour to admit you, but Oh, to no end,
Reason your viceroy in mee, mee should defend,
But is captiv'd, and proves weake or untrue.
Yet dearely I love you, and would be loved faine,
But am betroth'd unto your enemie:
Divorce mee, untie, or breake that knot againe,
Take me to you, imprison mee, for I
Except you enthrall mee, never shall be free,
Nor ever chast, except you ravish mee.

NARRATIVE

a) Elaborate Allegory in Spenserian Stanza. From Canto IV of *The Fairie Queene,* by Edmund Spenser (c. 1590):

Young knight, whatever that dost armes professe,
And through long labours huntest after fame,
Beware of fraud, beware of fickelnesse,
In choice, and change of thy deare loved Dame,
Least thou of her beleeve too lightly blame,
And rash misweening doe thy hart remove:
For unto knight there is no greater shame,
Then lightnesse and inconstancie in love;
That doth this *Redcrosse* knights ensample plainly prove.

b) Tragic Romance in Heroic Couplet. From the Second
   Sestiad of *Hero and Leander*, by Christopher Marlowe
   (c. 1593):

"O Hero, Hero!" thus he cried full oft;
And then he got him to a rock aloft,
Where having spied her tower, long star'd he on't,
And pray'd the narrow toiling Hellespont
To part in twain, that he might come and go;
But still the rising billows answer'd, "No."
With that, he stripp'd him to the ivory skin,
And, crying, "Love, I come," leap'd lively in:
Whereat the sapphire-visag'd god grew proud,
And made his capering Triton sound aloud,
Imagining that Ganymede, displeas'd,
Had left the heavens; therefore on him seiz'd.
Leander striv'd; the waves about him wound,
And pull'd him to the bottom, where the ground
Was strew'd with pearl, and in low coral groves
Sweet singing mermaids sported with their loves
On heaps of heavy gold, and took great pleasure
To spurn in careless sort the shipwreck treasure;
For here the stately azure palace stood,
Where kingly Neptune and his train abode. . . .

DRAMA.   The chief artistic glory of Early Modern English is its drama.
Drawing upon the examples of Plautus and Terence in comedy and of
Seneca in tragedy, Elizabethan drama moves from the melodramatic and
the religiously two-dimensional, to the secular serious and comic
three-dimensional. The plays of Early Modern English are seminal in
their realism, psychological depth, symbolic overtones, and social judgment. The Shakespearean stage spawns a bewildering variety of dramatic
genres, summed up in the words of Polonius (*Hamlet*, II, ii): "Tragedy,
comedy, history, pastoral, pastoral-comical, historical-pastoral, tragical-

historical, tragical-comical-historical-pastoral; scene individable, or poem unlimited." Constantly available to the people, and the great intellectual leaven of society, Elizabethan drama exercises the "mightly line" of blank verse until it becomes the fit instrument for the genius of Shakespeare.

That genius endows English with the richest literary heritage of all time—a heritage characterized by a masterly choice of diction, an exciting variety of themes, an objective reticence in religion, a brilliant adaptation of language to suit the needs of character and situation, a mature pruning of poetic excesses and provincialisms, a bold use of metaphor and imagery, a continual process of innovation in usage, a sharp acceleration of the acceptance of colloquialisms, a close approximation of the grammar of poetry with the grammar of prose, and a constant reminder that the spoken word of oral tradition is the vital formant of the highest literary expression. So magnificent is the artistic legacy of Shakespeare's Early Modern English that its finest prose often far exceeds the eloquence of the poetry of later periods, a fact demonstrable in Mistress Quickly's account of the death of Falstaff in *Henry V* (II, iii):

> Nay, sure he's not in hell: he's in Arthur's bosom, if ever man went to Arthur's bosom. 'A made a finer end and went away an it had been any christom child: 'a parted even just between twelve and one, even at the turning o' th' tide: for after I saw him fumble with the sheets, and play with flowers, and smile upon his fingers' ends, I knew there was but one way; for his nose was as sharp as a pen, and 'a babbled of green fields. "How now, Sir John!" quoth I; "what, man! be o' good cheer." So 'a cried out, "God, God, God!" three or four times: now I, to comfort him, bid him 'a should not think of God; I hoped there was no need to trouble himself with any such thoughts yet. So 'a bade me lay more clothes on his feet: I put my hand into the bed and felt them, and they were as cold as any stone; then I felt to his knees, and so upward and upward, and all was as cold as any stone.

PROSE.   Not all the prose of Early Modern English is a match for the sublime simplicity of Mistress Quickly's report, for the greatest poet of England is also its greatest prose writer. But Shakespeare aside, Early Modern English prose is marked by flexibility and exuberance. Experimental and innovating, it errs from excess rather than from lack. Overly poetic upon occasion, as in the euphuistic vein, it is gradually pruned of elaborate decoration into sobriety, clarity, and functional beauty. In its finest moments, it is unsurpassed in economy of means to ends, sensuous power, and cadential majesty.

The following samples of Early Modern English prose styles serve as a brief history of its evolution:

Historical Chronicle. From "Macbeth and the Weird Sisters," *Chronicles of England, Scotland, and Ireland*, by Ralph Holinshed (c. 1577):

> Shortly after happened a strange and uncouth wonder, which afterward was the cause of much trouble in the realm of Scotland, as ye shall after hear. It fortuned as Macbeth and Banquo journeyed towards Fores, where the king then lay, they went sporting by the way together without other company, save only themselves, passing through the woods and fields, when suddenly in the midst of a land, there met them three women in strange and wild apparel, resembling creatures of elder world, whom when they attentively beheld, wondering much at the sight, the first of them spake and said: "All hail Macbeth, thane of Glammis" (for he had lately entered into that dignity and office by the death of his father Sinell). The second of them said: "Hail Macbeth, thane of Cawdor." But the third said: "All hail Macbeth, that hereafter shalt be king of Scotland."

Decorative Poetic Romance. From *Euphues, The Anatomy of Wit*, by John Lyly (1578):

> Here shalt thou behold, as it were in a glass, that all the glory of man is as the grass; all things under heaven are but vain; that our life is but a shadow, a warfare, a pilgrimage, a vapor, a bubble, a blast; of such shortness that David saith it is but a span long; of such sharpness that Job noteth it replenished with all miseries; of such uncertainty that we are no sooner born but we are subject to death; the one foot no sooner on the ground but the other ready to slip into the grave. Here shalt thou find ease for thy burden of sin, comfort for the conscience pined with vanity, mercy for thine offences by the martyrdom of thy sweet Savior . . . .

Literary Criticism. From *The Defense of Poesie*, by Sir Philip Sidney (c. 1583):

> Chaucer, undoubtedly, did excellently in his *Troilus and Criseyde;* of whom, truly, I know not whether to marvel more, either that he in that misty time could see so clearly, or that we in this clear age go so stumblingly after him. Yet had he great wants, fit to be forgiven in so reverend antiquity. I account the *Mirror for Magistrates* meetly furnished of beautiful parts. And in the Earl of Surrey's lyrics, many

things tasting of a noble birth, and worthy of a noble mind. The *Shepherd's Calendar* hath much poetry in its eclogues, indeed, worthy the reading, if I be not deceived. That same framing of its style to an old rustic language, I dare not allow; since neither Theocritus in Greek, Virgil in Latin, nor Sannazaro in Italian, did affect it. . . .

Formal Essay. From "Of Studies," *Essays*, by Francis Bacon (1625):

Some books are to be tasted, others to be swallowed, and some few to be chewed and digested: that is, some books are to be read only in parts; others to be read, but not curiously; and some few to be read wholly, and with diligence and attention. Some books also may be read by deputy, and extracts made of them by others; but that would be only in the less important arguments, and the meaner sort of books: else distilled books are like common distilled waters, flashy things. Reading maketh a full man; conference a ready man; and writing an exact man. And therefore if a man write little, he had need have a great memory; if he confer little, he had need have a present wit; and if he read little, he had need have much cunning, to seem to know what he doth not. Histories make men wise; poets, witty; the mathematics, subtile; natural philosophy, deep; moral, grave; logic and rhetoric, able to contend. . . .

QUESTIONS FOR RESEARCH AND DISCUSSION

1. Phonemicize the famous third soliloquy from *Hamlet*, beginning with "To be or not to be," both as Shakespeare would have pronounced it and as a modern actor like Sir Laurence Olivier pronounces it today. What are the major differences in the phonology of Early Modern English and of the current version of the language? Be specific in your answer.

2. Organize a panel discussion among four members of the class on the rhyming habits of Chaucer and Shakespeare. Concentrate on the personal predilections of both and on the phonemic resources of Middle and Early Modern English. From this discussion, write a critique on the subject.

3. Organize another panel discussion among four members of the class on the rhythmical patterns in Chaucer's poetry and prose and in Shakespeare's poetry and prose. What are the major differences in the cadence units, suprasegmental features, and the rhythms in the work of these two great authors? Does Shakespeare's Early Modern English give him any rhythmical advantages over Chaucer? Does Chaucer's Middle English give him any rhythmical advantages over Shakespeare? Write a critical essay to answer these last two questions in detail.

4. Investigate the peculiar accent patterns of Early Modern English, based upon the poetry of Elizabethan drama. What are the major differences in the pronunciation stresses of polysyllabic terms in Early Modern English and in our language today? Using the many examples that this project has revealed, now write a critical paper on *the fronting of stress on foreign loans since the Elizabethan Age*.

5. Contrasting the language of Shakespeare with Chaucer's, write a major essay on the subject of *morphemic simplification in Early Modern English*. Pay particular attention to verbs and adjectives.

6. Let five members of the class each choose a different act of *King Lear* and study it for examples of functional shift. From these five separate reports, write a paper in support of the following observation: "Poetry comes into being at the moment when words (morphological essence) become deeds (syntactical function)." How well does Shakespeare illustrate this statement? Be specific and detailed in your answer.

7. Let ten members of the class each draw up a list of twenty-five different words from Shakespeare's plays that do not mean what they appear to in present-day semantics. Then let each member report his findings to the class in a mimeographed list of the terms and their Elizabethan definitions. Now write a critical paper, using the two hundred and fifty examples as primary evidence, on the subject of *the semantic evolution from Early Modern to Late Modern English*.

8. Organize a panel discussion among five members of the class on the morphological contractions in the plays of Shakespeare, Kyd, Marlowe, Jonson, and Beaumont and Fletcher. What are the major differences in this stylistic habit among the various playwrights of Early Modern English? Who is the most daring in his use of contractions? the most conservative? Does Shakespeare show any aesthetic advantages in originality or dramatic propriety in his use of contractions? Be specific in your answers.

9. Let five members of the class investigate the use of the idiomatic directive in the plays of Shakespeare, Kyd, Marlowe, Jonson, and Beaumont and Fletcher. Now let these same students conduct their own panel discussion on the leading idioms of this kind in Early Modern English, how they are used, and which playwright(s) seem(s) to be the master in his aesthetic control of them. What are the major differences in meaning between the idiomatic directives of Early Modern English and of those of the language as it is spoken today? Defend your answer with detailed examples.

10. Contrast the word order of the King James Version of the Bible with that of the Revised Standard Version and with that of the New English Bible. Which of these two twentieth-century versions is closer to the

prose stylistics of Early Modern English? Be specific and detailed in your answer. What are the major differences between the syntax of the King James Version and the more idiomatically contemporary of the two modern versions? Illustrate your answer with parallel examples.

11. From your study of Question 10, now write an essay on the need for each generation to make its own translation of the Bible or of any other literary masterpiece in a foreign tongue. Great as the King James Version is, it still has defects for the sensibility of contemporary man. What are some of these defects? Be specific in your answer.

SELECTED BIBLIOGRAPHY

Bloomfield, Morton W., and Leonard Newmark. *A Linguistic Introduction to the History of English.* New York: Alfred A. Knopf, 1963. See especially Chapter VI for a study of Early Modern English, from phonology to grammar, with special emphasis on the phrase-structure and transformation rules of the language of the Renaissance.

Bryant, Margaret M. *Modern English and Its Heritage.* Second Edition. New York: The Macmillan Company, 1962. See especially pp. 192–204 for a concise account of the phonology of Early Modern English, as determined by the Great Vowel Shift.

Ford, Boris, ed. *The Age of Shakespeare.* Volume 2 of *The Pelican Guide to English Literature.* Baltimore: Penguin Books, 1963. A fine collection of nineteen essays on various topics dealing with the English Renaissance, from social setting to literary achievements, all written by leading authorities in the period.

Kökeritz, Helge. *Shakespeare's Pronunciation.* New Haven: Yale University Press, 1953. A classic study in the phonology of Early Modern English.

Parrott, Thomas Marc. *William Shakespeare: A Handbook.* Revised Edition. New York: Charles Scribner's Sons, Scribner Library, 1955. A one-volume account of Shakespeare's life and times, his works and performers, with metrical statistics, chronological table, and selected bibliographies.

Robertson, Stuart, and Frederic G. Cassidy. *The Development of Modern English.* Second Edition. Englewood Cliffs, New Jersey: Prentice-Hall, 1954. See especially Chapters 7, 8, and 10 for scholarly discussions of the vocabulary, morphology, syntax, and usage of Early Modern English.

CHAPTER 9

Authoritarian English
1650-1800

❧

IMPORTANT DATES

1653-1659 Protectorates of Oliver and Richard Cromwell, symbols of Puritan domination in all things, including the English language.

1664 The Royal Society appoints a committee to "improve" English.

1667 Publication of John Milton's epic poem *Paradise Lost*, highest achievement in English literary baroque, source of authoritarian example, and heavily Latinic in influence.

1668 John Dryden's *Essay of Dramatic Poesy* initiates modern English criticism and is an important document in the development of a formal prose style.

1678-1684 John Bunyan publishes his masterpiece *The Pilgrim's Progress*, an allegorical forerunner of the English novel.

1679 In the Dedication to his *Troilus and Cressida*, John Dryden calls for "rules and standards" in the English language.

1688-1744 The life of Alexander Pope, finest satiric poet of Authoritarian English and a leading voice in the neoclassical aesthetics of the Age of Reason.

1697 In his *Essay Upon Projects*, Daniel Defoe calls for an Academy of thirty-six "gentlemen" to dictate English usage.

1712   In a letter to the Earl of Oxford, Jonathan Swift proposes an English Academy to correct, improve, and "ascertain" the language.

1721   Nathaniel Bailey publishes his *Universal Etymological Dictionary of the English Language,* a pioneer book in English lexicography: the first to feature current usage, etymology, syllabification, clarifying quotations, illustrations, and indications of pronunciation.

1726   Publication of Jonathan Swift's *Gulliver's Travels,* the supreme mythic satire of Authoritarian English.

1727   The death of Sir Isaac Newton symbolizes the impact of modern science on the growing vocabulary of English.

1740–1771   The English novel becomes a mature art form in the works of Samuel Richardson, Henry Fielding, Tobias Smollett, and Laurence Sterne.

1755   Samuel Johnson publishes his *A Dictionary of the English Language,* the authority on "correctness" that dominates English letters for more than a century.

1757   The British conquest of India: colonial expansion enriches the English language.

1759   British General James Wolfe defeats the French at the Battle of Quebec to further the growth of an empire, the source of the development of several major versions of English.

1760–1795   This thirty-five-year span marks the rise of the English grammarians and rhetoricians, whose prescriptions and proscriptions are still current in the handbooks: Joseph Priestly, Robert Lowth, James Buchanan, John Ash, Thomas Sheridan, George Campbell, William Ward, and Lindley Murray.

1775–1783   The American Revolution leads to the independent evolution of a colonial English into a national version of the language.

1783   The invention of the steam engine by James Watt begins the Industrial Revolution, which exercises an enormous influence on English.

1789–1799   The French Revolution and the rise of Napoleon put an end to the aristocratic world that has supported Authoritarian English.

1798   The publication of *Lyrical Ballads,* by William Wordsworth and Samuel Taylor Coleridge, marks the demise of the neoclassical aesthetics of Authoritarian English and introduces Romanticism into the literary efforts of Mature Modern English.

OUTSTANDING PERSONS

Joseph Addison (1672–1719) and Sir Richard Steele (1672–1729) Two champions of the rise of the periodical essay in Authoritarian English.

Nathaniel Bailey (d. 1742) Pioneer lexicographer and a founder of English etymological study.

James Boswell (1740–1795) Fountainhead of great English biography (*The Life of Samuel Johnson L.L.D.*, 1791) and a master of realistic details.

John Bunyan (1628–1688) Champion of "oral" prose and father of modern colloquial style.

Daniel Defoe (1659–1731) Outstanding pamphleteer of Authoritarian English and an early developer of the English novel in the form of rogue biography.

John Dryden (1631–1700) A perfecter of modern formal prose style and father of English literary criticism.

Henry Fielding (1707–1754) Chief aesthetician of the novel as a dignified art form and, in *Tom Jones* at least, the modern equivalent of the epic poem.

Samuel Johnson (1709–1784) Supreme lexicographer, literary critic, and arbiter of taste in Authoritarian English.

John Milton (1608–1674) Greatest poet of Authoritarian English and user of a ponderously Latinic prose style.

Alexander Pope (1688–1744) Master of the heroic couplet and the soul of satire in Authoritarian English.

Joseph Priestly (1733–1804) Champion of the doctrine of usage as the authority on correctness in English.

Samuel Richardson (1689–1761) Founder of the mature full-length English novel.

Tobias Smollett (1721–1771) Master of the picaresque in the English novel.

Laurence Sterne (1713–1768) Father of impressionism in the English novel.

Jonathan Swift (1667–1745) Finest prose stylist of Authoritarian English and yet the epitome of a conservative drive to purify and codify the language.

William Ward (fl. 1765) The first grammarian to draw up the complete set of prescriptions and proscriptions (*Grammar of the English Language*, 1765) that dominate even the handbooks of today.

MAJOR ATTRIBUTES OF THE LANGUAGE

Suffers the doctrine of "correctness" as the ideal, enforced by an authoritarian sense of order, regulation, and conforming to a standard.

Often imitative, derivative, falsely elegant, and snobbish in its aristocratic expressions.

Is codified by means of dictionaries and grammars.

Undergoes a divorce between spoken and written usage, intensified by emphasis on the proscriptions of logic and authority.

Experiences an immense vocabulary growth from all parts of the British Empire to become cosmopolitan in character.

Completes the Great Vowel Shift of Early Modern English.

Further refines the idiomatic structures and word-group patterns of an analytic syntax.

Develops a verb system of the progressive tenses, imperfect aspect, both active and passive.

Develops emphatic verb forms with the help of *do* and its morphological variants.

Modernizes the participial constructions of Renaissance English.

Is used by purists as a badge of social distinction: the start of class warfare in the English language.

THE HISTORY OF AUTHORITARIAN ENGLISH

FROM THE MIDDLE OF THE seventeenth century to the beginning of the nineteenth, English suffered a shift in the attitude of its educated speakers that can be called *authoritarian*. Gone was the gusto and the unselfconscious freedom of the Renaissance. With a diminished flexibility in speaking and writing, there arose a school tradition of prescriptive and proscriptive "rules" that hampered natural behavior in the language. Neoclassicism in literature resulted in satire, cold imitation of the ancients, stilted poetic diction, and a sharp separation from the vitality of the spoken word. With order and restraint prevailing in the Age of Reason, it was no accident that the greatest Englishman of this inhibited period of the language was Sir Isaac Newton (1642–1727), not a subjective artist but an objective scientist.

The shift from an era dominated by Shakespeare to one dominated by Newton is significant, for it indicates the gradual loss of the influence of poetry in the daily life of a nation. The novel became the popular form of literature. Authoritarian English, defined in dictionaries and regularized in grammars, was basically a language of prose. The major influences of Authoritarian English were a Puritan aesthetics; the authoritarian attitudes of a static society; the use of logic and classical example upon linguistic behavior; the codification of the language in dictionaries and grammars; the refinement of a literary prose style; the rise of the novel as the democratic equivalent of the Elizabethan drama; the impact of science upon the methods of research and the specialist terminologies of English; the expansion of the vocabulary attendant upon the global extension of the British Empire; the growth of Romanticism; and the Industrial Revolution.

THE IDEAL OF "CORRECTNESS."   In 1606 the Puritans prevailed upon the English Parliament to enact a law forbidding the use of profanity on the stage. It officially began the proscription of the social behavior of language. During the protectorates of the Cromwells, the theater itself was proscribed. With the Restoration of the monarchy in the person of Charles II in 1660, the French picture-frame stage dominated the English plays, and in the language what was once puritan had become purist. The purism of the Renaissance humanists had eliminated Latin as the international language of scholars, simply because that purism lamented the corruption of Latin by the medieval Scholastics and insisted on a return to the classical styles of Cicero and Virgil. That these styles were more difficult in construction and further removed from the linguistic habits of the European vernaculars made no difference to those obsessed with the erroneous notion of corruption. The notion, unfortunately, spread to include the vernaculars.

In the Age of Reason, intellectual leaders like Jonathan Swift believed passionately that ignorance and lack of taste were undermining the English language. Something must be done to arrest the process of decay in the native tongue—thus reasoned the English purists, who in their appeal to authority in usage turned to classical Latin for grammatical rules held to be universally applicable and eternally true. "Correctness" became the ideal of Authoritarian English. In the eighteenth century this ideal was to foster the methods of *ascertainment* that would reduce the language to rules, establish a standard of usage, eliminate the defects of ignorant corruption, and fix permanently a rational and polished form of the mother tongue.

What the purists mistook for "correctness," however, was a mixture of Latin grammar, poorly applied logic, and prejudice. They failed to realize that all living languages are subject to constant change. Desire for social graces on the part of a rising bourgeoisie united with a weakening landed aristocracy to demand class distinctions in language. The French Academy joined forces with a primitive psychological belief in the fixed nature of man and consequently in his language. The result was that soon after the founding of the Royal Society (1662), the voices of authority began to demand an ideal of correctness in English.

Among the most outspoken and prestigious of these voices were John Dryden, John Evelyn, Daniel Defoe, Jonathan Swift, and Thomas Cooke. As early as 1664, in the Dedication of the *Rival Ladies,* John Dryden lamented the fact that English was not so well measured as French and that his native land did not have an Academy to do the proper measuring. In the committee appointed by the Royal Society (in December of that same year) to "improve" the English language, Dryden was the moving spirit.

Such a snobbish classicist was Dryden that he often wrote his ideas in Latin and then translated them into English to give them more elegance and refinement. In his attempt to impose the dictates of an Academy on the democratic tradition of the language, Dryden was doomed to defeat. His desire to see the language written with the same "certainty of words and purity of phrase" as Italian and French was out of step with linguistic fact, for nothing in either literature has ever surpassed the masterpieces of his immediate predecessors the Elizabethans. But in his plea for rules and standards in English, Dryden revealed basic codification needs: an adequate dictionary, a sensible grammar, and a native system of prosodic analysis.

John Evelyn, a fellow member of the committee to improve English, believed that translations yield elegance in style. He was in favor of several major projects: a grammar of the language, a thorough reform of its spelling practices, a dictionary of "all the pure English words by themselves," and similar lexicons for derivations, symbolical terms, technical words, exotic words, dialect variants, and archaisms.

In his *Essay upon Projects* (1697), Daniel Defoe proposed an Academy of thirty-six "gentlemen"—twelve noble, twelve private, and twelve chosen by merit—to act as the arbiter of correctness in the language. With "liberty to correct and censure the exorbitance of writers," these thirty-six judges would assure a purity of style and diction. Defoe delighted in the fact that under the authority of such an Academy "it would be as criminal then to coin words as money." He obviously was not thinking of what crime he might be committing against either human rights or linguistic truth.

Nor was Jonathan Swift when he wrote his letter to the Earl of Oxford, then Lord Treasurer of England (1712), published later as *A Proposal for Correcting, Improving, and Ascertaining the English Tongue*. In this letter and in other writings like it, Swift showed himself to be a conservative, indeed a reactionary, in language. Objecting to such morphological processes as clipping and functional shift, the author of *Gulliver's Travels* opposed all change and every innovation in English. In seeking to reform the native tongue, Swift above all else desired to see it permanently "fixed," rid of "gross improprieties." But like Dryden before him, Swift failed to establish the Academy that was supposed to do the fixing.

By 1729 Thomas Cooke saw that an Academy was out of the question, but he was not deterred from publishing his "Proposals for Perfecting the English Language." In these "Proposals," Cooke suggested the weak regularization of all strong verbs, the formation of noun plurals by the standard morphology of -s and -es, and the formation of the comparative and the superlative forms of adjectives with the use of *more* and *most* alone.

LEXICOGRAPHY.   By the start of the eighteenth century, there was still no adequate dictionary to codify the lexical features of English. There had been, for Old English, Anglo-Saxon glosses on hard Latin terms, usually those from the Scriptures. By 1400 these isolated glosses were collected into a primitive Latin-English dictionary known as a *glossarium*. A century later Wynkyn de Worde printed the first dictionary of any kind in England: a redaction of the glossarium once known as *Medulla Grammatica,* but which appeared under the title *Promptorium Parvulorum sive Clericorum.*

In the following century foreign-language dictionaries were published: French-English, Welsh-English, Spanish-English, and Italian-English. With the influx of "inkhorn terms" during the sixteenth century, there arose the need for the "Dictionary of Hard Words," which became the real predecessor of modern lexicography in English. Men like Cawdrey, Bullokar, Cockeram, and Phillips supplied the impetus to a scholarly process that was to go far beyond explaining difficult terms and making efforts to reform the spelling habits of the language. With the publication of Thomas Blount's *Glossographia* in 1658, etymologies appeared for the first time in an English dictionary. Fifty years later, in 1708, Thomas Kersey's *Dictionarium Anglo-Brittanicum* explained legal terms, provincialisms, and archaisms, thus exerting the new influence of literary usage on English lexicography.

The standard of purity championed by Swift, Addison, and Steele demanded a codification of the linguistic changes of the age. In 1721 Nathanial Bailey published his *Universal Etymological Dictionary of the English Language,* followed ten years later by a handsome illustrated folio edition. Embodying many of the linguistic ideals of the Age of Reason, Bailey's dictionary was a revolutionary book. In the words of Harold Whitehall, it was "the first to pay proper attention to current usage, the first to feature etymology, the first to give aid in syllabification, the first to give illustrative quotations (chiefly from proverbs), the first to include illustrations, and the first to indicate pronunciation." Bailey's influence on Samuel Johnson was profound and became the basis for the future course of English dictionary-making.

DR. JOHNSON'S DICTIONARY.   In 1755 Samuel Johnson published his famous two-volume monument to eighteenth-century English: *A Dictionary of the English Language.* A great achievement for one man, who labored almost unaided for the brief period of eight years, the *Dictionary* revised Bailey's somewhat crude etymologies, made systematic use of quotations to illustrate usage, fixed the spelling of many troublesome words, developed a discriminating method of definition, and showed the range of the English vocabulary better than ever before. These were no mean accomplishments for Johnson, who had announced in his 1747 prospectus *The Plan of an English Dictionary* that his main purpose was fourfold: to fix pronunciations, to preserve the purity of the language, to ascertain its usage, and to lengthen its duration. Yet the man who had assumed the role of a nonexistent Academy had his idiosyncrasies and personal foibles, and these led to flaws in the work itself.

Judged by the standards of modern linguistics, as Baugh has said, the *Dictionary* was "painfully inadequate." What foolish etymologies did not mar in the work, personal prejudice and caprice often did. The definitions at times were truly Johnsonian—either heavily Latinic and obfuscating or simply whimsical and inaccurate. A few of Dr. Johnson's most delightful definitions may be listed as follows:

> *Cough:* A convulsion of the lungs, vellicated by some sharp serosity.
>
> *Excise:* A hateful tax levied upon commodities, and adjudged not by the common judges of property, but by wretches hired by those to whom Excise is paid.
>
> *Grub-street:* The name of a street in London, much inhabited by writers of small histories, *dictionaries*, and temporary poems; whence, any mean production is called *Grub-street*.
>
> *Lexicographer:* A writer of dictionaries, a *harmless drudge*.
>
> *Network:* Any thing reticulated or decussated, at equal distances, with interstices between the intersections.
>
> *Oats:* A grain given in England to horses and in Scotland to the people.
>
> *Pension:* An allowance made to anyone without equivalent. In England it is generally understood to mean pay given to a state hireling for treason to his country.

Amusing as these definitions are, they emphasize the flaws in Johnson's *Dictionary*. Johnson also had a penchant for including terms that Noah Webster rightly felt were not really English—for example: *denominable, opiniatry, ariolation, assation, ataraxy, clancular, comminuible, conclusible, detentition, deuteroscopy, digladiation, dignotion, cubiculary, discubitory, exolution, exenterate, incompossible, incompossibility,* and *indigitate.*

But the virtues of the *Dictionary* far outweighed its vices, justifying the epigram of praise written by the actor David Garrick:

> And Johnson, well arm'd like a hero of yore,
> Hath beat forty French, and will beat forty more.

The "forty French" of Garrick's reference were the members of the French Academy, for which Johnson had become an English equivalent.

With the middle class demanding authority to establish correctness, one immediate effect of Dr. Johnson's *Dictionary* was to make its author an arbiter of linguistic taste and a censor of wrong forms. Johnson relished being a censor, for in the Preface to the *Dictionary* he wrote that "every language has likewise its improprieties and absurdities, which it is the duty of the lexicographer to correct or proscribe." Lord Chesterfield, believing that "good order and authority" were then necessary in the language, was willing to accept Johnson as the oracle of English. In his letter "On Johnson's Dictionary," he made this act of submission: "I make a total surrender of all my rights and privileges in the English language to the said Mr. Johnson, during the term of his dictatorship." This statement in *The World*, November 8, 1754, was a symptom of the time, for the age was bent upon a course to remove "improprieties and absurdities" from the language.

So strong was the social influence of Dr. Johnson that his work became synonymous with the word *dictionary* itself, and *the* dictionary dominated English letters for over a century and remained in use until 1900. One measure of the dictatorial power of "the Dictionary" is the fact that a Bill was thrown out of Parliament in 1880 simply because one of its words had not been recorded by Dr. Johnson. This mystical power soon extended to other dictionaries in the latter half of the eighteenth century, especially with regard to proper pronunciation. Speakers of a middle-class dialect, eagerly engaged in social climbing, wanted authoritative keys to the articulations of polite society. As a result of this ready-made market, pronunciation dictionaries thrived during the last three decades of the eighteenth century: James Buchanan's *New English Dictionary* (1769), William Kenrick's *New Dictionary of the English Language* (1773), Thomas Sheridan's *General Dictionary of the English Language* (1780), and John Walker's *Critical Pronouncing Dictionary and Expositor of the English Language* (1791).

The major progress in lexicography during the eighteenth century was, as Whitehall has indicated, the authoritative recording of a literary vocabulary and the accurate exhibition of pronunciation patterns. In his *Dictionary* Johnson influenced spelling habits along conservative lines, for he was more interested in order and tradition than in innovations. In his search for consistency and uniformity, however, the good doctor often fell from grace, as can be seen in the following paired oppositions: *moveable, immovable; downhil, uphill, distil, instill; sliness, slyly; deceit, receipt; deign, disdain; install, reinstal; anteriour, posterior; interiour, exterior*. Johnson's verbal likes and dislikes have led many lexicographers into erroneous proscriptions and mythological taboos.

THE DOCTRINE OF USAGE.   For all his high-handedness with the language, Johnson admitted in the Preface to his *Dictionary* that no lexicographer can embalm his language and keep it from "corruption and decay." Change might be wrong, but change was here to stay, because "sounds are too volatile and subtile for legal restraints; to enchain syllables, and to lash the wind, are equally the undertakings of pride, unwilling to measure its desires by its strength." Johnson realized that "every man would have been willing, and many would have been proud to disobey" the decrees of an Academy founded upon the dictates of the linguistic purists. Others, like John Oldmixon and Thomas Sheridan, agreed with Johnson on this score.

From such agreement against the restraints of an Academy, English grammarians of the eighteenth century introduced the modern doctrine that usage is the key to "correctness." The fountainhead of this doctrine is Horace, quoted by John Hughes in his essay *Of Style* (1698): "Use is the sole arbiter and norm of speech." During the next half century Horace and Hughes were echoed by John Dennis, Lord Chesterfield, and Dr. Johnson himself. Although tempted into being untrue to his purpose, Johnson announced that the intention of the *Dictionary* was "to discover and promulgate the decrees of custom, who has so long possessed, whether by right or by usurpation, the sovereignty of words." The wording of Johnson's intention is a forecast of its violation, for when men are given the chance to play the king in language, most cannot refuse. But the term *custom* was out, whether Johnson cared or not, to be picked up with Lord Chesterfield's *usage* and turned into a modern formula by Joseph Priestly and George Campbell—namely, that prevailing custom, an arbitrary usage in language, yields the accepted standard.

In his *Rudiments of English Grammar* (1761) Priestly stated that "all-governing custom" decides language disputes through the passage of time. In *Theory of Language* (1762) he went further into the doctrine of usage by saying that "general prevailing custom, whatever it happen to be, can be the only standard for the time that it prevails." The inclusion of *only* in the dictum makes Priestly's position on the matter emphatic. In his *Philosophy of Rhetoric* (1776) George Campbell joined forces with Priestly to champion the cause of usage, which he characterized with the following three attributes: *present, national,* and *reputable.* Implicit in Campbell's observations is the present-day attitude in linguistics that correctness in language is merely a matter of usage plus social acceptability. But there were differences between Priestly and Campbell with regard to the doctrine of usage. Baugh has remarked, "Whereas Campbell expounded the doctrine of usage with admirable clarity and then violated it, Priestly was almost everywhere faithful to his principles."

THE "UNIVERSAL" GRAMMARIANS.   Seven years after the original publication of Dr. Johnson's *Dictionary,* an era of "normative and prescriptive" grammar was introduced with the appearance of Robert Lowth's *Short Introduction to English Grammar* (1762). Lowth, a clergyman aiming to be a bishop of London, represented the ex cathedra desire for infallibility in codifying the grammatical features of English. His work, based upon the application of classical grammar to an analytic and therefore relatively uninflected tongue, was scientifically a farce, but it suited the authoritarian ideal of correctness and the mania for rules that dominated the age. So popular was Lowth's grammar that it went through twenty-two editions before the end of the century, and it started an epidemic of authority-infected imitations. The rash of eighteenth-century English grammars included James Buchanan's *The British Grammar* (1762); John Ash's *Grammatical Institutes* (1763), a simplified version of Lowth; William Ward's *Grammar of the English Language* (1765); Robert Baker's utterly incompetent *Reflections on the English Language* (1770); Anselm Bayly's *The English Accidence* (1771); James Harris' *Philological Inquiries* (1781), and Lindley Murray's *English Grammar* (1795). Even Noah Webster in America was prescriptive and proscriptive in the second part of his *A Grammatical Institute of the English Language* (1784).

Thomas Sheridan had already gone beyond the demands of correctness, for in his work on the art of speaking, *British Education* (1756), he hoped to cure "the evils of immorality, ignorance and false taste." The eighteenth-century grammarians agreed on several principal aims that on the surface appear beyond reproach: to observe the grammar habits of the language and reduce them to codified principles and rules; to settle debated points of usage by condemning "wrong" forms; and to improve the language by correcting past errors. To achieve their aims, Lowth, Ward, Murray, and company proposed to use logic or reason, the analogy of classical languages, etymology, and propriety of sound. All these logicians of Authoritarian English overlooked the fact that language is primarily psychological, that what is true for one tongue may be false for another. They equated Latin grammar with a nonexistent "universal" grammar and believed that what was right and fitting in the language of Caesar was certainly right and fitting in the language of Pope. These "universal" grammarians were mistaken; yet despite modern linguistic science, their prescriptions and proscriptions still dominate the handbooks.

A measure of the inadequate methods of the "universal" grammarians is the triviality of the questions they discussed and the problems they solved. William Ward was the first compiler of the authoritarian rules of the handbook tradition, and ever since 1795 grammarians have continued to lay down such laws as these:

1) The distinction between *lie* and *lay*.
2) Proscribing *had* as the auxiliary of any idiomatic verb phrases in the present tense.
3) Rejecting *whose* as a possessive for *which*.
4) The preference for *different from* instead of *different than* or *different to*.
5) Condemning of *between you and I* and *it is me*.
6) Discouraging the ending of a sentence with a preposition.
7) The proper use of *between* (for two) and *among* (for several).
8) Proscribing the use of the superlative for the comparative (the *bigger* or *older* of two, not *biggest* or *oldest*).
9) Rejecting the comparison of incomparables (thus allowing no constructions like *rounder* or *most unique*).
10) Permitting *from hence*.
11) Proscribing *this here* and *that there*.
12) The preference for *you were* even in the singular.
13) The determination of the proper case for pronouns that follow *than* (I am taller than *he*, but she likes him better than *me*).
14) A final Websterian preference for the possessive case in front of a gerund (I don't like *his* doing that).

15) Proscribing the double negative (Lowth: "Two Negatives in English . . . are equivalent to an Affirmative").

16) Establishing a prescriptive mythology governing the use of *shall* and *will*.

17) The preference for not splitting the infinitive.

18) Proscribing functional shift, especially with regard to keeping adjectives adjectives and adverbs adverbs.

19) Prescribing proper agreement between pronoun references and their antecedents.

20) Proscribing a singular verb with a plural or compound subject and a plural verb with a singular subject.

21) Insisting on employing parallelism in grammatical constructions.

22) Proscribing contractions such as *'em* for *them*.

The linguistic evils fostered by the methods, results, and influences of the prescriptive tradition are evident. Because many borrowed words came into English from Latin via French, the eighteenth-century grammarians were often ridiculous in their etymologies. Lacking linguistic and historical perspective, they fallaciously applied the "universal rules" of a dead inflected language to a living analytic one. Many of their proscriptions continue to dominate the formal language habits of those who consider them divine pronouncements of *a priori* reasoning. Many handbooks today caution the college student against such idiomatic splittings of the infinitive as these: *to completely finish, to blindly follow, to falsely accuse, to secretly plot, to carefully consider, to promptly remit, to suddenly perceive, to gratefully acknowledge, to earnestly beseech, to loyally support, to faithfully serve, to utterly fail,* and *to finally expire.*

By ignoring what was really happening in English and concentrating on what the language should be doing, Bishop Lowth and his cohorts introduced a smug this-is-correct attitude into the study of English for all who share the-book-says-so frame of mind. The reverence for authority in language usage, still a marketable commodity among culture-shy immigrants and social-climbing suburbanites in America, has divorced the written word from the spoken, by encouraging snobbery and class warfare in language and by standardizing academic prose into a wordy dullness. Both the divorce between the spoken and the written word and the drab snobbism of modern academic prose can be heard in George Orwell's parody (in "Politics and the English Language") of the following passage from *Ecclesiastes:*

> I returned and saw under the sun, that the race is not to the swift, nor the battle to the strong, neither yet bread to the wise, nor yet riches to men of understanding, nor yet favour to men of skill; but time and chance happeneth to them all.

Here is that simple poetry in Orwell's deliberately contorted prose:

> Objective consideration of contemporary phenomena compels the conclusion that success or failure in competitive activities exhibits no tendency to be commensurate with innate capacity, but that a considerable element of the unpredictable must invariably be taken into account.

A pretentious Latinized style is only one of the many bad legacies handed down from the eighteenth-century grammarians. The inherited ignorance and confusion has crusted the study of English with such thick prejudice that most speakers believe that grammar is merely linguistic etiquette. Thus grammar as a set of formal patterns on the one hand and as a linguistic science on the other has been lost in what Francis Christensen calls the "school tradition." In his presidential address to the 1962 Conference of the California Association of Teachers of English, Christensen criticized that tradition for its "self-deception, misrepresentation, and misapprehension." He listed six major evils of the tradition:

1) Breeding general confusion over the teaching of English.
2) Fostering linguistic inertia and precluding scholarship.
3) Training insensitivity to language usage.
4) Discounting natural constructions in communication.
5) Encouraging mediocre conformity.
6) Further widening the gap between spoken and written English.

While the lexicographers and the grammarians were busy codifying Authoritarian English, the sound changes of the Great Vowel Shift were completed. Other advances included the development of a progressive verb system, the introduction of emphatic verb forms, the refinement of participial functions, and the modernizing of various syntactical idioms. With the evolution of the language and the vast influx of new words came fluctuations in word values and their attendant semantic shifts. The poetic diction dictated by neoclassic aesthetics encouraged the stilted euphemisms of a polite society.

In the hands of Milton, Bunyan, Dryden, Addison, Steele, Swift, Johnson, and Boswell, a nonfiction prose style came into being. Bunyan and Swift, with Defoe, were the stylistic progenitors of the great novelists of the eighteenth century. In poetry, on the other hand, the blank verse of the Renaissance gave way to the heroic couplets of the Age of Enlightenment; satire replaced tragedy, and the heroic became mock. Milton alone was a peer of the giants of the past.

PROSE STYLES.   Two prose styles slowly emerge and then diverge in the period of Authoritarian English: the academic and the fictional, shaped by John Milton and John Bunyan respectively. So stilted in diction was Milton that to describe an elephant curling his trunk in Book IV of *Paradise Lost* he created the following ponderosity:

> th' unwieldy Elephant
> To make them mirth us'd all his might, & wreathd
> His Lithe Proboscis . . . (345–347)

Milton's was a Latinic, convoluted, and rhetorically complex prose style out of touch with the spoken accents of men. His lumbering though balanced sentences were long, as seen in the following one chosen at random from *Areopagitica:*

> There needed no licensing of books among them, for they disliked all but their own laconic apophthegms, and took a slight occasion to chase Archilochus out of their city, perhaps for composing in a higher strain than their own soldierly ballads and roundels could reach to; or if it were for his broad verses, they were not therein so cautious, but they were as dissolute in their promiscuous conversing; whence Euripides affirms, in Andromache, that their women were all unchaste.

Milton's style was the parent of "Johnsonese," the notoriously periodic, antithetic, parallelistic, and Latinic style of Boswell's hero. In a statement cited by Jespersen as the epitome of "Johnsonese," the author of the *Dictionary* is comparing punch and conversation:

> The spirit, volatile and fiery, is *the proper emblem* of vivacity and wit; the acidity of the lemon will very *aptly figure* pungency of raillery and acrimony of censure; sugar is the *natural representative* of luscious adulation and gentle complaisance; and water is the *proper hieroglyphic* of easy prattle, innocent and tasteless.

In direct contrast to the academic, the opening paragraph of John Bunyan's *The Pilgrim's Progress*, a masterpiece of oral-tradition allegory, set the tone of the fictional:

> As I walked through the wilderness of this world, I lighted on a certain place where was a Den, and I laid me down in that place to sleep: and as I slept I dreamed a dream. I dreamed, and behold, I saw a man clothed with rags, standing in a certain place, with his face from his own house, a book in his hand, and a great burden upon his back. I looked, and saw him open the book and read therein; and as he read, he wept and trembled; and not being able longer to contain, he brake out with a lamentable cry, saying, "What shall I do?"

Bunyan's prose has the accents of the human voice: simple diction, concrete reference, breath rests based on the major junctures of the word groups, the urgency of direct and dramatic discourse, and the natural suspense induced by narrative conflict and crisis.

As Johnson was literary heir to Milton, so Jonathan Swift was to Bunyan. One of the paradoxes of Swift was the tension between his artistic achievements and his scholarly proscriptions. It is hard to believe that the man who wrote some of the best eighteenth-century prose should have wanted to embalm the language in Latinic rules. The greatness of Swift's prose may be seen in almost any passage from *Gulliver's Travels:*

> A dish of their meat was a good mouthful, and a barrel of their liquor a reasonable draught. Their mutton yields to ours, but their beef is excellent. I have had a sirloin so large, that I have been forced to make three bits of it; but this is rare. My servants were astonished to see me eat it bones and all, as in our country we do the leg of a lark. Their geese and turkeys I usually ate at a mouthful, and I must confess they far exceed ours. Of their smaller fowl I could take up twenty or thirty at the end of my knife.

Swift was thus the stylistic forerunner of the major novelists of the eighteenth century.

But "Johnsonese" was in the language to stay, as Orwell's Biblical parody has indicated. So sharp was the divergence between the two prose styles that James Russell Lowell saw the academic invading the journalese of the American newspapers of the nineteenth century. In the Introduction to the Second Series of his *Biglow Papers* (1848), Lowell listed such contrasts between the two styles as follows:

OLD STYLE	NEW STYLE
A great crowd came to see	A vast concourse was assembled to witness
Great fire	Disastrous conflagration
The fire spread	The conflagration extended its devastating career
Man fell	Individual was precipitated
Sent for the doctor	Called into requisition the services of the family physician
Began his answer	Commenced his rejoinder
He died	He deceased, he passed out of existence, his spirit quitted its earthly habitation, winged its way to eternity, shook off its burden, etc.

Authoritarian English—unlike its predecessors in that its chief literary glories were confined to prose, which took the popular appeal away from poetry and has never relinquished it—is characterized by 1) the prose domination of the Restoration and eighteenth-century drama; 2) the inception of literary criticism; 3) the development of the periodical essay; 4) the rise of the novel as a major literary art form; 5) the emergence of biography and autobiography as significant genres; and 6) the growth of intellectual prose, especially in the fields of history and philosophy.

With the reopening of the theaters during the Restoration, the Shakespearean stage was lost to the French picture-frame, with its elaborate scenery and separation from the audience. The passion and poetry of the Renaissance became the titter and prose of Authoritarian English. Dryden's attempts at poetry in drama were statuesque and imitative. Poetry in plays no longer conveyed the sense of the natural and the real; tragedy became melodrama, and the comedy of manners assumed the leading role. The playwrights William Congreve, Oliver Goldsmith, and Richard Brinsley Sheridan found prose the proper vehicle for their sentiment and wit. It was the poetry and the drama of the past that gave rise to John Dryden's famous *An Essay of Dramatic Poesy*, in which he defended Shakespeare and his contemporaries against the inflated reputations of the French classicists Corneille and Racine.

Dryden's essay was the wellspring of modern literary criticism, a prose genre developed in Authoritarian English by John Dennis, Lord Shaftesbury, Joseph Addison, Samuel Johnson, and a host of minor figures.

Addison and Sir Richard Steele, founder of *The Tatler*, perfected the periodical essay in some 555 numbers of *The Spectator* (1711–12). The essay was closely allied with journalism and the pamphleteering of the time, as championed by men like Ned Ward and Daniel Defoe. A literary critic, Samuel Johnson was also a biographer in his *Lives of the English Poets* (1779–81), fifty-two studies characterized by mature judgment and vigorous presentation. As the source for a study himself, Johnson imbued his disciple James Boswell with the goals and techniques of great biography. Prose of high quality appeared in philosophy, history, and politics in the work of three leading intellectuals: David Hume (1711–1776), Edward Gibbon (1737–1794), and Edmund Burke (1729–1797). Personal memoirs were a popular form in the late eighteenth century; as fictionalized autobiography in the tales of Defoe, this genre joined with letter writing in the work of Samuel Richardson (1689–1761) to form the basis of the English novel.

By the middle of the eighteenth century the novel, a new literary genre, had come of age in England. Tracing its beginnings back to Arabian tales, medieval romances, and Renaissance satiric picaresques, in Authoritarian English the novel became responsible prose literature. Bunyan had given it the natural rhythms of the human voice and the verisimilitude of the spoken word; Defoe had graced it with a spirit of adventure and realistic detail, and a middle-class morality; Swift had used mythic projection, symbolic behavior, metaphysical value, and social purpose. By 1740 the novel was a permanent addition to the art of English fiction.

From 1740–1770 the novel matured under the hands of Samuel Richardson, Henry Fielding, Tobias Smollett, and Laurence Sterne. In three novels—*Pamela, or Virtue Rewarded* (1740–1), *Clarissa* (1747–8), and *Sir Charles Grandison* (1753–4)—Richardson expanded the form and scope of the novel, enriched it with psychological depth and sentimental detail, and gave it an emotional appeal to rival that of contemporary French fiction. A master of fantasy and melodramatic suspense, Richardson venerated rank, respectability, priggish elegance, and poetic justice. He thus became the butt of satire from the pen of Henry Fielding (1707–1754) in that author's burlesque, *Shamela* (1741).

Drawn away from the theater into the field of the novel, Fielding gave the novel structure, style, and an aesthetic rationale. Fine as *Joseph Andrews* (1742) and *Jonathan Wild* (1743) were in farcical vitality and character portrayal, it was *Tom Jones* (1749) that exhibited the full range of Fielding's genius. In this novel, Fielding combines detail and episode in a masterfully conceived plot; the result is a structural unity difficult to match in the history of the genre. By means of eighteen essays which introduce the books of the novel, Fielding establishes a philosophical basis, an aesthetic rationale, for the novel as "the comic epic poem in prose." He closed out his career of seriously criticizing English manners with *Amelia* (1751), a novel more grim in its truth than graceful in its artistry. In defense of his commitments to realism, Fielding wrote as follows in his autobiographical *Voyage to Lisbon* (1754):

> I must confess I should have honoured and loved Homer more had he written a true history of his own times in humble prose, than those noble poems that have so justly collected the praise of all ages; for though I read these with more admiration and astonishment, I still read Herodotus, Thucydides and Xenophon, with more amusement and more satisfaction.

Tobias Smollett (1721–1771) shared Fielding's commitment to realism; he excelled with vivid burlesque, picaresque episode, racial characterization, and stylistic energy. In four novels—*Roderick Random* (1748), *Peregrine Pickle* (1751), *Count Fathom* (1753), and *Humphry Clinker* (1771)—Smollett savagely caricatured the vices and follies of polite society. In his inventiveness of dramatic situations and relish for scatological details, he resembled his great contemporary, Laurence Sterne (1713–1768).

Sterne had gifts that carried beyond Smollett's, and this Irish-born Anglican prelate of salacious wit used them to advantage in his masterpiece *The Life and Opinions of Tristram Shandy* (1759–1767). Capitalizing on the difference between psychic time and actual time, Sterne created uproarious comedy from the ruling passions of men, as based upon John Locke's principle of the association of ideas. Thus the "emotional aura" of the deed was more important to Sterne than the deed itself. By such mechanical tricks as the use of asterisks, black and marble pages, blank sheets, skipped pages, pointing index fingers, and elongated dashes, Sterne matched his texture with the brilliance of his structure. Mastering the repetitious rhythms of the emotional human voice, the double entendres possible between English and a foreign language, and the unpunctuated blend of spoken words and unspoken thoughts in any social gathering,

Sterne became the literary ancestor of James Joyce and the Brazilian novelist Machado de Assis (1839–1908).

NEOCLASSICAL POETRY.   The poetry during this period of prose development diminished in intensity, range, and influence. The epic baroque of Milton, Latinic in diction and written more for the ear than for the eye, gave way to the mock heroic of Alexander Pope (1688–1744), the most quoted and least read poet in the language. As a symbol of neoclassicism in literature, Pope typified the aristocratic attributes of the poetry written in his time. Formal in technique, imitative and importive in both theme and style, neoclassical lyrics were so chilly or so sentimental as to lead A. E. Housman to dismiss them as being either lumps of wet clay or fire that never burns clean of smoke. A basic fault was that aesthetics in the Age of Reason emphasized the lexical rather than the grammatical in the poem. Such atrocious "poetic diction" as *the finny tribe* for *fish* and *plumy burdens winnowing the waving element* for *flying birds* sapped the strength of the lyric. Believing that what man knew was more important than what he could imagine, the rational singers of the first half of the eighteenth century remained content to copy the ancients rather than nature.

As a result of this abdication of originality and creative invention, the highest poetic achievements of the age were confined to satiric narratives like Dryden's *Mac Flecknoe* (1682) and Pope's *The Rape of the Lock* (1714) and *The Dunciad* (1728–43). The polished heroic couplet dictated smaller thought patterns and permitted moral commonplaces to be turned into aphoristic epigrams. Less exciting in cadence patterns than the blank verse of either Shakespeare or Milton, the neoclassical satiric narrative supported a false elevation of style on bombast and periphrasis. Although Pope believed that "The sound must seem an Echo to the sense," his couplets were far removed from the natural accents of the common man. Politely conversational and suited to the demands of didacticism, these couplets employed discursive rather than imagic diction and achieved a decorative, drawing-room tone.

Elaborate epic machinery and borrowed mythology often fleshed out the triviality of theme in Pope's satires, which were basically prose dissertations and diatribes in verse form. The language of information in the Age of Rules had taken precedence over the language of formation. Even if Pope could claim that

> The rules of old discovered, not devised,
> Are Nature still, but nature methodized

his "method" became what was the matter with neoclassical poetry. Artificial tumidity, grammatical correctness, and moral propriety were no match for the majesty and primitive power of Homer, whom he reduced in translation to an eighteenth-century versifying gentleman.

EXPANSION OF EMPIRE. While Authoritarian English was undergoing lexical and grammatical codifications at home and the novel was replacing poetry as the most expressive art form of that language, the British Empire was extending its vast influence throughout the world. The American Revolution freed the American colonies from political domination by London, but the British victory over the French in the Battle of Quebec in 1759 had assured the triumph of the English language in North America. Two years earlier, Robert Clive had won a series of military engagements that gave India to the English Crown. A decade later, in 1768, the Royal Society prevailed upon the king to sponsor an astronomical expedition to the South Pacific to observe the passage of Venus across the sun. As a result of this scientific voyage, Captain James Cook planted the Union Jack on the soil of Australia and New Zealand. By 1787 the overcrowded English prisons were deporting convicts to Australia, and their language entered another area of conquest. Before the end of the century, in 1795, the British seized the Dutch settlement at Cape Town as an act of war against Napoleon, and began to extend their control over a good deal of South Africa. From all this eighteenth-century expansion of the British Empire, English came to enjoy its present-day global distribution and influence.

Commercial supremacy on the high seas and political supremacy among her far-flung colonies assured Great Britain of continual contact with strange climates, countries, cultures, and the words they engender. An enduring advantage of the Empire was the wealth of new terms that poured into English. Traffic with the many different tribes of North American Indians added some permanent loans to the version of the language spoken in the United States. These Indian loans include such botanical names as *catalpa, catawba, hickory, pecan, persimmon, pokeberry, pokeweed, scuppernong, sequoia, squash*, and *tamarack*; such terms for animals as *cayuse, chipmunk, moose, muskrat, opossum, raccoon, skunk, terrapin*, and *woodchuck*; such names for foods as *hominy, hooch, pem-*

mican, pone, succotash, and *supawn;* and such terms for general cultural items as *mugwump, Tammany, manitou, pot latch, powwow, sachem, skookum, totem, papoose, squaw, mackinaw, moccasin, tomahawk, wampum, hogan, igloo, kayak, tepee, wigwam, menhaden, muskellunge, quahog, Chautauqua, chinook,* and *podunk.*

Rivalry for trade within the New World brought the English language into commerce with Mexican, Caribbean, and South American Spanish and Brazilian Portuguese. From them came *chili, chocolate, coyote, tomato, barbecue, cannibal, canoe, hammock, hurricane, maize, potato, tobacco, alpaca, condor, jerky, llama, pampas, puma, quinine, buccaneer, cayenne, jaguar, petunia, poncho, pickaninny, tapioca, cashew,* and *tapir.* The British penetration into India added such exotic terms as *bandana, bangle, bengal, Brahman, bungalow, calico, cashmere, cheroot, china, chintz, coolie, cot, curry, dinghy, juggernaut, jungle, jute, loot, mandarin, nirvana, pariah, polo, pundit, rajah, rupee, sepoy, thug, toddy, tom-tom,* and *verandah.* East Indian versions of Malayan and Persian terms included *gingham, indigo, mango,* and *seersucker.* Africa contributed the native, Dutch, and Portuguese words *banana, Boer, boorish, chimpanzee, gorilla, guinea, gumbo, Hottentot, palaver, voodoo,* and *zebra.* Australia gave English a flavor from "down under": *boomerang, kangaroo, wombat, paramatta,* and *cooey.*

THE STRUCTURE OF AUTHORITARIAN ENGLISH

PHONEMIC STABILIZATION.   As the British Empire expanded, Authoritarian English experienced a gradual change in pronunciation that resulted in phonemic stabilization of the tense vowel clusters that were transitions from Middle English to Early Modern. At the outset of Authoritarian English in 1650, the language was still Shakespearean, with a touch of Irish brogue. By 1800, it had become Mature Modern English, with sound patterns like those of the present-day version. Milton at the outset and Wordsworth at the end of this evolution represent in their pronunciations the course of the phonemic stabilization. The following words, as pronounced by the two poets, illustrate this phonological process:

WORD	TENSE VOWEL PRONUNCIATION	
	Milton	*Wordsworth*
bide	/əy/	/ay/
rude	/ɫw/	/uw/
house	/əw/	/aw/
clean	/ey/	/iy/
lame	/eh/	/ey/
love	/uh/	/ə/

As a middle figure in this phonemic transition within Authoritarian English, Pope often leaned more toward Milton than toward Wordsworth—especially for the sake of a rhyme. Thus Pope could write this fine piece of anticlimax:

> Here thou, great ANNA! whom three realms obey,
> Dost sometimes counsel take—and sometimes tea.

The pronunciation of *tea* as /tey/ was aristocratic and dialectal in Pope's day, but conservative poetic license permitted it to become part of the sound texture of *The Rape of the Lock* in the same spirit that allowed Chaucer his Norman accents in *Troilus and Criseyde*. To base a scientific study of the standard phonology of eighteenth-century English upon Pope's rhymes would be a mistake. Pope's inexactness in sound-pattern agreements evoked this criticism from Jonathan Swift, in a letter to Pope on his first volume of translations from Homer: "I am angry at some bad rhymes and triplets; and pray in your next do not let me have so many unjustifiable rhymes to *war* and *gods*." But Pope continued to take liberties with his language, and hence he gave his readers a whole series of /ay/ rhymes on such words as *join* and *shine*. The centralizing of /ɔ/ to /a/ produced an Irish flavor, but in general Pope's archaisms were not in phonemic favor in Authoritarian English.

The typographical changes of *v* to *u* and *ʃ* to *s* in Authoritarian English were minor instances of the general modernization that was taking effect in the language. In Authoritarian English the seven distinctive acoustic features of vocality/consonantality, tension/laxness, interruption/continuance, gravity/acuteness, compactness/diffuseness, nasality/orality, and stridency/mellowness evolved into a complete accord with those of today. Early in this period, there was more centralizing of articulation and a lower positioning of the tongue on vocalic diphthongs, but by 1800 Authoritarian English had attained the overall sound patterns of the language of today.

The furtherance of phonemic weakening in stressless positions led to the present-day British tendency to swallow up unaccented syllables—usually the third in a series of four. Fronting of stress yielded accentual collocations in keeping with those of today. Shakespeare's *asPECT*, *char-ACTer*, *enVY*, and *welCOME* shifted to Pope's *ASpect*, *CHARacter*, *ENvy*, and *WELcome*. A sharper focusing of stress modification in Authoritarian English, however, could result in a backing of stress on verbs, so that Shakespeare's *perSEVer* became Pope's *perseVERE*. But for the most part, a general forwarding of stress strengthened the native tendency of converting word groups into compounds, a process seen in such modern examples as *STREETcar conductor*, *DANCing school*, and *FRENCH professor*.

As a determiner of the other suprasegmentals in the language, stress operated in four degrees: maximum /ˊ/, major /ˆ/, minor /ˋ/, and minimum /˘/. These four degrees of stress were paralleled, as in Early Modern English and present-day, by four levels of pitch, four kinds of juncture, and four major intonational contours. The language of Dr. Johnson was less guttural and grave than Old English, less tense and Normanesque than Middle English, and phonemically more diversified and well-balanced than either. From a growing linguistic inhibition, that language also was less rhetorical in stress energy, pitch height, and syllabic prolongation than the tongue of Shakespeare.

MORPHOLOGICAL FEATURES. In the area where morphology becomes grammar, Authoritarian English developed some new verb features that have made the language more expressive: the progressive active, the progressive passive, and emphatic forms of verbs. Verb forms using the various morphemes of *to be* with the present participle created the progressive active, a construction rare in the preceding history of English. Whereas Shakespeare said *I sing* and *sings he* for declarative and interrogative, Pope could say *I sing*, *I do sing*, *I am singing*, *does he sing*, and *is he singing*. If Pope wished to express critical surprise with his question, he might say *he sings* and apply the high-rising intonation pattern as a terminal contour. In the indicative, both French and German remain more restricted in construction than Authoritarian English was. In French the speaker says, *je chante*; in German, *ich singe*.

From the seventeenth century, the present participle evolved from a noun governed by the preposition *on*, through the intermediary *a-* form, which could be either nominal or verbal, to the modern morphology and function of the eighteenth century. This evolution may be traced in the following examples: *he was set on building a barn; he was a-building a barn; he was building a barn*. Present-day English uses the present participle in the progressive verb form throughout the tenses. Late in the eighteenth century, the progressive construction assumed the passive voice too. Shakespeare had inaugurated the progressive passive in this statement from *Hamlet: which, being kept close, might move more grief to hide*. But this new verb form languished until 1770. Generally employed only in the present and simple past, the progressive passive was and still is formed by uniting *being* with a past participle, with the entire verb phrase headed by some morpheme of *to be*—thus, *the barn is being built* or *the barns were being built*.

Meanwhile, the language was polishing its emphatic verb constructions with *do* and its morphological variants. So *he does too sing* came to have more emotional punch than *he sings too*. The emphatic verb forms were used effectively in negative constructions like *he doesn't sing very well* and in the interrogative constructions *does he sing well* and *doesn't he sing at all*. These verb developments modernized the syntax of Authoritarian English and gave the language a flexible grace often missing in its Renaissance predecessor.

Nineteenth-century purists, heirs to the proscriptive attitudes of the "universal" grammarians, objected to the progressive verb constructions on the grounds that they were "artificial neologisms." But no expression that develops from the mouths of the people can be considered artificial. The conservative authoritarians of the eighteenth century, Swift among the most outspoken, objected to three other innovations in the English of their time: clipping, verb contractions, and modish slang. For the sake of economy, Britons lopped off syllables and thereby clipped *hypochondriac* to *hyp*, *reputation* to *rep*, *ultimate* to *ult*, *penultimate* to *penult*, *incognito* to *incog*, *hypercritic* to *hyper*, and *extraordinary* to *extra*. This vital morphological process has given present-day English such standard clippings as *taxi, phone, bus, ad*, and *curio*. Believing that monosyllables were the disgrace of English, Swift fulminated against the contractions of verbs like *drudg'd, disturb'd, rebuk'd, fledg'd, rubb'd*, and "a thousand others everywhere to be met with in prose as well as verse, where, by leaving out a vowel to save a syllable, we form a jarring sound, and so difficult to utter, that I have often wondered how it could ever obtain."

The contractions were the graphemic way of indicating the phonemic zeroing of stressless syllables—a linguistic result of the fronting of accent. Swift should not have /æskɨd/ it to be different.

Swift was also critical of modish slang. Because slang is racy and metaphorical, it is close to poetry and rejuvenates every language. But Swift attacked new terms such as *sham*, *banter*, *mob*, *bubble*, *bully*, *cutting*, *shuffling*, and *palming*. So furious was he in his war on neologisms that he wanted Sir Richard Steele, editor of the *Tatler*, to condemn all such barbarisms by his "authority as Censor" in an annual *index expurgatorius*. In 1710 Swift wrote a letter to the *Tatler* (No. 230) illustrating the linguistic corruption of the time. In the following passage, Swift was quoting from a hypothetical letter to himself, written by "a most accomplished person":

> Sir,
>
> I *cou'dn't* get the things you sent for all *about Town*.—I *thôt* to *ha'* come down myself, and then *I'd ha' brout'um*; but I *han't don't*, and I believe I *can't do't*, that's *pozz*. Tom begins to *g'imself* airs because *he's* going with the *plenipo's*.—'Tis said, the French King will *bamboozl' us agen*, which *causes many speculations*. The *Jacks*, and others of that *kidney*, are very *uppish*, and *alert upon't*, as you may see by their *phizz's*.—*Will Hazzard* has got the *hipps*, having lost *to the tune of* five hundr'd pound, *thô* he understands play very well, *nobody better*. He has promis't me upon *rep*, to leave off play; but you know 'tis a weakness *he's* too apt to *give into, thô* he has as much wit as any man, *nobody more*. He has lain *incog* ever since. —The *mobb's* very quiet with us now.—I believe you *thôt* I *banter'd* you in my last like a *country put*.—I *sha'n't* leave Town this month, &c.

His imaginary letter demonstrates that Swift had a better ear than his linguistic prejudice should have permitted. From the clippings, contractions, slang phrases, and syntactical truncations recorded here, it is clear that a later generation of Shakespeare's countrymen was speaking a constantly changing version of living English. What Swift objected to was the human voice; he preferred a classically "correct" language that had fallen silent. The "reason" that Swift so exalted should have told him that when a language falls silent, it is dead.

The habit of contracting verbs in spoken discourse gave Authoritarian English an advantage over Old, Middle, and Early Modern English in the flexible economy of bound phonemic morphemes. Clipping joined affixing, compounding, and stress modification to add a fresh sound that the Elizabethans would have approved. Abbreviated spellings anticipated such present-day journalisms as *nite* and *thru*. Other morphological processes like internal modification, replacement, zeroing, and reduplication continued to wax strong in the language. Functional shift, back formation (as in *sherry* from *sherris sack*), and idea naming (encouraged by science and the Industrial Revolution) formed a part of the morphological riches of the language.

LINGUISTIC FEAR.   Much of the mania for "correctness" in the eighteenth century was a fear of change in the English language. Even Chaucer had felt that his version of English was doomed to either obsolescence or archaic quaintness by the progress of linguistic evolution. The author of *Troilus and Criseyde* prayed near the end of his masterpiece (V, 1793–98) that the great poem might continue to be understood by succeeding generations:

> And for ther is so gret diversite
> In Englissh and in writyng of our tonge,
> So prey I God that non myswrite the,
> Nor the mysmetre for defaute of tonge.
> And red wherso thow be, or elles songe,
> That thow be understonde, God I beseche!

Francis Bacon suffered a similar anxiety, writing in 1623 to his friend Sir Toby Matthew that his literary labors had been made permanent in Latin, a most felicitous event, because "these modern languages will, at one time or other, play the bankrupts with books." The Restoration poet Edmund Waller (1606–1687) wrote in his *Of English Verse* the following lines of gloom:

> Poets that Lasting Marble seek,
> Must carve in Latin or in Greek;
> We write in Sand.

And in his *Essay on Criticism* (1711), Pope agreed with Waller:

> And such as Chaucer is, shall Dryden be.

Pope's views were shared by Swift, Lord Chesterfield, Thomas Sheridan, and Richard Bentley.

What these men overlooked was that Sophocles had to read his Homer with the help of a lexicon and that Latin as a living language had become the Romance vernaculars. Historical and linguistic ignorance bred the insecurity that demanded fixing the language by inviolable rules. The English authoritarians of the eighteenth century equated change with corruption and decay, rather than with health and life.

A recent example of the lack of linguistic faith that produces mistaken notions of right and wrong has been the attacks on *Webster's Third New International Dictionary* in the *Atlantic, Saturday Review, Journal of the American Bar Association, New York Times*, and *Life*. The "disappointment," "shock," "calamity," "scandal and disaster" was sure to "accelerate the deterioration" of English, because the dictionary was "a flagrant example of lexicographic irresponsibility," a "serious blow to the cause of good English," and "a cause for dismay."

SYNTACTICAL REFINEMENTS.   Syntactical refinements in Authoritarian English made the language behave much like the present-day version. With the development of the progressive verb system, Authoritarian English refined its participial constructions to expand the use of the gerund as the nucleus of a verbal word group. This refinement led to the extended use of the nominative absolute. The emphatic verb forms permit the modern habit of initiating questions with verb auxiliaries rather than with the verbs themselves. A remodeling of the noun word group eliminated most of the Norman and French flavor of postnominal modifiers. With the marked tendency for single-word adjectives to precede their substantives, Authoritarian English supported far fewer constructions like *the lords dependants* than did Shakespearean.

A modernizing of prepositional usage in the language reduced the importance of *of;* increased the value of *by, through,* and *with* as markers of agency; expanded the employment of complex, compound, and word-group prepositions like *about, into,* and *in accordance with;* and strengthened the role of the idiomatic preposition as directive adverb in verb phrases and as noun formant in compound derivatives from those same phrases. A corresponding advance in the scale of specific meaning took place in the transitional adverbs and word groups of Authoritarian English. The entire connective system of the language underwent a further shaping and polishing to express better the newly developed hypotaxis of English. With the separation of the written word from the spoken, the periodicity of that hypotaxis became more pronounced than ever. To meet the demands of a growing literacy, Authoritarian English developed a utilitarian prose in literary criticism, the novel, biography, history, and scientific dissertation.

CULTURAL CHANGES.   In the latter half of the eighteenth century, major cultural changes prevailed—changes that were to mark the end of Authoritarian English and the beginning of Mature Modern. Science was on the rise; important discoveries in physics, chemistry, astronomy, mathematics, and medicine had emphasized the empirical method of Bacon and Newton. Improvements in the standard of living joined with an increased birth rate and better health measures to ensure a longer life expectancy and a radically larger population in Britain. More people meant more jobs; more jobs meant more money in circulation for expanded markets. Money gave its spenders a sharper desire to have their say in running the affairs of the nation. The extension of the British Empire turned attention outward. With the ideas of the French and American revolutions lapping against their shores, the English people began to demand Parliamentary reform; and the incipient Industrial Revolution was to make the laboring man's voice important. With the rise of Romanticism, individualism, emotionalism, nationalism were set free to make another new world.

QUESTIONS FOR RESEARCH AND DISCUSSION

1. Let four members of the class organize a debate, two affirmative and two negative, on the following subject: *That Authoritarian English needs an Academy, like that of the French, to police and purify the language.* Now let the entire class write a critical paper on the democratic resistance to the founding of an English Academy.

2. Let five members of the class engage in a panel discussion on the evolution of serious prose in Authoritarian English. Concentrate on the work of the following masters: John Dryden, John Bunyan, Daniel Defoe, Jonathan Swift, and Samuel Johnson. What stylistic attributes do these authors have in common? In what major respects are their prose works different? What virtues do they represent in English writing? What vices? Be specific and detailed in discussion.

3. Examine representative passages from the prose of John Milton and Samuel Johnson. Discuss the similarities and differences in style of the work of these two men. Pay close attention to such items as choice of diction, syntactical balance and antithesis, sentence length, complexity of constructions, periodicity and subordination, ease or difficulty of reading. Now write an essay either to attack or to defend the following value judgment: "The prose styles of both Milton and Johnson are best characterized by the epithet *Latinic elephantine*."

4. Conduct a classroom study of Johnson's famous *Dictionary*. How indebted is it to Bailey's earlier *Universal Etymological Dictionary?* What are the positive virtues of Johnson's *Dictionary?* its biased idiosyncrasies? its negative vices? How do you account for its century of popularity and almost absolute authority over the English language? Be specific in your answers.

5. Organize a series of reports on the linguistic methods of the famous grammarians and rhetoricians of Authoritarian English: Joseph Priestly, Robert Lowth, James Buchanan, John Ash, Thomas Sheridan, George Campbell, William Ward, and Lindley Murray. What language principles do these men hold in common? On what issues do they disagree and diverge? Who seems to be the most liberal and modern in approach? who the most reactionary and dated? Now write an essay on the grammatical and rhetorical heritage left by these seven men to the study and practice of Late Modern English.

6. Review the twenty-two prescriptions and proscriptions of Authoritarian English as listed in this chapter. Then conduct a detailed and lengthy class discussion, based upon independent study and thought, on the validity of these dictates in the usage of present-day English. Now write a critique on the prescriptions and proscriptions of Authoritarian English.

7. Phonemicize Alexander Pope's "Ode on Solitude" as the author would probably have pronounced it at a public reading. Now phonemicize the same poem as Shakespeare would have pronounced it if the poem were his. What are the major shifts in phonology between Early Modern and Authoritarian English? Be specific in your answer.

8. Organize a panel discussion among four members of the class on the subject of the rise of the novel in Authoritarian English. Let there be a detailed comparison and contrast of the prose styles of the four eighteenth-century masters in this genre: Richardson, Fielding, Smollett, and Sterne. What are the major contributions of each author to the development of the novel? Do these four novelists help widen or close the gap between spoken and written English? Support your answers with detailed examples.

9. Conduct a class discussion, based upon outside reading and reflection, on the following value judgment: *That the poetry of Alexander Pope is an aesthetic embodiment of the linguistic ideals of Authoritarian English— orderly correctness and purist refinement based upon the dictates of reason and classical example.* Now write a critical paper in which you either defend or attack the value judgment.

10. Organize a series of detailed reports on the following major occurrences in Authoritarian English: immense vocabulary growth, further refine-

ment of idiomatic structures and word-group patterns, development of a progressive verb system, emergence of emphatic verb forms, and modernization of Elizabethan participial constructions. From a deeper knowledge of these occurrences, as gained from the reports, now write a critical essay on the following proposition: *That ironical tension dominates the history of Authoritarian English—namely, that between the pole of an idealistic desire for codification and arrestment and that of a realistic drive for originality and change.* Concentrate attention on the dichotomy between authority and experience, between the dictators and the people.

11. From everything you have learned about Authoritarian English, now write a critique of the following literary judgment: The *neo*classicism of eighteenth-century England is really *pseudo*classicism. Support your attack or defense with detailed argument.

SELECTED BIBLIOGRAPHY

Baugh, Albert C. *A History of the English Language.* Second Edition. New York: Appleton-Century-Crofts, 1957. See especially Chapter 9 for study of the language during the period of "The Appeal to Authority, 1650–1800."

Bloomfield, Morton W., and Leonard Newmark. *A Linguistic Introduction to the History of English.* New York: Alfred A. Knopf, 1963. See especially Chapter VII for a study of "The Problem of Correctness and Good Usage, 1600–1850."

Jespersen, Otto. *Growth and Structure of the English Language.* Ninth Edition. New York: Doubleday, Anchor Books, 1955. See especially Chapter IX for a discussion of the evolution of English grammar.

Robertson, Stuart, and Frederic G. Cassidy. *The Development of Modern English.* Second Edition. Englewood Cliffs, New Jersey: Prentice-Hall, 1954. See especially Chapter 11 for an account of the evolution of English spelling and the growth of dictionaries, with a bibliography for further research.

Sherburn, George. *The Restoration and Eighteenth Century (1660–1789).* Volume III of *A Literary History of England,* edited by Albert C. Baugh. New York: Appleton-Century-Crofts, 1948. The best one-volume critical survey of the literary achievement in Authoritarian English.

Trevelyan, G. M. *History of England, Volume II: The Tudors and the Stuart Era; Volume III: From Utrecht to Modern Times.* New York: Doubleday, Anchor Books, 1953. See especially II, pp. 236–310, and III, pp. 12–94, for a discussion of the political and social backgrounds of Authoritarian English.

CHAPTER 10

Mature Modern English
1800–1920

---❧---

IMPORTANT DATES

1803   The Louisiana Purchase symbolizes the expansion of the United States and the extension of American English.

1805   Admiral Horatio Nelson defeats Napoleon's French fleet at the Battle of Trafalgar, giving England naval supremacy and a dominance in world commerce, and strengthening the prestige of the English language.

1816   The first cheap newspaper in England begins the process of mass-media communication and its impact on English.

1832–1868   The first period of the Progress of Reform, in which reorganization of Parliament, revision of penal codes and poor laws, restrictions on child labor, industrial reforms, and extension of the franchise contribute to the democratic leveling of classes that yields fewer social distinctions in the use of English.

1833–1870   The golden age of the Victorian novel, the most popular art form of the literate masses and an eloquent vehicle for the social satire that leads to reform.

1840   Cheap postage improves the means of written communication to further the spread of English.

1844   The invention of the telegraph by Samuel F. B. Morse is the first step in the development of rapid communication, a major influence on the growth and spread of Mature Modern English.

1845   The railroad furthers the cause of rapid transportation, another major influence on the development of Mature Modern English.

1850   William Wordsworth dies and Alfred Lord Tennyson becomes poet laureate: the Parnassian replaces the Romantic in English poetry.

1858   The seventy-year compilation of the *New English Dictionary* (1928) commences; this monument of English lexicography reflects the growth and diversity of the language and the development of linguistic principles and practices to describe it adequately.

1859   The publication of Charles Darwin's *On the Origin of Species* introduces survival-of-the-fittest and natural-selection theories that shake religious certitude and establish a secular basis for the study of human life. The book symbolizes the impact of science on Mature Modern English.

1861–1865   The American Civil War puts an end to wooden-ship navies, thereby making steel king of the industrial world; mass production leads to mass-media advertising and its impact on English.

1868–1902   The second period of the Progress of Reform results in more class leveling in England and a greater democratic influence upon English.

1875–1876   England gains control of the Suez Canal and Queen Victoria is proclaimed Empress of India. The British Empire is at the height of its wealth, power, influence, and prestige.

1876   The telephone invented by Alexander Graham Bell modernizes private communication, with vast implications for the development of English.

1890–1910   A period of great scientific and technological impact on English: radio and cinema, airplane and automobile, Freudian psychoanalysis and Einsteinian relativity.

1914–1918   World War I engenders twentieth-century aesthetics and the advances of present-day Late Modern English.

OUTSTANDING PERSONS

Robert Browning (1812–1889)   Father of the dramatic monologue and the narrative poem in Mature Modern English poetry.

Lewis Carroll (Charles L. Dodgson, 1832–1898)   Author of two masterpieces (*Alice's Adventures in Wonderland*, 1865; *Through the Looking-Glass*, 1871). A champion of parody, satire, illogical logic, and jabberwocky, Carroll has a light-hearted leavening effect on the serious development of English.

Charles Dickens (1812–1870)   The supreme novelist of Mature Modern English, Dickens champions the mass-media impact to reduce snobbery in the language.

Edward Fitzgerald (1809–1883)   The finest translator of poetry in Mature Modern English (*The Rubáiyát of Omar Khayyám*, 1859–79).

Alfred Lord Tennyson (1809–1892)   The poetic voice of the Victorian Age and epitome of the Parnassian aesthetics.

The Great Inventors Alexander Graham Bell (1847–1922), Robert Fulton (1765–1815), Henry Ford (1863–1947), Orville (1871–1948) and Wilbur (1867–1912) Wright, Guglielmo Marconi (1874–1937), Thomas A. Edison (1847–1931), Samuel F. B. Morse (1791–1872)   These men profoundly determine the growth of rapid transportation and communication.

The Great Lexicographers Herbert Coleridge (1830–1861), Frederick James Furnivall (1825–1910), Sir James A. H. Murray (1837–1915), Henry Bradley (1845–1923), Sir William A. Craigie (1867–1957), C. T. Onions (1863–1965) These men effect the long and scholarly compilation of the *New English Dictionary* (1858–1928), a remarkable study of meaning and usage in the English language.

The Great Scientists Charles Darwin (1809–1882), Thomas Henry Huxley (1825–1895), Louis Pasteur (1822–1895), Marie (1867–1934) and Pierre (1859–1906) Curie, Sigmund Freud (1856–1939), Albert Einstein (1879–1955)   These people provide the enormous acceleration of scientific discoveries and their subsequent impact on English vocabulary, morphology, idioms, literary subject matter, and aesthetic forms and attitudes.

The Romantic Essayists   Thomas DeQuincey (1785–1859), William Hazlitt (1778–1830), Charles Lamb (1775–1834)   These writers further refine the formal and the informal essay.

The Romantic Poets William Blake (1757–1827), William Wordsworth (1770–1850), Samuel Taylor Coleridge (1772–1834), Lord Byron (1788–1824), Percy Bysshe Shelley

(1792–1822), John Keats (1795–1821) These men free literary form from neoclassical restraint, modify poetic diction along homely and realistic lines, enlarge the sensibility of their age, and exalt the common.

The Victorian Critics Matthew Arnold (1822–1888), Thomas Carlyle (1795–1881), Thomas Babington Macaulay (1800–1859), William Morris (1834–1896), Walter Pater (1839–1894), John Ruskin (1819–1900) These men represent the continued development of English prose styles adequate for all nonfictional needs.

MAJOR ATTRIBUTES OF THE LANGUAGE

Experiences an enormous growth of vocabulary to extend its cosmopolitan character.

Achieves a relative stability in the pronunciation of its tense vowels.

Develops a genius for the portmanteau word.

Revitalizes old words with new meanings.

Uses journalism as a means of elevating the colloquial to the level of accepted written standard.

Begins the Late Modern English trend toward the informal and the utilitarian in usage.

Develops a tolerance for slang as a way of renewing the metaphoric and poetic content of the language.

Functionally shifts the present participle into an adjective.

Further modernizes grammatical idioms for greater flexibility and accuracy of expression.

Returns to the Anglo-Saxon tradition of compounding to create new words.

Further enriches the process of affixing.

Experiences an immense growth in the use of Greek and Latin morphemes in forming scientific terms.

Fully uses the idiomatic preposition as directive adverb and noun formant to create one of the most effective means of expression in present-day English.

THE HISTORY OF
MATURE MODERN ENGLISH

MUCH OF THE HISTORY OF Mature Modern English, a period in the language that ran for slightly over a century (1800–1920), was simply a matter of influences. Those influences, which resulted in important linguistic effects and aesthetic achievements, included the continued expansion of the British Empire; the growth in American power and prestige; the leveling of social classes; rapid methods of transportation, mass-media journalism, and instantaneous means of public and private communication; the extension of literacy and the raising of educational standards; modern research and technology; linguistic study and improved methods of lexicography; the support of informal and utilitarian usage; and the constant process of renewing the language itself.

Before the nineteenth century, English had been a poor European cousin of such "elite" vernaculars as French, Italian, Spanish, and even Dutch. English was considered no match for Latin, the universal language of the Middle Ages and the Renaissance. Even with the defeat of the Spanish Armada in 1588, the tongue of Shakespeare was looked down upon by the humanists on the Continent. Thus a curious linguistic anomaly came into being—at the very time English was accomplishing its greatest work in *belles lettres,* the rest of the civilized world was scarcely impressed with the language itself. The constant growth in economic and military power within the British Empire made English a tongue to be reckoned with, then respected, admired, imitated, and plagiarized. By the advent of Mature Modern English, the language was on the ascendancy throughout the world, attested by comparing the numbers of native speakers among the five leading European languages of the late nineteenth and the early twentieth century:

MILLIONS OF SPEAKERS PER LANGUAGE

Year	English	German	Russian	French	Spanish
1868	60	52	45	45	40
1890	111	75	75	51	42
1900	123	80	85	52	48
1912	150	90	106	47	52

By the outset of World War I, English was the most populated language of the Western world.

At the beginning of the nineteenth century, England had achieved an unrivaled naval supremacy. Admiral Nelson's victory over the French fleet in the Battle of Trafalgar in 1805 assured British domination over world commerce for a hundred years. To maintain the balance of power, and to protect her global lifelines of trade, England helped to populate and develop Australasia, extended her power over the Union of South

Africa and consolidated it in India, opposed Russian penetration into the Balkans, encouraged the rise of Prussia, and an independent Italy, finally made friends with France, gained control of the shipping route through the Middle East, and allowed the federation of Canada as the first step in the eventual establishment of a worldwide British Commonwealth. In the expansion of the Empire, the English language grew again in vocabulary, speakers, and prestige.

SOCIAL AND TECHNOLOGICAL INFLUENCES.   England's political achievements during the nineteenth century were schizophrenic, for the British Government while pursuing an imperialist policy overseas found itself of necessity sponsoring a series of progressive measures that in seven decades of social reform (1832–1902) turned England into a democracy, completed at last in the universal suffrage of 1918 and the Irish Home Rule of 1921. In the four great struggles for extending the franchise (1832, 1867, 1884, 1918), the people succeeded in appropriating the Magna Carta unto themselves. While they defined the nation to include more than the aristocracy, ten-pound householders, and tenant farmers, they also ended the rotten-borough system in Parliament and municipality, revised the penal code and the poor laws, protected children from economic exploitation by means of new labor bills, and championed a nationwide Primary Education Act (1870).

The opportunities for everyone to share in the economic and cultural advantages engendered by the Industrial Revolution increased. From the leveling of classes and the extension of advantages, it was natural that the language should reflect the psychology of the times by becoming less rule-ridden and snobbish, more utilitarian and informal. In its change from Authoritarian English, the language had several allies in the fields of communication and transportation.

With the establishment of the first cheap newspaper in England in 1816, the literate masses had a means of receiving propaganda and of exerting pressures upon the government. Aware of the dangers inherent in the sale of one-penny newspapers, Parliament slapped a fourpence-a-copy tax upon all periodicals in the island kingdom, but the tax was washed away in the swelling tide of reforms, and in 1836 the price of newspapers was only a penny. Large-circulation journalism provided a means not only of renewing the language but also of sanctioning its colloquial usage and of elevating the spoken standard to the written.

Journalists are notorious for their breezy styles, for these writers must make an instantaneous appeal to their audience or go out of business. They write for clarity, economy, and speed; they keep close to the accents of the human voice and an oral tradition constantly informs their writing. The union of the spoken and the written word often leads to neologisms and a dash of slang in what Joyce once called the *jinglish janglage.*

Today in both Britain and America the colloquial is king of the newspaper and the magazine. Thus *the beats* may very well be *pacifists* out *on a lark* that is not quite aesthetic *cricket*, but *the heavyweights* at the *summit eye-to-eye* know better than to *strike out* completely on the *ban-the-bomb pitch:* they might *lose their heads* in trying *to save face.* From politics to professional pugilism, present-day English journalese is a direct descendant of the cheap newspaper of the nineteenth century.

Accompanying the rise of popular journalism in Mature Modern English was the development of rapid methods of communication. The establishment of cheap postage in 1840 combined with use of the railroad to insure a swift exchange of correspondence in England. Twenty years later in the United States the expensive Pony Express from Missouri to California (1860–61) gave way to safer and cheaper railroad mail service. In the meantime, Samuel F. B. Morse had perfected the telegraph (1844). With the invention of the telephone by Alexander Graham Bell in 1876, an even faster and more personal method of communication entered the modern world. By the first decade of the twentieth century, Guglielmo Marconi had developed a system of wireless telegraphy, and Thomas A. Edison had invented the early stages of the modern cinema— the silent movie, a standard fare of entertainment in the nickelodeon theaters of pre-World War I.

James Watt discovered steam as an efficient form of energy. The growing mass production of goods and services accelerated technological demands and their attendant scientific inventions at an unprecedented rate. In 1803 Robert Fulton developed the first practicable steamboat. Sixty years later ironclad steamboats in the American Civil War ended wooden-ship navies and proved that steel was industrial king in an age of expanding markets. On land the railroads achieved a supremacy maintained well into the twentieth century. With the development of the gasoline engine, the automobile and the airplane added two new methods of transportation that further reduced the distances on earth and greatly increased human mobility.

The development of rapid methods of communication and transportation gave English a worldwide cohesiveness that, despite the local differences in vocabulary and pronunciation, kept future versions of British, American, and Commonwealth growing toward rather than away from one another. Lack of mobility and communication among the populace of any given tongue leads to dialect variants, which if allowed to further diverge can become separate languages, like Spanish and Portuguese. Both Old and Middle English supported major dialect variants and because of them, British English had to develop a Received Spoken Standard. Once achieved, this Standard spread throughout the various national versions of English in the farflung Empire. Rapid transportation and communication have kept Commonwealth English from becoming too unlike the parent language in Great Britain. In the United States, on the other hand, rapid transportation and communication accompanied the continental settling of a nation and prevented the rise of dialects at all. Only regional variants were permitted to exist. Today rapid transportation and communication continue to level what major differences remain among British, American, and Commonwealth English.

GROWTH IN VOCABULARY.   Every language is a mirror of the progress of the civilization for which it speaks. Mature Modern English reflected nineteenth-century advances in many different fields; its lexical enlargement included all areas of human endeavor. Such terms as *abolitionist, emancipation, rotten borough, suffragette, civil service*, and *proletariat* indicated developments in government affairs and political theory. *Horsepower, railway, dreadnaught, automobile, lorry, airplane, dirigible,* and *internal-combustion engine* pointed to the new achievements in the methods of transportation. Developments in electricity added the words *dynamo, commutator, alternating current*, and *arc light*. The *automobile* in America and the *motor car* in England, during the early twentieth century, contributed many technical terms to the language: *carburetor, spark plug, choke, clutch, gear shift, piston rings, throttle, differential, universal, steering wheel, ignition switch, starter, shock absorber, radiator, hood (bonnet), windshield (wind screen), bumper, chassis, hubcap, transmission, high, low, neutral, tire, crankshaft, crankcase, gas (petrol), skid, backfire*, and *garage*.

The progress in medicine during the period of Mature Modern English gave the language many words for new concepts: *acidosis, anemia, appendicitis, arteriosclerosis, bronchitis, diphtheria, osteopathy, bacteriology, immunology, orthodontia, adenoids, endocrine glands, hormones, enzymes, metabolism, proteins, carbohydrates, aspirin, iodine, anesthesia, morphine, strychnine,* and *allergy.* Physics contributed terms like *calorie, electron,* and *ionization,* whereas chemistry added words like *alkali, benzine, cyanide, formaldehyde, nitroglycerine,* and *radium.* Psychology with its *psychoanalysis* soon extended man's knowledge of himself with *ego, id, superego, libido, complex, apperception, egocentric, extravert, introvert, behaviorism, inhibition, repression,* and *frustration.* World War I brought Mature Modern English a new jargon of horror: *air raid, battleplane, antiaircraft gun, tank, whippet, blimp, gas mask, camouflage, sector, barrage, dud, hand grenade, dugout, machine gun, periscope, no man's land, doughboy, blighty, slacker, trench foot, cootie, war bride,* and *shell shock.*

To expand the size of its vocabulary, Mature Modern English—like all other languages—employed three basic processes of lexical growth: 1) creating new words from the morphological resources of the language; 2) extending use and meaning for words already in the language; and 3) borrowing new terms from other languages. Mature Modern English took *apéritif, bengaline, charmeuse, chauffeur, chiffon, consommé, garage, camouflage,* and *marquisette* from French; *confetti* and *vendetta* from Italian; *bonanza* from Spanish; *rucksack, zeppelin* and *zither* from German; *caracul* and *vodka* from Russian; *goulash* from Hungarian; *robot* from Czech; *afghan, loot,* and *thug* from the dialects of India; *pajamas* from Persian, and *chop suey* from Chinese. But the rate of borrowing had slowed down and Mature Modern English exploited its morphological resources to expand its vocabulary. In so doing, it proved itself strong in such methods of word formation as compounding, affixing, and the new process of blending.

Mature Modern English revived the key morphological process of Old English: *compounding.* But with a difference, for the compounds of the later version of the language tended to be *free* rather than *fixed.* As Jespersen has noted, the fixed compounds of English operate "as independent units, isolated from the component parts in sound and (or) meaning." Words like *daisy, woman, nostril, fifteen, Monday,* and *Christmas* furnish examples of this kind of compound. Speakers of the language may form free compounds, however, "after the pattern of already existing combinations." Such compounds may extend into sizable phrases like *railway station waiting room, New Year's Eve fancy dress ball*, and *dollar-a-week allowance*. Mature Modern English was especially rich in these phrasal "string compounds," as seen in such examples as *house-to-house call, cat-and-dog fight, summer garden party*, and *ringside seat*.

The capacity of the language for compounding, especially in epithet modifiers, was tested to the limit by the nineteenth-century poet Gerard Manley Hopkins. Some of Hopkins' most brilliant word combinations include *dapple-dawn-drawn Falcon, wanwood, leafmeal, mind-wandering, weed-winding, after-comers, couple-colour, fresh-firecoal chestnut-falls, wind-beat whitebeam, flake-doves, piece-bright, wimpled-water-dimpled, not-by-morning-matched face, girlgrace, dare-gale, flesh-bound, gold-vermilion, beam-blind, no-man-fathomed, lionlimb, rock-a-heart, shadow-tackle, root-room, lacklevel, prickproof, Amansstrength, selfyeast, day-labouring-out, raindrop-roundels, fawn-froth*, and *beak-leaved*. This creative predilection in Hopkins united with his metrical theories on "sprung rhythm" to give his poems some of the most energetic texture in the history of English literature, for the oldest resources of the language were fresh again through his use.

During Mature Modern English verb-object compounds came into vogue, a type of compound, illustrated by *pickpocket* (verb + object), that apparently originated in the Romance languages. From this new method of compounding came such combinations as *know-nothing, sawbones, breakwater, scarecrow, spoilsport*, and *turnkey*. The verb-object compound has also come to serve as an adjectival modifier, as in the following examples: *breakneck, telltale, lackluster, makeshift*, and *cut-rate*. In the twentieth century, verb-object compound modifiers have tended to include the definite article; thus a man with a *ban-the-bomb* philosophy asked a girl with a *wash-the-dishes* psychology for a date to hear a *love-the-enemy* lecture.

As a result of the advances of science during the nineteenth and the early twentieth century, there arose in Mature Modern English a need for new technical terms. The revival of compounding offered a morphological method, and the number of classical elements already a part of English usage became the elements. The *-scope*, from Greek *skopos* (watcher), moved far beyond the pseudoscience of astrology in *horo-*

scope, which predicted planetary influence on a person's life from the hour (*horo-*) of birth, to incorporate itself into the nomenclature of scientific instruments: with Greek *tele-* (*far*) as *telescope* in astronomy; with Greek *micro-* (*small*) as *microscope* in bacteriology; with Greek *stetho-* (*breast, chest*) as *stethoscope* in medicine; with Latin *fluoro-* (*flow*) as *fluoroscope* in X-ray examination; with Greek *peri-* (*around*) as *periscope* in submarine warfare.

Most of the morphology for scientific compounds in Mature and Late Modern English has been supplied by Greek, a language much like the Germanic tongues in its capacity for compounding. The fecundity of Greek morphemes in English scientific compounds has been great. The *tele-* of *telescope*, for instance, has accounted for *telecast, telecommunication, telegram, telegraph, telegraphoscope, telegraphy, telekinesis, telelectric, telemechanics, telemeter, telemotor, telepathy, telephone, telephoto, telephotography, teleprompter, telescript, telestereoscope, telesthesia, teletherapy, teletranscription, teletype, teletypesetter, teletypewriter, teleview, televise,* and *television.*

Scientific compounds in Mature and Late Modern English have been as fruitful in combinations upon their endings as upon their beginnings. In an age during which psychoanalysis has been able to isolate and treat man's basic fears, the category of fear itself has grown to enormous size. Hence the Greek base *-phobia* (*fear*) has combined with other classical morphemes to form the following list of scientific compounds that name the kinds of terror among human beings: *acrophobia*—fear of high places, *agoraphobia*—fear of open spaces, *androphobia*—fear of men, *astraphobia*—fear of thunderstorms, *autophobia*—fear of being alone, fear of self, *ballistophobia*—fear of missiles, *bathophobia*—fear of depths, *demophobia*—fear of crowds, *erythrophobia*—fear of the color red, *gynophobia*—fear of women, *haptephobia*—fear of being touched, *hemophobia*—fear of blood, *kinesophobia*—fear of movement, *mysophobia* —fear of contamination, *necrophobia*—fear of dead bodies, *neophobia*— fear of new things, *ophidiophobia*—fear of reptiles, *phonophobia*—fear of noise, *pyrophobia*—fear of fire, *taphephobia*—fear of being buried alive, *thanatophobia*—fear of death, *toxicophobia*—fear of poison, *zoophobia*—fear of animals.

Mature Modern English was also characterized by the extension of *affixing* as a chief morphological process. The vocabulary of English during the nineteenth and the early twentieth century was increased considerably by attaching familiar prefixes and suffixes to existent words in order to achieve new terms modeled by analogy upon the old. Thus the *trans-* of *transparent* joined with other bases to form such combinations as *transoceanic, transcontinental, trans-Siberian, transliteration, transformer, transfinite, transmarginal,* and *transpontine.* The *pre-* of *precede* and the *post-* of *postpone* formed new words like *prenatal, preschool, prehistoric, pre-Raphaelite, preheat, precool, preview, prerelease, prenuptial, postimpressionism, postprandial, postclassical, postgraduate,* and *postwar.*

A brief listing of the prefixes themselves include much morphological wealth: *up-, in-, an-, a-, n-, no-, non-, un-, dis-, de-, mis-, mal-, anti-, contra-, counter-, gain-, with-, ex-, for-, pro-, super-, sur-, hyper-, epi-, in-* (*il-, im-, ir-*), *en-* (*em-*), *intra-, intro-, by-, circum-, peri-, inter-, cis-, trans-, preter-, extra-, ultra-, through-* (*thorough-*), *sub-, hypo-, infra-, fore-, pre-, ante-, post-, mid-, co-, syn-, meta-, para-, be-, ana-, re-, retro-, demi-, semi-, hemi-, uni-* (*un-*), *mono-* (*mon-*), *bi-, poly-, pan-, panto-, proto-, neo-, palaeo-* (*paleo-*), *pseudo-, auto-, vice-,* and *arch-* (*archi-*). Impressive as this list of Jespersen's is, it is far from complete. When we consider the comparable use of suffixes in Mature Modern English, we realize that it would take a linguistic *super*man to final*ize* a study on the full range of neologistic affixing in Mature Modern English.

During Mature Modern English a new morphological process arose—*blending.* The initiator of this type of word formation was Lewis Carroll (1832–1898), the penname of Charles Lutwidge Dodgson, the professional mathematician who wrote two masterpieces of children's literature in England: *Alice's Adventures in Wonderland* (1865) and *Through the Looking-Glass* (1871). In the latter book, Alice has an encounter with Humpty Dumpty, the self-styled literary critic whose words mean just what he chooses them to mean:

> "You seem very clever at explaining words, sir," said Alice. "Would you kindly tell me the meaning of the poem called 'Jabberwocky?'"
>
> "Let's hear it," said Humpty Dumpty. "I can explain all the poems that ever were invented—and a good many that haven't been invented just yet."
>
> This sounded very hopeful, so Alice repeated the first verse:
>
> > "'Twas brillig, and the slithy toves
> > Did gyre and gimble in the wabe:
> > All mimsy were the borogroves,
> > And the mome raths outgrabe!"

"That's enough to begin with," Humpty Dumpty interrupted; "there are plenty of hard words there. '*Brillig*' means four o'clock in the afternoon—the time when you begin *broiling* things for dinner."

"That'll do very well," said Alice: "and '*slithy?*'"

"Well, '*slithy*' means 'lithe and slimy.' 'Lithe' is the same as 'active.' You see it's like a portmanteau—there are two meanings packed up into one word."

Thus did Lewis Caroll introduce a novel morphological process into English—one that could be either playful or serious: *Mimsy* is a facetious blend of *flimsy* and *miserable*. Lewis Carroll also contributed *chortle* (*snort* + *chuckle*) and *snark* (*snake* + *shark*) to the language. By 1900 the portmanteau *brunch* (*breakfast* + *lunch*) had come into English usage. The portmanteau of Carroll's invention is generally light-hearted and witty—like the following Late Modern English coinages: *paradoxology, alcoholiday, anecdotage, yellocution. Time* delights in this type of frothy blend: *cinemactress, cinemaddict, cinemagnate, cinemogul*. The city of Los Angeles has joined in with eye-watering *smog* (*smoke* + *fog*). As a blend, the portmanteau can also be dignified: *addressograph, linotype, stenotype, monotype, dictaphone, travelogue, bureaucrat, plutocrat, electrocute*, and *novocaine*.

When John Montagu (1718–1792), the fourth Earl of Sandwich, slapped a piece of meat between two slices of bread in order to dine without having to leave the gaming table, he invented an article of food that was to bear the proper name of his title: *sandwich*. Montagu thus gave impetus to expanding the English vocabulary by making a common word out of a proper name. Through this process English gained some useful terms during the nineteenth and the early twentieth century. In honor of James Watt, the father of the Industrial Revolution, the practical unit of electric power, activity, or rate of work was named a *watt*. Its derivatives and compounds include *wattage, watt-hour, kilowatt*, and *kilowatt-hour*.

In the scientific and technological advances achieved during Mature Modern English, other proper names became common words. Count Alessandro Volta (1745–1827), Italian pioneer in the study of electricity, received tribute in the term *volt*. By a similar method, *joule* honored James Prescott Joule (1818–1889), an English physicist; *ampere*, the French physicist Andre Marie Ampere (1775–1836); *ohm*, the German physicist Georg Simon Ohm (1787–1854). More recently, such scientific terms as *roentgen, curie,* and *einsteinium* have emerged through this morphological process. Some outstanding common words made from proper names in Mature Modern English were *tabasco sauce, camembert cheese, limousine, colt, wistaria, brougham, boycott, lynch law, to lynch, Mackintosh, raglan, Bakelite,* and *shrapnel.*

SEMANTIC SHIFTS.   When Humpty Dumpty says in *Through the Looking-Glass* that words mean what he wants them to mean, he is emphasizing the fact that meaning is determined by usage. One of the biggest mistakes of the purists is their habit of trying to hold a word to its original and "real" meaning, a mistake aptly called the *etymological fallacy.* Words mean what their speakers intend them to mean; words are always at the mercy of their users. Lexicographers are not at liberty to define a word according to what it may have meant a century or even a generation ago; they must define the word according to what it means at the moment, for that is the only meaning the word really has.

As a living language, English has continued to change semantically as well as lexically. Such change is not a sign of linguistic degeneration; on the contrary, it is a sign of regeneration, a process that must continue to operate lest the language die. English words are constantly free to undergo changes in meaning and social approbation. These changes may be called *semantic shifts.* The present-day term *deer,* for example, means "any member of the *Cervidae* family of ruminant animals that typically have deciduous antlers, usually in the male only, as the moose, elk, and reindeer." The word *deer* comes from the Old English *dēor,* which originally meant "any quadruped; a wild animal." Obviously the definition for the Old English word cannot be applied to its modern descendant. The word has undergone a semantic shift known as *specialization* or *restriction.*

In like manner, the word *lovely* has experienced a semantic shift from its original Old English meaning of "affectionate." Today the word has at least three categories of meaning: "possessing qualities that are capable of inspiring love and admiration"; "beautiful"; "delightful or pleasing." Whereas *deer* has experienced a restriction of meaning, *lovely* has enjoyed an *extension* of meaning that is properly called *generalization.* Old English *sēlig* has become modern English *silly,* with a meaning change from "happy and blessed" to "foolish"; Old English *cniht* became Middle English *knight,* with a meaning change from "boy or servant" to "feudal warrior of noble rank." *Silly* represents a semantic shift known as *pejoration*, a worsening of meaning; *knight*, on the other hand, represents a semantic shift known as *amelioration*, a bettering of meaning. The four great types of semantic shift active in Mature Modern English, therefore, were specialization, generalization, pejoration, and amelioration.

The native speakers of English have a habit of extending the meaning of a word until they have spent most of its value. Lord Chesterfield observed this linguistic phenomenon in an article in *The World* (No. 101, December 5, 1754), when he wrote:

> They take a word and change it, like a guinea into shillings for pocket-money, to be employed in the several occasional purposes of the day. For instance, the adjective *vast*, and its adverb *vastly*, mean anything, and are the fashionable words of the most fashionable people. A fine woman, under this head I comprehend all fine gentlemen too, not knowing in truth where to place them properly, is *vastly* obliged, or *vastly* offended, *vastly* glad, or *vastly* sorry. Large objects are *vastly* great, small ones are *vastly* little; and I had lately the pleasure to hear a fine woman pronounce, by a happy metonymy, a very small gold snuff-box that was produced in company to be *vastly* pretty, because it was *vastly* little.

Present-day speakers of the language might call Lord Chesterfield's observation either *awfully* good or *terribly* true or *just great.* Generalization, underway in the colloquial expressions of the polite society of Authoritarian English, gained momentum during the nineteenth and the early twentieth century and turned many terms into empty modifiers used by the cliché-ridden mind. Hemingway's characters use terms like *lovely* and *fine* to the point of boredom. Yet both words experienced extensions of meaning in Mature Modern English. So did *great* and *cute* and *dean.* As Baugh has indicated, the *proposition* of Lincoln's Gettysburg Address underwent quite a transformation of semantic possibilities—from a statement to be discussed or demonstrated to an offer of money, to almost anything. Every young woman in America and Britain around 1900 knew the difference between a *proposition* and a *proposal.*

But Mature Modern English also witnessed a corresponding restriction of meaning among words. A classic example of specialization is *doctor.* An urgent call at the theater in the nineteenth century, "Is there a doctor in the house?" could have only one meaning—a *physician* is needed. If the doctor failed at his task, then the recently deceased would require the attentions of an *undertaker*. This term is being replaced today by the euphemism of *mortician;* it originally meant someone who would undertake to do anything for pay. Similar restrictions of meaning in Mature Modern English included *wheel* for bicycle, *dress* for a lady's garment, *enlargement* for a large print in photography, *gas* for the fuel in a kitchen stove, *nickel* for a special type of American coin, and *Democrat* and *Republican* for specific political parties in the United States.

Union soldiers in the American Civil War usually expressed contempt for the *bomb-proofs* in Washington—that is, the civilian authorities safe from the front line fighting. To be *bomb-proof* today is a desirable thing. Thus words ameliorate in meaning. Mature Modern English sanctioned several terms that Dr. Johnson disparaged as not fit for standard usage: *budge, coax, nonplus, shabby, squabble, stingy, tiff, touchy*, and *wobbly*. *Sham* received approval in Mature Modern English, and the Victorian novelist Thackeray gave a respectability to the term *snob*. In Authoritarian English the adjective *sturdy* described the ruffian villain of the story; a century later the epithet suited the hero, for the word had ceased to convey a sense of "harsh, rough, intractable" and had assumed the primarily good meaning of "hardy and vigorous." *Smock* meant a woman's underwear as late as the eighteenth century; in Mature Modern English *smock* became an outer garment. The word *luxury* also rose in semantic value, for in Mature Modern English this term lost its exclusive association with sex in the original meaning of "lewdness."

In contrast, *peculiar*, which once meant, and still does mean "special, one's own," now also signifies something "queer, odd, or strange." The word *cunning*, originally meaning "knowledge" as a noun and "knowledgeable" as an adjective, came to epitomize the sense of clever machination for crooked gain, "crafty and deceptive guile." The adjective *smug* lost its good meaning of "neat and trim" and took on the objectionable significance of "self-satisfied and complacent." *Garble* furnishes another example of pejoration in Mature Modern English, for in Authoritarian English the word meant "to purify by sorting out the good from the bad." That many of the English grocers did not *garble* their spices, coffee beans, and rice grains properly must be assumed from what happened to the word, for in the nineteenth century the term achieved the bad meaning that it continues to carry: "to mix up, confuse, distort, mislead, or misrepresent." Other words which experienced pejoration were *pious, vulgar, amateur,* and *dilettante.* It was his use of the word *elegant* that proved the poet John Keats was not himself *genteel,* but a poor and rather unrefined Cockney. This critical charge against Keats was snobbish and cruel, but it illustrated the fact that usage in Mature Modern English was subject to amelioration and pejoration.

The decline in the linguistic gusto enjoyed by the Elizabethans, the purism of Authoritarian English, and the neoclassical aesthetics of the eighteenth century all combined to make stilted poetic diction. Though it did not infect the great novelists of the period, it joined with the cultural benefits of the Industrial Revolution to foster euphemisms among the social-climbing middle classes of Mature Modern English. Two sources for the obscene obtain in any language: sexual intercourse and the elimination of body wastes. The four-letter words that describe these biological functions are of vulgar usage and have always been taboo in polite society. Chaucer could get away with more in the way of spicy language than could even Shakespeare. With the enormous influx of polysyllabic foreign terms into English and the resultant development of a trilevel vocabulary (popular, literary, and learned), the possibilities for euphemistic expressions grew tremendously. The taboos kept pace, and called forth side-stepping language to avoid them.

In Margaret Mitchell's *Gone With The Wind* (1936), a decorous Mammy explains to an earthy young Scarlett O'Hara that horses *sweat* but young ladies *perspire.* Mammy's point is that there are some things that it is best not to talk about, but if we must, then we should use the least direct way of saying it. Indirection is the soul of euphemism, as seen in the following passage of *Roland for Oliver,* written in 1790 by the satirist Peter Pindar:

> I've heard that breeches, petticoats and smock,
> Give to thy modest mind a grievous shock
> And that thy brain (so lucky its device)
> Christ'neth them *inexpressibles* so nice.

The refinements of Mature Modern English changed *smock* to *shift, chemise, combinations,* and *step-ins,* and the *inexpressibles* became the *unmentionables.* Many a Victorian author, not wishing to bring a blush to a maiden's cheeks, called a *leg* a *limb.* In the evolution of the language, the terms for the place where a person "answers nature's call" have been such as these: *jakes, privy, outhouse, water-closet, W.C., toilet, bath-*

room, lavatory, smoking room, powder room, john, head, rest room, men's room, and *ladies' lounge.* In the United States during the late nineteenth century, a *barber* became a *tonsorial artist* and a *saloon* was often known as a *sample-room,* a *buffet,* an *exchange,* a *café,* or a *restaurant.* Pregnancy was a matter of *being in the family way.*

The thrust of euphemism from Mature Modern English has given impetus to a vast system of linguistic exaltations in present-day American English. With the disappearance of sharp class distinctions and the proliferation of scientific discoveries and technology, American English has a powerful tendency to confer sonorous titles upon commonplace occupations. Thus, H. L. Menken pointed out, there are such euphemisms as *realtor* for *real-estate agent, electragist* for *electrical contractor, aisle manager* for *floor-walker, beautician* for *hairdresser, exterminating engineer* for *rat-catcher,* and *superintendent* for *janitor.* Among recent euphemisms attendant upon the subject of death have been *body* or *patient* for *corpse, prepares* for *handles, preparation-room* or *operating-room* for *embalming-room, casket* for *coffin, funeral-car* or *casket-coach* for *hearse, invalid-coach* for *ambulance, négligé* or *slumber-shirt* or *slumber-robe* for *shroud,* and *memorial-park* or *cloister* or *burial-abbey* for *cemetery.* No *funeral director* in any *funeral home* in the United States would use the uncouth expression *graveyard.* Meanwhile the automotive marketing of America has been adept at changing *second-hand* to *reconditioned, rebuilt, repossessed* and *hardly used at all.*

SLANG.   Young men in America during the nineteenth century did not whistle at pretty young women; they cleared their throats instead. So widespread was this attention-getting habit during the Civil War that correspondents observed that the Army of the Potomac on the march to Gettysburg came down with a summer cold of epidemic proportions every time it passed through a town. Just as the *paralanguage* (nonverbal expressive sounds) of the American soldier has changed, so has his use of slang. And everybody uses slang.

Slang is a method of avoiding linguistic boredom; it springs from the desire for novelty and freshness. Slang has been growing constantly since the outset of the nineteenth century. As a matter of historical fact, the word *slang* itself was not included in Dr. Johnson's *Dictionary* of 1755. Advances in linguistics led to the objective study and approval of this feature of speech. In the nineteenth century, slang came into its own—

both as a vital method of rejuvenating English and as a subject for the descriptive analyses of lexicographers and linguists. What Noah Webster had dismissed as "low, vulgar, unmeaning language" in 1828 had come to be defined in the *Oxford Dictionary* in 1911 as "language of a highly colloquial type, below the level of standard educated speech, and consisting either of new words, or of current words employed in some special sense."

Slang has had a long history, as seen in the following terms and their dates of traceable origin: *to blow* (to boast), c. 1400; *duds* (clothes), 1567; *brass* (impudence), 1594; *to plant* (to hide), 1610; *bat* (a loose woman), 1612; *grub* (food), 1659; *to knock off* (to quit), 1662; *hush money*, 1709; and *racket*, 1785. *Booze*, as Mencken indicated, has remained slang since the fourteenth century. In the nineteenth century, these slang expressions became current: *to chisel* (1808), *to cheese it* (1811), *sap* (1815), *lip* (1821), *kibosh* (1836), and *to gas* (1847). Those same soldiers who kept clearing their throats on the way to Gettysburg were responsible for *bummer, coffee cooler, crawlies, Johnnies, lampposts, provos, rebs*, and *skedaddle*. They themselves were the *Willies*, and their wounds could be *bangers* or *poppers*, depending upon severity. Even if the slang in the mouths of the *bluesuits* differed from that of their *doughboy* and *GI* descendants, the habit of slang itself was in the language to stay.

FURTHER CODIFICATION.   Throughout the course of Mature Modern English there were further efforts to codify and refine the language. Isaac Pitman, the author of a system of shorthand (1837), promoted several plans for a phonetic spelling of English. By 1870 the English Philological Society was supporting simplified spelling; in 1883 the American Philological Society issued a long list of new spellings in cooperation with its British counterpart. The National Education Association by 1898 adopted twelve simplified spellings for its journals: *tho, altho, thoro, thorofare, thru, thruout, program, catalog, prolog, decalog, demagog*, and *pedagog*. In 1906 the American philanthropist Andrew Carnegie gave financial support to the organization of a Simplified Spelling Board, and Theodore Roosevelt endorsed its recommendation for the adoption of three hundred simplified spellings. Little came of this century of orthographic agitation, for a tradition of silent reading had placed emphasis on the visual morpheme, conventional spelling preserved the etymology of words, and homophones like *bred* and *bread* could enjoy their allographic distinctions under the old system.

In the meantime the purists of Mature Modern English were losing their battle against change. Thomas DeQuincey argued against using *implicit* in any sense other than the opposite of *explicit;* and George P. Marsh objected to the "vulgarism" of the phrase *in our midst* and attacked the use of the present participle as an adjective, a key morphological and syntactical refinement of Mature Modern English. This period of the language closed upon the founding of a Society for Pure English in 1913, but that society had the common sense not to attempt any "foolish interference with living developments." In the words of its poet laureate member Robert Bridges, the S.P.E. said that since "language is or should be democratic both in character and origin, and its best word-makers are the uneducated classes, we would prefer vivid popular terms to the artificial creations of scientists."

In the closing stages of Mature Modern and through the first two decades of Late Modern English, the Swedish philologist R. E. Zachrisson, Professor of English in the University of Uppsala, labored on a simplified spelling system that he felt would make English easier for foreigners to learn. For him it was the language with the two greatest claims on being an international tongue: simplicity of grammar and a cosmopolitan vocabulary. The major liability was its non-phonemic spelling. The phonetic modifications that Zachrisson made to achieve his international version known as *Anglic* were consistent and uniform, and they followed the old conventions whenever possible. The chief features of *Anglic* were 1) retention of the traditional spelling of "word signs"—about forty of the most common function words in the language; 2) use of the Roman alphabet without any change in its symbols; 3) consistent indication of the phonetic values of the principal vowels and diphthongs; and 4) marking of stress when it falls on some syllable other than the first by setting the accented vowel in bold face type.

Zachrisson's method of spelling was supposed to blunt the envy in the speakers of other languages by submitting English to the orthographic improvements of an "international form." An example of this "phonetically superior" Anglic may be seen in Zachrisson's version of the Gettysburg Address:

Forskor and sevn yeerz ago our faadherz braut forth on this kontinent a nue naeshon, konseevd in liberti, and dedikaeted to the propozishon that aul men ar kreeated eequel.

Now we are engaejd in a graet sivil wor, testing whedher that naeshon, or eni naeshon soe konseevd and soe dedikaeted, kan long enduer. We ar met on a graet batl-feeld of that wor. We hav kum to dedikaet a porshon of that feeld as a fienl resting-plaes for those who heer gaev their lievz that that naeshon miet liv. It is aultogedher fiting and proper that we shood do this.

But in a larjer sens, we kannot dedikaet—we kannot konsekraet—we kannot halo—this ground. The braev men, living and ded, who strugled heer, hav konsekraeted it far abuv our puur pour to ad or detrakt. The wurld wil litel noet nor long remember what we sae heer, but it kan never forget what they did heer. It is for us, the living, raadher, to be dedikaeted heer to the unfinisht wurk which they who faut heer hav dhus far soe noebli advaanst. It is raadher for us to be heer dedikaeted to the graet taask remaening befor us—that from these onerd ded we taek inkreest devoeshon to that kauz for which they gaev the laast ful mezher of devoeshon; that we heer hieli rezolv that these ded shal not have died in vaen; that this naeshon, under God, shal hav a nue burth of freedom; and that guvernment of the peepl, by the peepl, for the peepl, shal not perish from the urth.

Besides sounding very British, and therefore far removed from the frontier twang of Lincoln, Zachrisson's Anglic *looks* like a cheap novelist's attempt at mobster English. It violates the metaphysical pathos of visual morphology, because it is a test-tube language that has never been written by those who speak it.

Despite all the codification work of the eighteenth century, by the middle of the nineteenth century English still did not have an adequate dictionary, up-to-date and modern in its scholarship. In 1857 the Philological Society meeting in London appointed Herbert Coleridge, Dean Trench, and F. J. Furnivall to collect and publish a supplement to the incomplete dictionaries of the time. The project soon grew beyond supplement size, for Dean Trench convinced the society that the language needed a new dictionary that would record every word in use from about the year 1000 and depict its lexical history: in form, spelling, usage, and meaning. Hundreds of volunteer readers contributed illustrative quotations to the project, which gathered over six million examples before completion.

In the seventy-year period of its production (1858–1928), *A New Eng-*

lish Dictionary on Historical Principles (commonly known as the *NED* or the *OED*, a title added in 1895, *The Oxford English Dictionary*) had a succession of eminent editors: Herbert Coleridge, F. J. Furnivall, James A. H. Murray, Henry Bradley, William A. Craigie, and Charles T. Onions. Furnivall founded the Early English Text Society in 1864, Murray was knighted in 1908, and Craigie in 1928. Most important was the work itself: ten volumes, with 15,487 pages and 240,165 main words. The *NED* is the greatest dictionary of any language in the world. It has helped change dogma to science in linguistic study, has made speakers of English historically minded in the usage of their tongue, and has greatly increased the language perspective of the twentieth century. Despite an occasional unreliability in dates and etymologies the *NED* is a supreme monument to Mature Modern English.

THE STRUCTURE OF MATURE MODERN ENGLISH

GRAMMATICAL INNOVATIONS.   Certain grammatical features were meanwhile coming into focus. One such feature was the use of the present participle as an adjective preceding its substantive. In the nineteenth century the construction *you were* replaced *you was* in the singular and confirmed the plural use of *you* in all standard expressions of the verb. The weakened subjunctive mood all but disappeared from English usage; it maintained a twilight life in its morphological control over contrary-to-fact statements, in which *were* became the substitute for *was*. In colloquial speech especially, *don't* became—by analogy with *won't*—the clipped form of *doesn't*. In the relative pronoun *who/whom*, the objective-case form fell into disuse in interrogative statements. Most likely in analogy with unchanging *why*, *where*, *when*, and *how*, the uninflected *who* came to head all questions, even those in which the pronoun logically operates as an object—e.g., *Who did you hit?* As another grammatical feature of Mature Modern English, the *get/got* passive came into being—both as a dynamic substitute for the static *is/was* construction and as an informalizing alternate to the rather stiff *became*.

More important was the continued growth of the idiomatic preposition as adverb and noun formant. Acting somewhat like the separable prefixes in German, the idiomatic prepositions of Mature Modern English revitalized the language with such constructions as *put up, bring out, make over, shove off,* and *crack down.* Whereas similar Old English constructions usually placed the idiomatic preposition before the verb, as in *withstand* and *overcome,* a characteristic use of the idiomatic preposition in Mature Modern English was its positioning *after* the verb. The age of an idiomatic verb phrase or verb-adverb noun can generally be determined by this positioning. Thus to *overthrow* the government or witness a government *overthrow* is an older combination than to *hold over* a movie in the neighborhood theater or to go see such a *holdover.* Starting as simple intensifications of the verb, the idiomatic prepositions of Mature Modern English soon passed beyond that stage, as in *climb up* and *fall down,* and assumed figurative meanings. Thus *step up* means to accelerate, whereas *let up* means to slow down or stop. Epitomizing the vitality of the idiomatic preposition, *up* has entered into such popular expressions as *add up, ask up, bang up, break up, call up, cough up, crack up, dig up, dish up, drum up, ease up, foul up, goof up, gum up, hold up, jack up, join up, kick up, lay up, mash up, nick up, pass up, perk up, pop up, queue up, rip up, roll up, scrape up, shut up, stink up, talk up, tank up, wall up, work up,* and *wrap up.*

PHONOLOGY.   The similarity of Mature Modern English to Late Modern English was first of all a matter of phonology. The phonemes of both versions of English are identical: /p b m f v θ ð t s d j n l c š r j ž h k g y ŋ w/ as the consonants, /i ɫ u e ɘ o æ a ɔ/ as the simple vowels, and /y w h/ as the offset glides. Mature Modern English enjoyed the same distinctive acoustic features as does Late Modern. Against the rather colorless sound patterns of eighteenth-century neoclassical poetry, the phonemic texture of the Parnassian lines of Tennyson in the nineteenth is noted for its liquidity, nasality, and gravity. These characteristics, also present in the Romantic strains of Edgar Allan Poe in America, are a deliberate attempt to develop euphony and to avoid cacophony. Ruminative in tone and decorative in method (alliteration, assonance, consonance, and onomatopoeia), much of the poetry of Mature Modern English is phonologically "pretty."

The suprasegmentals of that poetry, as for the language itself, are the same ones that govern the intonation patterns of present-day English: four degrees of stress, four levels of pitch, four kinds of juncture, and four major intonation contours. In contrast with Authoritarian English, the language of the nineteenth and the early twentieth century supported more stability in the tense vowels and a greater tendency toward syllabic zeroing in stressless positions. Using the same tongue height as that employed in Late Modern English, stress modification was far more important in the phonemic morphology of the language of Tennyson than of the language of Pope. During Mature Modern English the pronunciations of the principal varieties of the language jelled, with their dialect and regional differences: British, American, and Commonwealth. A major difference between Mature and Late Modern has been the recent tendency toward leveling phonological variations, both within the national versions themselves and on an international basis.

MORPHOLOGY.   Parallel with the phonemic correspondence between Mature and Late Modern English runs a morphological similarity. Our language today supports the same basic types of morphemes as did the nineteenth and early twentieth century: bound phonemic, bound syllabic, and free word simple. Those morphemes combine in the same ways: by affixing, compounding, reduplication, blending, inflectionalizing, internal modification, stress modification, and the like. Compared with the current versions of the language, Mature Modern English had an underdeveloped system of acronyming. But World War I, with its armies, bureaus, code names, inventions, and civilian mobilizations, gave rise to the economy of shortening names on initial letters and syllables.

   Characterized by a return to the self-explanatory compound, by an extension of affixing, and by a rise of scientific terminology based upon Greek and Latin derivatives, Mature Modern English further refined the present participle, continued to weaken the subjunctive, and revitalized some of its shopworn diction with slang, colloquialism, coinage, and the idiomatic preposition. Lexically, the language grew at a rapid rate.

SYNTAX.   The linguistic advances of Mature Modern English were mirrored in its syntax. Built syntactically on the rhythmical structures of its major word groups, the English of the nineteenth and early twentieth century modified its analytic hypotaxis. A slow return to the flavor of the spoken word, evidenced in the informalizing influence of journalism, resulted in a more flexibly constructed sentence and in a greater range of nonstandard sentence types. With more gusto and variety, with less adherence to the proscriptive grammatical rules of Authoritarian

English, Mature Modern English loosened up idiomatic constructions and streamlined syntactical usage. The language supported the same major sentence features it does today: subject-verb-inner-complement-outer-complement word order under normal conditions, relatively fixed positioning of essential elements, general movability of nonessential elements, and a fully developed system of syntactical linkage to express both coordination and subordination.

The needs of mass-media communication and the accelerated pace of a world of scientific discovery and democratic policy influenced the language; Mature Modern English, unlike its Authoritarian forerunner, was syntactically more given to shirtsleeves and bare heads than to dress coats and periwigs. The informal and the utilitarian in the syntax of Mature Modern English united with a return to the speaking voice, obvious in the poetry of Byron and in the prose of Mark Twain, to develop a wealth of different styles that were the literary glories of the language in the nineteenth and the early twentieth century.

MATURE MODERN ENGLISH POETRY.   From the Scottish dialect verse of Robert Burns (1759–1796) to the imagistic manifestoes of the young Ezra Pound (b. 1885), Mature Modern English poetry was one of the supreme achievements of the language. The shift from the neoclassical tradition was epitomized in the difference between Pope's

> True wit is Nature to advantage dressed,
> What oft was thought, but ne'er so well expressed;

and the following lines of William Blake (1757–1827):

> To see a World in a grain of sand,
> And a Heaven in a wild flower,
> Hold Infinity in the palm of your hand,
> And Eternity in an hour.

It is the difference between imitative conformity and original intensity, between aristocratic correctness and democratic dignity, between retentive intellect and inventive imagination. With the publication of their *Lyrical Ballads* in 1798, William Wordsworth (1770–1850) and Samuel Taylor Coleridge (1772–1834) emphasized this difference in the natural and homely diction of the "common man."

The lyric in the hands of Blake, Wordsworth, and Coleridge became experimental; a return to Elizabethan exuberance was responsible for a vast variety of verse forms, subject matter, and stylistic techniques. The highest accomplishments in the poetry of Mature Modern English were in the narrative tradition. Extremely imagic, symbolic, and mythic, the narrative poem became a vehicle for philosophical meditation with Wordsworth, Robert Browning (1812–1889), and Walt Whitman (1819–1892); for exotic tales with Coleridge and Edgar Allan Poe (1809–1849); for lyric flights of reflection with Alfred Lord Tennyson (1809–1892) and Edward Fitzgerald (1809–1883); and for satiric digression with George Noel Gordon, Lord Byron (1788–1824). While the dramatic poetry in Mature Modern English remained statuesque and imitative, the nineteenth century saw the rise of great closet drama in the work of Byron and Percy Bysshe Shelley (1792–1822) and an innovational blend of the dramatic with the narrative in the monologues of Browning. Browning's inventive genius was matched by the experiments with the sonnet and the sensuous ode by John Keats (1795–1821). Byron wrote a masterpiece in the imported *ottava rima* of *Don Juan*, and Whitman, with his free verse, and Gerard Manley Hopkins (1844–1889), with his sprung rhythm, refined the rhythmical expression of the language. Meanwhile, Lewis Carroll created a new tradition of nonsense verse for both children and adults.

MATURE MODERN ENGLISH PROSE.   The prose of Mature Modern English luxuriated in a great variety of styles. In nonfiction, it was manifested in the theoretical criticism of Coleridge, the informal-essay whimsy of Charles Lamb (1775–1834), the titanic Teutonism in the historical writings of Thomas Carlyle (1795–1881), the eclectic classicism in the formal essays of Ralph Waldo Emerson (1803–1882), the simple eloquence of the political addresses of Abraham Lincoln (1809–1865), and the Cyrenaic decadence in the preciosity of Walter Pater (1839–1894). In fiction, that variety was apparent in the Gothic mood pieces of Emily Brontë (1818–1848), the historical descriptions of Sir Walter Scott (1771–1832), the ratiocinative stories of Poe, the dynamic caricatures of Charles Dickens (1812–1870), the Olympian prose-poetry of Herman Melville (1819–1891), the satiric realism of William Makepeace Thackeray (1811–1863), the illogical logic of Lewis Carroll, and the sensuously exotic rhythms of the fairy tales of Oscar Wilde (1854–1900).

As the dictatorial prudence of Dr. Johnson spoke for late eighteenth-century criticism, so did the touchstone "sweetness and light" of Matthew

Arnold (1822–1888) speak for the late nineteenth. Adequate for both literary criticism and philosophical exegesis, the prose of Mature Modern English was flexible enough to accommodate also the novel, drama, and children's literature. Mature Modern English prose experienced the beginnings of specialist scientific vocabularies and scholarly jargons, which in Late Modern English have become serious obstructions to clear communication. In its tendency toward the informal and the utilitarian, Mature Modern English prose prepared the way for the present-day flood of advertising. Yet in its return to spoken English and the accents of the human voice, the prose of the nineteenth and the early twentieth century expressed the deepest realities of the human heart.

Nowhere did those realities talk with greater honesty than in the fictional truth of Huckleberry Finn. As the master of a classically colloquial prose style, his creator Mark Twain (1835–1910) graced Mature Modern English with the perfection of a method that may be called "the American natural." In that method, Twain demonstrated that the United States had, in three centuries of development, achieved its own brand of English.

QUESTIONS FOR RESEARCH AND DISCUSSION

1. Organize a research project on the impact of journalism upon the development of Mature Modern English. Pay attention to the rise of the informal and the utilitarian in usage. In what ways were British and American English different in such usage during the nineteenth and the early twentieth century? In what ways were they alike?

2. Let five members of the class organize a panel discussion on the "phonological prettiness" of nineteenth-century English poetry, using the works of Coleridge, Keats, Tennyson, Arnold, and Swinburne as the bases for the discussion. What sound-pattern features do these poets master in common? In what features do they differ? Do they support Pope's theory that "The sound must seem an Echo to the sense"? Defend your answer in detail.

3. Organize a series of class reports on the vocabulary growth of Mature Modern English. Let one student concentrate on each of the following topics: borrowings from Romance languages; borrowings from Asia; borrowings from Africa; borrowings from India; scientific compounds based on Greek and Latin; coinages based on native morphology.

4. Investigate the rise of the humorous portmanteau and the serious blend in Mature Modern English. From this investigation, collect a dictionary

of the portmanteaus and blends formed between 1800 and 1920. What are some of the most outstanding examples of this morphological process?

5. Let four members of the class use the *New English Dictionary* to study the semantic shifts of Mature Modern English and then report on the central features of amelioration, pejoration, generalization, and specialization during the nineteenth and the early twentieth century.

6. Let five members of the class organize a panel discussion, based upon intensive research, on the following major attributes of Mature Modern English: elevation of the colloquial to written standard; tolerance for slang; use of the present participle as an adjective; extension of affixing; emergence of the idiomatic preposition as directive adverb and noun formant. Use the poetry of Byron and the prose of Dickens to illustrate these attributes.

7. Let two members of the class report on the compound adjectives of Gerard Manley Hopkins and Dylan Thomas. How do these two poets differ in their revival of this Anglo-Saxon poetic resource? In what ways are they alike?

8. Conduct a series of classroom reports on the rhythm contributions to Mature Modern English made by the poetry of Shelley, Browning, and Hopkins, and by the prose of Carlyle, Pater, and Wilde. Mimeograph and distribute representative passages from the works of these writers for the purpose of organizing a classroom analysis of their word-group cadences.

9. Let four members of the class organize a debate, two pro and two con, on the following proposition: *That the democratic leveling of classes during Mature Modern English constituted a major influence upon the language*

10. Investigate the euphemisms and taboos of Mature Modern English. Have these euphemisms and taboos carried over into Late Modern English? What evolution has taken place in these features of the language? Is present-day English more inventive of euphemism than was Victorian? Defend your answer in detail.

SELECTED BIBLIOGRAPHY

Baugh, Albert C. *A History of the English Language*. Second Edition. New York: Appleton-Century-Crofts, 1957. See especially Chapter 10, pp. 356–405, for an account of the evolution of Mature Modern English in "The Nineteenth Century and After," with splendid bibliography.

Bloomfield, Morton W., and Leonard Newmark. *A Linguistic Introduction to the History of English*. New York: Alfred A. Knopf, 1963. See especially

Chapter VIII, pp. 326–366, for a study of the growth of English vocabulary and the extension of its morphological processes.

Bryant, Margaret M. *Modern English and Its Heritage*. Second Edition. New York: The Macmillan Company, 1962. Section III ("Words"), pp. 223–433, provides a detailed account of the major lexical, morphological, and grammatical features of Mature and Late Modern English.

Chew, Samuel C. *The Nineteenth Century and After (1789–1939)*. Volume IV of *A Literary History of England*, edited by Albert C. Baugh. New York: Appleton-Century-Crofts, 1948. The best one-volume critical survey of the literary effort in the British version of Mature Modern English.

Robertson, Stuart, and Frederic G. Cassidy. *The Development of Modern English*. Second Edition. Englewood Cliffs, New Jersey: Prentice-Hall, 1954. See especially Chapter 12, pp. 375–418, for a study of the problems of pronunciation, variations, and standards in Mature and Late Modern English, with an excellent bibliography.

Trevelyan, G. M. *History of England, Volume III: From Utrecht to Modern Times*. New York: Doubleday, Anchor Books, 1953. See especially pp. 95–296 for a discussion of the political and social background of Mature Modern English, with emphasis upon the Industrial Revolution and the transition to democracy.

CHAPTER **11**

American English

IMPORTANT DATES

1607–1790 The first period of European immigration, predominantly British. The language is Colonial American English.

1790–1860 The second period of European immigration, predominantly Irish and German. The language is now Continental-Expansion American English.

1816 John Pickering compiles and publishes the first dictionary of Americanisms.

1828 Noah Webster publishes his two-volume *An American Dictionary of the English Language,* a key document in the growing awareness of the independent nature of American English, and a great influence on American spelling and pronunciation habits.

1848 John R. Bartlett's *Dictionary of Americanisms* furthers the cause of American independence in the use of English.

1855 The first edition of Whitman's *Leaves of Grass,* symbolizing the rise of an independent American literary tradition.

1860–1890 The third period of European immigration, predominantly British and Teutonic. The language is now Independent-Status American English.

1866 James Russell Lowell champions the use of American regionalisms, helping to end deference to the Received British Standard.

1884 Mark Twain's *The Adventures of Huckleberry Finn* introduces a prose style of the natural conversational, with marked influence on all subsequent writing of fiction in America.

1890–1910 Rapid transportation, mass-media communication, and modern science exercise great influences on American English.

1890–1920 The fourth period of European immigration, predominantly Italian and Slavic. The United States becomes a true melting pot, and its language is Nationalist American English.

1917 T. S. Eliot's *Prufrock and Other Observations* modernizes American poetry.

1919 H. L. Mencken's *The American Language* is a pioneer study in the history of a major national version of English.

1920–1930 The Jazz Age intensifies the use of the informal, utilitarian, pragmatic, colloquial, and slangy in Modern American English.

1920–present The period of modern technology and worldwide immigration. The language is now World-Power American English, with immense linguistic and literary prestige.

1925 George P. Krapp publishes his two-volume *The English Language in America*, the first comprehensive and scholarly treatment of the subject.

1925–1930 Commercial radio and talking motion pictures begin their influence on Modern American English.

1930 Sinclair Lewis is the first American author to win the Nobel Prize in literature—official recognition of the aesthetic maturity of American English.

1931 Work begins on the *Linguistic Atlas of the United States and Canada*, an important document in modern linguistic geography.

1933 Leonard Bloomfield publishes *Language*, the foundation of modern linguistic science in America.

1939 John Crowe Ransom starts the *Kenyon Review*, an important journal in the rise of the New Criticism in America.

1948 Commercial television begins its enormous impact on modern American English through the "folk poetry" of advertising.

1949 Hans Kurath's *A Word Geography of the Eastern United States* is a linguistic landmark in the scientific study of American regionalisms.

1957 Noam Chomsky publishes his *Syntactic Structures*, a key document in generative and transformation grammar.

OUTSTANDING PERSONS

Emily Dickinson (1830–1886) Greatest woman poet of American English and founder of a modern idiosyncratic style.

Ralph Waldo Emerson (1803–1882) The catalytic agent for an original American literature and intellectual culture.

William Faulkner (1897–1962) Great American novelist and master of a modern Gongoric style.

Robert Frost (1874-1963) Father of the easy blend of the conversational and the philosophical in modern American poetry.

Henry James (1843–1916) The supreme aesthetician for the modern American novel as a literary art form.

Thomas Jefferson (1743–1826) and James Madison (1751–1836) Fathers of the American Constitutional prose style.

Sinclair Lewis (1885–1951) As the first American to win the Nobel Prize in Literature, Lewis symbolizes the enormous influence of the American novel in the twentieth century.

Abraham Lincoln (1809–1865) The American statesman who elevated the political address to the level of *belles lettres*.

H. L. Mencken (1880–1956) Popular pioneer in the study of American English.

Eugene O'Neill (1888–1953) The playwright who elevated American dramatic prose to the level of world stature.

Edgar Allan Poe (1809–1849) Founder of the American short story and forerunner, by French adoption, of twentieth-century American and English poetry.

John Crowe Ransom (b. 1888) Dean of the New Criticism in twentieth-century American English.

J. D. Salinger (b. 1919) Master of present-day teenage slang and of an informal conversational prose style.

Carl Sandburg (b. 1878) Poet and Boswell of American biography.

Edward Taylor (1645–1729) The supreme poet of Colonial American English.

Mark Twain (1835–1910) Father of the natural-conversational in modern American prose style.

Noah Webster (1758–1843) Nineteenth-century lexicographer, Webster has had the largest single impact on the spelling and pronunciation habits of American English.

Walt Whitman (1819–1892) The creator of a new metrical tradition in American poetry and the founder of a native literature of world stature.

MAJOR ATTRIBUTES OF THE LANGUAGE

Supports regional variants rather than true dialects.

Is arrested and conservative in some of its evolutionary features, especially in folk speech.

Develops a vocabulary diverging from native British English.

Is flatter in intonation and less weak in secondary stressing than British English.

Is generally less tense in pronunciation than British English.

Becomes more dynamic in idiomatic usage than British English.

Operates more by hyperbole (exaggeration) than by litotes (understatement).

Suffers from the snobbery of the culturally insecure.

Experiences a journalistic leveling of prose style to fit the lowest common denominator of mass-media intelligence.

Undergoes rapid exhaustion of lexical meaning and originality of expression under the constant impact of high-pressure advertising.

Constantly renews itself via the elevating of slang and the colloquial to the level of standard written usage.

Is flexible, daring, and imaginative in its morphological processes.

Becomes informal and utilitarian, with natural simplicity and sincerity.

Maintains a vast proliferation of specialist jargons.

Has achieved a finer creative prose tradition than discursive.

THE HISTORICAL DEVELOPMENT OF American English, a major offspring of the parent British, has taken place in five general stages, through five distinct periods. The first stage was the Colonial Period, which ran from the settling of Jamestown in 1607 to the ratification of the Federal Constitution in 1789. In this period Elizabethan English was transplanted to a new soil, where different surroundings yielded new names in the form of Indian, French, and Dutch imports. The derivative culture of the Colonial Period resulted in a highly imitative American literature. The second stage in the development of American English was the Continental Expansion, a period that extended from 1790 to 1860, the eve of the American Civil War. A transplanted Eastern conservatism met with a frontier spirit that disregarded tradition, and the language grew in morphological flexibility. Imports from Spanish, German, and Irish swelled the vocabulary of American English during the Continental Expansion. The third stage of development was the period of Independent Status, which extended from 1860 to 1890, when immigration from Latinic and Slavic countries began. In the three decades of this period, a national literature was founded, and Webster, Bartlett, Lowell, Whitman, and Twain opposed both purists and deference to the Received British Standard. American English was truly on its own.

The fourth stage of development, the Nationalist, was a period of thirty years (1890–1920) that witnessed the growth of rapid transportation and communication and of scientific discoveries and technological inventions. World War I, the "Lost Generation," a new aesthetics, and the first edition of Mencken's *The American Language* prepared the way for the fifth and present stage—the period of World Power. This period began with the "Roaring Twenties" and has continued through today. From 1920 on, American English has undergone the influences of the Jazz Age; the impact of such mass-media communications as radio, television, and the movies; World War II and the emergence of the Atomic Age and the Space Age; further developments in the novel, the drama, and linguistic science, and the rise of the New Criticism.

COLONIAL AMERICAN ENGLISH, 1607–1790

THE LANGUAGE BROUGHT TO THE New World by the early colonists was basically Elizabethan English, the tongue of Shakespeare. But within this English, the Puritans spoke an East Anglian bourgeois lingua franca; the landowners of the Southern plantations, a version of the cultivated and aristocratic speech of London. Thus the /o/ of New England *cot* is due to the fact that East Anglian English, having "loose contact" after stops, did not undergo the aristocratic "close contact" change from /o/

to /a/. Colonial American English varied rather markedly from the present-day version of the language; *clerk* rhymed with *dark, convert* with *art, serve* with *carve,* and *heard* with *regard.* Six complex vowel clusters were transitions from Middle English: /ih ɬw uh eh əy əw/. The /ey/ of such words as *meat, teach, sea, tea, lean,* and *beard* was often the substitute for present-day /iy/. The phonemic value of *oo* in such words as *flood, good,* and *mood* was quite flexible, but the *ir, er, ur* in words like *bird, fern,* and *turn* had merged into the same phonemic cluster: /ɬr/. The *o* in *fog* generally had the sound of /ɔ/.

The stress patterns of Colonial American English were frequently different from those of today. Trisyllabic words like *character'd* often received maximum accent on the middle syllable, whereas two-syllable terms like *turmoil* were usually stressed on the terminal syllable. The forwarding of stress in English was still going on when the British colonists came to America. Nor were morphological and syntactical refinements yet complete. Colonial American English had inherited the inflectional simplicity of forming noun plurals and the weak past tense and past participle. But the use of *thou/thee* and *ye/you* was far from settled, and generated a morphemic tolerance in the present tense of the indicative singular of the verb, for *thou* dictated an *-est* inflection to supplement the still unresolved rivalry between *-eth* and *-s* in the third person of the verb. Archaic usage in the language of the colonists allowed such forms as *inacomodate, hasted, yea, unto,* and *beholden.* The pronoun *other* was often used in the plural, and the adverb did not demand the *-ly* morpheme so strongly as it does today.

The spelling habits of Colonial American English were as chaotic as those of Early Modern English—everybody seemed to have his own system, as seen in the orthography of William Bradford (1590–1657), the second governor of Plymouth Colony: *togeather, moneths, ther, espetialy, sadd, lothsome, cloaths, homly, quesie, cherfully, shewing, lamnes, doute, cann, beere, begane, maisters, tould, boatson, allmost, halfe, lustyest,* and *dyed.* Colonial American English was also deficient in syntactical and stylistic refinements. Besides the frequent lack of agreement between subject and verb and the universal pronominal preference for *that* over *who,* the language of the colonists showed poor subordination, violations of parallelism, dangling modifiers, and unconventional sentence fragments. The prose style of the colonists, like the language, was unpolished.

INDIAN INFLUENCE.   Once the colonists had settled in the New World, they found their language inadequate for all the needs of a culture unlike the one they had left in England. A different flora, fauna, landscape, and people met the colonists at every turn, and the new surroundings demanded new words to name, describe, and understand. When Jamestown was founded in 1607, there were between a million and a million and a half Indians in North America. Grouped into twenty-five major families, they spoke approximately three hundred and fifty different languages. From these languages American English was to adopt and adapt the lexical items that it needed. Of the 1700 Indian words still active in American English, about half entered the language during the seventeenth century, mostly from the Algonquian family of languages; the other half was equally divided between the eighteenth and the nineteenth century.

But the death rate of Indian loans has been enormous—of 132 Algonquian loans only 34 have survived to the present day. With the ascertained dates of their entrance into American English, these are *caribou* (1610), *chinquapin* (1645), *chipmunk* (1832), *hickory* (1618), *hominy* (1629), *mackinaw* (1812), *menhaden* (1643), *moccasin* (1612), *moose* (1613), *mugwump* (1663), *muskellunge* (1789), *oppossum* (1610), *papoose* (1634), *pecan* (1773), *pemmican* (1791), *persimmon* (1612), *podunk* (1666), *poke* (1634), *pone* (1612), *powwow* (1624), *raccoon* (1608), *sachem* (1622), *scuppernong* (1811), *skunk* (1588), *squash* (1634), *squaw* (1634), *succotash* (1751), *Tammany* (1771), *terrapin* (1672), *toboggan* (1829), *tomahawk* (1612), *totem* (1609), *wigwam* (1628), and *woodchuck* (1674). This list of Mencken's shows that the Indian influence on American English has been like the Celtic on British English. Indian words that have remained vital in the language deal with Indian civilization, its culture and institutions; many of these words are the names of plants, animals, and foods that the Indians introduced to the colonists.

The colonists altered the Indian loans by simplifying and shortening them, as in *squash* from *askutasquash* and *raccoon* from *raughroughcums*, and they had to Anglicize their Indian borrowings, for the Indians often nasalized their vowels and made strange consonant sounds with pharynx and epiglottis. Initial clusters like *mt*, *psh*, and *kch* must have been close to impossible for the speakers of English. The American colonists applied their folk etymology to Indian morphemes and produced equivalents like *woodchuck* from the Cree or Ojibwa word for "fisher" or "weasel": *wuchak, otchak,* or *odjig.*

Despite the compounds and derivatives formed from Indian loans, this earliest influence on American English has been neither extensive nor profound. A good linguistic test of the impact of one language on another is the appropriation of verbs; only four verbs remain as a result of Indian influence: *caucus, powwow, tomahawk,* and *skunk.* Expressions built upon *Indian*—like *Indian claim, Indian summer, Indian file, Indian giver*—and the few translations such as *paleface, firewater,* and *Great White Father* do not hide the fact that a subjugated people usually do not offer much to the language of the conqueror.

FRENCH INFLUENCE. In the struggle to control and settle the New World, English-speaking colonists encountered French-speaking explorers, trappers, traders, and missionaries. What the British transplants did not learn from the Indians they picked up from the French, for the French mingled more freely with the Indians, traded with them regularly, lived among them, and married them. Thus French became a linguistic bridge from Indian tongues to the nascent American English. Unlike the Indian languages of North America, French was prestigious and influential. As Albert H. Marckwardt has said, French "was important in New England because Calvin had written in it; in the South because it constituted part of the equipment of a gentleman."

Though many French loans to the language of the New World have died out, quite a few remain. They are terms for plants and animals, for foods, for the terrain of the continent and its local features, for exploration and travel, for general culture, and even for coinage: *caribou, crappie, gopher, pumpkin; brioche, chowder, jambalaya, praline, sazarac; bayou, butte, chute, coulee, crevasse, flume, levee, prairie, rapids, sault; bateau, cache, carry-all, pirogue, portage, toboggan, voyageur; apache, brave* (Indian), *bureau, Cajun, calumet, Canuck, chambray, charivari* (shivaree), *depot, lacrosse, lagniappe, parlay, picayune, rotisserie, sashay, shanty; cent, dime,* and *mill.* Since French was easier to pronounce than Indian languages, the English-speaking colonists did not have to adapt its loans so much. In general, Anglicizing French linguistic imports amounted to forwarding stress and naturalizing the French *u* in words like *butte, flume,* and *bureau.* The imports from French were all nouns, except for *sashay,* a verb later joined by three widely used functional shifts: *portage, cache,* and *toboggan.* The scarcity of French verbs as direct loans to American English indicates that French did not exercise anything like the enormous impact it had made earlier upon British English.

DUTCH INFLUENCE. In 1664, New Amsterdam was taken over by the English-speaking colonists who were to organize New York City. Thus the influence of the Dutch was felt early in the course of American English, though they did not offer so large a lexical contribution to American English as did the French. But what the Dutch gave in loan words went deep into the permanent vocabulary of American English; their contribution was less extensive but more penetrating than the French. It is to the Dutch that American English owes the name *Yankee.* The term *Jan Kees,* meaning "John Cheese," was the contemptuous label of the Dutch for the hard-headed, shrewd-bargaining, small-farming New Englander of the seventeenth century. Mistaken as a plural by the New Englanders and Anglicized into a back-formation, the name *Jan Kees* got singularized into *Yankee,* first a regional, then a national term for an American.

Other important Dutch contributions to American English are *boodle, boss, bush* (back country), *caboose, cole slaw, cookie, cruller, dingus, dope, dumb* (stupid), *hay barrack, hook* (of land), *logy, patroon, pit* (stone or seed), *poppycock, pot cheese, Santa Claus, saw buck, scow, sleigh, snoop, span* (of horses), *spook, stoop* (porch), and *waffle.* Most Dutch words, like the Indian and the French, were borrowed as nouns. *Dumb* and *logy* were and remain adjectives; *snoop* was a verb, now also functionally shifted into a noun; *pit, boss,* and *sleigh* have all been shifted to verbs. The term *boodle* has entered into several derivatives: *boodleize, boodleism, boodleistic, boodler, boodlerism, boodlery,* and *boodling. Caboose* has evolved semantically through "ship's galley," "outdoor oven," "hut," and "freight-train crewcar."

PURITAN LITERATURE. Colonial American English was dominated by a Puritan tradition that nearly turned New England into a theocracy. Emphasizing piety and religious sobriety, this tradition placed a premium on pragmatic will rather than on aesthetic sensibility. As a result of the anti-imaginative Puritan attitude and the frontier habit of rewarding the doer rather than the thinker, the interested action rather than the disinterested act, most early American literature championed the "language of information" rather than the "language of formation." That literature was characterized by the fanaticism of those who preferred preaching to art: John Winthrop (1588–1649), Michael Wigglesworth (1631–1705), Increase Mather (1639–1723), Cotton Mather (1663–1728), and Jonathan Edwards (1703–1758). The literary output of Colonial American English, heavily weighted with dogma, was mainly theology, chronicled history, and the private journal. The novel and the drama were practically nonexistent, and poetry was a rhyming tool of moral instruction. Wigglesworth's *Day of Doom* (1622) defends the damnation of those who "never had good or bad effected pers'nally" because they died in infancy:

> A crime it is, therefore in bliss
>   you may not hope to dwell;
> But unto you I shall allow
>   the easiest room in Hell.
>
> The glorious King thus answering,
>   they cease, and plead no longer:
> Their Consciences must needs confess
>   his Reasons are the stronger.

A better poet was Anne Bradstreet (1612–1672), but even she choked off true feeling with the constricting hand of pietistic orthodoxy—as seen in the following lines of lament for her dead child:

> By nature trees do rot when they are grown
> And plums and apples thoroughly ripe do fall,
> And corn and grass are in their season mown,
> And time brings down what is both strong and tall.
> But plants new set to be eradicate,
> And buds new blown, to have so short a date,
> Is by his hand alone that guides nature and fate.

The finest Puritan poet was Edward Taylor (c. 1644–1729), discovered and published so recently as 1937. A baroque metaphysical, Taylor's religious ecstasy found expression through symbolic logic, homely conceits, simple proverbs, provincial or newly coined language, complex and packed syntax, and syncopated cadences. Often compared with Quarles and Crashaw, at his best Taylor was more like Donne. His verbal power is seen in the opening lines of "The Preface" to *God's Determinations Touching His Elect*:

> INFINITY, when all things it beheld,
> In Nothing, and of Nothing all did build,
> Upon what Base was fixt the Lath, wherein
> He turn'd this Globe, and riggalld it so trim?
> Who blew the Bellows of his Furnace Vast?
> Or held the Mould wherein the world was Cast?
> Who laid its Corner Stone? Or whose Command?
> Where stand the Pillars upon which it stands?
> Who Lac'de and Fillitted the earth so fine,
> With Rivers like Green Ribbons Smaragdine?
> Who made the Sea's its Selvedge, and it locks
> Like a Quilt Ball within a Silver Box?
> Who Spread its Canopy? Or Curtains Spun?
> Who in this Bowling Alley bowld the Sun?

Sublime as these questions by Taylor are, they symbolize the parochial nature of the literature of Colonial American English—the consequence of a culture reared upon too narrow a base. A corresponding provincialism led the Revolutionary poet Philip Freneau (1752–1832) to ask one overwhelming question:

> Can we never be thought
> To have learning or grace
> Unless it be brought
> From that damnable place?

That "damnable place" was not the nethermost region of another world but the dictatorial island kingdom known as Great Britain. It was not the conscience of the Puritans so much as the reason of the Deists that offered an answer in the field of political action.

POLITICAL INDEPENDENCE.   The American Revolutionary War (1775–1783) and the subsequent political independence of the United States under a Federal Constitution (1789) were profoundly influenced by the European Age of Enlightenment. In the philosophy of John Locke (1632–1704) and Jean-Jacques Rousseau (1712–1778), republicanism and democracy waged a violent conflict with absolutism, as represented in the thinking of Thomas Hobbes (1588–1679), among the American colonists. As a result of that conflict, the natural rights of man were restated, in the words of Thomas Jefferson, as those of "life, liberty, and the pursuit of happiness." If a conservative protection of the rights of property often ran counter to the message of *Liberté, Egalité,* and

Fraternité, the political gains of the American Revolution were still enormous: government in the New World was henceforth fiduciary and not sovereign. The divine right of the monarchy was forever dead in America; authority was a matter of delegation rather than of surrender.

As the instrument of the majority of the electorate, dedicated to the well-being of everybody, the government became the servant rather than the master of the governed. By 1790 the pragmatic will of that government was informed by the Deistic rationale of Benjamin Franklin (1706–1790) and his Thirteen Virtues—temperance, silence, order, resolution, frugality, industry, sincerity, justice, moderation, cleanliness, tranquility, chastity, and humility—that the "pursuit of happiness" could best be served by a "tradesman's attitude" that was to make an idol of success. Such success demanded the conquest of the continent.

CONTINENTAL-EXPANSION AMERICAN ENGLISH, 1790–1860

SPANISH INFLUENCE.   The Louisiana Purchase of 1803 committed the United States to settling the vast lands beyond the Mississippi River. In the struggle for Texas, in exploring the Southwest, and in the California Gold Rush of 1849, American frontiersmen and pioneers encountered what Marckwardt has called the "hacienda culture" of Mexico. The Spanish influence became a major attribute of Continental-Expansion American English.

Loans from Spanish had entered American English in the seventeenth century—*tomato, barbecue, savannah, chocolate,* and *sarsaparilla.* But it was primarily during the nineteenth and into the twentieth century that Mexican Spanish influenced American English, especially in the terms used for ranching, mining, building, and cooking. Mexican Spanish also offered American English new words for plants and animals, for clothing, for legal and penal activities, for topography, for naming races and nationalities, and for general linguistic use. The following Mexican Spanish loans are important in American English as it is spoken today: *alfalfa, marijuana, mesquite, yucca; armadillo, bronco, burro, barracuda, bonito, pompano; chigger, cockroach, coyote, mustang, palomino, pinto, vinegarroon; buckaroo, chaparral, cinch, corral, cuarta, hacienda, lariat, lasso, peon, quirt, ranch, reata, rodeo, stampede, wrangler; chile con carne, enchilada, frijole, jerk* (jerked meat), *mescal, pinion nuts, taco, tamale, tequila, tortilla; adobe, patio, plaza, pueblo; bonanza, placer; chaps, poncho, serape, sombrero, ten-gallon hat; calaboose, cuartel, desperado, hoosegow, incommunicado, vigilantes; arroyo, barranca, canyon, key, mesa, sierra; conch, coon, creole, dago, mulatto, octoroon, quadroon; coquina, fiesta, filibuster, hombre, loco, marina, mosey, pronto, rumba, savvy, stevedore, temblor, tornado,* and *vamoose.*

Most of the Spanish loans to American English have maintained their native endings in *o* or *a.* The Anglicizing of these loans, however, is apparent in the changing of *juzgado* to *hoosegow,* of *cucaracha* to *cockroach,* of *vaquero* to *buckaroo,* of *caballerango* to *wrangler,* and of *mesteño* to *mustang.* Folk etymology was responsible for equating the Spanish word for *braid* with liquid capacity: thus *galón* became *gallon* for the modifier of *hat.* As with French and Indian loans, most Spanish terms have entered American English as nouns, but the adjective *loco* and the adverb *pronto* represent exceptions. The profound nature of the American borrowing from Mexican Spanish is evident in the use of such verbs as *vamoose, mosey,* and *savvy,* and in the functional shift of such noun-derived verbs as *stampede, lasso, ranch, barbecue, filibuster,* and *jerk.* With the entrance of *cafeteria* into American English in 1918, the Spanish suffix *-eria* became almost as productive as the French *-ee.*

GERMAN INFLUENCE.   The largest group of non-English speaking people in the United States today are the Germans. The German language was the first major influence *of an immigrant people* upon American English, for Indian, French, Dutch, and Spanish were the languages of subjugated aborigines and defeated colonial rivals. In the late seventeenth century, Germans began to settle in Pennsylvania; by the American Revolution about 90,000 Germans had created a language all their own: Pennsylvania Dutch. In the first half of the nineteenth century, a second wave of German migration washed into the United States and deposited many immigrants in the cosmopolitan centers of the country: Milwaukee, Chicago, Cleveland, Cincinnati, St. Louis, Detroit, Buffalo, and New York. So large was the influx of the Germans that at the time of Chancellorsville (May 1863) in the Civil War, half of Major General O. O. Howard's Union Corps XI could scarcely understand a word of English.

Until the United States entered World War I in 1917, the German immigrants in America maintained their cultural traditions and identity and preserved their foreign tongue. As a result, German has made a strong impact upon American English. In food and drink, for example, German tastes have led to the following household words: *beer soup, blutwurst, bock beer, delicatessen, dunk, fossnocks, frankfurter, hamburger, lager beer, liverwurst, noodle, ponhaus, pretzel, pumpernickel, sauerbraten, sauerkraut, schnitzel, smear case, snits, springerle, stollen, sweitzer cheese, thick milk, wienerwurst,* and *zwieback.* The influence of German education on the colleges and universities of America is evident in the entire research program of the Ph.D. degree; and apparent in *festschrift, semester,* and *seminar.*

Other German terms that have remained active in American English bear witness to a pervasive social and linguistic influence: *beer garden, bub, bum, Christmas tree, fresh* (impudent), *hausfrau, katzenjammer, Kris Kringle, loafer, nix, ouch, phooey, pinochle, poker, rathskeller, saengerfest, spiel, spieler, stein,* and *wunderkind.* Such words as *kosher, kibitzer, mazuma, schlemiel,* and *schmaltz* are ultimately from German by way of Yiddish. German affixes like *ker-, -fest,* and *-burger* have been active in the word-formation habits of American English: *kerflop, kerplunk, kerboom, kersmash; gabfest, talkfest, swatfest, slugfest, swimfest; cheeseburger, chickenburger, turkeyburger, fishburger, shrimpburger,* and *sputnikburger.*

MORPHOLOGICAL INGENUITY.   Much of American culture has been the outgrowth of a frontier spirit. A chief characteristic of that frontier spirit, fed by Yankee ingenuity, was an independent disregard for the dictates of linguistic tradition—a disregard made evident in the morphological processes of American English.

1) *Functional Shift.* As a result of the leveling of inflections, American English shared the possibilities of functional shift with British English, but American English has permitted more shifts to take place without temporary disfavor. In converting nouns to adjectives, American English has become more extreme than British, with such an astounding combination as *Chocolate Coffee Frosted Walnut Marble Icebox Layer Cake.* Since most loans have entered American English as nouns, the resultant need for verbs has initiated functional shifts like *clapboard, scalp, tomahawk, portage, lynch,* and *deed.* The reverse of this process has made

nouns out of the verbs *dump, drool, scoop, beat, release, strike, cut, drive,* and *probe.*

2) *Compounding.* As a Teutonic language, English has had a long record in the word-formation process known as compounding. In the primitive world of the frontier, American English returned to its Anglo-Saxon source and named the new surroundings with the colorful compounds of linguistic pioneers: *live oak, bullfrog, groundhog, swamp oak, coach-whip snake, bottom land, water gap, underbrush,* and *cold snap.* All these compounds were part of the language by the time of the Declaration of Independence. After the Louisiana Purchase in 1803, the expeditions of Lewis and Clark added *arrowwood, bull snake, ground squirrel, tumblebug, cutoff, copperhead, cottonwood, catbird,* and *tow cord.* The development of the railroad resulted in *boxcar, handcar, cow-catcher, jerkwater, stopover, sideswipe, sidetrack, milk train,* and *round-house.* Social and economic conditions in an agriculture-dominated frontier gave American English compounds like *log house, log cabin, split-rail fence, corn belt, cotton gin, roundup, land office, cattle ranch, hog ranch, hired hand,* and *hired help.* Gambling offered the following poker terms to the growing pot of American compounds: *full house, inside straight, straight flush, jackpot, penny ante, seven-card stud, five-card draw,* and *fourflusher.*

The tendency to form compounds in American English was appropriated by baseball, the national pastime invented before the Civil War by one of its Union heroes—Abner Doubleday: *pinch-hit, double play, squeeze bunt, sacrifice fly, chest protector, infield, outfield, home plate, first base, second base, third base, strikeout, pop up, home run, relief pitcher, double-header, bush league, grandstand play, charley horse, college try, strike zone, southpaw,* and *rain check.* Even the terms of American politics rely upon compounding: *lame duck, boss rule, favorite son, dark horse, carpetbagger,* and *political football.* The great vitality of American compounds is seen in their metaphorical quality: *soap opera, wetback, disk jockey, rat race, ghost town, double talk,* and *cow college.*

3) *Affixing.* Yankee ingenuity has given American English a wealth of affixes that "superize" it into a language distinct from the parent tongue of Great Britain. Among the most prolific American prefixes have been *anti-, de-, pro-, semi-,* and *super-,* seen in such derivatives as *anti-secession, anti-Mormon, delouse, destinger, pro-labor, prorate,*

semifinal, semipro, superannuate, and *superintend.* The leading suffixes have been *-ee, -ette, -eer, -ster, -ite, -itis, -ist, -ician, -tor, -ize, -er,* and *-ery;* thus the language has witnessed the development of such derivatives as *contestee, escapee, evacuee, draftee, trainee, usherette, drum-majorette, kitchenette, dinette, bathinette, commandeer, racketeer, sloganeer, black marketeer, mobster, gangster, speedster, roadster, dopester, New Jersey-ite, socialite, laborite, trailerite, third-termite, appendicitis, convention-itis, golfitis, headlinitis, machinitis, receptionist, moralist, cosmetist, agri-culturist, liberalist, beautician, mortician, janitor, realtor, accessorize, itemize, demoralize, slenderize, winterize, hospitalize, corder, schooner, hauler, trucker, cutter, grocery, groggery, deanery, beanery, toggery, greenery, printery, rocketry,* and *missilery.*

4) *Clipping.* In direct contradiction to the purism of eighteenth-century British English, the American English of the nineteenth century reveled in the morphological process of clipping. Such early truncations as *stogie* for *Conestoga* (1847) and *pike* for *turnpike* have been followed by *phone, coon, possom, pop, coed, fan, gym, gyp, gas, movie, talkie, ad,* and *prefab.* So characteristic is this tendency to shorten a word whenever possible in American English that people have lost sight of the fact that British English was responsible for such clippings as *cab, photo, spats, van,* and *wig.*

5) *Back Formation.* Closely allied with clipping is the morpho-logical process of back formation. The oldest back formation in Ameri-can English is *locate,* which came into being in the seventeenth century. At the close of the Civil War, the term *commute* was formed from *commutation* and was applied to regular railroad travel to and from the city. Other back formations achieved during the continental expansion include *housekeep, burgle, enthuse, donate, injunct,* and *jell.* American English in its disregard for tradition has been more adept than British English at changing an *-ation* noun into an *-ate* verb: *create* from *crea-tion, deviate* from *deviation, delineate* from *delineation, placate* from *placation,* and *ruminate* from *rumination.* Terms like *electrocute* and *emote* are easier to come by in American English.

In these five areas of morphological ingenuity American English has been livelier than British English.

HYPERBOLE. When a twentieth-century comedian like Jimmy Durante says that he is *discompooperated* over the *stupendispotama-*

cheeneous world premier of a *giganticolossoloscious* movie, he is making the most of an American frontier tradition of "tall talk." Typical terms of the American frontiersmen of the nineteenth century were *kankarriferous, rambunctious, angeliferous, splendiferous, teetotaciously, bodaciously, ripsniptious, helliferocious, elegantiferously, exfluncticate, absquatulate, obfusticate, ramsquaddle, flusticate, jumpsecute, slantindicular, conbobberation, hornswoggle, cahoots, catawampus, snollygoster,* and *rickaboo racker*. Given to braggadocio and metaphorical language, the American frontiersmen lived in terms of constant hyperbole. They were heirs to the ornate diction of the Elizabethan "inkhorners" and to the overblown style of John Marston (c. 1575–1634), and their immediate colonial ancestor was Nathaniel Ward, the author of the turgid book *The Simple Cobler of Aggawam* (1647), in which appears the following edifying observation on religious liberty: "If the whole conclave of Hell can so compromise, exadverse and diametricall contradictions, as to compolitize such multimonstrous manfrey of heteroclytes and quicquidlibets quietly; I trust I may say with all humble reverence, they can doe more than the Senate of Heaven." In discussing women's fashions, Ward outdid himself:

> But when I heare a nugiperous Gentledame inquire what dresse the Queen is in this week: what the nudiustertian fashion of the Court; I mean the very newest: with egge to be in it in all haste, whatever it be; I look at her as the very gizzard of a trifle, the product of a quarter of a cypher, the epitome of nothing, fitter to be kick't, if shee were of a kickable substance, than either honour'd or humour'd.
>
> To speak moderately, I truly confesse, it is beyond the ken of my understanding to conceive, how those women should have any true grace, or valuable vertue, that have so little wit as to disfigure themselves with such exotick garbes, as not only dismantles their native lovely lustre, but transclouts them into gant bar-geese, ill-shapen-shotten-shell-fish, Egyptian Hyeroglyphicks, or at the best into French flurts of the pastery, which a proper English woman should scorne with her heels: it is no marvell they weare drailes on the hinder part of their heads, having nothing as it seems on the fore-part but a few Squirrils brains to help them frisk from one ill-favored fashion to another.

Davy Crockett (1786–1836) exemplified the bombast of Ward turned into the hyperbole of the American frontiersman, for Crockett once described himself as "fresh from the back-woods, half horse, half alligator, a little touched with snapping turtle, can wade the Mississippi, leap the Ohio, ride a streak of lightning, slide down a honey locust and not get scratched. I can whip my weight in wildcats, hug a bear too close for comfort, and eat any man opposed to Jackson." Self-admittedly a "retail dealer" in the tall tales of the frontier, Abraham Lincoln developed a talent for satiric hyperbole. In 1848, young Congressman Lincoln ridiculed the military record of General Lewis Cass, the Democrat candidate for President:

> Speaking of General Cass's career reminds me of my own. I was not at Stillman's defeat, but I was about as near it as Cass was to Hull's surrender; and, like him, I saw the place very soon afterward. It is quite certain I did not break my sword, for I had none to break; but I bent a musket pretty badly on one occasion. If Cass broke his sword, the idea is he broke it in desperation; I bent the musket by accident. If General Cass went in advance of me in picking huckleberries, I guess I surpassed him in charges upon the wild onions. If he saw any live, fighting Indians, it was more than I did; but I had a good many bloody struggles with the mosquitoes, and although I never fainted from loss of blood, I can truly say I was often hungry.

Many another language has spawned the tall tale, the myth larger than reality, but the distinguishing trait of the American big story is its intention to be funny.

EMERGING LINGUISTIC NATIONALISM.   In 1816, John Pickering published *A Vocabulary, or Collection of Words and Phrases which have been supposed to be Peculiar to the United States of America.* The work was the first dictionary of Americanisms, but the attitude was British: Pickering wanted to purify the language of his country by isolating all departures from the usage of the island kingdom. In a published *Letter to the Honorable John Pickering on the Subject of His Vocabulary* (1817), Noah Webster objected to restricting American usage so that it coincided with the British. Believing such restriction "impracticable," "improper," and "arrogant," Webster stated: "New words will be formed and used, if found necessary or convenient, without a license from Englishmen."

The very term *Americanism* had been coined in 1781 by John Witherspoon, a signer of the Declaration of Independence and an early president of Princeton University. The conservative Benjamin Franklin, another signer of the Declaration, was all for conforming to British usage, as were William Cullen Bryant and Richard Grant White. But Thomas Jefferson favored the adoption of all good innovations, and believed that "should the language of England continue stationary, we shall probably enlarge our employment of it, until its new character may separate it in name, as well as in power, from the mother tongue." Though Jefferson represented a minority view of the American usage of English, he did not stand alone. In addition to Webster, there were John R. Bartlett and James Russell Lowell.

In 1848, Bartlett published the first edition of his *Dictionary of Americanisms*, which he enlarged considerably in 1859. He not only gathered many terms from prairie culture and frontier life but also studied regionalisms. Thus Bartlett saw that American English was diverging from British English, that it was futile to try to make an American use his language like an Englishman, that "the pure old idiomatic English style" could never be restored in the United States, but that the new style of an emerging American literature would have its own "beauties and merits." In *The Biglow Papers* (1848), often called "the high point of Yankee humor," James Russell Lowell did his best to fashion a new and native style based upon the mastery of a regional dialect. A champion of the use of Americanisms, Lowell argued in 1866 that many of them were archaic holdovers from earlier British usage. In his lengthy Introduction to the Second Series of *The Biglow Papers*, Lowell demonstrated the linguistic lag of folk speech. His work helped to focus national consciousness on the use of American English.

To supply a demand for schoolbooks at the close of the American Revolutionary War, Noah Webster (1758–1843) published three elementary English texts—a speller, a grammar, and a reader—under the title of *A Grammatical Institute of the English Language* (1783–85). The speller made such a hit with the public that it soon appeared separately as *The American Spelling Book*, had many editions, supported Webster for life, and eventually sold more than eighty million copies. Freed from financial worry by the steady income from his speller, Webster turned his attention to other linguistic matters. In 1789 he published a volume entitled *Dissertations on the English Language, with Notes Historical and Critical*. For the next four decades, he worked on the masterpiece of his life, *An American Dictionary of the English Language*, which was published in two quarto volumes in 1828. As Mencken said, "Webster himself worked better than he knew. His American Dictionary was not only thoroughly American; it was superior to any of the current dictionaries of the English."

Believing that a national language "is a band of national union," Webster felt that American independence required a truly American language, which would reflect the new ideas and names of the different social and political laws, institutions, and customs of the United States. How far Webster carried his patriotism is seen in the following statement, penned after the War of 1812:

> . . . numerous local causes, such as a new country, new associations of people, new combinations of ideas in arts and sciences, and some intercourse with tribes wholly unknown in Europe, will introduce new words into the American tongue. These causes will produce, in a course of time, a language in North America, as different from the future language of England, as the Modern Dutch, Danish and Swedish are from the German, or from one another.

If rapid transportation, mass-media communications, and a constant cultural interpenetration among the English-speaking nations have combined to prove Webster wrong in his prediction, his *American Dictionary* was nevertheless a vindication of his major linguistic insight. As Baugh remarked, "by stressing American usage and American pronunciation, by adopting a number of distinctive spellings, and especially by introducing quotations from American authors alongside of those from English literature, he contrived in large measure to justify the title of his work."

Webster ultimately did more than merely justify a title. In the first place, he advocated the distinctively American spellings of his day and incorporated them into his dictionary. Although some of his proposals for spelling reform—in which all superfluous letters were to be omitted, *ee* would be the graphemic equivalent of /iy/, and *k* would replace *ch* for the sound of /k/—fell upon deaf ears, Webster urged a general improvement and modernization of American spelling. Because of the authority that he gave to simplification, Americans today prefer *or* to *our* in such words as *honor* and *color;* they write one medial consonant instead of two in *traveler* and *wagon;* they use *er* rather than *re* in *fiber* and *center;* they employ an *s* in place of a *c* in *defense* and *offense;* and they write *ax* for *axe, plow* for *plough, tire* for *tyre, story* for *storey, czar* for *tsar, jail* for *gaol,* and *medieval* for *mediaeval.* In his dropping of final *k* in words like *music, physic,* and *logic,* Webster helped to set

British spelling habits as well; his *ck* for *que* in *check, mask,* and *risk* is standard practice.

Although he failed to achieve uniform pronunciation based upon his own Connecticut Yankee speech, Webster succeeded in influencing a careful articulation of syllables. Combined with the pronunciation values fostered by the spelling bee, it resulted in the American habit of maintaining stressless syllables rather than zeroing them as in current British English. Far beyond his impact on spelling and pronunciation, however, has been Webster's influence as a symbol: of the rise of American lexicography and linguistics, of the emergence of American English as a major revision of and expansion upon the British, of the curious paradox of a frontier taste for the uninhibited neologism and the suburban mania for correctness and conformity, of an American reliance upon authority and a contradictory rejection of tradition. Webster's name has become the household word of American English, the magic pass to proper meaning and usage.

NATIVE LITERATURE.   In 1789, Noah Webster saw that although the American colonies had achieved political independence, their culture remained a pale imitation of the English: "However they may boast of Independence, and the freedom of their government, yet their *opinions* are not sufficiently independent; an astonishing respect for the arts and literature of their parent country, and a blind imitation of its manners, are still prevalent among the Americans." But during the period of continental expansion American English achieved a truly native literature of aesthetic maturity.

Walt Whitman believed that only second-rate talents immediately please and succeed in literature; first-rate geniuses have to bide their posthumous time. The history of native American literature is, in the main, a proof of Whitman's critical understanding. Between 1790 and 1860, lesser figures loomed large: Washington Irving (1783–1859), James Fenimore Cooper (1789–1851), Ralph Waldo Emerson (1803–1882), Henry David Thoreau (1817–1862), Nathaniel Hawthorne (1804–1864), Henry Wadsworth Longfellow (1807–1882), and Oliver Wendell Holmes (1809–1894). With John Greenleaf Whittier (1807–1892) and William Cullen Bryant (1794–1878), these nineteenth-century American writers reaped the early harvest of a cultural independence. Yet all but one of them lacked that essential of great art, passion.

Irving was not imaginative; he depended heavily upon the plots of others and was much given to history. Cooper visualized nothing and permitted a stilted diction to devour his aesthetic texture. Emerson and Thoreau, those thorny blossoms in the flowering of New England, were both eclectic and therefore derivative transcendentalists. Longfellow, the best craftsman among his fellow poets Holmes, Whittier, and Bryant, combined an aristocratic imitation with a rather commonplace sensibility. Hawthorne alone had the potential of artistic heights, but he choked reality with coils of indirection: emblem, symbol, moral, analogy, type, image. As D. H. Lawrence said in *Studies in Classic American Literature*, "That blue-eyed darling Nathaniel knew disagreeable things in his inner soul. He was careful to send them out in disguise." But despite the failure inherent in the work of Hawthorne and his nineteenth-century compatriots, these men formed a sound base upon which to build a great native American literature.

Walt Whitman once contended that Edgar Allan Poe (1809–1849) belonged to the electric lights of American literature. True, for the heroism of Poe was that, surrounded by crass Yankee commercialism and priggish and didactic criticism, he burned so bright and clear. Poe's central achievement was his insistence upon the language of formation over that of information as the proper vehicle for poetry and creative prose. He demanded that the imagination dictate to the will so that the "rhythmical creation of beauty" would never be vitiated by the intrusion of moral propaganda. A master of ratiocination and Gothic horror, Poe invented the detective story and initiated an ever growing craze for science fiction and juvenile adventure. He was the literary progenitor of such widely divergent writers as Jules Verne, Robert Louis Stevenson, Arthur Conan Doyle, H. G. Wells, and Mickey Spillane. Aware of his psychic limitations and his facile sentimentality, Poe resorted to "mythic projection" to enrich his poetry with fable, allusion, allegory, and symbolism. By so doing, he became the fountainhead of modern poetry as it developed under the influence of Baudelaire, LaForgue, and other French Symbolists. Despite the handicaps of what James Russell Lowell called the "fudge" in his genius, Poe constantly served an "elevating excitement of the soul" that was a model for the artistic passion needed for a great American literature.

Had Poe's aesthetic position been at all appreciated during the middle of the nineteenth century, perhaps Herman Melville (1819–1891) would not have succumbed to the rejection that turned him in the last thirty years of his life to composing mediocre poetry. At any rate, America's first novelist of world stature met with misunderstanding and opposition from almost every quarter. A master at describing physical violence and of creating the essence of stillness, Melville wrote one supreme book that soars above all his other work: *Moby Dick* (1851). In this greatest of sea novels, Melville used the opposing rhythms of the universe (e.g., sea vs. land, stasis vs. motion, time vs. space, light vs. dark, withdrawal vs. return) to create his symbolic myth of life and death. A false Prometheus (Ahab), emasculated by his preference for knowledge over love, is destroyed, along with representatives of the three major races of man, by the western world's mechanical conception of good and evil (Moby Dick). The prose style that depicts this destruction is titanically American: a melting pot of journalism, poetry, drama, and scientific essay.

In the meantime, another giant freed American poetry from the meters of an outworn tradition—Walt Whitman (1819–1892). In 1855, Whitman set the type and wrote the reviews for the first edition of his life's work, *Leaves of Grass*. Although John Greenleaf Whittier threw his gift copy into the fire, *Leaves of Grass* announced the arrival of a major poet who helped to fulfill Webster's promise of a great native literature, who, in the words of Van Wyck Brooks, "favored everything that broke down fences and brought together the East and the West, creeds, classes, races, customs, colors, and tongues." Through Whitman a new and independent culture spoke in the rhythms of an original form, free verse. Whitman, above all other poets, created in the word-group cadences of English a tradition of poetic expression that can be simultaneously the universal and the intimate, as seen in the following passage from *Song of Myself:*

> I believe a leaf of grass is no less than the journey
>   work of the stars,
> And the pismire is equally perfect, and a grain of sand,
>   and the egg of the wren,
> And the tree-toad is a chef-d'oeuvre for the highest,
> And the running blackberry would adorn the parlors of
>   heaven,
> And the narrowest hinge in my hand puts to scorn all
>   machinery,
> And the cow crunching with depress'd head surpasses
>   any statue,
> And a mouse is miracle enough to stagger sextillions
>   of infidels.

Whitman matched the termini of his lines with the major junctures of his cadences and banished the concept of the classical foot from the practice of much American poetry. Speaking *democracy* as the password primeval, he championed the doctrine of sympathy, the miracle of the common, the beauty of death, and the wonder of life. The freshness of his insight matched the originality of his style, for in the words of Lewis Mumford, "Whitman took in the quaker, the puritan, the cosmopolitan, the pioneer, the republican; and what came out in his poems was none of these things: it was a new essence. . . . It had the smell of reality which was science; it had the largeness of comprehension which was philosophy; and it had the doubts, searchings, quests, achievements, and consummations which are the stuff of life itself." In that stuff, D. H. Lawrence saw the creative power of a supreme poet: "Ahead of all poets, pioneering into the wilderness of unopened life, Whitman. Beyond him, none."

INDEPENDENT-STATUS AMERICAN ENGLISH, 1860–1890

RISE OF A NATIVE PROSE STYLE.   Important as Poe, Melville, and Whitman were to the development of an American literature of world stature, none of these writers was fully American in his use of English. Poe's scientific Gothicism was perfumed with the sentimentalism of the English Romantics; Melville's Biblical grandiloquent was Jonathan Swift turned Elizabethan; Whitman's "barbaric yawp" was occasionally a medley of artificial English, finishing-school French, and borrowed Spanish and Italian. By the Civil War, "the whole American empire," said H. L. Mencken, "was closer to a mining camp in its life and thought than to the grove of Academe. Emerson had shrunk to a wraith almost as impalpable as his own Transcendentalism, and the reigning demigod was a river boatman and rail splitter of the West." The American English need of this demigod developed a mature native prose style. In that development the language had several advantages: a Western habit of flexibility and inventiveness, a frontier tradition of hyperbole and humor, and the utilitarian demands of a rising national form of journalism.

The neologisms of the time included *to strike oil, boom, jack rabbit, cuss word, hoodlum, grubstake, holdup, freeze-out, crook, joint, spellbinder, to a frazzle, concededly, to go through* (plunder), *to go back on, to light out,* and *to side-track.* The hyperbole and humor abounded in the Southern hill country, on the Western frontiers, and along the Mississippi River. Young Sam Clemens had a good ear for tall talk, as seen in the following sample from his *Life on the Mississippi* (1883):

> Whoo-oop! I'm the old original iron-jawed, brass-mounted, copper-bellied corpse-maker from the wilds of Arkansaw! Look at me! I'm the man they call Sudden Death and General Desolation! Sired by a hurricane, dam'd by an earthquake, half-brother to the cholera, nearly related to the smallpox on the mother's side! . . . Blood's my natural drink, and the wails of the dying is music to my ear! Cast your eye on me gentlemen, and lay low and hold your breath, for I'm 'bout to turn myself loose!

By 1860 the chief characteristics of American English, as observed by Mencken, had jelled: "its disdain of all scholastic rules and precedents, its tendency toward bold and often bizarre tropes, its rough humors, its not infrequent flights of what might almost be called poetic fancy, its love of neologisms for their own sake." The newspaper was king of a new prose style that was simple, racy, and direct. William Cullen Bryant and Charles A. Dana were to rid the journalism of American English of long flowery terms and vague circumlocutions. Headlines demanded short words and back formations.

In the meantime, a commoner was in the White House. Abraham Lincoln tried deliberately to speak and write in a manner that was truly American. As Carl Sandburg has said—

> The new words of the American language streamed across the Lincoln addresses, letters, daily speech. The Boston *Transcript* noted old Abe's use of "the plain homespun language" of a man of the people who was accustomed to talk with the "folks" and "the language of a man of vital common sense, whose words exactly fitted his facts and thoughts." That ex-President John Tyler should protest his grammar was natural. W. O. Stoddard wrote that the President knew how some of his plainer phrasing would sound in the ears of millions over the country and did not "care a cornhusk for the literary critics."
>
> (*Abraham Lincoln: The War Years,* II, 305.)

With the divorce between the spoken and the written word, decreed by the eighteenth-century English grammarians, one law became central to the aesthetic abuse of the language: *self-consciousness makes a mess of literary stylistics.* Nurtured on the formal written British Standard and imitative in diction and tone, for two and a half centuries American creative prose was a stuffy affair. Mark Twain (1835–1910), above all others, introduced the speaking voice into the literary heritage of the United States. A lack of self-consciousness in Twain taught him the virtues of colloquial American speech, which gave him ease and freedom in sentence structures, word-group cadences, and intonation patterns. In *The Liberal Imagination* (1950), Lionel Trilling credits Twain with having created a "classic" American prose:

> The adjective may seem a strange one, yet it is apt. Forget the misspellings and the faults of grammar, and the prose will be seen to move with the greatest simplicity, directness, lucidity, and grace. . . . He is the master of the style that escapes the fixity of the printed page, that sounds in your ears with the immediacy of the heard voice, the very voice of unpretentious truth.

Twain was not always a complete master of the necessary lack of self-consciousness. Stylistically, *The Adventures of Huckleberry Finn* (1884) is calculus to the arithmetic of *The Adventures of Tom Sawyer* (1876)— the gain in power and depth and verisimilitude in the former was enormous. This gain is seen in the following two descriptions of dawn over the Mississippi; the first, taken from *Tom Sawyer*, is told in the person of Twain himself; the second, taken from *Huckleberry Finn*, comes from the mouth of Huck:

> When Tom awoke in the morning, he wondered where he was. He sat up and rubbed his eyes and looked around. Then he comprehended. It was the cool gray dawn, and there was a delicious sense of repose and peace in the deep pervading calm and silence of the woods. Not a leaf stirred; not a sound obtruded upon great Nature's meditation. Beaded dew-drops stood upon the leaves and grasses. A white layer of ashes covered the fire, and a thin blue breath of smoke rose straight into the air. Joe and Huck still slept.
>   Now, far away in the woods a bird called; another answered; presently the hammering of a woodpecker was heard. Gradually the cool dim gray of the morning whitened, and as gradually sounds multiplied and life manifested itself. The marvel of Nature shaking off sleep and going to work unfolded itself to the musing boy. . . .
>   (*Tom Sawyer*, Chapter XIV)

> . . . Next we slid into the river and had a swim, so as to freshen up and cool off; then we set down on the sandy bottom where the water was about knee-deep, and watched the daylight come. Not a

sound anywheres—perfectly still—just like the whole world was asleep, only sometimes the bullfrogs a-cluttering, maybe. The first thing to see, looking away over the water, was a kind of dull line— that was the woods on t'other side; you couldn't make nothing else out; then a pale place in the sky; then more paleness spreading around; then the river softened up away off, and warn't black any more, but gray; you could see little dark spots drifting along ever so far away—trading-scows, and such things; and long black streaks —rafts; sometimes you could hear a sweep screaking; or jumbled-up voices, it was so still, and sounds come so far; and by and by you could see a streak on the water which you know by the look of the streak that there's a snag there in a swift current which breaks on it and makes that streak look that way; and you see the mist curl up off of the water, and the east reddens up, and the river, and you make out a log cabin in the edge of the woods, away on the bank on t'other side of the river, being a wood-yard, likely, and piled by them cheats so you can throw a dog through it anywheres; then the nice breeze springs up, and comes fanning you from over there, so cool and fresh and sweet to smell on account of the woods and the flowers; but sometimes not that way, because they've left dead fish laying around, gars and such, and they do get pretty rank; and next you've got the full day, and everything smiling in the sun, and the song-birds just going it!

(*Huckleberry Finn*, Chapter XIX)

Although lovely in its own right, the passage from *Tom Sawyer* is scented with adult and Latinic vocabulary, romantic cliché, eighteenth-century personification, decorative alliteration, and weak passive voice. Twain is doing the telling, without the informal easiness, the utter lack of self-consciousness, of Huck—who just talks and lets his talk do the telling. The growth in *sensuous concreteness* between the two passages is immense. The air is fresh, unperfumed, with a healthy touch of stink. Always—by emphatic additions, heavily junctured appositions, poetic cadences in the word groups, a climactic shift from past tense to historical present, and the long flow of the syntax (broken by the snags of only three full stops)—there is the immediacy of the speaking voice, which flows as naturally as the Mississippi. No wonder Ernest Hemingway remarked that "all modern American literature comes from one book by Mark Twain called *Huckleberry Finn*."

THE GENTEEL TRADITION.   While Mark Twain was leading the attack of the "redskins" against deference to the British Standard in

American English, the "palefaces" were retreating into the comfortable stockade of authority and purism. That retreat, the last major rear-guard action of the genteel tradition, resulted in what Marckwardt has called "the glorification of the commonplace"—the American habit of using an elegant word for an unelegant situation. Any small-town American theater of 1870 was called an *opera house*, though *opera* was often pronounced *op'ry*. Scarcity values on the frontier produced both a verbal glorification in the names of occupations and a proliferation of titles of honor in American English.

In a reaction to the linguistic abuses of the Civil War, the genteel tradition was strengthened by the concern for propriety on the part of women as represented by the schoolmarm and by the euphemistic sensibility of a powerful middle class. American English has since been noted for its sexual reticence, taboos, euphemisms, social promotions, and laundered profanity. The taboo on mentioning *breast* led to the euphemism of *white meat* in the consumption of poultry; *memorial parks* have taken the place of *cemeteries;* an *exceptional* child has become a designation for a *subnormal* one; and people can cuss now without really doing so: *darn, drat, doggone, blasted, Sam Hill, gee whiz,* and *judas priest.*

For a generation after the Civil War, the genteel tradition promoted a drive to make American English agree with the dictates of British usage. Led, as Mencken has indicated, by Edward S. Gould and Richard Grant White, this drive was supported by "schoolma'ms, male and female, on the one hand, and from Anglomaniacs on the other." Believing in the superiority of British authors over American, Gould held the ignorant masses and the neologistic journalists in contempt. In his *Good English* (1867), Gould permitted only "educated men" to engage in linguistic innovation; he inveighed against such Americanisms as *to jeopardize, controversialist, leniency, standpoint, over his signature,* and *to open up.* White seemed to champion the usage of the common man, but he mistook the Boston regionalism for the American Standard, and he was a linguistic snob. Among White's proscriptions were such solid Americanisms as *reliable, gubernatorial, presidential, editorial, real estate, railroad, dirt road, ice water, to locate, to enthuse, to aggravate,* and *to resurrect.*

The remnant of American purism is largely responsible for the present-day academic enthusiasm for the prose of Henry James (1843–1916), the expatriate Anglophile novelist who decried American barbarisms and called the pronunciation of *r* in the United States "a morose grinding of the back teeth." He blamed most departures from the spoken British Standard on "the American school, the American newspaper, and the American Dutchman and Dago." As a consequence of his snobbery, James is the very antithesis of Twain.

THE GROWTH OF AMERICANISMS.   In direct opposition to purist inhibitions, Independent-Status American English continued to make its fresh expressions and linguistic innovations. Under the influence of journalese, after the Civil War the language indulged in clipping and back formation. The terms *photo* (1863) and *phone* (1886) are two examples of the clipping that made such classics as *gas, auto, Coke, pen* (for *penitentiary*), *beaut, copter, combo, champ, sap, lube, semi* (for *semi-trailer*), *Yank, sleeper, flu, drapes,* and *memo.* As a back formation, *co-ed* (1889) became a sample of the college slang that also produced *prof, grad, medic, dorm,* and *plebe.* Simplifications that developed as a result of the Civil War include *con* (for *convict*), *doc, pard, sarge, prelim, ad, boob* (for *booby*), *bum* (from *bummer*), *bo* (for *hobo*), and *bunk* (from *buncombe*). *Bike* for *bicycle* came into being in 1882; it was followed by *fed* for *federal, gat* for *Gatling gun, Met* for *Metropolitan, legit* for *legitimate,* and *flat* for *flat tire.*

As for the process of blending, American English came up with *cablegram* (1868) and *insinuendo* (1885), followed by such native neologisms as *radiogram, telecast, Aframerican, Dixiecrat, pulmotor,* and *travelogue.* In the three decades of independent status, American English invented a host of picturesque new compounds: *college widow* (1871), *section hand* (1873), *summer kitchen* (1874), *storm door* (1878), *barb wire* (1880), *monkey business* (1883), *bargain counter* (1888), and *shanty town* (1888). Joined by metaphor, compounding produced *rubberneck, barfly, doghouse, tightwad, stuffed shirt, bulldozer, hayseed, skin game, skyscraper, square deal, hot dog, cowpuncher, screwball, dust bowl,* and *road hog.* By means of functional shift, post-Civil War American English made nouns out of idiomatic verb phrases: *showdown* (1884), *strikeout* (1887), *shake-up* (1887), *get-up-and-get* (1888), *hangover* (1894), and *shoot-the-chutes* (1895). The *dingus* of 1876 illustrates how American English created artificial words of idiomatic grandiloquence. Other examples of this habit are *lallapalooza, rambunctious, whangdoodle, scallywampus, doodad, floozy, blurb, moron, sundae,* and *goof.*

As Mencken has indicated, the West was the source of most of the Americanisms of the late nineteenth century. With the rise of immense cosmopolitan centers in the industrialized East and the enormous influx of immigrants into those centers, the chief area of neologisms shifted back across the Mississippi by the turn of the century. And the sources of neologisms changed from amateur to professional, for in the twentieth century American English has been constantly enriched by professional word makers: journalists and press agents and hucksters of advertising.

NATIONALIST AMERICAN ENGLISH
1890–1920

IN 1890 THE FOURTH PERIOD of European immigration into the United States began, dominated by the Italians and the Slavs. During the next generation, while the country became a true melting pot of various ethnic groups, the growth of rapid transportation, mass media, and modern science and technology coincided with the development of an American nationalism that liberated Cuba and ended Spanish control over the Philippines (1898), built the Panama Canal (1903–1914), and "made the world safe for democracy" through a late entrance into World War I (1917–18). Ford and the Wright brothers gave American nationalism an internal mobility that spread to the rest of the world; Marconi and Edison made it possible for American English to mix its several regional variants without the immediate presence of the speaker.

The American nationalism that led to the expatriate aesthetics of Eliot and Pound also produced a generation of postwar isolation. The nationalism itself was manifested in the very language of the American doughboy, who did not particularly like his English-speaking ally the British Tommy. Even as wartime patriotism at home sought to drive all German loans from American English by such linguistic idiocies as changing *sauerkraut* to *liberty cabbage*, *hamburger steak* to *Salisbury steak,* and *German measles* to *liberty measles,* so the strong sense of nationalist identity in American English made it triumphant abroad. As a direct result of the increased prestige of the United States after World War I, Americanisms came to dominate English on a universal scale.

THE AMERICAN INVASION OF BRITISH ENGLISH.   After the successful completion of the War of 1812 and the subsequent Americanization of the United States under Andrew Jackson, the traffic of linguistic exports within the English language began to change directions: what had been a westerly flow became easterly. American English started to infiltrate British English with *talented, reliable, influential, lengthy, prairie, caucus, bluff*, and *to belittle*. In the quarter century following the Civil War, popular American humorists led an immense invasion of British English by the idiomatic neologisms of the United States. In the half century that followed World War I, the beachhead expanded into a linguistic conquest and occupation. By radio and television, movies and popular musical recordings, American English has entered British English to stay.

Among the Americanisms "naturalized" by British English, as Mencken has indicated, are these early twentieth-century exports: *hot air, comeback, highbrow, jaywalker, roundup, boom, kick, publicity, to park, to rattle, to get away with, to make good, to get a move on, to turn down, bargain counter, bellboy, comedown, joyride, holdup, horse sense, soap box, frame-up, roughhouse, close-up, goldbrick, logrolling, bromide, rally, cut, quitter, political pull, pointer, mixer, cereal, to ditch, to feature, to fire, to pass, to hustle, to bank on, to get busy, to try out, to hand-pick, to iron out, to soft-pedal, to sandbag, to sit up and take notice, to snow under, to stay put, to side-step, to side-track*, and *to win out*. Idiomatic adoptions include *good and, on the side, up to*, and *up against*. British authors have become so enamored of Americanisms that they must guard against an automatic inclusion of them at inappropriate points in their creative texture.

By the time Hitler launched the Third Reich, American English had penetrated the usage of the British Parliament itself. Thus the Sunderland *Echo* of October 31, 1934, reported on a speech of Mr. Stanley Baldwin, three-time Prime Minister, in the following manner:

> Even Mr. Baldwin, one of the few authorities on the King's English in the House, used in his speech yesterday the expressions *backslider, best-seller*, and *party dog-fight*. I have heard him use *to deliver the goods*. The House is undoubtedly Americanized in some of its phrases. I have heard *whoopee* and *debunked* in the debating chamber, and *oh, yeah* and *you're telling me* in the lobby. *To pass the buck* is a well-known House expression and it is often used.

Long before World War II, British politics had admitted such American-isms as *caucus, buncombe, graft, platform, carpetbagger, wirepuller, logrolling, on the fence, campaign, to stump,* and *to electioneer.*

LITERARY DEVELOPMENTS.   In the period of Nationalist American English, six American writers contributed to the rise of realism in the prose fiction of the United States: William Dean Howells (1837–1920), Hamlin Garland (1860–1940), Stephen Crane (1871–1900), Frank Norris (1870–1902), Jack London (1876–1916), and Theodore Dreiser (1871–1945). Seeking an unvarnished truth with honesty and accuracy, the realists as a group wanted to represent life as it is; their realism therefore was opposed to such terms as *idealism, romanticism,* and *sentimentality.* Promising as Crane was, it was Dreiser—the first important American author whose name was not English-sounding—who deepened realism to naturalism and distilled the essence of modern life in the United States with feeling and thought.

American life proved to be a suffocating atmosphere of monotony for the four leading expatriates of the time: Henry James (1843–1916), Edith Wharton (1862–1937), Henry Adams (1838–1918), and Gertrude Stein (1874–1946). Seeking to convey psychological truth with economy and precision, James was the finest craftsman among them. Though a precious aestheticism led him into ever greater complexities in which motive crowded out event and his language lost contact with American idiom and usage, James wrote exactingly formal fiction that transcended the limitations of mere narration and didactic sermonizing. Gertrude Stein, on the other hand, emphasized concentration and penetration. Extremely experimental, she was a catalytic agent for the making of a modern professionalism in the *methods* of literary activity. Cosmopolitan and avant garde, Miss Stein was a major influence on the achievement of a modern American prose style, for among her disciples were Eugene O'Neill (1888–1953), Sherwood Anderson (1876–1941), and Ernest Hemingway (1899–1961).

The American poets of the period stayed at home and contributed to a native tradition. Two of them, Edwin Arlington Robinson (1869–1935) and Robert Frost (1874–1963), exhibited a New England dryness, a Yankee reticence, which kept them from a deeper contemporary aware-ness and gave them Pulitzer-prize popularity. Two Illinois poets, on the other hand, worked at creating an American, as distinct from either a

cosmopolitan or a regional, movement in twentieth-century poetry: Carl
Sandburg (b. 1878) and Nicholas Vachel Lindsay (1879–1931). Sandburg
used slang and the colloquial in a modern Whitmanesque line; Lindsay
revived the oral impact of bardic verse by his creation of "jazz rhythm"
from the musical model that sang of "booze, brothels, and blues." William Carlos Williams (1883–1963) joined the real and unreal, the sentimental and the antipoetic with much of the technical excellence achieved
by the hermitic Wallace Stevens (1879–1955). And the exuberant expatriate Ezra Pound (b. 1885) was Gertrude Stein's counterpart in
fashioning a really new poetry. In 1913 Pound co-authored with F. S.
Flint, in *Poetry*, the following three rules for aspiring young versifiers:

> 1) Direct treatment of the "thing," whether subjective or ob-
> jective.
>
> 2) The use of no word that does not contribute to the pres-
> entation.
>
> 3) Rhythmical composition in the sequence of the "musical
> phrase," rather than in that of a metronome.

Pound became the fountainhead of post-World War I aesthetics, which
from T. S. Eliot to Ernest Hemingway has allowed American writers to
dominate the English language ever since.

WORLD-POWER
AMERICAN ENGLISH, 1920–present

BY THE END OF WORLD WAR I, the United States had achieved the prestige
of a military power, and most of the civilized world owed it money.
Since more than twice as many people spoke the American version of
English than spoke the British, the American version inevitably gained
ascendancy. Through radio shows, musical comedies, New York advertising blurbs, and Hollywood movies, American English became a chief
export of the United States. By 1934 Wyndham Lewis could observe in
an article ("The Dumb Ox") in *Life and Letters* that

> While England was a uniquely powerful empire state, ruled by an
> aristocratic caste, its influence upon the speech as upon the psychology
> of the American ex-colonies was overwhelming. But today that
> ascendancy has almost entirely vanished. The aristocratic caste is
> nothing but a shadow of itself, the cinema has brought the American

scene and the American dialect nightly into the heart of England, and the Americanizing process is far advanced. . . . There has been no reciprocal movement of England into the United States; indeed, with the new American nationalism, England is kept out.

American English let in a few Briticisms like *commando, rating, alert, quisling,* and *paratroops,* but it sent many more Americanisms to Britain. As Mencken indicated, by 1944 the following American terms had become respectable British usage: *stopover, peanut, cooler* (jail), *calaboose, flop, to put the heat on, tuxedo, through* (finished), *radio, what it takes, can take it, double-cross, four-flush, pin-up girl, to lay off,* and *racket* (swindling conspiracy). With the rise of commercial television in the United States, American English has witnessed the emergence of a "folk poetry" of advertising, the elevation of the colloquial to the spoken and written standard, and an emphasis on informal and utilitarian usage. American English today revels in fresh idioms, startling new compounds (like an *ouchless* bandage), and slangy metaphors. Examples of twentieth-century Americanisms include *fan, highbrow, tightwad, strong arm, loan shark, hard-boiled, he-man, nuts, getaway, square shooter, panhandler, third degree, to bump off, to take for a ride, to shake down, to hijack, the once-over, neck-and-neck, by a nose, to scratch, to tout, hop-up, understudy, barnstormer, star, angel, box office, to ring down the curtain on, to blast off, nineteenth hole, to stymie, to birdie, to sing* (squeal), and *to wisecrack.*

The three hallmarks of American English today are, as Mencken has indicated, uniformity, freedom in usage, and inventive genius. They are responsible for the following peculiar characteristics of the language:

    1) A remarkable degree of sameness throughout the United States in the basic features of pronunciation: phonemics, stressing, intonation, and syllabicity.

    2) An evolution of regional differences in American speech rather than of true dialects that hinder communication.

    3) A dynamic lexical flexibility, as seen in simplified spellings, vocabulary expansion, rapid growth of popular idioms, and experimental language temperament.

    4) A conservative grammatical usage that makes for social distinctions in American English, as seen in the mistakes of an overly correct snobbism and the substandard constructions of "folk speech."

5) A utilitarian worship of advertising, occupational euphemism, technical jargon, and official bureaucratese.

Today, in the latter half of the twentieth century, Americans are fa-
natic in their development of the last-mentioned characteristic of their
language. Everybody is selling somebody something: from breakfast food
to filter cigarettes, from religious salvation to political freedom. As a
result of all this American huckstering, about ten thousand new trade
names are registered in the United States each year, thus illustrating the
lexical flexibility of American English. The leading methods of trade-
name coinage, as indicated by Louise Pound, are:

Derivation from a proper name, as in *Listerine* (Sir Joseph Lister)
and *Postum* (C. F. Post).

Shortenings or extensions of descriptive words, as in *Jello, Shinola,
Wheatena.*

Diminutives, as in *Chiclet.*

Compounds, as in *Palmolive, Papermate,* and *Easy-On.*

Disguised spellings, as in *Prest-O-Lite, Uneeda, Ibuya,* and *Hol-
sum.*

Blends, as in *Triscuit, Vaporub, Eversharp,* and *Philco.*

Acronyms, as in *Pebeco* from P. Beirsdorf & Company, *Reo* from
R. E. Olds, and *Nabisco* from National Biscuit Company.

Arbitrary coinages, as in *Kodak, Kotex,* and *Zu-Zu.*

The occupational euphemisms of American English are almost as prolific
as the trade names. Present-day classics in this category are *ecdysiast* for
strip teaser and *experienced tires* for big rubber donuts with no tread
at all.

Technical jargon has grown to enormous proportions. Between 1925
and 1950, linguistic science coined the following jawbreakers: *inter alia,
alternation morph, belch timbre, constructional meaning, determinative
compound, epilegm, fluctuant, glosseme, initiating stricture, literics,
macrotagmeme, nonnucleus, operational sandhi, presequential* (noun),
*referential symbolism, suprasegmental, tonomechanics, vocoid, zero affix,
terminal contours, morphophonemics,* and *complementary distribution.*
The jargon of Washington became a *gobbledygook* of sententious cliché
and obfuscating abstraction, in which *contracts were finalized, programs
pointed up, plans activated, patterns effectuated,* and *dynamics imple-
mented.* Among the favorite terms of the New Deal were *coordinator,
pool, roll-back, rationale, objective, clearance, to be severed, to process,*

of the essence, to contact, and *processing centers.* Today the State Department is constantly seeking *to strengthen the peace, stabilize the situation,* and *consolidate the advantage.*

PHONOLOGICAL SAMENESS. A major characteristic of American English today is the general uniformity in its pronunciation throughout the United States. Regional differences exist to be sure, but they are slight when contrasted with the dialect variants of contemporary British English. This phonological sameness has been inherited from colonial days; the homogeneity of American English received the praise, in 1791, of the British editor of David Ramsey's *History of the American Revolution:*

> It is a curious fact that there is perhaps no one portion of the British empire in which two or three millions of persons are to be found who speak their mother tongue with greater purity or a truer pronunciation than the white inhabitants of the United States. This was attributed, by a penetrating observer, to the number of British subjects assembled in America from various quarters, who, in consequence of their intercourse and intermarriages, soon dropped the peculiarities of their several provincial idioms, retaining only what was fundamental and common to all—a process which the frequency or rather the universality of school-learning in America must naturally have assisted.

Population mobility, rapid transportation, mass-media communication, and universal education maintain the relative uniformity, characterized by the following features of American English:

1) A nasalized pronunciation.

2) A somewhat monotonous system of intonation.

3) Full articulation even of stressless syllables.

4) A general preference for the flat /æ/ over the broad /a/, except in Eastern New England, in words like *dance* and *aunt.*

5) The retention of a clear terminal *r*—except in Eastern New England, much of Middle Atlantic, and Southern—in words like *father* and *rather.*

6) A substitution of low-central /a/ for the British mid-back /o/, except in Eastern New England and Western Pennsylvania, in words like *hot, box,* and *stop.*

7) The prevalent use of high-central /ɨ/ in place of British mid-central /ə/ or mid-front /e/ in words like *hurry, worry,* and *thorough.*

Because of the high concentration of immigrant speakers, who tend to articulate precisely in learning their adopted tongue, American English phonology corresponds with its spelling to a higher degree than does British English. Together with the tendency not to reduce stressless syllables to zero, American English also stresses the first syllable of a word more than British—a predilection heard in *LABratory* as against *labORRat'ry*. British English, on the other hand, Anglicizes foreign loans more readily than American, perhaps because England has a much smaller percentage of foreign-born citizens than the United States. The decay of the consonants *r*, *l*, *d*, *g*, *t*, and *h* in British English is generally more advanced than in American. Most important is that strong dialect variants in British English have made a Received Pronunciation Standard a necessity, whereas small departures from phonological sameness in American English are responsible for its *regionalisms*.

AMERICAN REGIONALISMS.   George P. Krapp declared in 1919 that "Relatively few Americans spend all their lives in one locality, and even if they do, they cannot possibly escape coming into contact with Americans from other localities. . . . We can distinguish with some certainty Eastern and Western and Southern speech, but beyond this the author has little confidence in those confident experts who think they can tell infallibly, by the test of speech, a native of Hartford from a native of Providence, or a native of Philadelphia from a native of Atlanta, or even, if one insists on infallibility, a native of Chicago from a native of Boston." Despite some minor regional vocabulary differences, a leveling of speech habits has been a primary factor in the similarity of American regionalisms. The reasons for that leveling, according to Mencken, are "The railroad, the automobile, the mail-order catalogue, the movie and, above all, radio and television. . . ." As a present-day indication of regional leveling in American English, the omitted *r* in the pronunciation of Eastern New England, New York City, and the South is beginning to reassert itself.

Regionalisms do, nevertheless, exist. They now constitute three major speech areas in the United States: Northern, Midland, and Southern. These speech areas foster their own regional subdivisions, which at times have little to do with geographical location. Thus the pronunciation habits of the Southwest area of Arizona, Nevada, and California are generally of Northern derivation, whereas the speech patterns of the Northwest (Montana, Idaho, Oregon, and Washington) are basically of

Midland origin. West Texas speech shows the dominance of Appalachian; East Texas speech is an outgrowth of Southern. Since Appalachian is a regional version of Midland, the differences between the pronunciations of East and West Texas are marked.

American English, then, is characterized by three major speech areas that have generated ten leading regionalisms:

Northern

1) *Eastern New England.* This Atlantic seaboard regionalism, with Boston as its center, lengthens the vowel /a/ to compensate for the loss of r in a word like *barn* /bahn/; tends to use the broad British /a/ in words like *ask, dance, path, aunt,* and *rather;* interjects a final r in words like *idea* and *Cuba;* distinguishes the low-central vowel of *cot* /kat/ from the low-back vowel of *caught* /kɔt/; prefers /æ/ as the stressed vowel of *barren;* lowers the stressed vowel of *hurry* to /ə/; often interjects the glide /y/ after /d/ in a word like *due* /dyuw/; centers the low-back vowel of *log* to /a/; either lengthens or *schwa*-glides the vowel of *horse* and *hoarse* to compensate for the loss of r: /hɔhs/ or /hoəs/; pronounces *greasy* with an /s/.

2) *North Central.* This regionalism extends from Western New England across the Champlain and Great Lakes basins to the central Dakotas; Hartford, Syracuse, Cleveland, Detroit, Chicago, and Minneapolis are centers. North Central American English pronounces its medial and final r's; prefers the flat /æ/ in words like *ask;* does not interject a final r in words like *idea;* also distinguishes *cot* from *caught;* usually prefers /e/ as the stressed vowel of *barren;* heightens the stressed vowel of *hurry* to /ɨ/; does not interject the glide /y/ into the pronunciation of *due* /duw/; employs the low-back vowel /ɔ/ in the word *log;* uses r in both *horse* and *hoarse* so that they sound alike: /hɔrs/; pronounces *greasy* with an /s/.

3) *Southwest.* This regionalism covers Arizona, Nevada, and California; Phoenix, San Francisco, and Los Angeles are centers. Southwest American English is almost identical with North Central. A higher incidence of Mexican Spanish vocabulary constitutes the primary difference.

Midland

1) *New York City.* This regionalism covers a small area (southern New York, southwestern Connecticut, and northeastern New Jersey), but it is big in importance because of the population and prestige of its center. Agreeing with Eastern New England in many of its pronunciation

patterns, New York City American English is different in several major respects, for it often articulates medial and final *r's;* does not interject a final *r* after a terminal vowel; makes a clearer phonemic distinction between the /a/ of *cot* and the /ɔ/ of *caught;* and refuses to employ the glide /ə/ in any actualization of *hoarse.* Known for its heavy nasal quality and Yiddish influence, this regionalism is often hard and metallic in intonation; it also permits such variants as /c/ for /j/, /t/ for /θ/, /d/ for /ð/. Brooklyn versions of /ɔy/ and /ɪr/ are notorious.

      2) *Middle Atlantic.* Extending from New Jersey to Maryland and from Delaware to the mountains of Pennsylvania, with Philadelphia as center, this regionalism does not permit the complex /ah/ to replace the *r* in *barn;* allows /z/ as a phonemic variant of /s/ in the pronunciation of *greasy;* often rounds and elevates the /ɔ/ of *horse* to /o/; permits both /lag/ and /lɔg/ for *log;* and resembles New York City in the use of either /e/ or /æ/ as the stressed vowel of *various.*

      3) *Western Pennsylvania.* This small regionalism covers western Pennsylvania, the eastern tip of Ohio, and the northern portion of West Virginia. With Pittsburgh as center, Western Pennsylvania American English is noted for its "Pennsylvania Dutch" vocabulary and idioms. Much like Middle Atlantic, Western Pennsylvania differs in that it backs the /a/ in *orange* to /ɔ/; it makes absolutely no distinction between *cot* and *caught;* it does not permit /æ/ as the stressed vowel of *various;* it consistently pronounces *log* as /lɔg/.

      4) *Central Midland.* This vast regionalism covers the heartland of the United States from Ohio to Utah and from west Texas to Wyoming, with such centers as Cincinnati, Indianapolis, St. Louis, Kansas City, Denver, Albuquerque, and Salt Lake City. Because it dominates such a large area of the country and is the immediate progenitor of Northwest American English, Central Midland is perhaps the best candidate for the office of Standard American, the outstanding characteristics of which are the articulation of medial and terminal *r;* the distinction between the vocalic phonemes of *cot* and *caught;* the preference for /e/ over /æ/ as the stressed vowel of *barren;* the universal use of the flat /æ/ in words like *ask* and *path;* the tolerance of /s/ and /z/ as phonemic variants in the pronunciation of *greasy;* the preference for /ɪ/ over /ə/ as the stressed vowel of *hurry;* the rejection of interjectional /y/ in words like *due* /duw/; the interchangeability of /ɔ/ and /o/ as the stressed vowel of *hoarse;* and the exclusive use of /ɔ/ as the stressed vowel of *log.*

5) *Northwest*. With Seattle as center, this regionalism covers Washington, Oregon, Idaho, and Montana, and small portions of northern California, Nevada, Utah, of northwestern Wyoming, and of western North Dakota and South Dakota. In most respects, Northwest American English is identical with Central Midland. It differs slightly by permitting a higher-tongued and tenser pronunciation of the stressed vowel in *various* and by allowing /lag/ as a variant of /lɔg/.

6) *Appalachian*. Commonly referred to as "hillbilly" American English, this regionalism covers the eastern area of the United States known as Appalachia (most of West Virginia, Kentucky, Tennessee, and portions of eastern Virginia, North Carolina, South Carolina, and northern Georgia, Alabama, and Mississippi). Noted for the archaic features of its grammar and the substandard usage of its "folk speech," Appalachian partakes of certain Midland characteristics that distinguish it from Southern—especially in retaining *r* in words like *barn;* in refusing to add the breaking glide /ə/ to diphthongs; in maintaining /æ/ as a simple vowel without tension and in adding the breaking glide /ɨ/; in backing Southern /a/ to /ɔ/ in words like *orange;* in permitting /e/ as a phonemic variant of /æ/ in the pronunciation of *barren;* and in the preference for /duw/ over /dyuw/. Appalachian is like Southern in its distinction between *cot* and *caught;* in its use of flat /æ/ in words like *ask* and *path;* in its complete use of /z/ in the pronunciation of *greasy;* in its universal preference for /ə/ as the stressed vowel of *hurry* and for /ɔ/ as the stressed vowel of *log*.

Southern

A complex of various subregionalisms, this vast speech variety extends from Virginia through most of the old Confederacy to western Texas. With centers in Richmond, Charleston, Atlanta, Miami, Montgomery, New Orleans, and Houston, Southern American English is famous for its loss of final *r;* for its conversion of *r* to either the breaking glide /ə/ or the offset glide /h/ when the *r* is followed by another consonant or by a juncture; for its transmutation of simple vowels to diphthongs, as in *dog* /dɔəg/ and *class* /klæɨs/; for reducing complex narrow vowels to complex wide vowels, as in *time* /tahm/ and *oil* /ɔhl/, so that words like *Mike* and *Mark* sound identical: /mahk/; and for a generally slower rate of speech that gives the intonation a "honey-and-molasses" effect.

The characteristics for each of these regionalisms are merely representative and not exhaustive. Both Hawaiian and Alaskan American English, furthermore, need detailed study. But the ten major regionalisms listed above are *speech varieties;* they are not confined within arbitrary borders. From the migration of munitions workers during World War II, for example, Appalachian gained an entrance into, and thus an influence upon, North Central American English. Appalachian, as a matter of fact, spills way beyond its traditional confines—into Texas as far east as the Brazos River, into southern Missouri, Illinois, Indiana, and Pennsylvania. Some of the most interesting phonemic features of American English have to do with Southern pronunciations. The nasalizations of the South tend to raise the preceding vowel; hence it is that *pin* is articulated as /piyn/, *pen* as /pin/, and *pan* as /pen/. Southern American English shows several signs that a major sound shift is taking place within its area of dominance: 1) back vowels tend to be fronted whenever possible; 2) checked "short" vowels generally develop a high-central glide before voiceless consonants and a mid-central glide before voiced consonants: /ɨ/ and /ə/ respectively; 3) the /ɨ/ glide tends to form before post-apical consonants, as in /θeɨŋk/ for *thank*, /bæɨs/ for *bass*, and /puɨš/ for *push*; 4) tense vowels, therefore, tend to break into two segments (or syllables) at points of pitch change—hence the Southern *drawl*, as in /rihəst/ for *wrist*.

Far more important than the phonemic features of Southern speech habits, however, is the gradual wearing away of pronunciation differences among the four regionalisms that cover most of the land mass of the continental United States: North Central, Southwest, Central Midland, and Northwest. Because of the vast increase in population mobility and the immense impact of the mass media, at present these four regionalisms constitute an Emerging General American, which in time may become the accepted American Standard. The resultant seven major speech varieties of present-day American English are distributed as shown in Map 3.

FOLK SPEECH.   Whereas regionalisms generally indicate the geographical distribution of various forms of American English, *levels of usage* indicate the status of the speaker of the language. The four major levels of usage in American English are standard formal (literary), standard informal (well-bred colloquial), trade or technical (commercial, scientific, diplomatic, etc.), and popular or illiterate (uncultivated folk

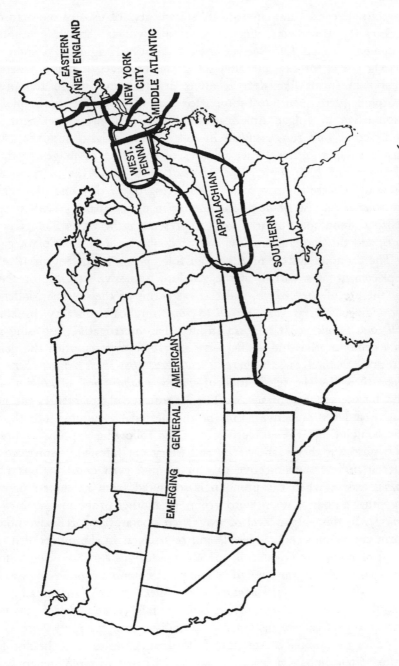

MAP 3. MAJOR AMERICAN ENGLISH SPEECH VARIETIES, CA. 1965

EASTERN
NEW ENGLAND

NEW YORK
CITY

MIDDLE ATLANTIC

WEST.
PENNA.

APPALACHIAN

SOUTHERN

GENERAL
AMERICAN

EMERGING

speech). Because "ungrammatical" statements are usually more forceful and clear than their refined equivalents, vulgar American English—commonly called *folk speech*—is a fascinating linguistic phenomenon. Strong verbs, for example, find refuge in this level of usage, where the final *t* in forms like *slept* is often dropped and where the preterit morphology frequently substitutes for that of the perfect participle. The subjunctive in vulgar American English is virtually nonexistent. The contraction *ain't* runs rampant in folk speech; so also does the archaic past participle *gotten.* Other features of this level of usage are the replacement of *have* with *gotta,* of *must* with *hafta;* the preference for *useta* to indicate the past tense; the slurring of *n't* to *n* and of *can't you* to *cancha;* the use of *don't* for *doesn't* in direct analogy with *won't;* a reliance upon the vulgar historical present, as in verbs like *gives* and *says;* and the constant employment of double or even multiple negation.

The pronoun system of American folk speech is characterized by the replacement of *s* with *n* in the absolute possessive (*theirn* for *theirs*); by the use of *they, them,* and *their* as forms of the common indefinite; by adding either *-s, -uns,* or *-all* to *you* to indicate plurality; by affixing *-all* to *who* and *what* to form an intensive interrogative; by using *them* as a demonstrative and adding *here* and *there* to strengthen the demonstratives themselves: *this-here, these-here, that-there, those-there,* and *them-there;* by the substitution of *who* for *whom* and of *em* for *them;* and by the scarcity of *whose.* The American vulgate merges the nominative and the objective forms of the personal pronouns into those of the conjoint and the absolute so that the following expressions prevail: "*Us* girls was there" and "*Him* and Mary got hitched." American folk speech prefers the objective case in all post-verb constructions (*that's him*), except when the pronoun is separated from its governing word by either a noun, a noun word group, or another pronoun (*between you and I*). In this vulgar level of usage, *self* operates as a reflexive noun to form compounds such as *hisself* and *theirselves.* In the inflectional treatment of nouns American folk speech is notorious for indicating plurality and possession at the end of a compound noun or noun phrase (*two mother-in-laws, the girl around the corner's glove*); for creating false singulars (*Chinee, Portugee*), double plurals (*oxens, sheeps, womens*), and an objective-case disregard of plurality (*give me forty bushel*).

As for the adjective, American folk speech chooses *-y* as the distinctive suffix, often omits *-ed* from the converted past participle, generally prefers -*er* for the comparative and -*est* for the superlative, and almost always slurs *than* to '*n*. The so-called flat adverb in the American vulgate, by which the adjectival form predominates, is admission of the importance of stress and syntactical positioning in determining grammatical function. As a matter of fact, use of the "flat" adverb indicates the native wisdom inherent in this level of usage, which has given Modern American English such standard constructions as the split infinitive; the use of *between, either*, and *neither* when more than two items are involved; the comparative formula of *different than;* the use of *like* as a conjunction; the terminal positioning of the idiomatic preposition; the preference for *loan* over *lend* as a verb; the choice of *their* as the reference to an indefinite singular; and the prevalence of such accepted idioms as *good and, try and*, and *it's me*.

So vigorous is American folk speech that it proves that communication and communion in language need not be either elegant or universally socially acceptable to be effective and eloquent. Literary art is most tolerant of the American vulgate—in fact, cannot do without it. Since what is frowned on today may be praised tomorrow, American folk speech is indispensable for the future development of the language. People yield usage; usage yields language; language yields literature. Without the impact of the vulgate upon its authors, twentieth-century American literature would not occupy the position it does.

MODERN AMERICAN LINGUISTICS.   Although the Modern Language Association of America was founded at Johns Hopkins in 1883, it was not until 1908 that a purely descriptive and scientific grammar came into being in the United States. The MLA was not speech oriented, but narrowly literary: with emphasis on sources, influences, movements, and dates. With the organizing of the Linguistic Society in 1924, a new force came into the study of American English. By 1930, S. A. Leonard of Wisconsin had published a piece of inductive research on contemporary usage which revealed such preferences among language experts as *as regards, none-are, all dressed up, go slow, I don't know if, it is me, who are you looking for?, the reason was because, invite whoever you like, to loan, but what, I wish I was, everyone-they*, and the use of *only* before the verb, of *providing* in place of *provided*, and of *awfully* as a general intensive.

In 1932, Robert C. Pooley made the following recommendations:

"Whenever traditional grammatical classification ignores or misrepresents current usage, it must be changed. When custom has established two forms or usages on approximately equal standing, both must be represented. When current established usage conflicts with traditional rules, the rules must be modified or discarded." A year later, Leonard Bloomfield published his epoch-making *Language*, which established the use of linguistic science as the basis for understanding the habits and patterns of any native tongue, emphasizing the primacy of speech and the grammar of the vulgar. In 1940, C. C. Fries published his *American English Grammar*, a rather conservative analysis of "Standard, Common, and Vulgar" English as evidenced in the written word. Though Fries failed to create a realistic grammar of American common speech, he gave impetus to the eventual attainment of such a grammar—an impetus that was followed up by his own work in *The Structure of English* (1952) and by the grammatical data assembled in the *Linguistic Atlas*.

In 1951 George L. Trager and Henry Lee Smith, Jr., published *An Outline of English Structure* to intensify scholarly awareness of phonology, morphemics, and metalinguistics as necessary elements in the scientific study of Modern American English. With the appearance of Noam Chomsky's *Syntactic Structures* in 1957, structural linguistics was augmented by the findings of generative grammar and its mathematical formulas of constructional transforms. Seeking to be as *formal, explicit, complete,* and *simple* as possible, generative and transformational grammar defines a language as a "concatenation of strings" and seeks to determine which strings of the language are permitted and what the structure of each permitted string is. Tending to be exhaustive, abstract, and somewhat naive in approach, generative and transformation grammar is the latest instrument in the laboratory of American linguistics.

QUESTIONS FOR RESEARCH AND DISCUSSION

1. Dividing the work evenly over the alphabet, let the entire class compile a dictionary of contrasting terms in the vocabularies of British and American English. From this project, let every student write a critical essay on the lexical divergence of British and American English.

2. You have just read that Webster's *An American Dictionary of the English Language* is far superior as a piece of lexicography to Johnson's *A Dictionary of the English Language*. In a study of comparison and contrast, either prove or refute this value judgment.

3. Have five members of the class engage in a panel discussion on the use of Indian place-names in American English. In which area of the country are such place-names the most common? In which area are they the most rare? Account for the relative density of such place-names in the various areas of the United States. From their linguistic influence, which were the ten leading Indian tribes in North America during the seventeenth, eighteenth, and nineteenth centuries? Which tribes have had the greatest influence on the regionalisms of the students who are engaged in this panel discussion?

4. Mimeograph and distribute to the class representative prose passages from the work of James Fenimore Cooper, Henry James, Mark Twain, Ernest Hemingway, and J. D. Salinger. Discuss the relative merits of these five American styles. Now write an essay on the evolution of American fictional prose style, from the written to the spoken word.

5. With every student sharing the work equally, let the class do a word-group analysis of Walt Whitman's "When Lilacs Last in the Dooryard Bloom'd." From this analysis, answer the following questions in detail: What are the salient features of Whitman's free verse? What is the syllabic range of his cadences? How does Whitman maintain a uniformity in his diversity? Now let each student either attack or defend this value judgment from Robert Frost: *Writing free verse is like playing tennis without a net.*

6. Investigate the speech patterns of the various students in the course. Using key words to determine regional differences in pronunciation, let the entire class try to map its own geographical constituency and linguistic influences. Which member of the class is the most easy to place? Which the most difficult? From this study, what evidence has been discovered to support a theory of regional leveling in American English? What lessons have you learned from this project?

7. Let five members of the class give a series of reports on contemporary American slang among teen-agers; soldiers; sailors and marines; athletes; astronauts and airmen. Now let each student write an essay on this subject: *What's your brand of slanguage?*

8. Let the class engage in a discussion of the use of folk speech among its various members. From this discussion, let each student write an essay on the vitality of folk speech in American English.

9. Let five students engage in a panel discussion on the legacies of the Genteel Tradition in American English. Pay particular attention to euphemism, linguistic taboo, anemic diction, circumlocution, and honorifics for the commonplace. Let the other members of the class join in on this discussion with examples drawn from political addresses, Sunday sermons, academic prose, stilted fiction, and amateur poetry. What are

the major dangers of the Genteel Tradition for the achievement of a vigorous style in both speaking and writing?

10. Let the class make a group study of H. L. Mencken's *The American Language* (One-Volume Abridged Edition, 1963). What are Mencken's virtues as a linguistic scholar? What are his defects? Be specific in your answers.

11. Let three members of the class give a series of reports on the impact of contemporary American English upon other languages, concentrating particular attention upon French, German, and Japanese. Now write an essay on the subject of American linguistic exports.

SELECTED BIBLIOGRAPHY

Baugh, Albert C. *A History of the English Language*. Second Edition. New York: Appleton-Century-Crofts, 1957. See especially Chapter 11, pp. 406–465, for a study of "The English Language in America," with a full bibliography.

Cunliffe, Marcus. *The Literature of the United States*. Baltimore: Penguin Books, Pelican Books, 1955. A fine account of the entire range of literature in American English, as seen through the critical sensibility of a present-day Englishman.

Francis, W. Nelson. *The Structure of American English*, with a chapter on "American English Dialects" by Raven I. McDavid, Jr. New York: Ronald Press, 1958. A fine popular textbook.

Kerr, Elizabeth M., and Ralph M. Aderman, eds. *Aspects of American English*. New York: Harcourt, Brace & World, 1963. This anthology of thirty essays by leading authorities on American English deals with principles, historical evolution, regional variations, literary and colloquial usage, social levels.

Krapp, George Philip. *The English Language in America*. Second Edition. New York: Frederick Ungar Publishing Co., 1960. Reissue of a pioneering classic in the study of the language as it is spoken in the United States.

Lawrence, D. H. *Studies in Classic American Literature*. New York: Doubleday, Anchor Books, 1955. The most provocative literary criticism of the early giants of American letters.

Lewisohn, Ludwig. *The Story of American Literature*. New York: Random House, Modern Library, 1939. A one-volume critical survey of the literary achievements in American English, with emphasis upon the essences of the personalities involved and their ideas.

Marckwardt, Albert H. *American English*. New York: Oxford University Press, 1958. An account of the historical evolution of the English language in the United States—clear, economical, and precise.

Mencken, H. L. *The American Language*. The Fourth Edition and the Two Supplements, abridged, with annotations and new material, by Raven I. McDavid, Jr., with the assistance of David W. Maurer. New York: Alfred A. Knopf, 1963. The best one-volume study of American English; for sheer readability it is unmatched by any other work in the field.

Spiller, Robert E. *The Cycle of American Literature*. New York: New American Library, Mentor Books, 1957. A succinct account of the development of American literature, valuable for its lucid scholarship, graceful economy, and lively style.

Thomas, Charles Kenneth. *An Introduction to the Phonetics of American English*. Second Edition. New York: Ronald Press, 1958. This book offers keen insights into the problem of American English phonology and the resultant pronunciations of its various regionalisms.

CHAPTER 12

The Future of
the English Language

———————◦❦◦———————

THROUGH THE SIMPLE STATISTICS OF births and deaths, English will experience a steady increase in the number of its native speakers. The population of the United States alone is expected to jump to around 300 million by the year 2000. In its expanding role as the lingua franca of the world, there will be an even greater increase in the number of people who adopt English as their second tongue. As H. L. Mencken has said, English

> . . . is not only the first—and in large part, the only—language of one of the world's two strongest powers and of several of the second rank; it is also the second language of large and populous regions beyond their bounds. Its teaching is obligatory in the secondary schools of countries as diverse as Germany and Argentina, Turkey and Denmark, Portugal and Japan. No ship captain can trade upon the oceans without some knowledge of it; it is the common tongue of all the great ports, and likewise of all the maritime Bad Lands, from the South Sea Islands to the West Coast of Africa and the Persian Gulf. Every language of the free world that still resists its advance—for example, Spanish and Portuguese in Latin America, Italian and French in the Levant, Japanese and Hindi in Asia—has made large concessions. Everywhere in Latin America, Spanish has taken in many English and American words. Japanese has gone even further. . . .

English will continue to flourish because of the power and wealth of the United States, the traditional prestige of culture-laden Great Britain, and the far-flung usage among the independent nations of the Commonwealth. Use of English as a second language generally means increased economic effectiveness and social prestige for the individual.

The language itself offers several outstanding reasons for its further growth as the second tongue of the world: an ever expanding cosmopolitan vocabulary, a simple inflectional system, an orderly natural gender, and a functional syntax. These major attributes of Late Modern English are responsible for the clarity, directness, and force of the language. The economy of English is undeniable. As Walter Kirkconnell discovered in 1927, in a count of the number of syllables needed to translate the Gospel of St. Mark, English proved to be the most flexible and succinct language on earth:

LANGUAGE	NUMBER OF SYLLABLES
English	29,000
Teutonic languages	32,650 (average)
French	36,000
Slavic languages	36,500 (average)
Romance languages	40,200 (average)
Indo-Iranian languages	43,100 (average)

In addition to the intrinsic merit of economy, present-day English employs a basic vocabulary of 850 words: 600 nouns, 100 adjectives, 100 adverbs, 30 verbs, and 20 function words. In contrast with the complexity of Russian—with its six cases, three genders, palatalized consonants, and confusing pronouns—English is simple in structure.

The major fault with Esperanto—or any other "universal" language created by scholars to assume the role of international communicator—is lifelessness. No artificial tongue can become the lingua franca of the world: it has no blood and breath from the mouths of native speakers. As a living language, English will continue to grow and change. Certain features of its future evolution are clear; others are somewhat obscure. Any linguist would predict a constant increase in vocabulary through borrowing, new word formation, and fresh meanings for old terms. There will be further development in the specialist jargons of the various sciences and technologies of the post-Freudian and post-Einsteinian world. At the same time, American English will probably continue to slow down its absorption of immigrant words. But what tomorrow holds for the verb auxiliaries of the language—in their function, meaning, and relative importance—is far from evident.

PHONOLOGY. Ever since the time of Chaucer, only one new phonemic consonant has been added to the English language: the /ž/ of the Renaissance. True, the /j/ of *Jack* saw usage in initial positions for the first time in Early Modern English, and the /x/ of *knight* dropped from the language at that time. Otherwise, for over four centuries the consonant system of English has remained very constant and stable. It will continue to remain so.

The lax (short) vowels, always more stable than the tense (long) vowels, seem to have jelled into permanence. Even the /ə/ and the /ɫ/ of stress-reduced syllables have become pronunciation fixtures in English. If there is to be change in the lax vowels, it will undoubtedly involve *a general drift toward the front,* as seen today in Received Standard British and Southern American. As for the vocalic diphthongs of Late Modern English, they will probably maintain their present tongue height and oral positioning in most non-deviant versions. The increasing tendency to level dialect and regional differences within national boundaries, and among the English-speaking nations in general, will probably lead to the gradual reduction of the breaking of simple vowels with the syllabic glides /ɫ/ and /ə/ in such versions of the language as Southern American. If there is to be change in the tense vowels, it will most likely involve the fronting of the first formant element in the diphthong /aw/ so that it becomes /æw/, and the backing and lowering of the offset glide in the diphthong /ay/ so that this narrow complex becomes the wide /ah/ before voiced consonants and in final position. A general tendency toward a full isochroneity of phrase pacing, furthermore, will probably abolish /ey/ for *a* and /ðiy/ for *the,* and encourage the rapid articulation of unstressed syllables in the valleys between stressed heights.

The growing cultural exchange among English-speaking nations will be intensified in the future through rapid transportation and instantaneous mass-media communication, and eventually put an end to the traditional divergence of British and American English. Isolation breeds dialects and regionalisms; togetherness produces language standards and norms. Healthy minor differences will remain among the leading brands of English. But it is doubtful, for example, how long the Cockney inheritance in Australian pronunciation can survive. The broad /a/ of Eastern

New England is already weakening before the onslaught of the flat /æ/ of most American speech; in time the /a/ will give way.

From the sheer weight of numbers of speakers, American English will assume preëminence in modeling an international standard. English as a whole will continue the habit of forwarding stress whenever possible. The maintenance of syllabicity in weakened positions—a strong American habit—will probably arrest the British practice of swallowing unaccented vowel clusters. In the give and take of intonation compromise, the tendency will be to obliterate extremes. British English will very likely cease to be as musical as in the past, and American English will no longer be quite so monotonous and nasalized. Education in the form of cultural interchange will kill off many of the most colorful deviants in the phonology of Late Modern English. That is the price which the language has to pay for the benefit of achieving an international standard.

MORPHOLOGY.   The morphological habits of present-day English will continue to evolve along established lines. Thus the -*s* form of the noun plural will continue to grow. Just as *automata* became *automatons* when it left the realm of the learned and entered the popular, so did *indices* become *indexes*. Many foreign plurals are similarly doomed to Anglicizing. In like manner, because of regularization in the past, the -*ed* form of both the preterit and the past participle of the verb will strengthen its hold on English. The result will be a further reduction in the number of irregular verbs. Meanwhile, the subjunctive mood will all but disappear from Late Modern English. The *if* itself, for example, conveys the sense of condition in *If I was you . . .* ; there is no need to repeat the contrary-to-fact state in the morphology of *were*. The loss of the subjunctive will be analogous to the leveling of inflections, for English continues to reduce scholarly redundancy.

The language also shuns unemphatic verbosity, and this antipathy will probably keep the -'*s* possession in popular favor over the use of *of* in constructions of the possessive genitive. The *world's fair* will prevail over the *fair of the world*. In the partitive genitive, on the other hand, simplicity will lead to the preference for such material-construction forms as *the table leg* rather than *the leg of the table;* the forwarding of stress, that is, will make compounds out of word groups whenever possible. As for the comparative and the superlative morphology of the adjective, the use of *more* and *most* will be preferred in terms of several syllables and where *-er* and *-est* make pronunciation difficult (e.g., *interestinger* and *honestest*). Otherwise, the greater urgency of *-er* and *-est*, as felt especially in folk speech, will demand the further use of these morphemes in forms like *stinkier* and *jazziest*.

In the morphological processes themselves, tomorrow's English will emphasize compounding, affixing, and functional shift. Scientific terminology will result in a marked growth of serious blending, and an intensified bureaucratese will undoubtedly lead to more acronyms. In the international exchange between British and American English, clipping and abbreviation will probably increase in the island kingdom, whereas capitalization, hyphenation, and use of the apostrophe will decrease.

SYNTAX.   In the future syntax of English, a further fixing of word order will help in determining function and in expressing essential importance. Thus *I only had a dollar* conveys the psychological urgency of the speaker better than does the logical placing of the modifier in *I had only a dollar*. For, let it be said again, language is primarily psychological rather than logical. The emphatic forwarding of movable modifiers seems to be in the English language to stay; it is a direct syntactic parallel to the phonemic forwarding of stress. Syntactically, forwarding of stress will continue to make noun compounds out of the idiomatic verb groups that are created by using the preposition as a directive adverb. Constructions based upon the idiomatic preposition will proliferate. The idiomatic *it*, especially in phrases like *beat it, make it up to, step on it, hurry it up, see it through, work it over, jazz it up, talk it down*, and *lay it out*, will surely increase in use.

A continued refinement of verb auxiliaries—in function, importance, and meaning—will be accompanied by a rising use of the objective form of the pronoun in all post-verb constructions. The colloquial correctness of *It's me* will generate acceptability in linking-verb statements such as *That's her* and *I'm him*. But in the future syntax of English, *who* will probably be considered correct in all positions; like *that, who* will remain an uninflected relative. Meanwhile, the textbook use of *his* as the referent to such common indefinites as *everyone, each person*, and *everybody* will give way in American English to the British *their*. In like manner, *he* will be replaced by *they* in the nominative construction. That replacement is already underway and no amount of purist carping can arrest the process. As with *who*, the *they/their* preference is an out-growth of psychological economy and ease. Major changes in the English syntax of the future are out of the question.

USAGE.   Because of the impact of the mass media, the future usage of English will be dominated by the informal and the utilitarian. Slang will rapidly rise to the level of the colloquial and the colloquial to the level of the standard. As a consequence of the speed-up of acceptability, which with usage is another name for correctness, a modern cavalier attitude towards new word formations, syntactical idioms, and specialist jargons will also intensify. On October 16, 1964, *Time* observed that "English teachers curse Madison Avenue for institutionalizing bad grammar with such calculated lapses as 'us Tareyton smokers' and 'like a cigarette should.' " What the English teachers and *Time* overlook is the central linguistic fact of the post-TV era—folk speech is here to prevail.

The poetry of folk speech can be seen in the alliteration and rhyme of the slogans of twentieth-century huckstering, whether commercial or political: *I like Ike; All the way with L.B.J.; Keep cool with Coolidge; All outcleans them all; Winston tastes good like a cigarette should; The new flavor-filter . . . ; Ban the bomb; Better Red than dead,* and *Put a tiger in your tank!* Appealing to the auditory imagination, modern sloganeering—of whatever stripe—is liberal in language outlook and flexible in morphological and syntactical behavior. Thus one brand of coffee may be *coffee-er* than another, one type of peanut butter the *P-nuttiest*, and one kind of hair rinse *always ash, never brash*. Because true meaning in the propaganda of all forms of advertising is easily ex-hausted, English will constantly have to renew itself. Present-day promises of a *free gift* are indications that tomorrow may call for an *absolutely free gift*. Consumer suspicion, in other words, has robbed *gift* of its time-honored semantics.

The need for constant renewal of meaning is an advantage for the evolution of English, for challenge is good. How will the folk poetry in future mass-media advertising meet the challenge? By *paradox* ("We have nothing to fear but fear itself"), *metonymy* ("The full dinner pail"), *parody* (as in the Norwegian travel-folder slogan that says, "There's a Fjord in your future"), and *punning* ("Every litter bit hurts"). The use of *metaphor* (as in "Just the kiss of the hops") will thrive in informal and utilitarian usage. Future English usage, in short, is bound to be popular and dynamic.

Attitudes about what constitutes correct usage will change—an inevitable result of the failure of the "school tradition" to create an adequate grammar of English. That failure has been the outcome of too much adherence to the nonscientific prescriptions and proscriptions of the eighteenth-century authoritarians, who sought to apply the principles of a "universal grammar," based upon the various structures of Latin, to their analysis of English. The development of linguistic science during the twentieth century has resulted in the emergence of several doctrines of correct English usage. Those different doctrines may be summarized as follows:

1) *Rules:* Dogmatically applies reason and example, by means of the Latin grammar of the eighteenth century, to the function of English. Correct usage under this doctrine is simply a matter of nonviolation of the rules. Lip-service is paid to usage by the adherents of this doctrine, who equate that usage with the dictates of a conservative handbook tradition.

2) *General Usage:* Recognizes four levels of linguistic acceptability: literary English; standard cultivated colloquial English; trade or technical English; naive and uncultivated popular English (folk speech). Although C. C. Fries championed the doctrine of general usage, he tempered it with the need to be *appropriate* in speaking and writing.

3) *Appropriateness:* As fostered by George P. Krapp, states that there is no such thing as "absolute" English. The appropriateness of three kinds of "good" English (popular, colloquial, formal) may violate a "general standard," but it insures a constant revitalizing of the language. Tension between the "standard" and the "good" leads to improvement in expression.

4) *Linguistic Norm:* Asserts that language is "responsible to an expressive ideal." In the opposition between the need for new expressions and the grammar of a conservative tradition, the linguistic norm must consider the intention of the speaker, the nature of his language, and the probable effect on his audience. As championed by Otto Jespersen, the doctrine of the linguistic norm understands the folk dynamism that results in a *maximum*

of expressiveness with a *minimum of effort*. This doctrine emphasizes that economy is power and that psychology dominates logic.

Through the interaction of these doctrines of correct English, different ideas about what constitutes a standard practice will develop. The speakers of English will come to see that there is a range of tolerance within the standard and that all standards change because of the constant impact of the spoken word upon the written, of the informal upon the formal.

In the future usage of English, the "school tradition" and the general public will become increasingly enlightened about the flexibility of the language, and greater latitude in correct usage will develop. The range of tolerance within the various levels of usage will tend to broaden. There will be in the English of tomorrow a greater emphasis on the use of what Louis Zahner has called "inventive" language—language that produces a desired effect in an imaginative way, as in expressions like *pussyfoot, lounge lizard*, and *armchair strategist*. The user of "preventive" language, on the other hand, will be awakened to the dangers of his imprecise and sterile clichés, which prevent meaning by abandoning it for the comfort of the tried-and-trite formulas like *nice girl, terrific day*, and *delicious meal*.

Several recent tolerances of usage indicate a further breakdown among the handbook proscriptions: 1) *will* for *shall* in all constructions of futurity and intention; 2) the split infinitive; 3) *like* as a conjunction; 4) the comparative phrase *different than;* 5) the separation of singular substantive and verb by a plural construction, as in *He is one of those who is . . .;* 6) the formulaic *the reason . . . is because . . . ;* 7) the polite substitution of *myself* for *me* in statements like *You can go with Mr. Smith and myself;* 8) the objective form of the pronoun, rather than the possessive, before a gerund, as in *I don't mind him doing that.*

In a 1960 issue of the *English Journal*, Robert C. Pooley declared that the schools of America are "committed by duty and by conscience to bring every student as close as possible to the attainment of a decent standard of English usage by every means" at their command. What constitutes a "decent" standard is fraught with argument. But Pooley was certain that twenty-five proscriptions form the core of the standard he would "rightfully set" for public and private use:

1) Don't use baby-talk and "cute" expressions.

2) Don't misuse, in both speech and writing, *I* for *me*, *he* for *him*, *she* for *her*, *they* for *them*, and vice versa.

3) Don't violate number and tense in the use of *is*, *are*, *was*, and *were*.

4) Don't use an incorrect form of the past tense in such common irregular verbs as *see*, *give*, *take*, *bring*, *buy*, and *stick*.

5) Don't use an incorrect form of the past participle in these same irregular verbs after an auxiliary.

6) Don't use the double negative.

7) Don't use such analogical forms of folk speech as *ain't*, *hisn*, *hern*, *ourn*, and *theirselves*.

8) Don't use incorrect forms of the possessive pronouns *my*, *mine*, *his*, *hers*, *theirs*, *ours*.

9) Don't confuse *its*, a possessive pronoun, with *it's*, a contraction of *it is*.

10) Don't leave out *have* or its phonetic reduction to *v* between *I* and a past participle.

11) Don't use *them* as a demonstrative pronoun.

12) Don't say, much less write, *this here* and *that there*.

13) Don't be incorrect in the use of articles *a* and *an*.

14) Don't misuse personal pronouns in compound constructions, whether as subject (*John and I*) or object (*Mary and me*).

15) Don't confuse *us* and *we* before appositional nouns.

16) Don't violate number agreement after the expletive phrases *there is*, *there are*, *there was*, *there were*.

17) Don't use *don't* with a third person singular subject.

18) Don't use *learn* for *teach*, *leave* for *let*.

19) Don't use such pleonasms as *my brother he*, *my mother she*, *that fellow he*.

20) Don't violate agreement in number between such antecedent pronouns as *one*, *anyone*, *everyone*, *each*, *no one*, *somebody*, *anybody*, *everybody* and their postcedent referents.

21) Don't confuse *who* for *whom* and vice versa.

22) Don't use *says* for *said* in reporting past discourse.

23) Don't confuse *lay down* with *lie down*.

24) Don't use the adjective *good* for the adverb *well*.

25) Don't use such barbarisms as *can't hardly*, *all the farther* (for *as far as*), *Where is he (she, it) at?*

Adhering to these proscriptions constitutes a systematic *convention* that may be called a standard. It is not, however, "decent." It merely is. Violation of these proscriptions also constitutes a conventional standard. It is not "indecent." It merely is. The rivalry between academic English and popular English will wear away many of Pooley's negative commandments. Some of them are already out of date. Literary art uses baby-talk and "cute" expressions as a means of characterization and textural emphasis. The double negative is a psychological intensive and not an illogical contradiction. *Who* is winning out in all constructions. *Their* refers to all indefinite singular antecedents. *Lay* is becoming a middle-voice intransitive, whereas *lie* is falling into disuse. *Good* acts as an adverb by means of stress and post-verb positioning (*He pitched real good*). Folk songs delight in pleonasms (they are rhythmically appropriate), and only a stuffed shirt shuns the historical present at moments of crisis.

GENERATIVE GRAMMAR.   Since the end of World War II, an important linguistic event has transpired in the formal study of English syntax: the rise of generative grammar. From his work in analyzing the many different sentence structures in spoken and written English discourse, in 1952 Zellig Harris developed an idea of "grammatical transformation," a language process whereby one construction or set of constructions can become another construction or set of constructions. This concept concerning grammatical transformation led the way to a re-examination of general linguistic theory and of the abstract systems upon which the description of language constructions is based. In *Syntactic Structures* (1957, 1962), Noam Chomsky systematized and expanded upon the new insights of Harris. Taken together, the work of these men has developed into generative grammar, a study still in the state of rapid growth and development.

Generative grammar seeks to describe *all* the sentences that can be constructed in English (its *inclusive* dimension) and *only* the sentences that can be constructed in English (its *exclusive* dimension). These sentences, in turn, are determined by the "phrase structure" and the "transformation" rules of the language. The "phrase structure" rules account for, or generate, the simple, or "kernel," sentences of English. The kernel sentences are non-derived in that they do not depend on any structures other than their own. Thus the following phrase structure rule (also known as a "rewrite" rule) underlies the kernel sentence *The man drank tea:*

$$S \longrightarrow CS + CP$$

(Sentence is "rewritten" as Complete Subject + Complete Predicate) This formula means that *The man drank tea* is composed of two major "immediate constituents": Complete Subject (*The man*) and Complete Predicate (*drank tea*). Other phrase structure rules determine syntactical units of meaning smaller than a sentence. Every phrase structure rule of generative grammar uses a single arrow (——→) to indicate "is rewritten as."

From two or more kernel sentences of English, each non-kernel sentence, or "transform," is "derived" via the transformation rules of the language. These transformation rules demand the use of a double arrow (=>) to indicate "is transformed into." The transforms themselves occur in two types: *singulary* (as in passive-voice constructions and interrogatory inversions) and *generalized* (as in conjunction and relative-clause transformations). A simple generalized transform based upon use of a conjunction may be illustrated as follows:

KERNEL SENTENCES   TRANSFORM

George loved his mother.
George idolized his father.   => George loved his mother and idolized his father.

A similar generalized transform with the relative clause would look like this:

KERNEL SENTENCES   TRANSFORM

This is the house.
Jack built the house.   => This is the house that Jack built.

Using phrase structure rules as a means of *direct* representation of English sentences, and transformation rules as a means of *indirect* representation, generative grammar is thus far the most accurate and complete system of linguistic analysis. In company with its own cognate transformational grammar, this academic discipline makes the following series of observations about English: *The grammatical relations of the phrase structure rules of kernel sentences plus their transformations into derived sentences yield the complex structures of an "infinite recursiveness," which in turn constitute the creativity of the language.*

The advantages of generative grammar are in the aims of the grammarians themselves: *formality, explicitness, completeness,* and *simplicity*. Drawing upon the best features of conventional eighteenth-century grammar and of structural (descriptive) linguistics, generative grammar transcends their weaknesses: the misapplication of reason and example, based upon a foreign language; failure to describe the immediate constituents of *every* sentence structure; the tendency to isolate the immediate constituents, when adequately described, into a closed system of classes that has no opening to an infinite recursiveness; the inability to show how transformations change underlying structure, which is the basis for sentence interpretation; and an insufficient awareness of the importance of "context sensitivity," the total semantic environment. Generative grammar alone furnishes a scientific rationale for understanding creativity in the English language.

Generative grammar unites linguistic theory with linguistic description to arrive at a "state of predictability" about language behavior beyond the reach of the more conventional grammars. Although the depths of human psychology continue to escape the probings of linguistic science, generative grammar nevertheless emphasizes the importance of semantics in communication—and communion. In an implied hierarchy of linguistic values, generative grammar underscores the fact that style takes artistic precedence over mere "grammaticality." By showing the deviation which is true language creativity, this new discipline is a valuable ally of literary criticism in the task of evaluating poetry as a matter of idiom rather than of adherence to rule. Since transformational procedures constantly test constituent structures, generative grammar also brings nearer the achievement of a set of "linguistic universals," from which a mature and accurate theory of language itself may be evolved.

No human discipline, however, is infallible. Generative grammar, good as it may be, has already manifested certain dangers. The more mathematically accurate and inclusive a subject becomes, the more it tends toward a complete abstraction. As an interruptive analysis of a continuant action and a continuant projection of an interruptive action, generative grammar is tempted beyond the realm of reality. Thus the *mathematical* possibility of infinitely expanding any sentence is both a physical and a psychological absurdity. In their search for linguistic universals, a process reminiscent of the eighteenth-century authoritarians, the generative grammarians have already showed signs of becoming prescriptive and proscriptive in their analyses of permitted "strings." An inherent danger abides in the very term *rule*, a misnomer if applied to a linguistic habit. Thus conventional and arbitrary behavior takes on the significance of law. But it is not phrase structure rules and transformation rules that communicate and commune with other phrase structure rules and transformation rules. Human beings speak and listen to other human beings. Hence this observation cannot be too strongly emphasized—*men, not grammatical rules, generate sentences.*

Because generative grammar is an abstraction of a concretion, relying heavily upon mathematics and modern logic, the schemata of its analyses dominate the information. The terminology can become a deadly gobbledygook. Often a clarifying statement in "ordinary English" is more concise than the set of symbols used to methodize the statement. Although generative grammarians are aware of the functions of grammatical rules—deletion, replacement, expansion, reduction, addition, and permutation—in their drive for "rigorous" results they rely too heavily on automatically mechanical procedures. Their method tends to confuse the possible with the idiomatic and the probable. Because the people who speak English do not create "an ideal abstract system," their so-called "ungrammatical" statements are often more exciting than those that follow the rules of correctness. Since the psychology of human speech remains an "elusive notion" to the generative grammarians, they gear their language predictions to the rational norm of what is logically acceptable.

If a mathematical diagramming of sentences is not to make future generations of students unhappy with the prescriptions and proscriptions of English, generative grammar must constantly insist that the "rules" are fallible *ex post facto* observations on a special kind of human behavior and not infallible *a priori* dictations of that behavior. English cannot be adequately described by any system, and the rigidity of a mathematical system cannot explain the flexible mystery of man's imagination and the marvelous creativity of his neural system.

FUTURE DEVELOPMENTS.   In the proliferation of specialist jargons, English will continue its processes of popular simplification. Thus when an invention like a *transistor* becomes a widget for the gadget of a type of radio, the people will short-circuit the whole technological process by making the gadget bear the name of the widget. As English must resist the overspecialization of technology, it must also demand a simpler and clearer scholarly prose style. As computational linguistics develops from high-speed data processing, there will be an increased demand for modern linguists to undergo a rigorous training in both logic and mathematics. Such training will necessitate a conscious effort for the expert to communicate with the layman on the subject of his language.

In the future search for a "universal grammar," there will be an increasing need *to compare and to evaluate* every kind of grammar. The criterion of simplicity will become the *sine qua non* of the search, which itself will reveal the need for more refined methods of testing existing language theories. Just as an incomplete grammar does not have to be incorrect, so a defective sentence does not necessarily cease to be a sentence. Future grammars of English will have to answer the following pressing questions: How does context sensitivity narrow the range of ambiguity? How accurate can an objective and empirical study be of a subject that is neither objective nor empirical? What are the bases for human correlation of phonology and semantics? Are the generative "rules" for speech and for writing the same? What role does psychological emphasis play in changing the practices of the transforms themselves? How can generative grammar account for social acceptability as a key to the doctrine of correctness? What is really meant by the phrase "a grammatical sentence"?

The greatest need in any future study of English is to broaden the base of inquiry to include as many relevant disciplines as possible. Just as every man who speaks English is a total pychological being, made up of many subtly blended physical and spiritual characteristics, so the study of what he says must inform itself upon the knowledge offered by every academic discipline. The linguists of the future will have to go to school with poets and mystics, anthropologists and historians, physiologists and theologians, psychologists and philosophers, chemists and physicists. They will not be permitted the luxury of associating only with their own kind, because they and their fellow lexicographers, philologists, semanticists, symbolic logicians, structuralists, transformationalists, and recursive mathematicians simply do not know enough to do an adequate job of revealing the greatest secrets underlying the mystery, the majesty, the miracle of the English language.

Language instruction in English must foster the observance of a few positive prescriptions. Since use of language is primarily a matter of synthesis, more attention must be given to the process of doing rather than of naming, of making rather than of inspecting, of putting together rather than of pulling apart. Too often in the past, schools in Britain and America have inculcated a picayunish desire to label everything and to master nothing in English. Too many students can analyze their language perfectly without being able to say or write anything of artistic value in it. Unfortunately, the academics who jam the learned journals with their opaque research into the trivia of their disciplines constitute too large a group among the ranks of professional scholarship.

Thus a vicious circle has been drawn to encompass all levels of language instruction, from grammar school to graduate school. To break that circle, the schools of tomorrow must meet the following challenges:

1) To understand usage rather than to judge and condemn it.

2) To describe disinterestedly rather than to proscribe with prejudice.

3) To encourage creative imagination and inventive language rather than merely to discourage lapses in logic and violations of the rules.

4) To abandon a half-educated snobbism in the use of English.

5) To remarry the spoken word with the written.

6) To insist on the primacy of speech as the living basis of English and therefore never to let formal writing dictate what is proper or improper.

7) To eradicate both the fear of error and the mania for correctness in speaking and writing English.

8) To promote pragmatic communication and aesthetic communion in English.

9) To respect function rather than rule in the study and use of English.

10) To draw upon the best features of all English grammars.

11) To demand a new handbook tradition to keep pace with the rapid evolution of English.

12) To liberalize language study in order to liberate the student in the use of his native tongue.

Shakespeare wrote with such flexible power and linguistic abandon because he was not inhibited by a restrictively proscriptive English grammar. If the schools of the future bear this lesson in mind, perhaps they can help nurture a modern equivalent of Shakespeare.

CONCLUSION.   The distinguished history of English forecasts a distinguished future, with ever increasing influence and prestige. The great shaping force of its popular spirit will keep English free from the tyranny of reason and emphasize linguistic liberty and creative flexibility. Aided by mass-media communications, regional, dialect, and national differences will be levelled within the three major brands of Late Modern English: American, British, and Commonwealth. The informal and utilitarian in the language will demand equality among the various levels of usage, and class-consciousness and the barriers of snobbery will tend to weaken. Extremely rich in lexical resources, English will maintain its pattern of immense vocabulary growth, although its exports will undoubtedly out-number the imports. The two thousand different ways to spell the basic three score sounds of present-day English will continue to exasperate professional linguists, confuse immigrants, and delight the formal fol-lowers of Noah Webster. Like poor spelling habits, the difficult idioms of English are here to stay—and to grow, for idiom is its poetic soul.

Just as the phonology of the language will probably remain fairly stable, so regularization will continue in such areas of morphology as the plural form of the noun and the principle parts of the verb. Modern lin-guistic studies should make the native users of English aware of the wealth of its syntactical devices and of the central importance of formal stylis-tics in transforming pragmatic communication into artistic communion. Linguistic science will draw upon the best features of the available gram-mars—traditional, structural, generative, and transformational—to achieve a new handbook discipline for the schools, a discipline that will emphasize instructive and creative synthesis rather than destructive and restrictive analysis. Linguistic science will have to refine and expand its processes of understanding to meet the demands of an evolving English, for the healthy worldwide rivalry of the language, both within its various na-tional versions and among the other leading tongues of earth, will keep it dynamically alive.

QUESTIONS FOR RESEARCH AND DISCUSSION

1. Discuss the use of idiomatic *it* in such constructions as *beat it* and *jazz it up*. How widespread is the use of this idiomatic *it?* How many examples of its use can the class gather?

2. Let five members of the class conduct a panel discussion on the cavalier attitude in contemporary American English usage. Concentrate attention on such items as word coinages, syntactical idioms, specialist jargons, television advertising, and political slogans. How important is the impact of folk speech on this cavalier attitude? Let the class answer in detail.

3. Let five other members of the class give a series of reports on the folk poetry of mass-media advertising, with special attention to paradox, metonymy, parody, punning, metaphor, alliteration, and rhyme. Do such advertising tactics make the aesthetic use of American English easier or more difficult? Let the class answer with a critical essay.

4. Using Bach's *An Introduction to Transformational Grammars*, Chomsky's *Syntactic Structures*, and Rogovin's *Modern English Sentence Structure* as source books for research, organize a panel discussion among five members of the class on the merits and defects of generative grammar. Concentrate attention on the methods and aims of this new linguistic discipline.

5. Read Chapter VI of Bloomfield and Newmark's *A Linguistic Introduction to the History of English*. From a mastery of this demonstration of generative grammar, do a discourse analysis of Lincoln's Gettysburg Address. Does such an analysis enhance your appreciation of Lincoln's verbal mastery? Defend your answer with detailed argument.

6. Let each member of the class read a different essay in Saporta's *Psycholinguistics: A Book of Readings* and give an oral report on it. From all these reports, now let every student write a critical essay on the future needs of linguistic science in the study of the English language.

7. From your study of this book—*A Structural History of English*—what do you predict for the future of English in its phonology, morphology, syntax, and formal stylistics? Defend your predictions with detailed arguments.

SELECTED BIBLIOGRAPHY

Allen, Harold B., ed. *Readings in Applied English Linguistics*. Second Edition. New York: Appleton-Century-Crofts, 1964. A collection of sixty-two essays on the various aspects of English; both diachronically and synchronically, this book reflects the wide variety of scholarly studies available in the linguistics of the future.

Bach, Emmon. *An Introduction to Transformational Grammars*. New York: Holt, Rinehart and Winston, 1964. An avant garde study of what may become the future grammar of the English language as it evolves in the post-Chomsky era.

Chomsky, Noam. *Syntactic Structures*. The Hague: Mouton, 1957, 1962. The blueprint for the generative grammar of tomorrow.

Gleason, H. A., Jr. *Linguistics and English Grammar*. New York: Holt, Rinehart and Winston, 1965. A brilliant book—historically, linguistically, pedagogically—which attempts to make the study of English grammar a liberal art for both teachers and students, with extended bibliography and well-balanced critical comments.

Hall, Robert A., Jr. *Linguistics and Your Language*. New York: Doubleday, Anchor Books, 1960. A popular representation of the impact modern linguistic science exerts on the layman's changing attitudes about the usage of English.

Jespersen, Otto. *Language: Its Nature, Development, and Origin*. New York: W. W. Norton & Company, 1964. This classic of theoretical linguistics symbolizes the need for the development of sound language theory and a universal grammar that does not violate the particular habits of individual tongues.

Marckwardt, Albert H. *American English*. New York: Oxford University Press, 1958. See especially Chapter 9, pp. 170–185, for a discussion of the probable future of the language.

Mencken, H. L. *The American Language*. The Fourth Edition and the Two Supplements, abridged, with annotations and new material, by Raven I. McDavid, Jr., with the assistance of David W. Maurer. New York: Alfred A. Knopf, 1963. See especially Chapter XII, pp. 762–777, for an account of what may happen in the future of English.

Rogovin, Syrell. *Modern English Sentence Structure*. New York and Syracuse: Random House/Singer, 1964. This recent workbook in English grammar symbolizes the importance of both rewrite and transformation rules in the study of the language.

Saporta, Sol, ed. *Psycholinguistics: A Book of Readings*. Prepared with the assistance of Jarvis R. Bastian. New York: Holt, Rinehart and Winston, 1961. This collection of essays in psycholinguistics represents the need for language scholars to probe the human personality in order to understand the fascinating creations of speech.

APICAL   Describing those consonants articulated with the tip of the tongue, as in /θ ð t s d z n l r/.

ARGOT   The specialized vocabulary of a tightly knit group, e.g., the underworld.

ARTICULATION   The movements of the organs of speech in producing a speech sound; such a speech sound, especially a consonant.

ARTICULATOR   A movable organ of speech, especially the tongue.

ASSONANCE   The phonemic correspondence of accented vowels, but not of consonants, as in *main raid*.

AXIS OF SIMULTANEITY   The vertical dimension of a language utterance in which the segmental and suprasegmental phonemes combine to produce an instantaneous minimum unit of meaning, characterized by the distinctive-acoustic-feature oppositions.

AXIS OF SUCCESSIVENESS   The horizontal dimension of a language utterance in which morphology and syntax combine to produce a discursive minimum unit of statement, characterized by the rhythmical features of a cadence.

BACK FORMATION   The creation by analogy of a new word from an existing word, through the mistaken assumption that the existing word is a derivative of the new word (*enthuse* from *enthusiasm*, *edit* from *editor*).

BASE MORPHEME   In the formation of derivatives, the root or stem to which prefixes, suffixes, or infixes are attached (*man*, in *manly*, *-duce* in *produce*).

BLEND   A serious word formed by telescoping parts of two distinct words, as in *astronaut* and *teleprompt*.

BOUND MORPHEME   A minimum unit of non-free meaning, either phonemic (the /z/ of possession) or syllabic (the *-ing* of the present participle) in nature.

CADENCE   Basic unit of Late Modern English rhythm, bounded by two major junctures and carrying one maximum stress as its nucleus.

CLIPPING   The morphological shortening of polysyllabic words, as in *ad* from *advertisement* and *phone* from *telephone*.

CLOSE JUNCTURE   The three suprasegmental phonemes of transition that define word-group boundaries (/|/), phrasal and clausal boundaries (/||/), and sentence boundaries (/#/). These three forms of juncture are *close* because they momentarily close off the flow of speech; two of them demand written punctuation: /||/ and /#/.

Selective Glossary

ACRONYM   A word formed by combining initial letters (*UNESCO*) or syllables and letters (*sonar*) of a series of words or a compound term.

ACUTENESS   A distinctive acoustic feature of English, characterized by a sharp non-muffling of articulation in the front vowels /i e æ/ and the apical and post-apical consonants /s š z ž t c d j θ ð n l r/.

ADDITION   In generative grammar, a transformation rule symbolized as a → a + b, as in the derivation *He can't come* from *He can come.*

AFFIX   A bound syllabic morpheme attached to a base, stem, or root as a prefix (*pro*duce), a suffix (produc*tion*), or an infix (re*pro*duction).

ALLITERATION   The repetition of initial phonemes on stressed syllables: *Silly Sally saw the sinking sun.*

ALLOGRAPH   A variant alphabetical spelling for the same sound. In Old English, *ea* is an allograph of *æ.*

ALLOPHONE   A non-distinctive variant of a phoneme, as determined by positional environment. The velar (k) of *coop* and the palatal (k) of *keep* are allophones of the phoneme /k/.

ALVEOLAR   The hard ridge behind the upper front teeth; when the tongue touches or approaches this ridge, it produces an alveolar consonant.

ALVEOLOPALATAL   When the blade and front of the tongue either touch or approach the alveolar ridge and the hard palate, they produce an alveolopalatal consonant.

AMELIORATION   A semantic shift, in which the meaning or value of a word is improved or elevated in the historical evolution of a language, as in *knight.*

ANACRUSIS   One or more unemphatic introductory syllables in a line of verse that properly begins with a stressed syllable.

ANALYTIC SYNTAX   The syntax of a language in which word order determines grammatical function.

COGNATE   A word allied to another word by derivation from the same source, stock, or root; English *cold* is a cognate of Latin *gelidus*.

COHERENCE   The principle of maintaining logical consistency in the detailed development of a written composition. The integrity of texture.

COLORLESS I   The high-central vowel /ɨ/ heard often in unstressed positions, as in the second syllable of *women* /wimɨn/.

COMPACTNESS   A distinctive acoustic feature of Late Modern English, produced by the presence of a central formant region, which characterizes the articulation of the low vowels /æ a ɔ/ and the back consonants /h k g ŋ w/.

COMPLEX VOWEL   The union of a simple vowel /i ɨ u e ə o æ a ɔ/ with one of the Late Modern English offset glides /y w h/; the 18 complex vowels formed with /y/ and /w/ are *narrow* in articulation, whereas the 9 complex vowels formed with /h/ are *wide*.

COMPOUND   A word formed by the union of two or more free morphemes, with a stress pattern falling usually from maximum /ˊ/ to minor /ˋ/, as in *stréetcàr* and *dáncǐng schòol*.

CONCATENATION OF STRINGS   In generative grammar, the entire range of grammatical representations of the permitted sentences of a given language.

CONCRETISM   The aesthetic theory that a poem is a *graphic* thing, with the attendant practice which places emphasis upon sight-patterns, as in the experimental work of Apollinaire and cummings.

CONSONANCE   The phonemic correspondence of consonants, but not of vowels, on stressed syllables, as in *bad ride*.

CONSONANTALITY   A distinctive acoustic feature of Late Modern English that forms non-syllabic phonemic nuclei.

CONTEXT SENSITIVITY   The semantic environment of a word or phrase that helps to determine its function and to define its meaning; this environment operates on five levels: phonemic, morphemic, lexical, syntactic, and stylistic. In generative grammar, context sensitivity is essential in determining only and all the sentences of Late Modern English.

CONTINUANCE   A distinctive acoustic feature of Late Modern English that does not impede the flow of speech breath, as in all vowels, semivowels, and the consonants /f v θ ð h s š z ž m n ŋ l r/.

COVERT GENDER   The attribution of gender to animate or inanimate objects, without regard to sex, under the shelter of rhetorical license, as in *she* for a country or a ship.

DEICTIC   Demonstrative (i.e., pointing), as in the pronouns *this* (close by) and *that* (far away).

DELETION   In generative grammar, a transformation rule symbolized as a + b ⟶ b, as in the derivation of *John ate* from *John ate a sandwich*.

DERIVATIVE   A word developed from another by the use of one or more bound morphemes, as in *reproduction* from *produce*.

DESCRIPTIVE LINGUISTICS   The *synchronic* study of a language or languages, with emphasis upon making a complete grammar.

DIACHRONIC   As distinct from *synchronic*, the study of a language or a linguistic feature through its historical evolution or development.

DIALECT   A variant version of a language distinguished by its peculiar idiom, vocabulary, phonology, and morphology. A dialect usually impedes speech communication, as in the Cockney of British English.

DIFFUSENESS   A distinctive acoustic feature of Late Modern English, produced by the absence of a central formant region, which characterizes the high vowels /i ɨ u/ and the apical and post-apical consonants /s š z ž t c d j θ ð n l r/.

DIPHTHONG   The blend of two vocalic phonemes into one syllabic unit, as in the /ay/ of *right;* the blend of two consonantal phones into one phonemic unit, as in /š ž c j ŋ/.

DIPODIC RHYTHM   The accentual rhythm of Anglo-Saxon alliterative poetry, characterized by having two primary stresses or "feet" to each half line.

DISPLACED SPEECH   Man's capacity to talk of absent and abstract things as though they were physically present and concrete. A kindergarten discussion of the redness of apples and Plato's dialogue on justice are two examples of displaced speech.

DISTINCTIVE ACOUSTIC FEATURES   The basic phonemic oppositions within a language. In Late Modern English they are seven: vocality/consonantality, tension/laxness, interruption/continuance, gravity/acuteness, compactness/diffuseness, nasality/orality, stridency/mellowness.

EMPHASIS   The stylistic habit in good writing that puts first things first and last things last: the attribute of proportioning rhetorical energy to the value of what is being said.

EMPTY WORD   A word that has no lexical content, but only grammatical function, as in the preposition *of*, the indefinite article *a*, and the verb auxiliary *would*.

ENCLITICIZE   To pronounce as part of a preceding word, with the attendant loss of independent accent, as in encliticizing *is* in the statement *Tom's going.*

ENDOCENTRIC   A syntactic construction that has a nucleus which can substitute for the entire construction, as *book* can in *the good book.*

ETYMOLOGY   The history of a word as shown by analyzing its basic elements or by tracing its evolution in form and meaning.

EXOCENTRIC   A syntactic construction that has no nucleus which can substitute for the entire construction, as in *George smiled.*

EXPANSION   In generative grammar, a transformation rule symbolized as a $\longrightarrow$ b + c, as in the derivation of *I know John is good* from *I know John.*

FOLK ETYMOLOGY   Popular modification of an unfamiliar word by metaphoric or morphological misuse so that the modification corresponds with better known forms, as in *sparrow grass* for *asparagus.*

"FOLK POETRY"   A term applied to the poetic devices of present-day mass-media advertising, especially on television: alliteration, assonance, consonance, metaphor, metonymy, musical jinglet, paradox, punning, rhyme, and rhythm.

FOLK SPEECH   The vulgate of American English, noted for its uncultivated vitality and illiterate constructions.

FORMAL STYLISTICS   The rhetorical principles employed to achieve aesthetic grace in the written and the formal spoken word. These principles deal primarily with unity, coherence, and emphasis; economy, proportion, and radiance.

FREE MORPHEME   A minimum unit of meaning that is free to stand alone or to combine into compounds and derivatives. Simply, it is a word.

FRICATIVE   A *spirant* consonant produced by the passage of breath through a narrow aperture with audible friction, as in /f v θ ð s š z ž/.

FULL WORD   A word that carries lexical meaning as well as grammatical function and is characterized by its stress, practicality, and nonomissiveness in a statement.

FUNCTIONAL SHIFT   The assumption of a new syntactic function by a word without its undergoing any change in form, as when an adjective becomes a noun (*On the village green*).

GENDER   A category of words or affixes based upon differences of sex or absence of sex. The major bases for forming gender are nature, grammar, and common attribution.

GENERALIZATION   A semantic shift, in which the meaning of a word is broadened or extended beyond its original definition, as in *lovely*.

GENERATIVE GRAMMAR   A system of linguistic analysis that seeks to generate only and all the formation rules (which construct kernel sentences) and the transformation rules (which construct derived sentences) of a given language, with formality, explicitness, completeness, and simplicity.

GLIDE   A transitional phoneme used in passing from the position of one speech sound to that of another. The breaking glides of Late Modern English are /ɬ ə/; the offset glides are /y w h/.

GLOTTAL STOP   A sound produced in the larynx by closing the glottis and then releasing the impounded breath with a coughlike explosion. Nonstandard in Late Modern English.

GLOTTIS   The cleft between the vocal chords at the upper orifice of the larynx.

GRAPHEME   The basic unit of writing in any language; Late Modern English has 26 graphemes: a b c d e f g h i j k l m n o p q r s t u v w x y z, together with their capitals.

GRAPHEMICS   The spelling practices of a language; a study of those practices.

GRAVITY   A distinctive acoustic feature of Late Modern English, produced by long oral cavity and small lip aperture, as heard in the muffling of the back vowels /u o ɔ/, the labial consonants /p b m f v/, and the back consonants /h k g ŋ w/.

GREAT VOWEL SHIFT   The term invented by Otto Jespersen to characterize the dramatic change in the pronunciation of the complex vowels of English that took place during the sixteenth and seventeenth centuries.

HOMOGRAPH   The correspondence of one word with another in spelling, though never in meaning and usually not in pronunciation, as in *wind* /wind/ (air current) and *wind* /waynd/ (to coil).

HOMOPHONE   The correspondence of one word with another in pronunciation, though differing from it in origin, spelling, and meaning, as in *read* and *reed*.

HYPERBOLE   The art of exaggeration, a chief characteristic in the usage of American English.

HYPOTAXIS   The syntax of subordinate or dependent arrangement and relationship.

IDEA NAMING   A morphological process in Late Modern English whereby a human being gives his name to some scientific discovery, technological invention, or moral concept, as in *einsteinium*, *quisling*, *Van Allen radiation*.

IDIOM   Any expression peculiar to a language, not easily understood from either its morphology or its grammatical construction, as in *to put up with* (endure, tolerate).

IMAGERY   A morphological process in Late Modern English that relies upon figures of speech for its lexical creations, as in *squirt* (a small or young impudent person).

IMMEDIATE CONSTITUENT   One of the component word groups in a grammatical construction. In the statement *The black dog jumped swiftly over the fence*, the immediate constituents are *The black dog*, *jumped swiftly*, and *over the fence*.

INFLECTION   A bound morpheme used to denote the grammatical function of a word. The *'s* in *boy's* indicates the possessive case.

INNER COMPLEMENT   The number 3 position in the four-position syntax of Late Modern English, usually denoting the indirect object in a sentence of active voice.

INTERDENTAL   A *dentilingual* consonant produced with the tip of the tongue between the teeth: /θ ð/.

INTERNAL CONTOUR   The pitch pattern achieved with either of the two forms of close internal juncture. Optional /|/ produces the internal contour /2/ – /2/; obligatory /|||/ produces the internal contour /2/↗/2/.

INTERNAL MODIFICATION   A morphological process of Late Modern English in which phonemic replacement within a word indicates a change in function and/or meaning, as in *sang* for the past tense of *sing* and *mice* for the plural of *mouse*.

INTERRUPTION   A distinctive acoustic feature of Late Modern English, characterized by the momentary obstruction of the breath stream, as in the voiceless stops /p t k c/ and the voiced obstruents /b d g j/.

INTONATIONAL SYSTEM   The suprasegmental phonemes of Late Modern English, which determine the patterns of speech delivery according to volume (stress), intonation height (pitch), and transition (juncture).

ISOCHRONOUS   Of equal duration in pronunciation, as in the half-line measures of dipodic rhythm.

JARGON   The technical or specialized vocabulary or phraseology used by members of a particular profession, sect, or socially restricted group; to the uninitiated, jargon is meaningless or confusing.

JUNCTURE   The transition from one speech utterance to the next with either a catch in or a stoppage of the breath stream, thereby indicating a demarcation of grammatical boundaries. Late Modern English has four kinds of juncture, one open and three close.

KERNEL SENTENCE   In generative grammar, a non-derived sentence constructed upon the formation (phrase structure) rules of a given language. A kernel sentence in English is therefore dependent upon no phrase structures other than its own, as in *The boy ran home* and *The boy is tall. The tall boy ran home*, however, is derived from the other two sentences and is therefore non-kernel.

LABIAL   Articulated or modified by the lips, as in /p b m w/.

LABIODENTAL   Articulated with the lower lip and the upper front teeth, as in /f v/.

LAXNESS   A distinctive acoustic feature of Late Modern English, characterized by a relative relaxation of tongue and jaw in the act of articulation.

LAX PHONEME   Articulated with the tongue and jaw relatively relaxed, as in the simple vowels /i ɪ u e ə o æ a ɔ/ and the voiced consonants /b m v ð d z n l r j ž g y ŋ w/.

LEXICAL   A term denoting words or morphemes as *semantic* items in a vocabulary and not as *grammatical* items in a linguistic structure.

LINGUISTIC GEOGRAPHY   The study of the distribution of languages among areas and peoples, with emphasis on dialect boundaries.

LIQUID   A term applied to the vowel-like consonants that are produced without friction: /l r/.

LITOTES   The art of understatement, a chief characteristic in the usage of British English.

LOAN WORD   A word adopted from another language and partly or completely naturalized, as in English *chauffeur* from French, *creed* from Latin, and *poet* from Greek.

LONG VOWEL   In Late Modern English, a complex vowel formed by uniting a simple vowel with one of the offset glides /y w h/ and pronounced as one vocalic cluster, as in the /aw/ of *house*.

MELLOWNESS   A distinctive acoustic feature of Late Modern English, characterized by a muffling of the friction in the spirants /θ ð/.

METALINGUISTICS   The linguistic study concerned with the interrelationship of linguistic and other cultural factors in a society.

METATHESIS   The transposition of letters, syllables, or sounds within a word; Old English *bridd* became Modern English *bird*.

METRICS   The artistic discipline that studies meter in prosody.

MORPHEME   The basic unit of meaning in any language. Late Modern English has three kinds of morphemes: bound phonemic (the /z/ of possession in *John's*), bound syllabic (the -*ly* of adverbial function in *slowly*), and free word simple (*John* and *slow*).

MORPHEME WORD   The minimum unit of free meaning in any language; morpheme and word boundaries coincide to form one free and simple semantic unit, as in *cat*.

MORPHOLOGICAL PROCESS   A method of word formation, such as compounding, affixing, or telescoping.

MORPHOLOGY   The arrangement and interrelationship of morphemes in words. Also the branch of linguistics which studies this subject.

MORPHOPHONEMIC   Pertaining to the alternation of phonemes within a morpheme according to the context of articulation, as in /z/ for /s/ or /d/ for /t/ in voicing environments.

MUFFLING   The deadening of articulation by the use of oral cavity, lips, or dental ridge so that phonemic sharpness is reduced. Muffling is responsible in Late Modern English for the distinctive acoustic features gravity and mellowness.

NARROW NUCLEI   A term applicable to the complex vowels formed by use of the offset glides /y w/, which constrict both the oral cavity and the lip aperture.

NASAL   A term applied to the consonantal phonemes formed by use of the nasal passage: /m n ŋ/.

NASALITY   A distinctive acoustic feature of Late Modern English, characterized by use of the nose in phonemic formation and articulation.

OBLIGATORY INTERNAL CLOSE JUNCTURE   The suprasegmental phoneme of transition, symbolized as /|||/, which discriminates phrasal and clausal boundaries with the need for written punctuation. In Late

Modern English, this juncture is accompanied by the internal contour /2/ ↗ /2/.

OBLIGATORY TERMINAL CLOSE JUNCTURE   The suprasegmental phoneme of transition, symbolized as /#/, which discriminates sentence boundaries with the need for written punctuation. In Late Modern English, this juncture is accompanied by either one of the terminal contours: /3/ – /1/ or /3/ – /4/.

OBSTRUENT   A term applied to the voiced stops of Late Modern English /b d g j/, because they obstruct the breath stream without fully cutting it off; a resonant hum, denied to the voiceless stops, makes for a less abrupt transition.

OFFSET GLIDE   Any one of the three semivowels of transition /y w h/ used *after* a vowel to make a complex nucleus of one syllabic value.

ONOMATOPOEIA   A morphological process of Late Modern English, in which words are formed in imitation of natural sounds, as in *bang*, *splash*, and *zoom*.

ONSET GLIDE   Any one of the three semivowels of transition /y w h/ used *before* a vowel, as in *fuse* /fyuwz/.

OPEN JUNCTURE   The suprasegmental phoneme /+/ of transition that defines morphemic and word boundaries on stressed elements, as in *that + stuff*. This form of juncture is open because it does not close off the flow of speech.

OPTIONAL INTERNAL CLOSE JUNCTURE   The suprasegmental phoneme of transition, symbolized as /|/, which discriminates word-group boundaries without the need for written punctuation. In Late Modern English, this juncture is accompanied by the internal contour /2/ – /2/.

ORALITY   A distinctive acoustic feature of Late Modern English, characterized by articulation in the oral cavity without any use of the nasal passage.

ORTHOGRAPHY   A mode or system of spelling correctly according to a standard usage.

OUTER COMPLEMENT   The number 4 position in the four-position syntax of Late Modern English, usually denoting the direct object in a sentence of active voice.

PACING   The speed of speech delivery, as determined by the intonational system of the speaker.

PALATAL   A consonantal phoneme produced by placing the front (not the tip) of the tongue near or against the hard palate, as in Late Modern English /h k g y/.

PARADIGM   An ordered list of all the inflected forms of a word or class of words, as in a particular declension or conjugation.

PARALANGUAGE   A system of non-phonemic articulations which nevertheless convey some sense of morphological meaning and semantic value, as in a child's babbling and cooing or an adult's sighs and groans.

PARATAXIS   The syntax of coordination, not subordination, especially when conjunctions are omitted as in *I came, I saw, I conquered*.

PEJORATION   A semantic shift, in which the meaning or value of a word is worsened or lowered in the historical evolution of a language, as in *knave*.

PERIPHRASIS   Circumlocution; a roundabout method of saying something.

PERMITTED STRINGS   In generative grammar, the direct grammatical representations of the permitted sentences of a given language.

PERMUTATION   In generative grammar, a transformation rule symbolized as a + b ⟶ b + a, as in the derivation of *Home went George* from *George went home*.

PHONEME   The minimum unit of distinctive (significant) sound in a language; the smallest contrastive unit in the sound system of a language, functioning to distinguish utterances from one another. The English phonemes /p/ and /t/ distinguish the words *pan* and *tan*.

PHONEMIC MORPHEME   A bound morpheme of phonemic rather than syllabic value, usually affixed to a stressed base as in the /z/ of possession in *John's* or in the /s/ of plurality in *tops*.

PHONEMICS   A phonemic system or the study of phonemic systems.

PHONETICS   The branch of linguistics dealing with the analysis, description, and classification of speech sounds, including the physiological processes (*articulatory*) and the physical attributes (*acoustic*). The system of sounds in a language, more finely described than the phonemes.

PHONOLOGY   Phonemics. Phonemics and phonetics taken together. The history of the sound changes that have occurred in the evolution of a language.

PHRASE STRUCTURE RULES   In generative grammar, the formation rules that govern the construction of the various immediate constituents of the kernel sentences of a given language.

PITCH   Tone accent. The intonation heights of spoken discourse. Late

Modern English supports four degrees of pitch, the suprasegmental phonemes /4/ (highest), /3/ (high), /2/ (normal), and /1/ (low).

PITCH CONTOURS   The significant patterns of transition from one intonation segment to another, as in the terminal contour of high-falling /3/ – /1/ or in the internal contour of normal-rising /2/ ↗ /2/.

PORTMANTEAU   A humorous word formed by telescoping parts of two distinct words, as in *brunch* and *globaloney*.

POST-APICAL   Describing those consonants articulated just behind the tip of the tongue, as in /c š j ž/.

PREFIX   A bound morpheme attached at the beginning of a base, stem, or root, altering or modifying its meaning, as in the *re-* of *renew*.

PROLONGATION   The phonemic lengthening of a maximum-stressed syllable for rhetorical emphasis, usually accompanied in Late Modern English by the intonation height of /4/, as in the state-
$$/4/$$
ment *Givve me the book.*

REDUCTION   In generative grammar, a transformation rule symbolized as $a + b \longrightarrow c$, as in the derivation of *I know that John is good* from the two kernel sentences *I know the fact* and *John is good*.

REDUPLICATION   A morphological process of Late Modern English, in which the doubling of a word, usually with some internal modification, creates an emotional emphasis that is echoic in nature, as in *fiddle-faddle* and *namby-pamby*.

REGIONALISM   The speech variety, as distinct from dialect, of a language, which does not hinder communication or necessitate the adoption of a spoken standard. Appalachian is a regionalism of American English.

REPLACEMENT   A morphological process of Late Modern English, in which one morpheme is semantically identified with another, but with no conceivable phonemic connection, as in *went* as the past tense of *go*. In generative grammar, a transformation rule symbolized as $a \longrightarrow b$, as in the derivation of *John went home* from *John goes home*.

ROOT   Etymologically, the minimum irreducible base common to all cognate forms; morphologically, a base to which affixes may be added to form a word, as *know* in *unknown, knowable, knowingly*.

SCHWA   The mid-central vowel /ə/ heard often in unstressed positions. as in the first syllable of *abide* /əbayd/.

SEGMENTAL PHONEME   A minimum unit of distinctive sound on the segmental plane; hence, the basic sound structure along the axis of successiveness, from which morphology and syntax emerge. Late Modern English supports 33 segmental phonemes: 24 consonants and 9 vowels.

SEMANTICS   The study of the meanings of speech forms, especially of the evolution in meaning of words and word groups. Also, in logic, the relation between signs or symbols and what they signify or denote.

SEMANTIC SHIFT   A process in the historical evolution of a language wherein a word undergoes changes in definition, application, or value.

SEMIVOWEL   A vowel-like sound used as a consonant. In Late Modern English the glides /y w h/ consistently act like semivowels; the liquids /l r/ do so upon occasion.

SHORT VOWEL   In Late Modern English, one of the simple and lax vowels: /i ɨ u e o ə æ a ɔ/.

SLANG   Language, words, or phrases of a vigorous, colorful, metaphoric, or taboo nature, invented to transfuse fresh life into a vocabulary gone stale from too much standard and conventional usage; also used to obscure meaning from the uninitiated outsider.

SOUND OPPOSITIONS   The phonemic contrasts that constitute the distinctive acoustic features of a language. In Late Modern English, these sound oppositions are vocality/consonantality, tension/laxness, interruption/continuance, gravity/acuteness, compactness/diffuseness, nasality/orality, stridency/mellowness.

SPECIALIZATION   A semantic shift, in which the meaning of a word is narrowed or reduced within the boundaries of its original definition, as in *deer*.

SPIRANT   A *fricative* consonant produced by the passage of breath through a narrow aperture with audible friction, as in /f v θ ð s š z ž/.

STEM   A root plus thematic vowel, as *luci-* in *lucifer*.

STOP   A Late Modern English voiceless consonant that momentarily cuts off the flow of speech breath: /p t k c/, with voiced obstruent equivalents /b d g j/.

STRESS   A suprasegmental phoneme of intonation volume, denoting the relative loudness of an utterance. Late Modern English has four degrees of stress: maximum /ˊ/, major /ˆ/, minor /ˋ/, and minimum /ˇ/.

STRESS MODIFICATION   A morphological process of Late Modern English, in which grammatical function is indicated by the mutual morphemic interchange of rising and falling stress patterns, as in the distinction between *ímport* as noun and *impórt* as verb.

STRIDENCY   A distinctive acoustic feature of Late Modern English, characterized by the sharpness of articulation in the fricatives /s š z ž/.

STRINGS   In generative grammar, the grammatical representations of sentences, wherein each sentence may have more than one representation. Thus the following two strings are both grammatical representations of the same sentence *The bell rang:*

    1) Noun Phrase + Complete Predicate
    2) Article + Noun + Complete Predicate

STRUCTURAL LINGUISTICS   A study of the distribution of form classes in a language or languages, with emphasis on syntactic function rather than upon lexical meaning.

STRUCTURE   The form of an utterance, whether phonemic, morphemic, or syntactic.

SUBSTITUTE WORD   A grammatical word, empty of lexical meaning, which systematically substitutes for a full word. In Late Modern English, substitute words include the personal, possessive, and relative pronouns, the expletives, and the deictic adverbs of time and place.

SUFFIX   A bound morpheme attached to the end of a base, stem, or root, functioning as a derivative or an inflectional element, as in the *-hood* of *manhood.*

SUPERFIX   The intonational pattern of an utterance, as determined by the interrelation of its suprasegmental phonemes of stress, pitch, and juncture.

SUPRASEGMENTAL PHONEME   A phoneme occurring *above* the segmental plane of the axis of successiveness and therefore a part of the intonational system of the language; hence, a minimum unit of either stress, pitch, or juncture.

SYLLABIC MORPHEME   A bound morpheme, syllabic in extent, usually operating as a prefix, suffix, or inflectional ending, although such a morpheme may also act as a base, as in the *-duce* of *produce.*

SYNCHRONIC   As distinct from *diachronic*, the study of a language or a linguistic feature at a certain time or stage in its development and not historically.

SYNCRETIZE   To fuse two or more inflectional forms that were originally different, as in declensional cases or conjugational endings.

SYNTAGMEME   A minimum unit of syntax. In Late Modern English, one of the endocentric or exocentric word groups.

SYNTAX   The arrangement and interrelationship of words in word groups, phrases, clauses, and sentences. Also the branch of linguistics which studies this feature of language.

SYNTHETIC SYNTAX   The use of inflectional affixes or bound morphemes as the principal means of expressing grammatical relationships, as in Old English, Latin, and Russian. Opposed to analytic syntax, as in Late Modern English.

TELESCOPING   A morphological process of Late Modern English, in which parts of two distinct words, often of similar meaning, are combined to form a new word, whether serious blend or humorous portmanteau.

TENSE PHONEME   Articulated with the tongue and jaw relatively tense, as in the voiceless consonants /p f θ t s c š h k/. The complex vowels of Late Modern English, based upon the glides /y w h/, are all diphthongs of tension.

TENSION   A distinctive acoustic feature of Late Modern English, characterized by a relative tenseness in tongue and jaw in the act of articulation, as in the voiceless consonants and the complex vowels.

TERMINAL CONTOUR   The intonation pattern that accompanies obligatory terminal close juncture /#/, the discriminator of sentence boundaries. Late Modern English has two terminal contours: high-rising /3/↗ and high-falling /3/ – /1/; the high-rising produces an abrupt voice cutoff, the high-falling a gradual voice fade.

TEXTURAL INTENSITY   The deliberate aesthetic control of the sound features of a language for the achievement of a desired poetic effect.

TEXTURE   The specific content or constituency, whether immediate or ultimate, of a linguistic form or structure. Thus /k/, /ə/, and /p/ are the phonemic texture of the word *cup* /kəp/.

THEMATIC VOWEL   A vowel added to a root to form a stem or theme.

THEORETICAL LINGUISTICS   The branch of linguistics that deals with the theory or theories concerning the origin, growth, development, divergence, and interpenetration of languages. Often abstract and mathematical in nature, theoretical linguistics seeks to apprehend the unknown or demonstrate the still unproved in the past, present, and future of a language or languages.

TRANSFORM   Any grammatical construction that is a transformation of some other grammatical construction or constructions. Thus the statement *This is the house that Jack built* is a transform of the two kernel sentences *This is the house* and *Jack built the house.*

TRANSFORMATION   A change from one grammatical construction to another considered more or less equivalent according to the syntactic laws of the language. In Late Modern English, the passive voice is a transformation of the active; a question is a transformation of a statement. In generative grammar, a transformation is indicated by the use of the symbol =>.

UNITY   The principle of adhering to one subject, point of view, tone, mood, thesis, and topic in the detailed development of a written composition. The oneness of structure.

VARIANT   Any positional or contextual form of a linguistic unit, such as allophone, allomorph, allostress.

VELAR   Formed with the back of the tongue touching or approaching the soft palate, as in the guttural /k/ of *cool* and /g/ of *goal*. The phonemes /ŋ/ and /w/ are regularly velar.

VOCALIC NUCLEUS   The nucleus of a syllable based upon a vowel, whether simple or complex. Also the simple vowel formant, as distinct from the semivowel glide, of a complex vowel.

VOCALITY   A distinctive acoustic feature of Late Modern English, characterized by the syllable-forming capacity of the vowels. Intermediately, the semivowel glides /y w h/ and the liquids /l r/ share in this feature; occasionally the nasals /m n/ act syllabically like liquids.

VOICED   Uttered with a resonant hum from the vibrating vocal chords; a feature of all Late Modern English vowels and the lax consonants.

VOICELESS   Uttered without any resonant hum or vibration of the vocal chords; a feature of all tense consonants in Late Modern English.

VOWEL TRANSMUTATION   The phonemic change of Late Modern English vowels in stressed positions to indicate a shift in function and/or meaning of the words they inhabit, as in the plural *mice* /mays/ from the singular *mouse* /maws/, the verb *gild* /gild/ from the noun *gold* /gowld/. Thus a means of internal modification.

WIDE NUCLEI   A term applicable to the complex vowels formed by use of the offset glide /h/, which expands both the oral cavity and the lip aperture.

WORD   Minimum unit of free meaning.

WORD GROUP   A minimum unit of syntax, usually carrying one maximum stress and bounded by two major junctures, though not always. Late Modern English has four major endocentric word groups (noun, verb, modifier, verbal) and two major exocentric (subject-predicate, prepositional).

WORD ORDER   The sequence of words in any syntactical construction. In Late Modern English, word order, rather than inflectional endings, joins with stress to determine grammatical function.

WORD SIMPLE   In Late Modern English, a free morpheme the boundaries of which coincide with those of a word that is neither compound nor derivative.

ZEROING   A morphological process of Late Modern English, in which the absence of an addition to or modification of a word implies meaning, as in the lack of *-s* in *bear* to indicate non-distinctive number. Also a phonological swallowing up of a minimum stressed syllable so that it is no longer pronounced, as in British *secret'ry*.

Index

Note: The main concern of this index is with concrete guidance rather than with abstract conceptual analysis. Linguistic symbols may be found in the Linguistic Key; linguistic terms, in the Selective Glossary. Other major items (and their related topics) such as important dates, outstanding persons, major attributes of the language, phonology, morphology, syntax, and formal stylistics are readily available through the Contents. Questions for research and discussion and selected bibliographies appear at the end of each chapter.